The Book of

CHAPEL-EN-LE-FRITH

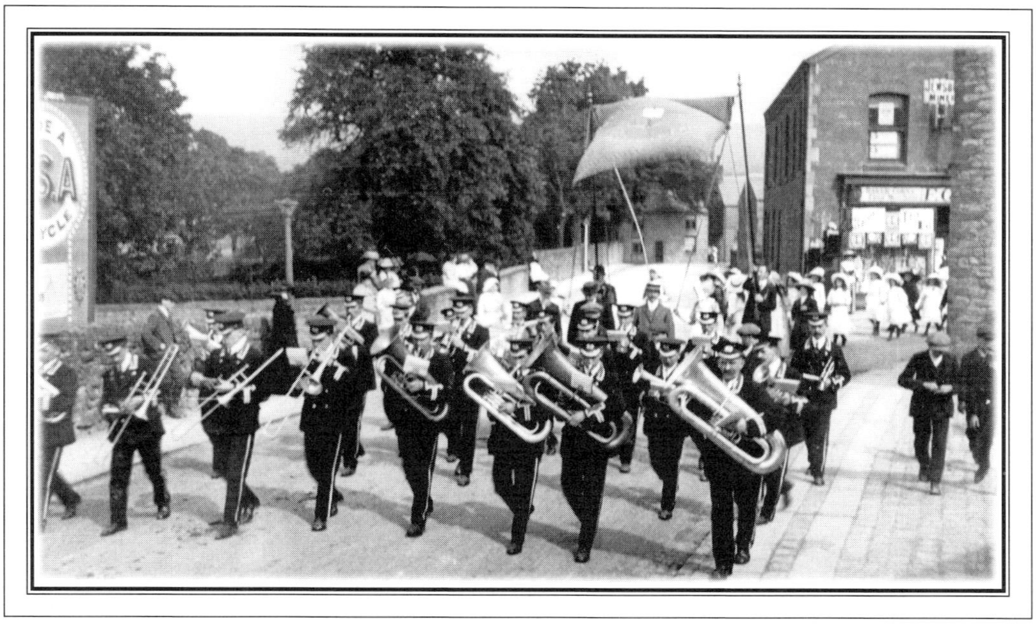

A Community History of the Parish

COMPILED & EDITED BY MIKE SMITH

HALSGROVE

First published in Great Britain in 2003.

British Library Cataloguing-in-Publication Data.
A CIP record for this title is available from the British Library.

ISBN 1 84114 234 4

HALSGROVE

Halsgrove House
Lower Moor Way
Tiverton, Devon EX16 6SS
Tel: 01884 243242
Fax: 01884 243325
email: sales@halsgrove.com
website: www.halsgrove.com

Frontispiece photograph: *The Town Band in 1912.*

Printed and bound by CPI Bath.

Foreword

In October 2001, I was pleased to accept an invitation to open an exhibition organised by Chapel-en-le-Frith Parish Council to celebrate the 150th anniversary of their Town Hall. The illustrations, maps, historical documents and memorabilia on display gave a fascinating account of a High Peak parish whose origins date back to the thirteenth century and the days of the Royal Forest of the Peak.

During my tour of the exhibition, I met parish councillors, pupils and staff from local schools, leaders of the various churches in the parish and representatives from more than 20 local groups. As in other Peak District towns and villages, life in Chapel-en-le-Frith is greatly enriched by the activities of those organisations which are sustained entirely by the efforts of enthusiastic volunteers.

I am delighted to find that the long history of this High Peak parish and its rich and varied community life have now been recorded in the form of a book. This publication will be valued as an historical account of Chapel-en-le-Frith and I hope that it will also inspire local people to continue the good work of the parish's many organisations into the twenty-first century.

His Grace, The Duke of Devonshire

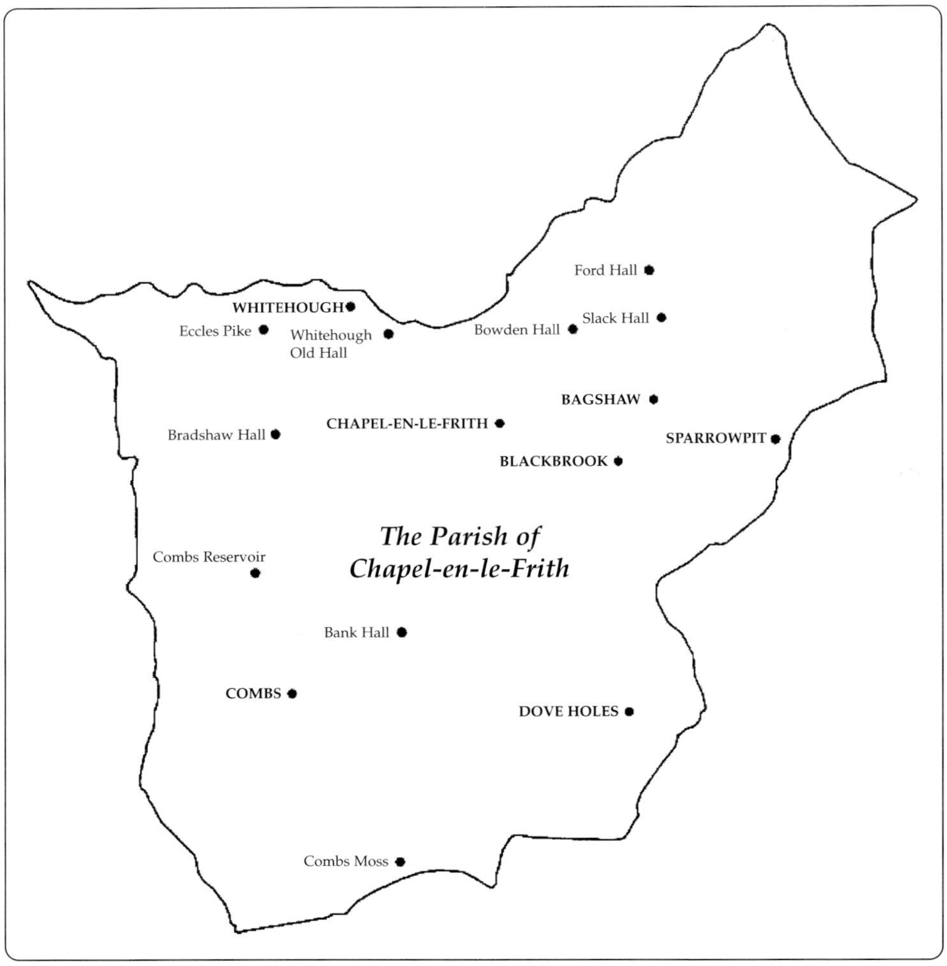
Ford Hall
WHITEHOUGH
Slack Hall
Eccles Pike
Whitehough Old Hall
Bowden Hall
BAGSHAW
CHAPEL-EN-LE-FRITH
Bradshaw Hall
SPARROWPIT
BLACKBROOK
The Parish of Chapel-en-le-Frith
Combs Reservoir
Bank Hall
COMBS
DOVE HOLES
Combs Moss

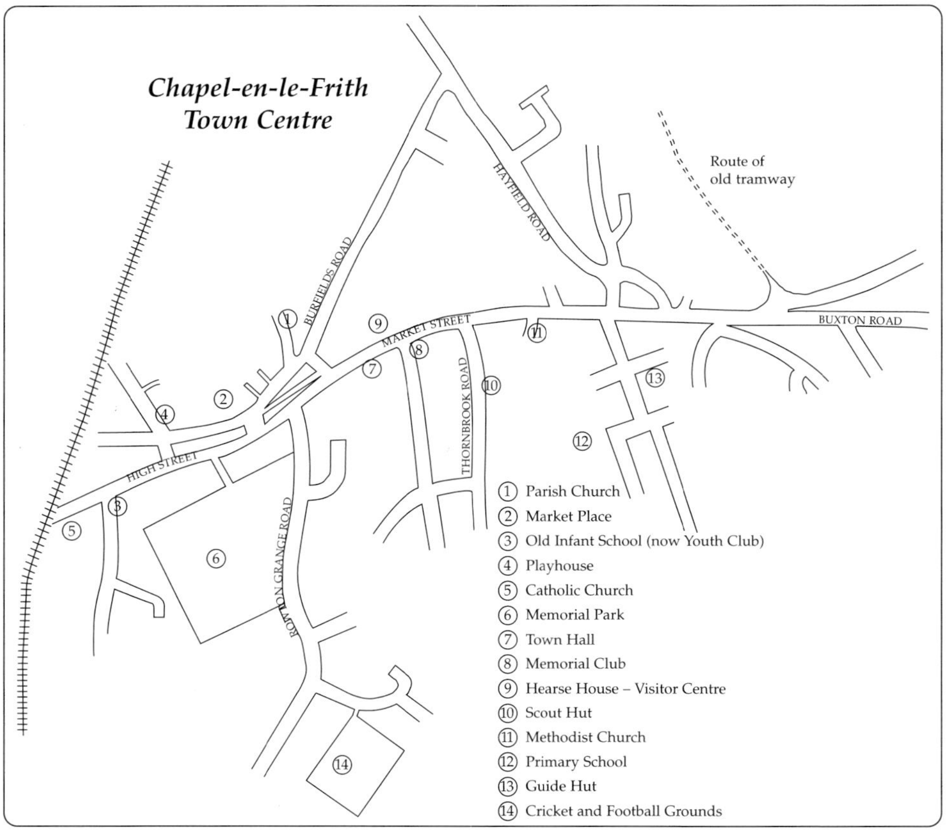
Chapel-en-le-Frith Town Centre
Route of old tramway
HAYFIELD ROAD
BURRFIELDS ROAD
MARKET STREET
BUXTON ROAD
THORNBROOK ROAD
HIGH STREET
BUXTON GRANGE ROAD
① Parish Church
② Market Place
③ Old Infant School (now Youth Club)
④ Playhouse
⑤ Catholic Church
⑥ Memorial Park
⑦ Town Hall
⑧ Memorial Club
⑨ Hearse House – Visitor Centre
⑩ Scout Hut
⑪ Methodist Church
⑫ Primary School
⑬ Guide Hut
⑭ Cricket and Football Grounds

Contents

Acknowledgements

I am greatly indebted to the following people who wrote chapters or part-chapters for this publication: Brian Aries, Joanne Carrington, Muriel Carrington, Ron Cooke, Roy Danson, Mary Davies, Jean Evanson, Mike Evanson, Peter Goddard, Mike Harrison, Gordon Helps, Peter Helps, Frances Hibbert, Tom James, Bryan McGee, Janet McNicol, Robert Mulholland, Julie Murdy, Jenny Nicholson, Beryl Pilkington, Elaine Radford, Tony Read, David Ripley, Jeanette Saxby, Dorothy Simpson, Patricia Simpson, Elizabeth Stafford, Alan Watson, Bernard West, Nona Williams and Bernice Wood.

The following people contributed to discussions which enabled accounts to be written: Christine Ashbury, Julian Barber, Alastair Carrington, Hector Carrington, Bryan Cooper, Avis Curry, Ron Davidson, Randall Dawson, Jim Hirst, Michael Hough, Donna Kadzewska, Kevin Kelly, Shaun King, Nigel Lloyd, Joe Lomas, Jean McDowell, Will Newman, Norman Prime, Joyce Taylor, Doreen Vernon, Linda Vernon, Gerald Williams and Bill Wilson.

The following individuals and organisations kindly loaned archive material: Bryan Cooper, Roy Danson, Margaret Dyson, Michael Hough, Bryan McGee, Ruth Mullis, Enid Phillips, Beryl Pilkington, Norman Prime, Pauline Turner, Bill Wilson, Revd David Youngs, Chapel Amenity Society, Chapel Golf Club, Chapel High School, Chapel Memorial Institute, Chapel Parish Council, Chapel Town Football Club, Combs Sailing Club and Combs School.

I am grateful to the following people and organisations who contributed photographs to this publication: Terry Abigail, Brian Aries, Dr Ron Bedell, Mary Beswick, Baz Brown, Jean Cartledge, Ron Cooke, Betty Cooper, Bryan Cooper, Avis Curry, Ron Davidson, Mary Davies, Mike Evanson, Ada Fox, Margaret Garner, Peter Goddard, Harry Hall, Michael Harrison, Ralph Harper, Linda Harper, Mike Hazlewood, Gordon Helps, Frances Hibbert, Ada Hitchens, Michael Hough, Brenda Jackson, David Jackson, Tom James, Beryl Johnson, Donna Kadzewska, Jean Kadzewska, Debbie Langford, Nigel Lloyd, Hetty Marchington, Gordon Millner, Julie Murdy, Jean McDowell, Janet McNicol, John Needham, Robert Mulholland, Tim Norton, Mr Parker, Enid Phillips, Beryl Pilkington, David Pilkington, Norman Prime, Tony Read, Jeanette Saxby, Joanne Smith, Alan Watson, Bernard West, Fred Williamson, Bernice Wood, the Boys' Brigade, Dove Holes Community Association, the Girls' Brigade, Chapel Amenity Society, Chapel Band, Chapel High School, Chapel Memorial Club, Chapel Youth Club, the Male Voice Choir, the National Westminster Bank, Peak Press and Town End Methodist Church.

The following gave permission for articles which had been published elsewhere to be used in this publication: Chapel Parish Council, Peter Helps, Silk Press Ltd and Revd David Youngs.

Last, but not least, I should like to thank my wife, Jo-Ann, my daughter, Charlotte, and my mother-in-law, Donna, for their tolerance during the many hours I spent in preparation of this book. I am grateful to Donna and Charlotte for their help in research and to Jo-Ann for her meticulous reading of the entire proofs and for her many helpful suggestions. Any errors which remain are, of course, entirely my responsibility.

Introduction

One of the highlights of my term of office as chairman of the Parish Council was a two-day exhibition to celebrate the 150th anniversary of Chapel-en-le-Frith Town Hall. The exhibition, which was coordinated by Margaret Dyson (then vice-chairman of the Parish Council, and now chairman) brought together 22 different groups and organisations which had used the Town Hall as a venue over the years. Throughout the anniversary weekend, the main hall and the annexe of the building were packed with photographic displays, press cuttings, video presentations, minute-books, maps, banners and all manner of other memorabilia and artefacts.

His Grace the Duke of Devonshire opened the exhibition, which was attended by over 500 local people during the weekend. The Chapel-en-le-Frith Male Voice Choir and the Children's Kinder Choir both gave concerts to capacity audiences, a recorder group from Warmbrook Junior School performed at the opening ceremony and an extensive display of old maps and photographs of the parish decorated the walls.

As pictures in the exhibition illustrated, Chapel-en-le-Frith is an ancient parish set against the beautiful backdrop of the High Peak, a landscape that contains evidence of human habitation stretching back to Neolithic times.

Above all, the exhibition was a tribute to the people and organisations that enriched the lives of the people of Chapel throughout the twentieth century. The parish has been fortunate in having scores of energetic and committed individuals who have provided educational, religious, cultural, sporting and social opportunities for people of all ages in the community. Many of those who benefited by their membership of groups and organisations went on to become the leaders, organisers, movers and shakers of the next generation. Thanks to the energy and spirit shown by all these people throughout an often troubled twentieth century, Chapel-en-le-Frith enters the twenty-first century as a vibrant community.

When Margaret and I closed the doors of the exhibition at the end of the weekend (two hours later than scheduled, because visitors were still arriving) we both concluded that the subject matter which had been on display ought not be lost, but should be put on permanent record in some way. Margaret favoured the establishment of a local history museum; I favoured a book.

When Halsgrove publishers invited me to write this book, I was delighted to take the opportunity to put on record the work of the people and organisations that made Chapel-en-le-Frith tick in the twentieth century.

Scores of people in the parish have unearthed their photographic and written records and dug deep into their memories for the cause of this book; no fewer than 32 people have contributed to the publication by writing chapters or part-chapters. This is a book about the community, by the community.

Mike Smith, January 2003

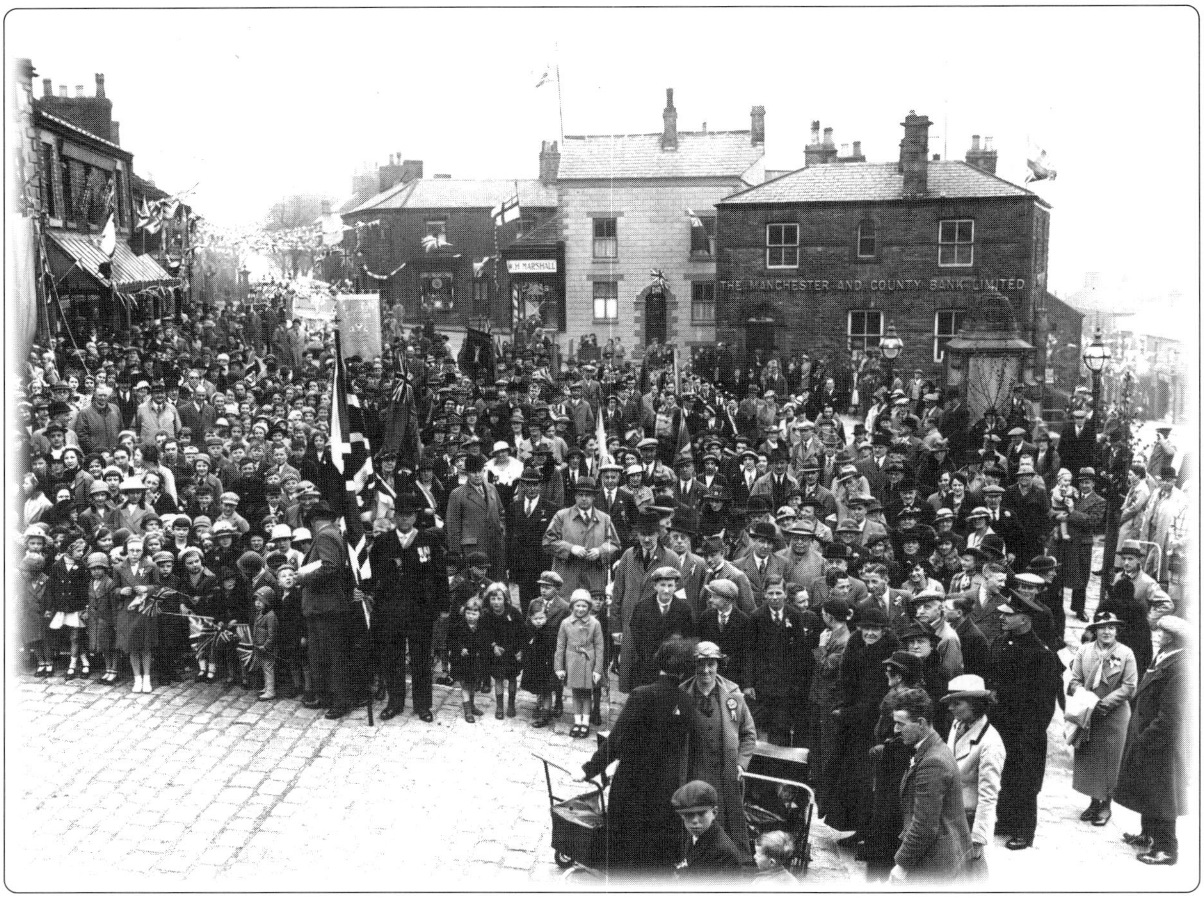

Townspeople gathering on Market Place on 12 May 1937 to celebrate the coronation of King George VI.

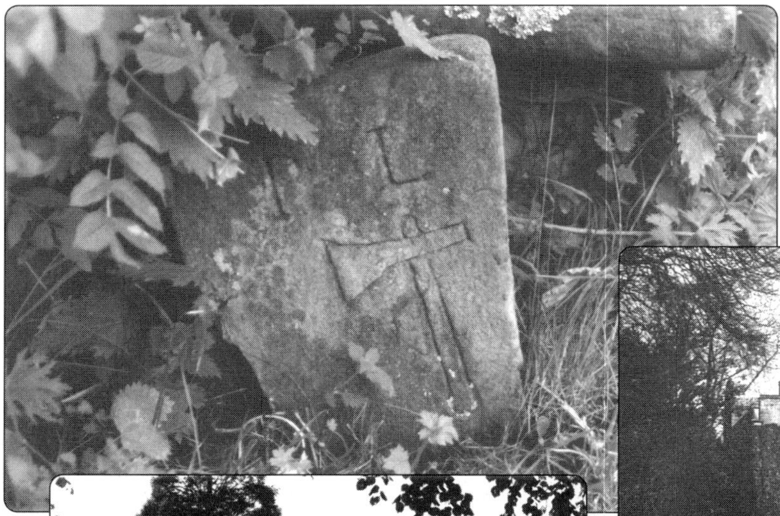

The Woodcutter's Grave, said to date from the days of the Royal Forest of the Peak.

Below: *Bowden Hall.*

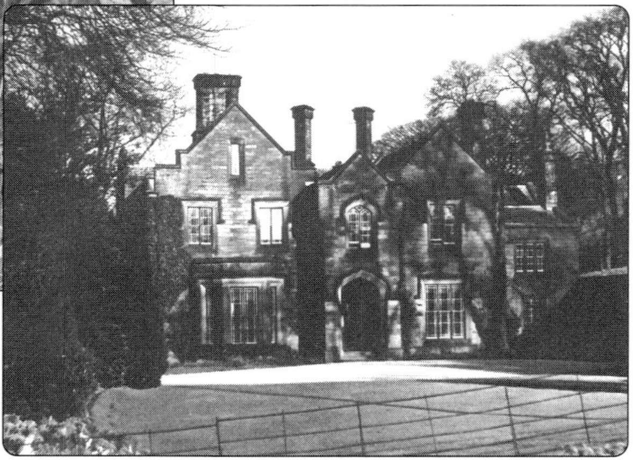

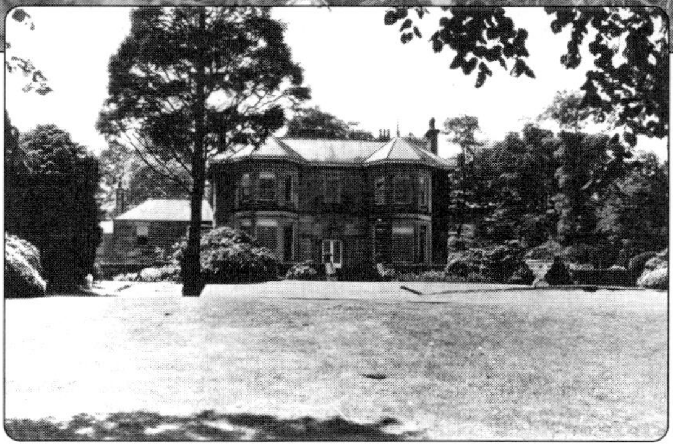

Bank Hall, the former residence of Squire Frith.

Chapter 1

THE CHAPEL IN THE FOREST

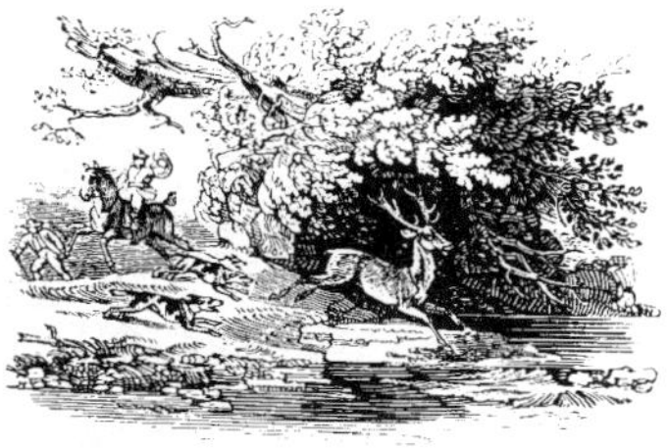

In the thirteenth century, a vast area of the High Peak, bordered by the Rivers Goyt, Etherow, Derwent and Wye, was covered by a royal hunting forest. In 1225, a group of foresters in a ward of the forest known as Campana petitioned the Earl of Derby for permission to build a chapel of ease, which would relieve them of the 11-mile trek to their Parish Church at Hope. Their request was granted and a chapel in the forest (a chapel-en-le-frith) was duly constructed on a spur of land running eastwards from Eccles Pike, a conical peak that rises from the centre of a wide bowl in the gritstone hills of the Dark Peak.

The church, which was dedicated to St Thomas Becket, who had been murdered 55 years earlier, became the centre of a new township that grew rapidly in importance, not least because it stood on a natural route through the Pennines, much used by salt carriers from Cheshire. The town became the venue for forest courts and inquiries; the new chapel soon became a Parish Church in its own right and the people of Chapel-en-le-Frith acquired the privilege of electing their own vicar, a right which they still hold to this day.

The present church of St Thomas Becket, which was largely remodelled in a Georgian style in 1733, stands on the site of the foresters' chapel, but has almost no vestiges of the original building. However, the churchyard contains a simple tombstone, which is inscribed with a crude drawing of an axe and is said to be the grave of a woodcutter in the Royal Forest of the Peak.

Those inhabitants of the forest who carried out specific duties for the Crown were granted small plots of land. The new landowners were soon building rather grand houses on their little estates in the hills, with the result that the area around Chapel-en-le-Frith contains a remarkable profusion of country houses. Writing in 1888, the historian Henry Kirke claimed, 'Perhaps there is no other parish in England at the present time where there are so many freeholders of land for the number of inhabitants.'

HALLS IN THE HILLS

Thanks are due to Chapel-en-le-Frith Parish Council for permission to reproduce this article, by Mike Smith, which first appeared, in a slightly different form, in the Council's *Guide to the Capital of the Peak*, published in 1990.

Exploration of the narrow roads which criss-cross the high gritstone hills surrounding Chapel-en-le-Frith reveals a remarkable feature of the area. In the wooded hollows of the hills, there is a high concentration of halls and estates which have been in existence since the fourteenth century. Many generations of Chapel families, including the Bowdens, Bagshawes, Shallcrosses, Bradshaws and Ollerenshaws, have lived in these solid stone houses of the High Peak. Some of the halls have changed hands by purchase and most have been altered over the years, but they remain romantic places. Many local people have tales to tell about the halls and their inhabitants.

Bradshaw Hall, in a secluded hollow below Eccles Pike, was rebuilt in warm brownstone in 1620 by Francis Bradshaw. On first discovery, the building provides one of the most delightful visual surprises in the Peak District, appearing like a sudden vision of the Cotswolds in the heart of dark Pennine hills. Local people like to believe that John Bradshaw, who presided over the trial of Charles I, lived at Bradshaw Hall. This is not the case, but the regicide was a relative of the Chapel Bradshaws.

Bank Hall is situated on a spectacular site on the slopes of Combs Moss, high above the town. Its most famous past resident is Squire Frith, a Georgian country gentleman, Justice of the Peace, Deputy Lieutenant and High Sheriff, but, above all, huntsman. The story of a chase which took place in 1788, when a poor fox was pursued relentlessly for 40 miles, is told in Squire Frith's 'Hunting Song', which ends with the lines:

In a full flowing bowl,
We will drink a health all,
To that great and true sportsman,
Squire Frith of Bank Hall.

The present house is largely early Victorian, but a dining-room was added in the mid-1870s by W.E. Nesfield, a partner of the famous architect, Norman

Right: *Slack Hall, with the route of the turnpike running through its garden.*

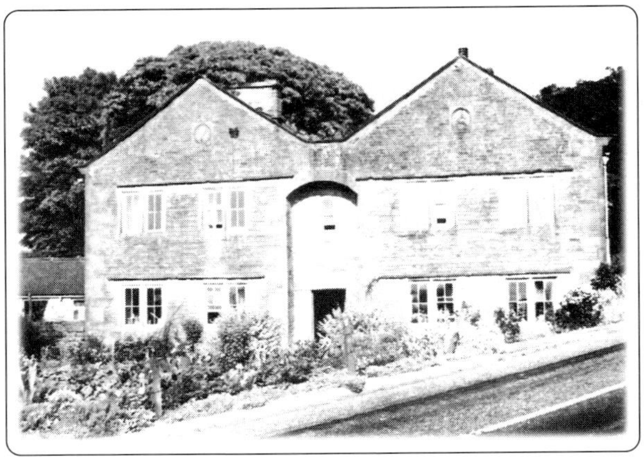

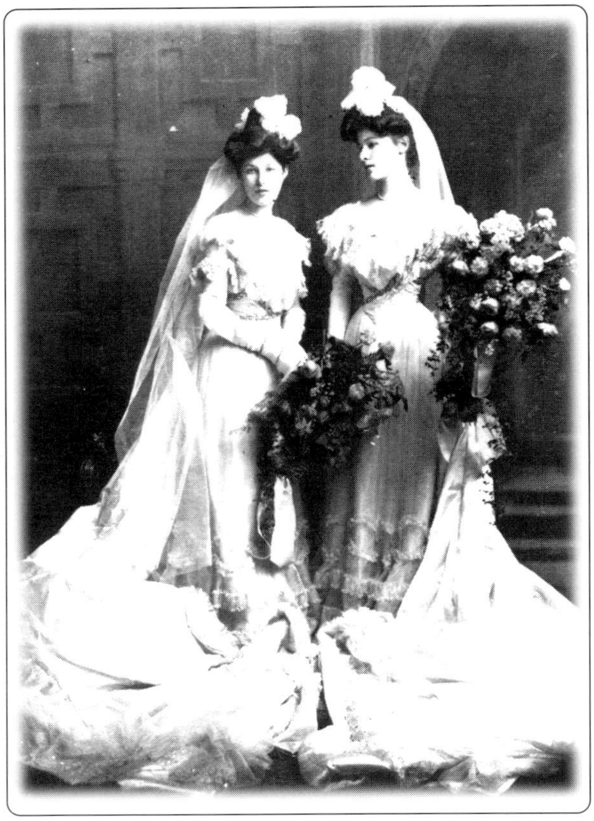

Above: *Lillian and Dorothy Bagshawe, the beautiful twin sisters of Ford Hall.*

Below: *Chapel Market Place before the jubilee horse trough was put in place in 1897.*

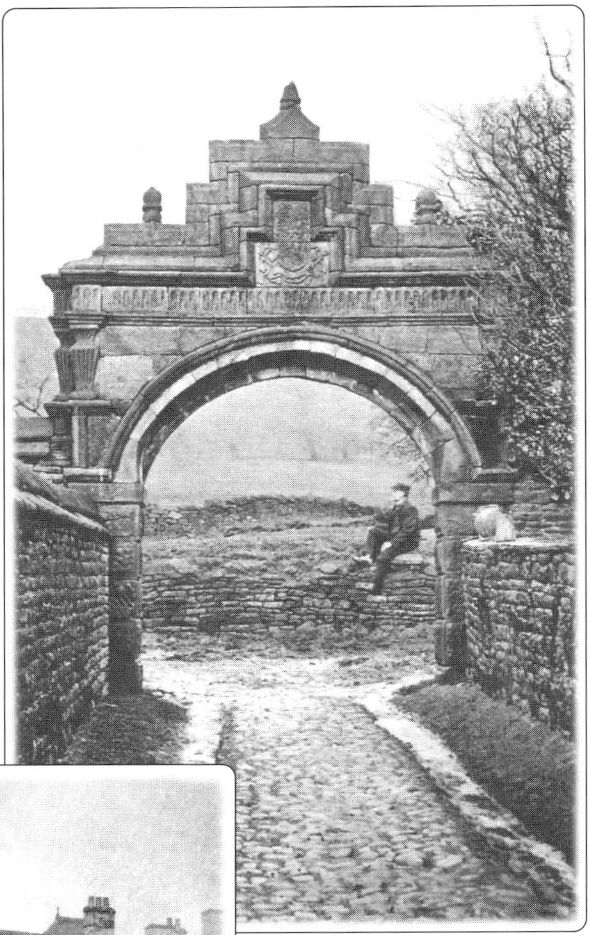

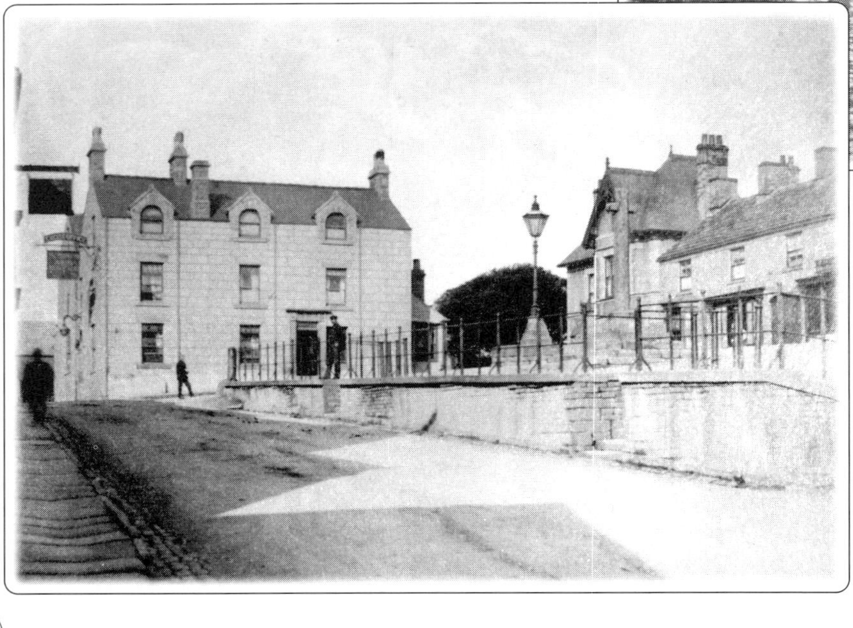

Above: *Locating Bradshaw Hall is quite difficult, but the search is worthwhile, because it is a very beautiful Jacobean house, which is entered through a fine gateway adorned with the arms of the Bradshaws. There are tales of secret passages running from the hall; one leading to Shallcross Hall, the other to the church.*

Shaw. Unfortunately, the extensive panel paintings in this room were sold some years ago, but the delicate stained-glass floral designs on the bay window remain in situ.

Most romantic of all the halls is Ford Hall, which occupies a deep, lonely valley in the hills to the east of Chapel and is the ancestral home of the Bagshawes. Nikolaus Pevsner called the building a *'mixtum compositum'*, and with plenty of justification, for there is a mullioned seventeenth-century portion, a Georgian wing, some nineteenth-century extensions and twentieth-century neo-Georgian additions. The hall is associated with William Bagshawe, the famous Apostle of the Peak. In 1662, William lost his ministry at Glossop because he refused to conform to the *Book of Common Prayer*. Undeterred, he continued to hold secret services in the area, including many meetings at Ford Hall.

The beautiful seventeenth-century Independent Chapel, situated between the railway viaducts at Chapel Milton and founded in 1662, is clear evidence of the strength of Nonconformist feeling in the area.

Other halls in the parish include Whitehough Hall, a charming late-Elizabethan, mullion-windowed building, which adjoins the Old Hall Hotel, and the twin-gabled Slack Hall, which stands almost in the path of the A625 Castleton road. The newer Slack Hall, which was built when the turnpike was routed right through the garden, hides in a wooded hollow to the south of the road.

The Old Town

Writing in the nineteenth century, Britten and Brayley described Chapel-en-le-Frith in their book *Beauties of England and Wales* as:

> *... a small, but neat town, situated in the declivity of a high convex hill, which rises in the midst of a spacious concave, formed by the mountains at the extremity of this county.*

Although Chapel stands in an upland valley, it is, in reality, a hill town, whose oldest houses huddle around a church which stands almost 800ft above sea level.

The lovely cobbled street of Church Brow, which bears a remarkable similarity to the famous Gold Hill in Dorset, drops steeply from the church to Market Street. Its houses, characterised by their peculiar asymmetrically arranged stone lintels and door jambs, form a picturesque terrace. Another street runs westwards from the church to Market Place, whose ancient monuments are scattered about a sloping, cobbled area, which is raised above the modern main road through the town and is therefore largely hidden from the view of passing motorists.

At the eastern extremity of Market Place, there is a set of stocks, which have been much renovated

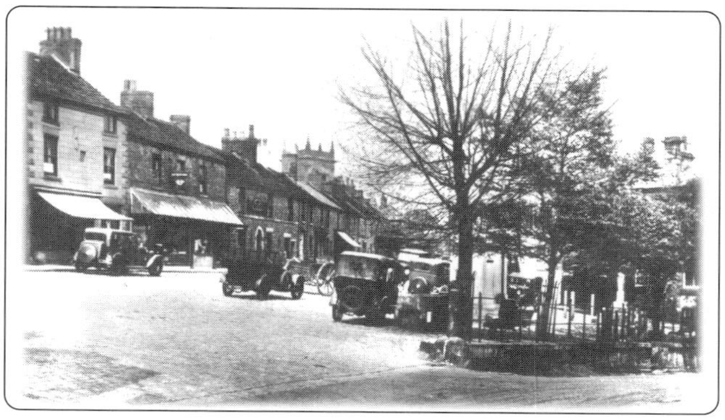

Chapel Market Place between the two world wars, with cars and carts parked at random.

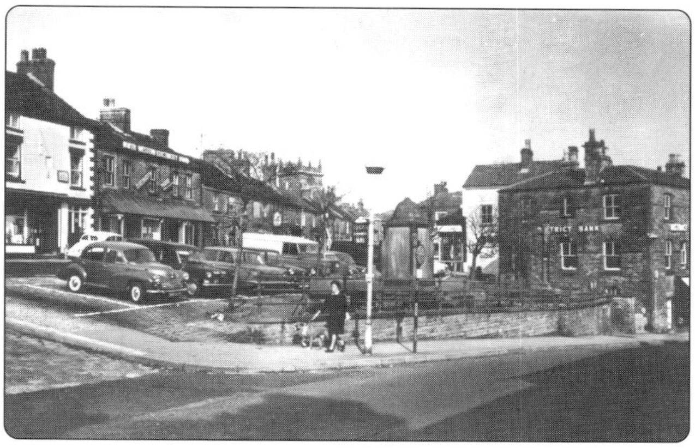

Chapel Market Place after the Second World War, with cars arranged in regimented fashion.

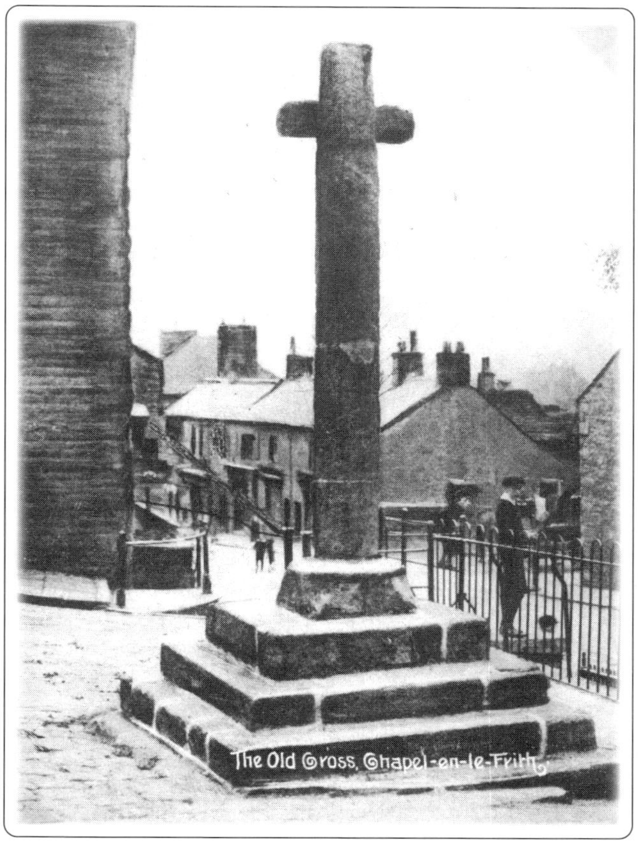

The old market cross, possibly dating from the seventeenth century.

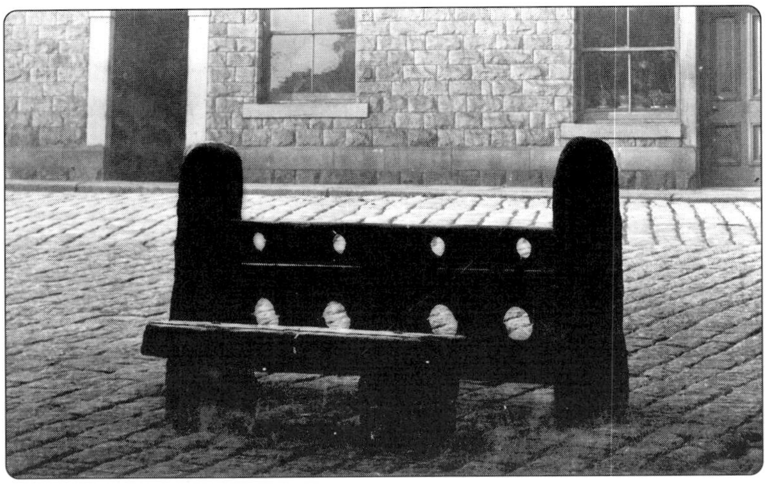

The stocks, possibly originating from the Cromwellian era.

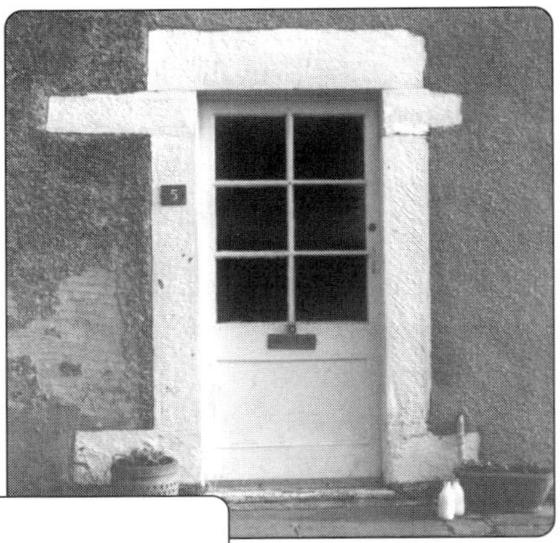

Above: *Asymmetric door decoration, characteristic of old Chapel.*

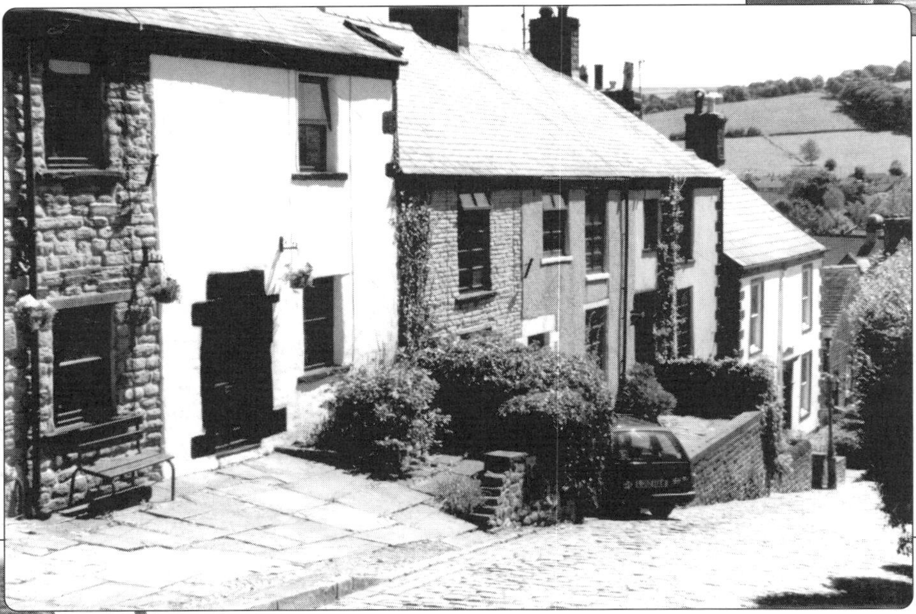

Church Brow, Chapel's most picturesque street, as it is today.

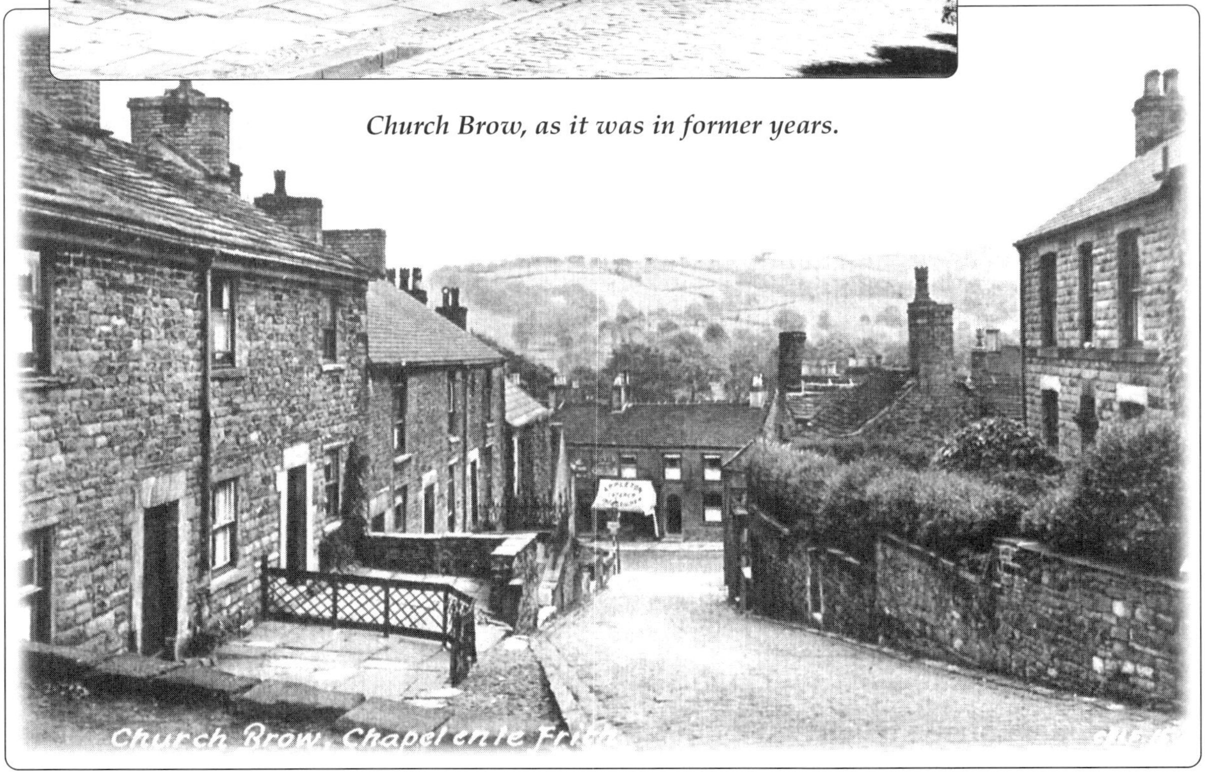

Church Brow, as it was in former years.

over the years but were possibly erected in the Cromwellian period. Close to the stocks is an ancient market cross, of uncertain origin but said by some to contain surface markings that indicate a date of 1636. To the west of the cross is the war memorial, erected by public subscription in 1919, and a horse trough, constructed to celebrate the diamond jubilee of Queen Victoria in 1897. A small weekly stall market is still held on Market Place every Thursday morning.

Chapel at War

The church at Chapel-en-le-Frith became known as 'Derbyshire's Black Hole' in 1648 after 44 Scottish soldiers imprisoned in the building by Cromwell were found dead after two weeks' incarceration.

Many of Chapel's townspeople have served in battle, from the time of the Spanish Armada, when 17 men from Chapel were enlisted, to the two world wars of the twentieth century. The war memorial is a more generous tribute to the fallen than similar monuments in other towns, because it lists all the local men who served in the First World War, rather than just those who died – the soldiers who perished in battle are identified by a cross. Of 599 Chapel men who served, 78 were killed.

An idea of the horror and carnage of the First World War can be gleaned from some descriptions of battle gathered by Fred Heather during his time in the Western General Hospital, where he was recovering from his wounds. One private wrote:

> *After being at the Front for just over four months, I was unlucky enough to get wounded in the face. When the men came to get the wounded out, they passed me by, saying, 'Let him stay there – he won't last much longer.' I was left for 12 hours before I was finally rescued.*

Far fewer local men lost their lives in the Second World War, but there were tragic fatalities. Colin Wilson, whose parents lived at Greyfriars in Combs, was a member of No.90 Squadron and flew bombing missions to Orleans, Hamburg, Remscheld, La Rochelle, Nuremberg, Turin, Munich, Gladbach, Berlin, Manheim, Boulogne, Hanover and Leverkusen, and went on two other more mysterious sorties to North Africa. After being awarded the DFC for his bravery, he was grounded on account of his age, but pleaded to fly again. He volunteered for a squadron of pathfinders, a group of airmen whose task was to fly out and pinpoint targets. Their life expectancy after their first flight was said to be just six weeks. Colin was sent on a pathfinder mission to Nuremberg, but never returned. Having no definite news of his fate, his wife Joyce held out hope that he might have been taken prisoner but she eventually had to accept that he had been killed.

Other tragic losses included three air cadets from Chapel, P. Bond, L. Fox and L. Hall, who were taken on a cross-country flight from their base at RAF Elsham Wolds by an Australian pilot, Flight Sergeant A.W. Buxton and his crew. At 13.20 hours, on 8 September 1943, the aircraft crashed a couple of miles south-east of Wymeswold airfield. All six crew and cadets lost their lives, with Peter Bond becoming the youngest member of the ATC to lose his life on duty. He was just 14 years of age.

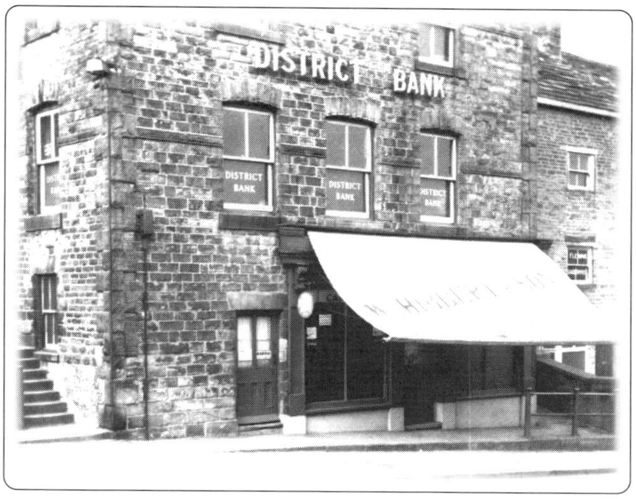

Hibbert's cycle shop and the District Bank – both have now gone to make way for the new NatWest building.

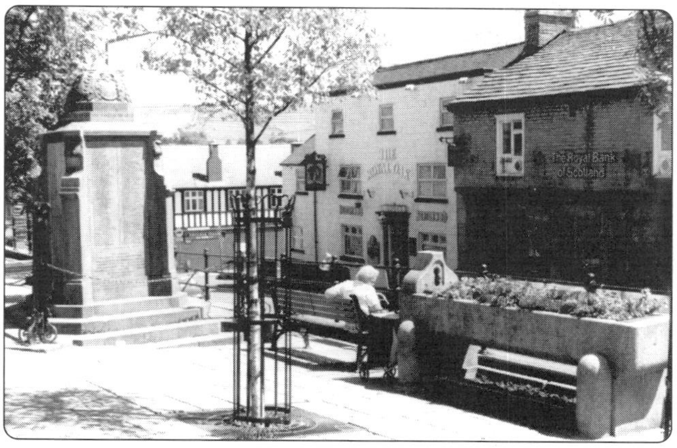

The war memorial and the jubilee horse trough.

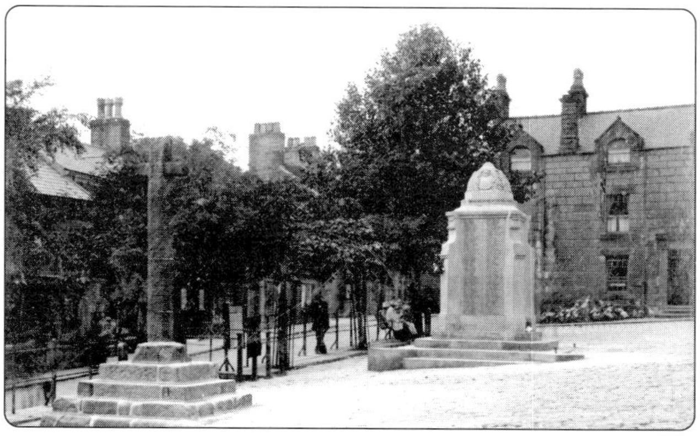

The war memorial (right), *which lists all the Chapel men who served in the First World War. Those who died in the conflict are indentified by small crosses next to their names.*

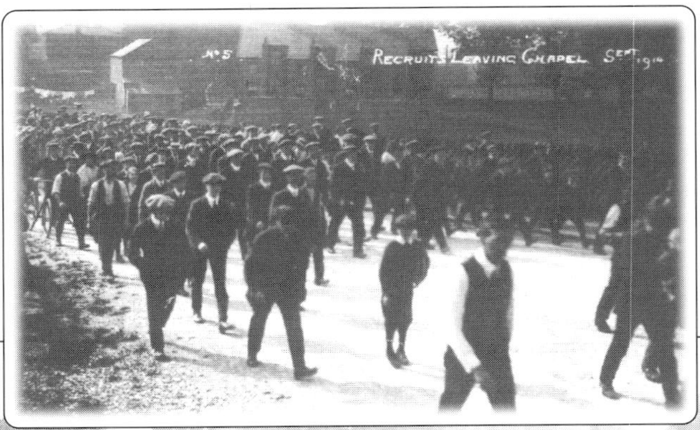

Recruits leaving Chapel in 1914.

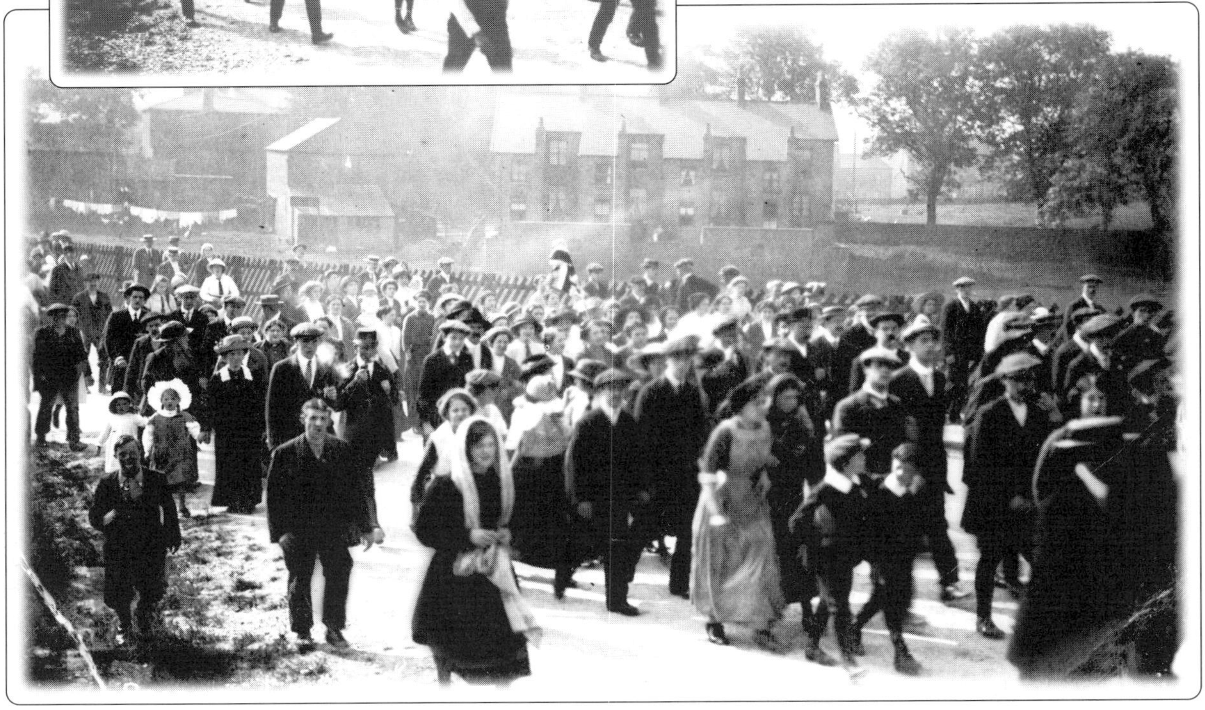

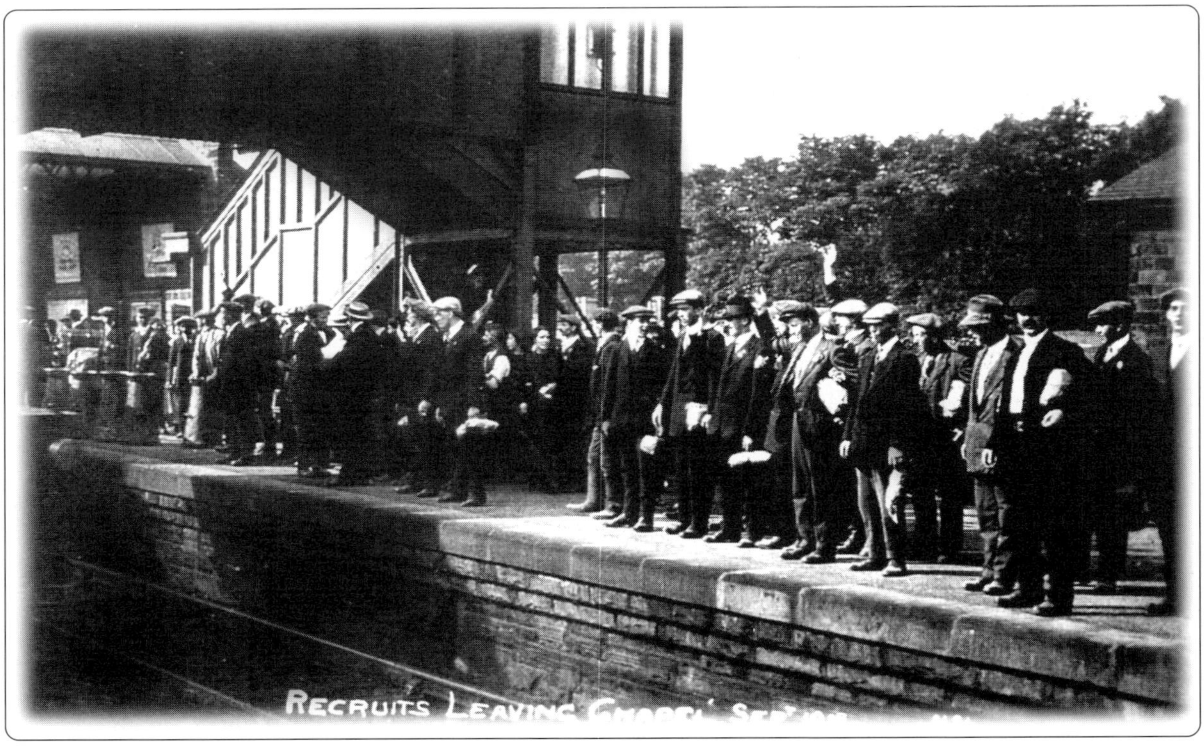

Recruits leaving Chapel Station in 1914.

The British Legion

Described by Bernard West (chairman and secretary of the Chapel Branch of the British Legion).

The British Legion looks after the welfare of people who have served in the Forces. The Chapel Branch has 93 full members, all of whom have served at least seven days 'under the flag', and ten associate members. The president is 85-year-old Derek Eley, while Bernard West is the chairman and secretary. The majority of the Chapel Legion members served in the Second World War; there are now no survivors from the First World War.

From 1938, the British Legion had the use of a room in the Chapel Institute on two evenings per week. After the war, the Institute was renamed the Chapel Memorial Institute and new rules were passed whereby ex-servicemen made up half the committee of the club and three out of seven trustees. From 1954 until 1977, the Memorial Institute served as the Legion's headquarters, but the group now meets bi-monthly, on Thursday nights, at the Pack Horse.

A coffee morning is held annually in April or May, in order to raise funds for the group and poppies are sold in the weeks leading up to Remembrance Day.

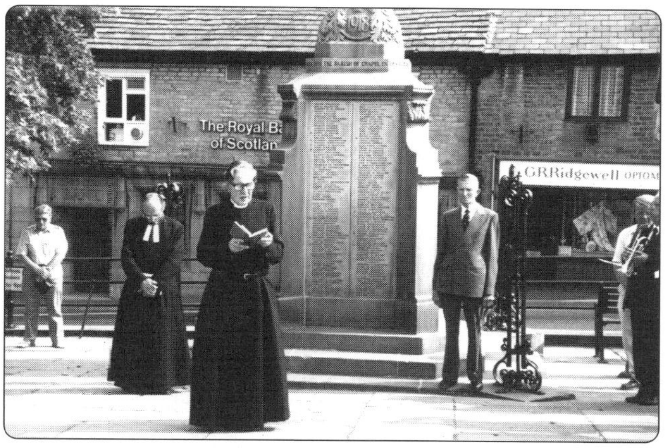

A Remembrance Day service in Market Place, with Bernard West, Revd Bentham and Revd Willey.

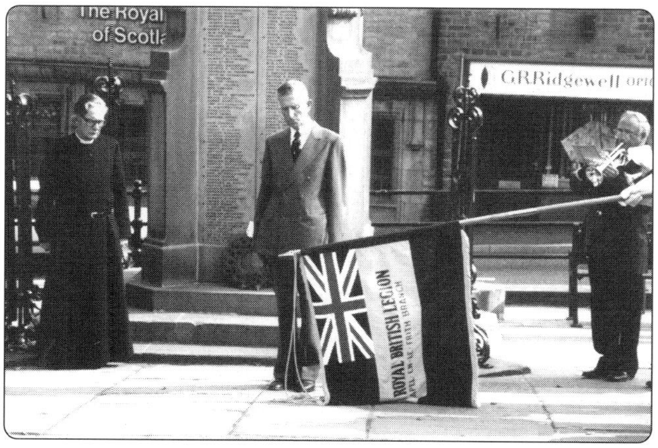

A Remembrance Day service, with Bernard West and Revd Willey.

The money is used to help ex-servicemen, members and non-members alike. Hampers are distributed at Christmas to ex-servicemen as well as to women who have been widowed during the previous year.

A Remembrance Sunday parade, with representatives from all the uniformed organisations, as well as the Parish Council and other groups, follows a route from Thornbrook Road to St Thomas Becket's Church, where a Remembrance Service is held. Wreaths are then placed on the war memorial in Market Place by a variety of organisations in the town. The ceremony is always well attended by Chapel people who still take heed of the last lines of 'For the Fallen', by Laurence Binyon, which ends with the line, 'We will remember them'.

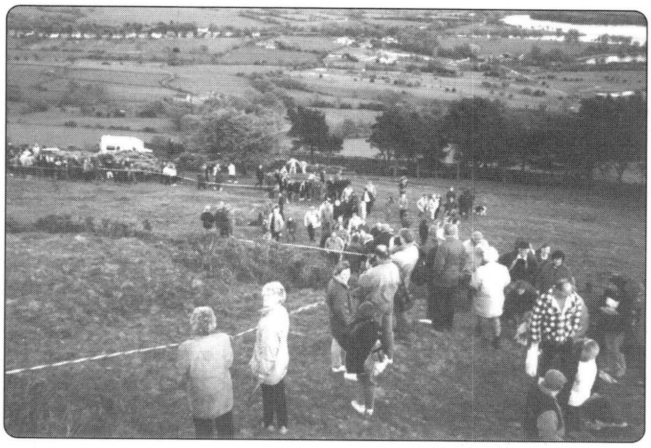

Walking to the summit of Eccles Pike on the 50th anniversary of VE Day.

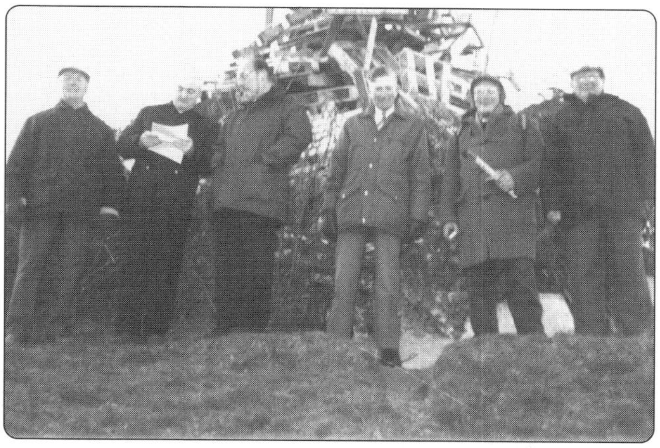

The VE anniversary bonfire with local clergy and members of the British Legion, including Bill Belfield, the last remaining Chapel POW to be held by the Japanese.

The Story of Transport

The large number of inns clustered around Chapel's Market Place is testimony to the town's importance as a staging post on routes across the Pennines. Today, there are four inns overlooking the little cobbled market area, but there were many more in former days. Greyhound Cottage is the former Greyhound

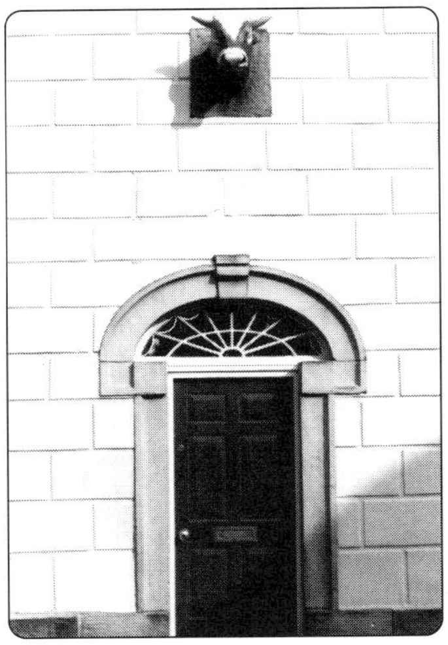

The house on Market Place which formerly housed the Bull's Head Inn.

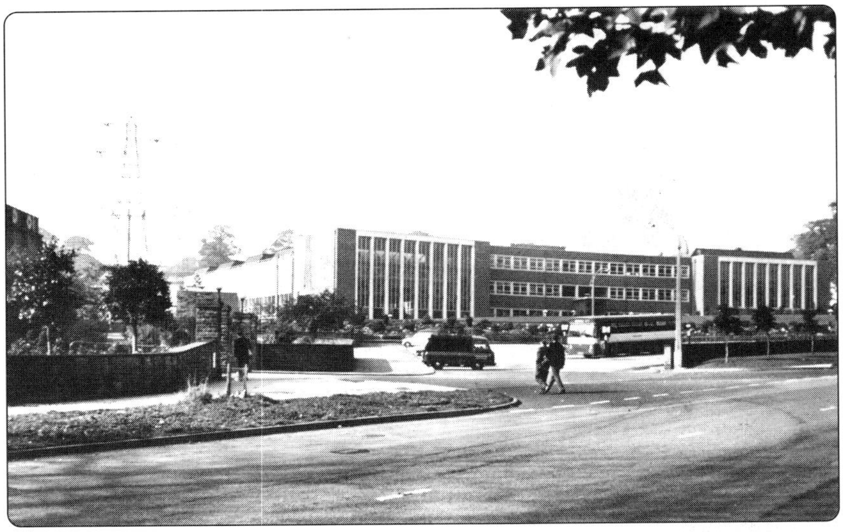

The Ferodo laboratory block, which was opened by the Duke of Edinburgh in 1958.

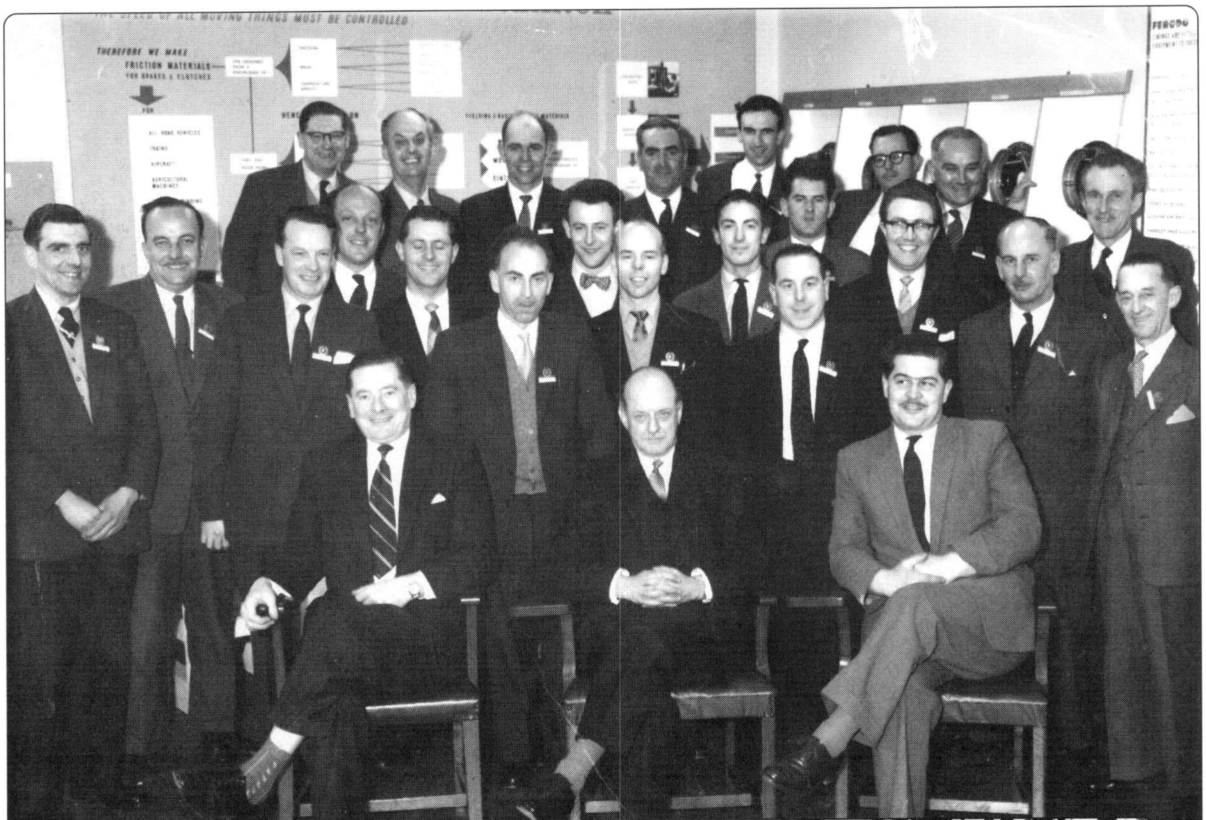

Senior managers at the Ferodo brake-lining company in the 1960s.

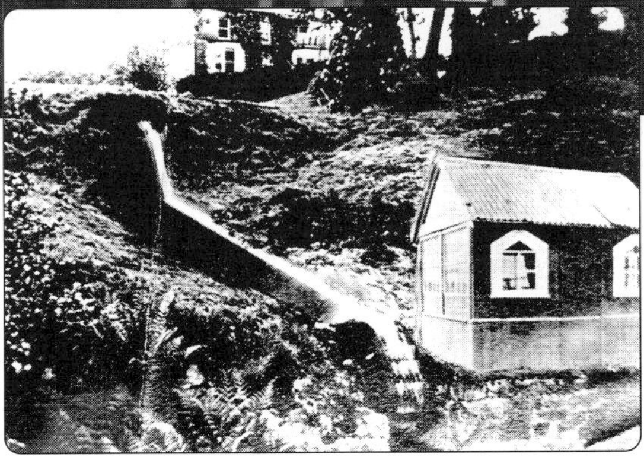

A picture of the garden shed where Herbert Frood carried put his experiments on friction materials.

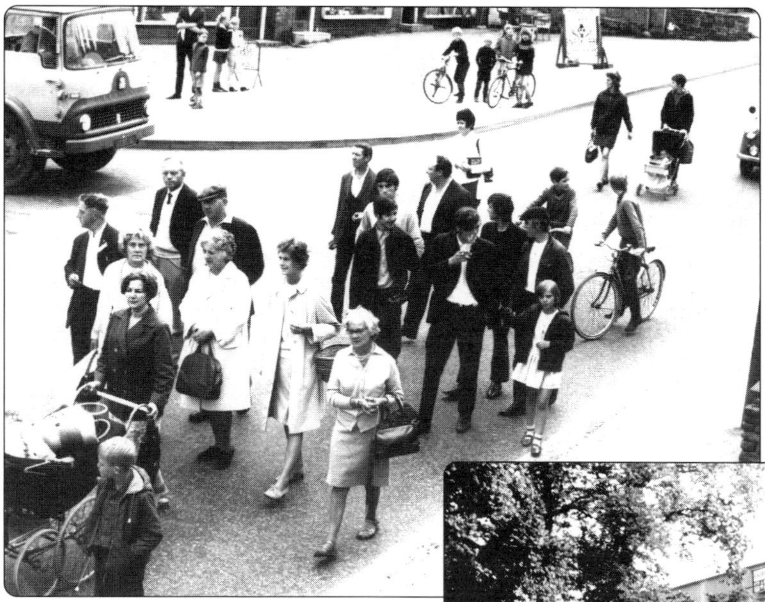

March of townspeople demanding a bypass in 1969.

The new bypass bridge being put in place over Hayfield Road.

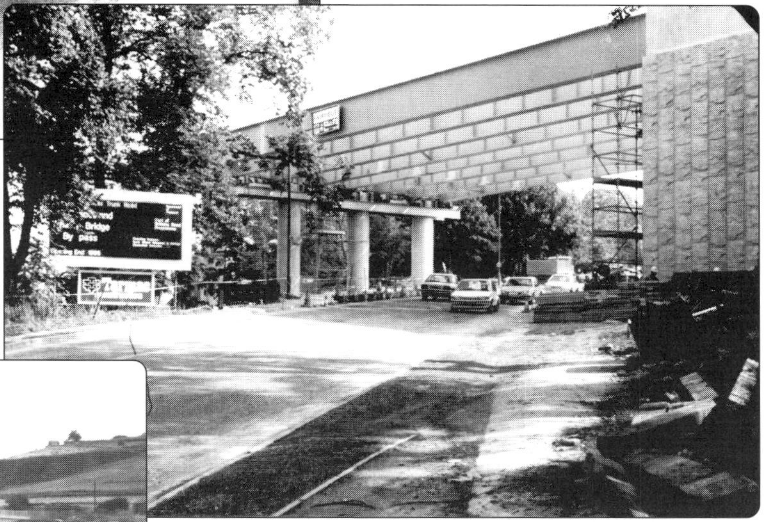

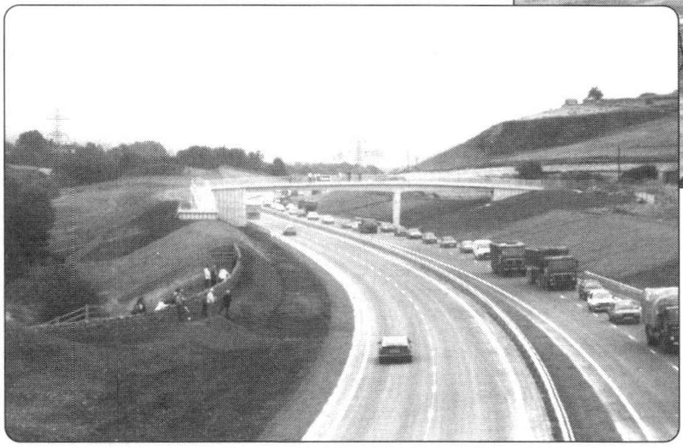

First traffic on the bypass, 1987.

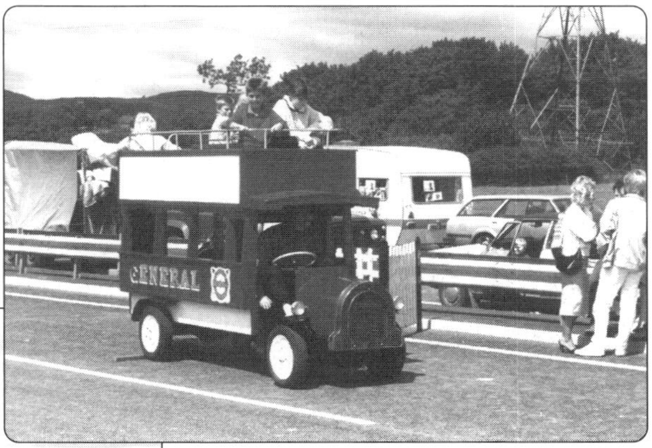

Coach rides for children on the bypass before the road was opened to general traffic in 1987.

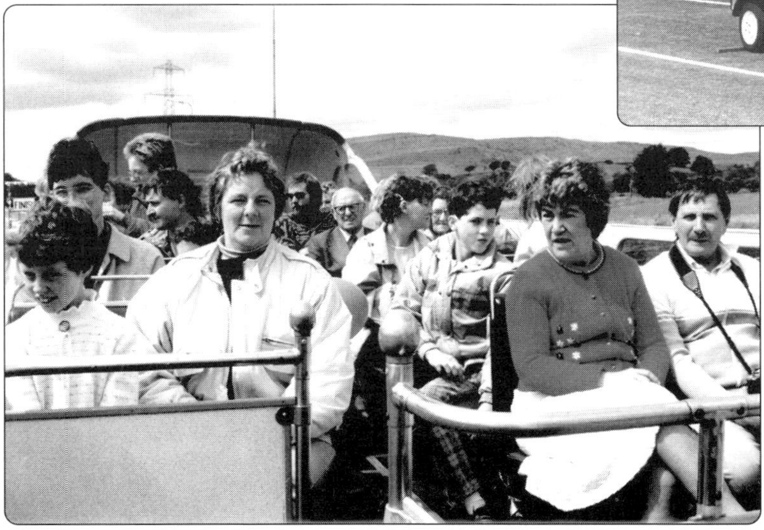

Coach rides for adults on the bypass before it opened in 1987.

Inn and the present Post Office, which bears the inscription TOB 1773, was once the Swan with Two Necks. In addition, a rather grand house with a relief of a bull's head above its doorway housed the Bull's Head Inn up to the time of the Second World War. The Royal Oak was the departure point for the Peak Ranger and Celerity stagecoaches which ran to Stockport and Manchester.

The age of canals impacted on Chapel-en-le-Frith at the end of the eighteenth century with the construction of a tramway to link the quarries at Dove Holes with the Peak Forest Basin at Bugsworth. For much of the tramway's length, the wagons were horse-drawn, but they were carried along the steepest section by a gravitation railway. The wagons travelling up the incline were connected to those which were descending by a hemp rope. The weight of the loaded descending wagons was sufficient to haul the empty wagons up the hill. As the hemp rope had a nasty habit of snapping, chain links were used from 1809, but controlling the wagons was always a risky business, especially for the brakemen who would ride on the descending truck and thrust a pin into a socket between the iron spokes in order to lock the wheels. The path of the old tramway can still be seen clearly on land to the east of the town.

The age of canals was superseded by the age of railways. Chapel, being on a natural routeway, had two stations, one of which has now closed. Tunnels and great viaducts were constructed to take the new lines across the difficult terrain of the High Peak. The twin curving viaducts at Chapel Milton are great monuments to the railway age.

This period was in turn superseded by the age of automobiles, which brought a personal fortune to one enterprising local man. Herbert Frood, who lived in Combs, had become alarmed at the 'untidy and ragged brakes' on wagons which he saw negotiating the steep hills of the High Peak, and set to work in his garden shed to produce something better. Pasteur once said, 'Chance favours the prepared mind', and Frood had the good fortune to come across some discarded, oil-soaked belts on the floor of his father-in-law's belting factory at Rossendale. When he tested the belts in his shed, he found that they had surprising friction properties. As a result of this chance discovery, he hit upon the idea of using oil-impregnated woven cotton as a braking material. In 1897, he began manufacturing his superior brake blocks at Gorton in Manchester. Five years later, he established his first factory at Chapel-en-le-Frith, and, in 1909, after carrying out further research and development work, he obtained the first patent for his product.

Frood's fortune was assured when he convinced the London Omnibus Company, which ran 5,000 horse-drawn trams, that his brake blocks were 'much superior to the old rope currently in use'. Frood went on to produce brake linings for the new motor buses and many other commissions followed. The Ferodo Company eventually became an international organisation with factories on four continents. The firm's laboratory block on Hayfield Road was erected in the 1950s and officially opened by the Duke of Edinburgh. Despite a reduction in the workforce as a result of automation, the brake-lining works are still the major employer in the town and the Ferodo name lives on. However, the company has since been acquired by the American firm, Federal Mogul.

Regeneration

The motor car not only brought employment to Chapel, but also congestion. By the mid-1980s, the town's main road was becoming choked with vehicles. In 1987, a four-mile bypass was built through the Blackbrook Valley. The new road has diverted much of the north–south traffic away from the town, but has done little to relieve Chapel of east–west traffic. In the mid-1990s, traffic-calming measures were introduced on Market Street in the form of 'pregnant pavements', which are designed to slow down traffic by a series of chicanes. The Parish Council decided to take advantage of the new arrangement by installing a series of colourful planters on the pavement projections. This heralded the slow regeneration of the town, which is managed by a Regeneration Committee with representatives from the County, Borough and Parish Councils, the Traders and the Amenity Society. Heritage Economic Regeneration Scheme (HERS) grants have been obtained to restore buildings in the Conservation Area, pavements have been resurfaced with aggregate, setts have been restored, lamppost flower baskets have been installed and interpretation boards have been placed in car parks. In 2000, the Regeneration Committee secured funding from the East Midlands Development agency and the Countryside Agency to enable a six-month 'Health Check' to be carried out by Parish Clerk, Sue Bamford. This involves checking on the town's well-being, in terms of its economy and tourist potential as well as its leisure, social and transport facilities. The Health Check period has been followed by a three-year development programme with a Development Officer, Helen Pakpahan, at the helm.

New Structures

Four brand-new buildings in Chapel-en-le-Frith are of particular significance. Firstly the Safeway store, which opened in 1998, brings over 12,000 shoppers every week to the heart of the town. Secondly the new Infant School building, which opened in 1999, is now part of the newly formed Primary School, which is one of the largest in Derbyshire. Thirdly the new High School and Leisure Centre, scheduled to open on Long Lane in May 2003, will bring with it much-needed and long-awaited improvements in educational and leisure facilities to the town, and fourthly the new High Peak Hospice, financed by volunteer fund-raisers and benefactors, is now playing a key role in bringing relief and care to local people.

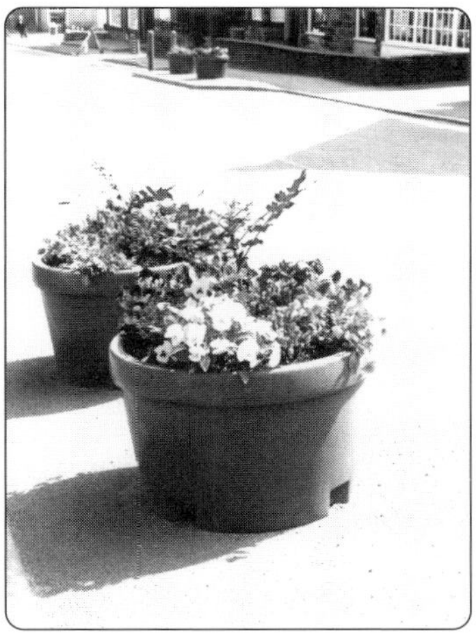

First efforts at regeneration – planters on the pregnant pavements.

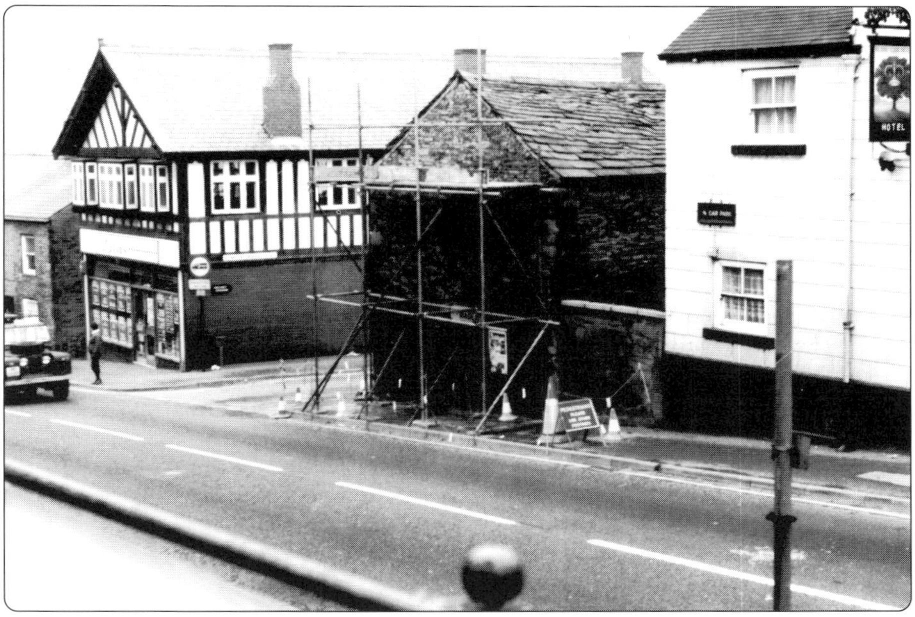

Above: *Park Garage being demolished – the unsightly gap which was created is about to be filled at the time of going to press.*

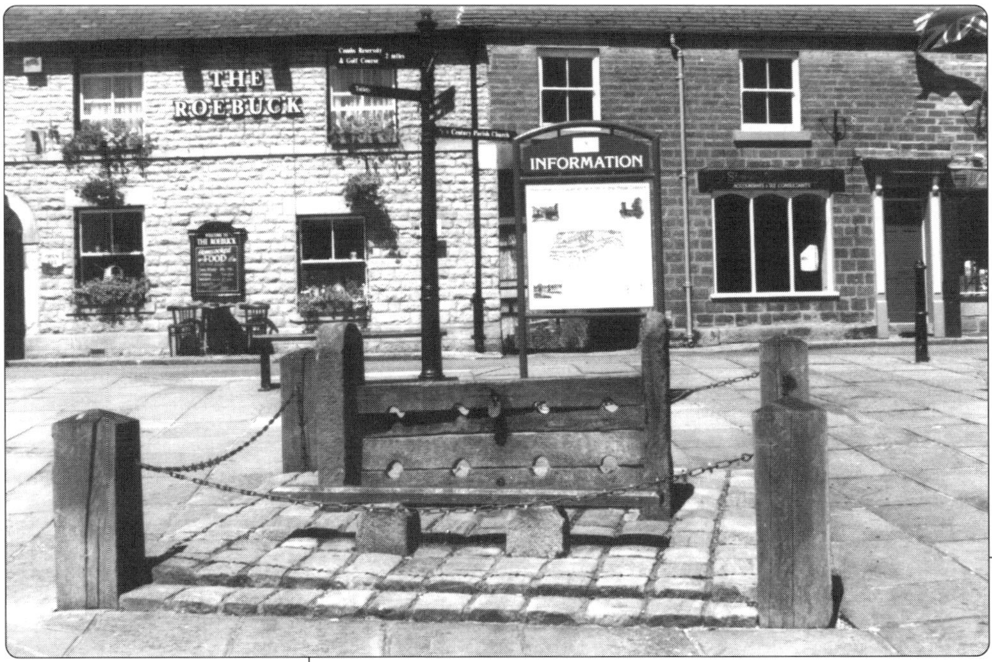

More regeneration – interpretation boards next to the stocks.

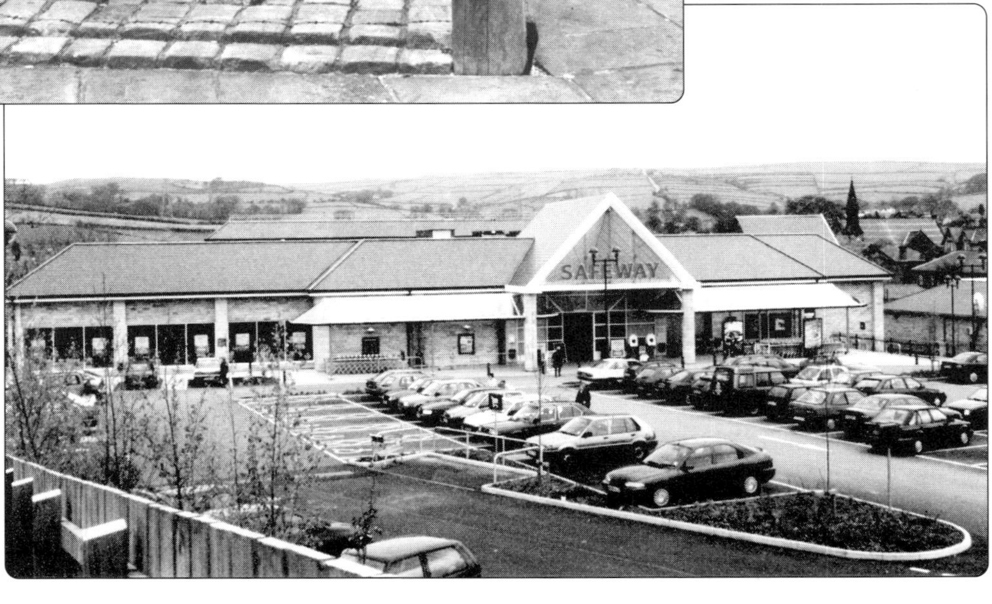

The new Safeway store, which opened in 1998.

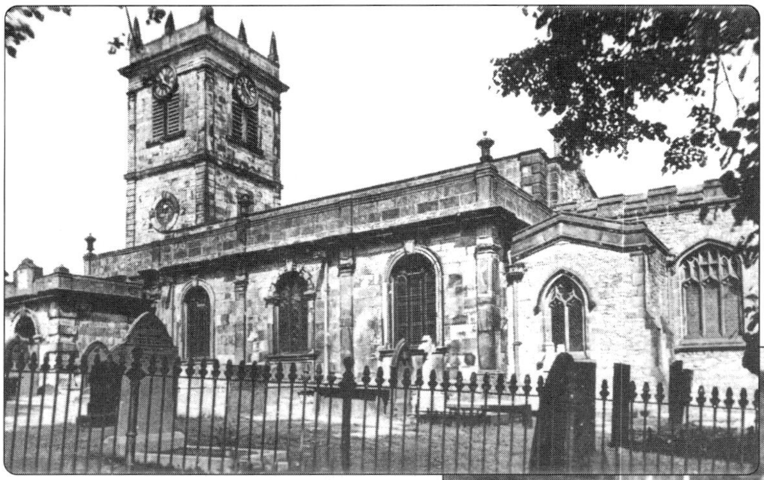

Church of St Thomas Becket from the south-east.

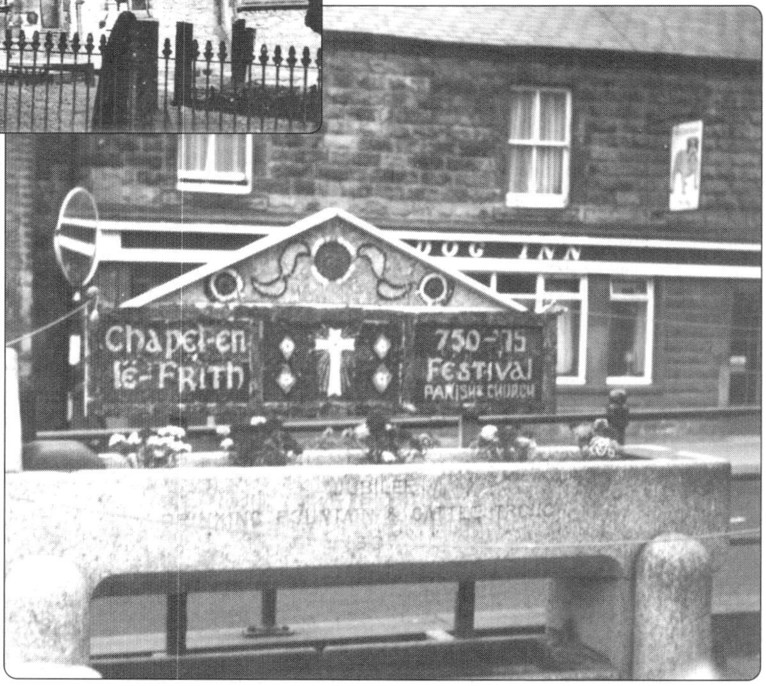

Celebrating the 750th anniversary of the Parish Church with Chapel's only well dressing before 1995.

Celebrating the 750th anniversary of the church in the 1975 carnival.

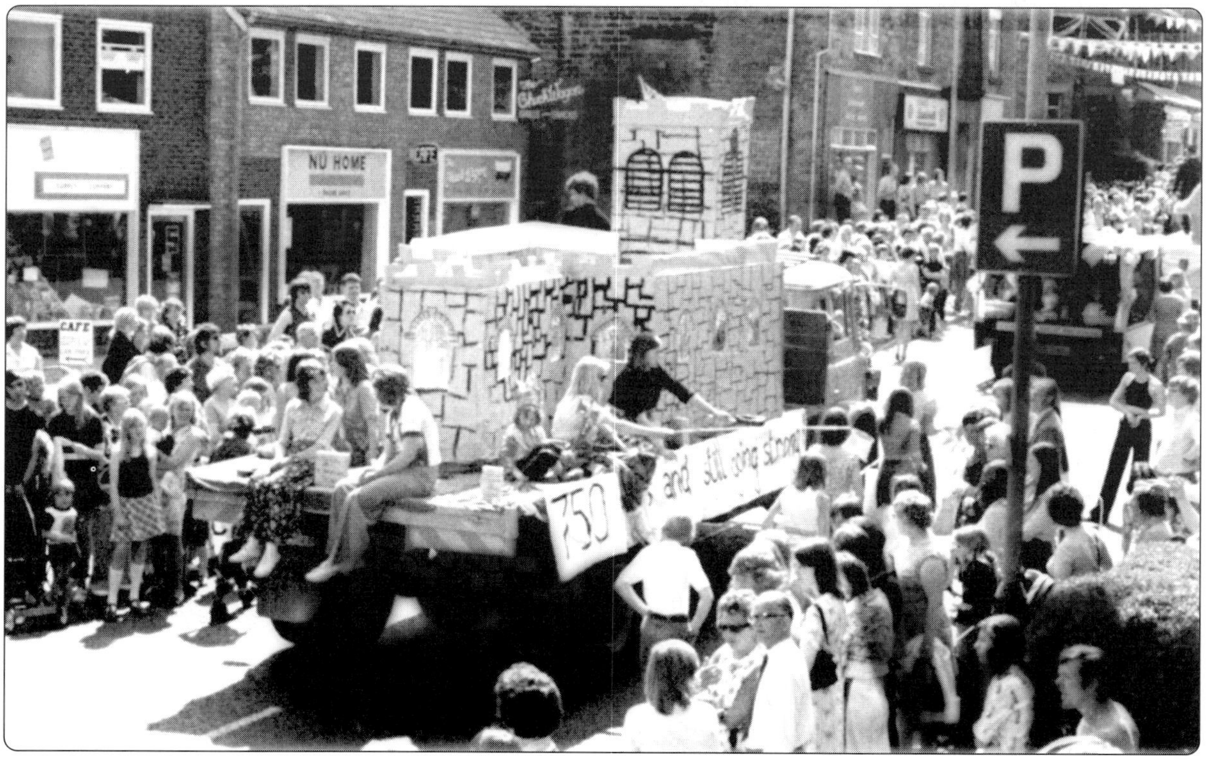

Chapter 2

GOING TO CHAPEL

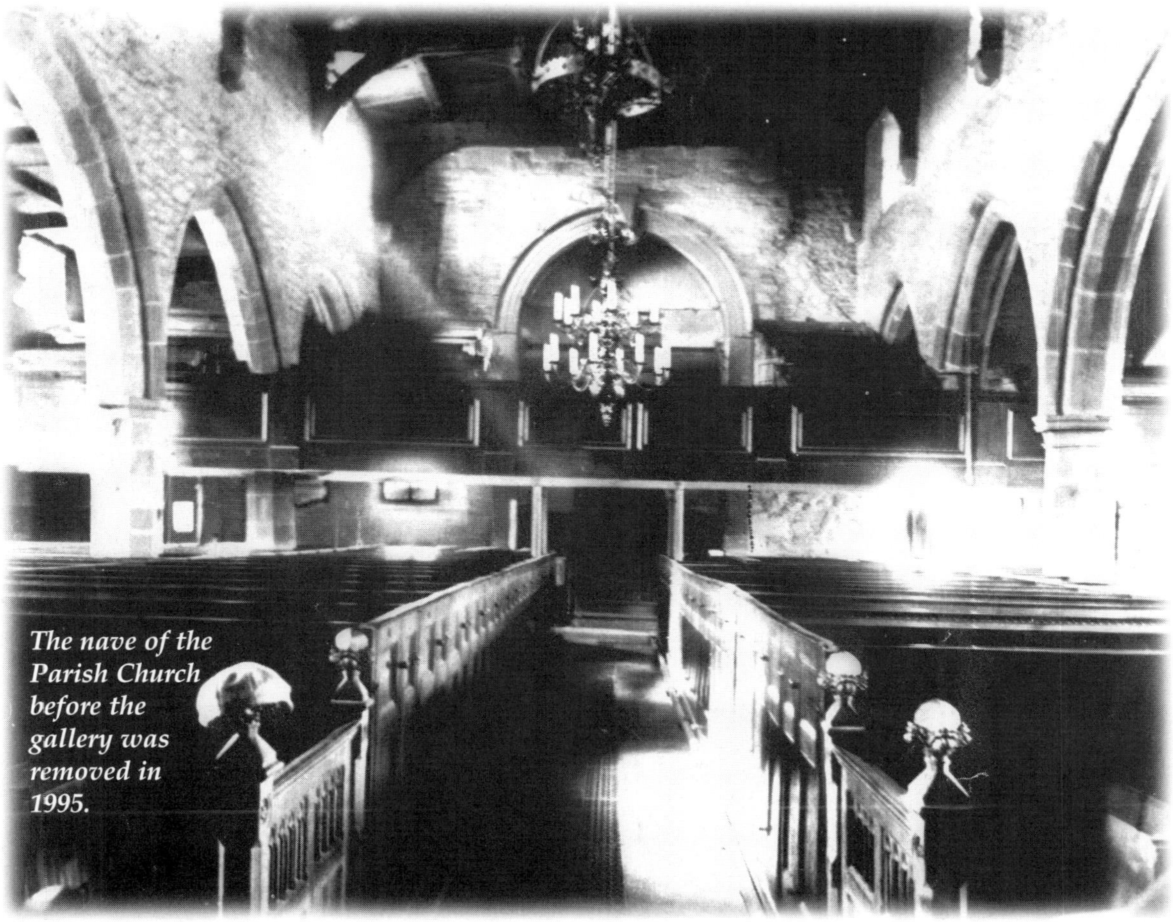

The nave of the Parish Church before the gallery was removed in 1995.

A place of worship has stood on a spur of land below Eccles Pike since 1225, when foresters in the Royal Forest of the Peak were given permission to erect a chapel. The building has been much altered over the years, but a curious stone slab in the churchyard is said by some historians to date back to the days of the Royal Forest. The church is a prominent landmark at the heart of the Dark Peak. It has been at the centre of life in Chapel-en-le-Frith for almost eight centuries.

Methodism was brought to Chapel in the eighteenth century by John Wesley, who made four separate visits to the area. The present Wesleyan Chapel at Town End was described in the local paper as a 'singularly beautiful building' when it was completed in 1874. Chapel-en-le-Frith has another, more surprising connection with John Wesley: one of its long-term residents, Grace Bennett, was engaged to be married to the preacher until Wesley's brother put a stop to their liaison.

The Peak-District town is also home to a Roman-Catholic community, which not only raised sufficient money to build its own church, but also bought its priest a house and a car!

THE PARISH CHURCH OF ST THOMAS BECKET

By David Ripley and Frances Hibbert.

Records exist showing that permission for a chapel of ease was granted in 1225 to foresters and others who looked after King Henry III's interests in the Royal

Forest of the Peak, a hunting preserve for the Norman kings. The chapel was built to serve the many hamlets which had sprung up in the area. It was constructed on high ground close to the crossing of two trackways, one from the salt mines of Cheshire into Yorkshire, and the other a drovers' road, which followed, in part, the Roman road from Derby to Glossop and the North.

It is believed that the chapel was dedicated to St Thomas Becket on 7 July 1225, this being five years after St Thomas Becket's body was moved from the crypt of Canterbury Cathedral to a new shrine in Trinity Chapel, at the eastern end of the cathedral choir. The original chapel, which was no doubt built of stone from a quarry on the lower slopes of Eccles Pike, would have been quite small and probably stood on the area now occupied by the chancel. The little church soon became a focus for the area, and a new town, which became known as Chapel-en-le-Frith (chapel in the forest), began to grow up around it. By 1377, the foresters' chapel had become recognised as a separate Parish Church with its own parochial rights and boundaries.

In 1380, a nave was added, using warm, pink stone from local quarries; later additions included a tower and side aisles. The first tower was situated on the north side, but it was noticed during the rebuilding of the north aisle in 1712 that the structure had become dangerous. As a result, the tower was taken down in 1729 and replaced by a tower at the west end in 1733, when a Classical façade was also added to the south aisle.

The church has, at times, served as a school, a courthouse and, most notoriously, a prison. In 1648, 1,500 Scottish soldiers, who had been taken prisoner by Cromwell at the Battle of Ribbleton Moor, were locked in the church for two weeks. It is said that 44 men were found to be dead when the doors were opened and a further ten collapsed and died while being marched to Chester. For a short period, Chapel's church became known as 'Derbyshire's Black Hole'. However, it is not known where the prisoners are buried and no record of their deaths has been found in any parish records.

The church is known for its box pews. The existing ones, which date from the 1830s, are floored in wood in order to prevent parishioners' feet suffering from the effects of cold stone on damp earth. A church school was constructed on High Street in 1839 and the building served as a school for over 150 years until it was replaced by a new building at Warmbrook in the millennium year. In addition to the school in Chapel-en-le-Frith, the church built and equipped schools at Dove Holes and Whitehough and chapels of ease at Whitehough, Whaley Bridge and Dove Holes, as well as a Mission Hall at Cockyard. Dove Holes eventually became an ecclesiastical parish in its own right; the Mission Hall at Cockyard is still in use, but the other chapels of ease have closed.

During the second half of the nineteenth century, the Parish Church needed extensive repairs. The chancel was rebuilt and an organ chamber was added. The positions of several windows were changed and, as a result of donations from the local gentry, stained-glass windows were installed. At this time, the altar-back of Caen stone was added – this was later used as a memorial to those who died in the First World War. A few more minor changes took place immediately prior to the 700th anniversary of the church in 1925. This event was celebrated by special services conducted by the Bishop of Lichfield, an ox-roast on Market Place and a parade, which included Sunday-school pupils, the choir and members of various church organisations. A local solicitor, William Braylesford Bunting, published a history of the church to mark the anniversary.

In common with many towns in other country areas, life in Chapel-en-le-Frith was markedly affected by the Second World War. Many young men, and some young women, joined the Forces; evacuees arrived and went, and local schools had to resort to part-time schooling, with local children being taught for one half of the day and evacuees for the other half. The church is often visited by former evacuees anxious to trace the families with whom they lodged. Two schools that were evacuated en masse were housed at Bank Hall. The pupils from Westcliffe High School for Girls arrived in 1940, followed by pupils from Chetham's Music School in Manchester. After the war, a carved wooden plaque was installed at the back of the church to commemorate those servicemen who made the supreme sacrifice.

The Becket Room

An extension known as the Becket Room was built between 1973 and 1975 at a cost of £21,000, a sum raised without the benefit of raffles or gaming. The new room was dedicated in 1975 by the Bishop of Derby to commemorate the 750th anniversary of the founding of the church. Designed by George Robb, a local architect, it is employed as a meeting-room and refreshment area after Sunday service and is used for Holy Communion, Healing and Blessing on Thursdays. It also houses the Sunday school, the Rainbow Group (under fives), the Ladies' Guild, Men's Fellowship, meetings of the Parochial Church Council and church events such as the Harvest Supper. The complex incorporates a kitchen and toilets, plus a small passage with a sink for use by the flower arrangers. The Becket Room also allows entrance to the tower and belfry from inside the building. The local Male Voice Choir rehearses in the room, which also serves as a choir vestry, replacing an oblong curtained area at the head of the north aisle, the removal of which has enhanced the internal appearance of the church.

The Becket Room has proved to be of great benefit to the town and is used most days of the week, both

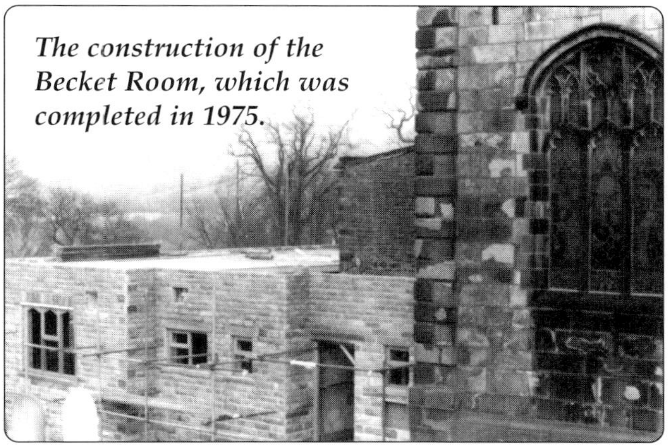

The construction of the Becket Room, which was completed in 1975.

during the day and in the evening. Current members find it hard to believe that the church managed without this facility for 750 years!

The New Window

In recent years the church has suffered at the hands of vandals, who have stripped lead from the roof and set fire to a wooden shed, resulting in damage to two stained-glass windows. The lead roof has now been replaced by a steel one and although one of the damaged windows was repairable, the other was replaced by a new stained-glass window designed and made by local craftsmen.

The new window at the head of the north aisle was constructed by Steven Parsonson, imaginatively designed and engraved with lettering by David Pilkington and dedicated by the Bishop of Repton in 1997. The window's semi-abstract motifs are brilliantly coloured. Red areas at the top are remains from the previous window and represent the fire that destroyed it. Descending gold flashes, set against a heavenly blue, symbolise spiritual food and drink, while royal purple is used to represent the King of Kings. The design also features a background cross. Although the new window is uncompromisingly modern, its vertical grid is designed to match the older stained-glass windows in the church.

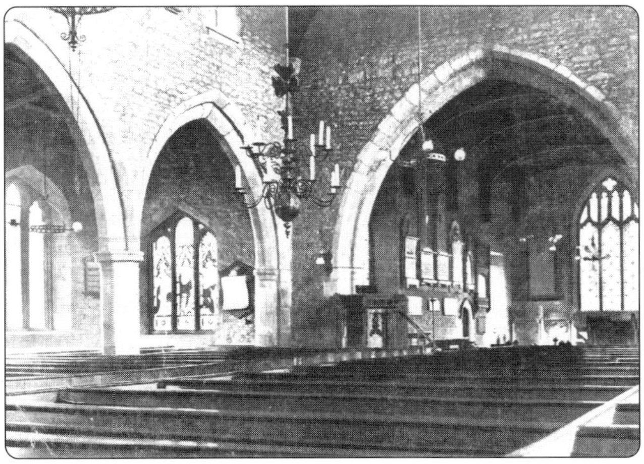

The interior of the church before the window at the head of the north aisle was destroyed by fire.

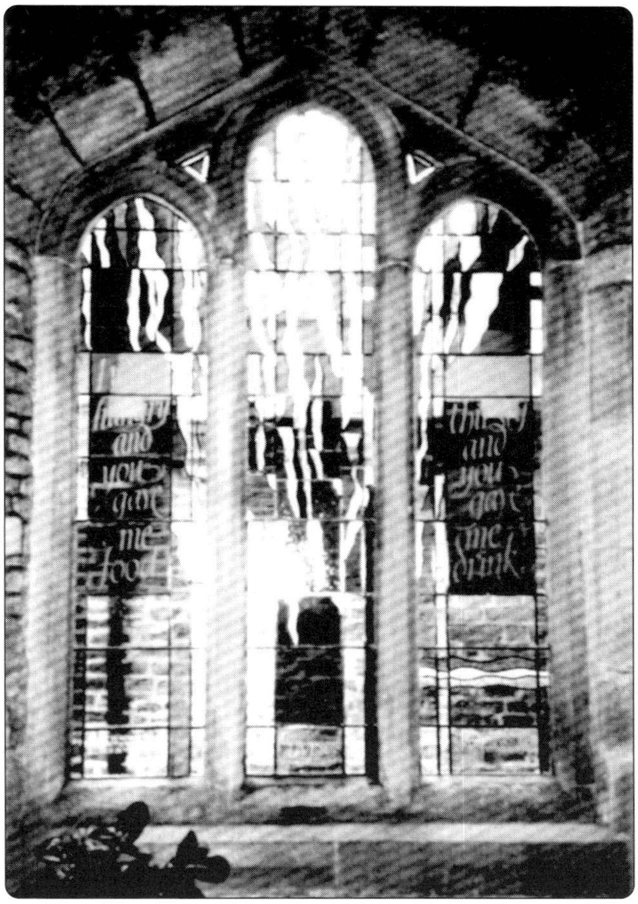

The new window, designed by David Pilkington.

The Tower & Bells

There was at least one bell in the old tower, which was demolished in 1729 by John Platt at a cost of £10.10s.6d. In 1731, a contract was signed between George Platt (brother of John) and the 'Gentlemen of the Parish' for the building of a new tower. The contract is still preserved in the church records.

The new tower was erected in 1733 and given a peal of six bells, five of which were cast by Abraham Rudhall of Gloucester (whose business became part of the Whitechapel Bell Foundry in London). The fourth of these bells does not bear any inscription and it is thought that this could be the Great Bell mentioned in the parish registers as having been cast in Wigan in 1701.

When the bells were rehung in 1895, a new timber and iron bell frame was provided, and the rehanging of 1933, on the 200th anniversary of their installation, saw the introduction of ball bearings. It is interesting to note that the five bells cast by Abraham Rudhall were transported by sea from Gloucester to Liverpool, and then carried by horse-and-cart teams to Chapel-en-le-Frith. Another rehanging took place in 1990, when new wheels, crown staples and head stocks were provided for the fifth bell and the tenor bell (which weighs 11cwt). The work was carried out by Eyre & Smith of Melbourne, Derbyshire.

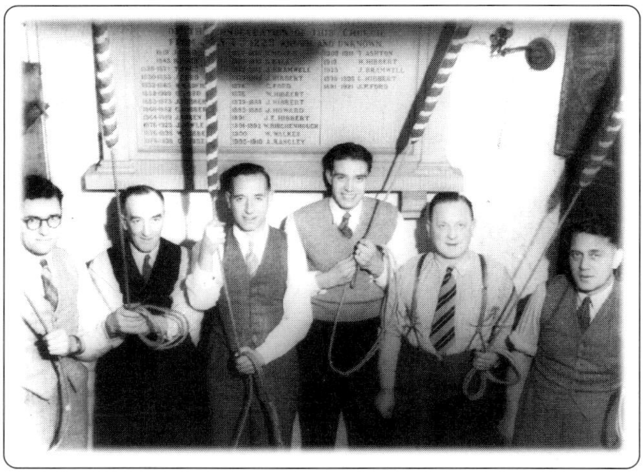

Bell-ringers of old, in 1948. Left to right: *Arthur Hibbert, Billy Fryer, George Ashmore, Hector Smith, Walter Pearson, Harold Pearson.*

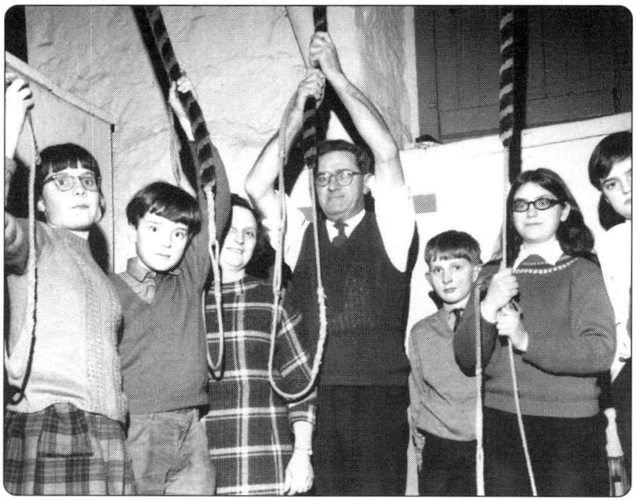

Young bell-ringers, in 1972. Left to right: *Valerie Croft, Peter Hibbert, Frances Hibbert, Arthur Hibbert, Peter Ripley, Elizabeth Hibbert, William Hibbert.*

At one time, midday bells and curfew bells were rung daily and passing bells were rung to mark the passing away of parishioners. During the Second World War all these customs ceased and the bells were not even rung for services or weddings. Unfortunately, most of the bell customs were not revived after the war, but the Shrove bell, originally used to mark the holiday given to the apprentices before the rigours of Lent, is still rung at 11a.m. on Shrove Tuesday. The bells are rung regularly for Sunday services and on local, national and royal occasions. The bells were rung to mark the millennium and on New Year's Eve 1988, to mark the 400th anniversary of the defeat of the Spanish Armada.

The five bells cast in 1733 bear the following inscriptions: treble: 'Peace and good neighbourhood', Note E; 2nd: 'Prosperity to this parish', Note D; 3rd: 'We were all cast at Glocester by A Rudhal', Note C; 4th: does not bear an inscription, but is thought to be the old Great Bell of 1701, Note B; 5th: 'Jasper Frith and John Wainwright, Churchwardens', Note A; tenor: 'I to the Church the living call And to the grave do summon all', Note G.

The Clock

There have been three clocks in the tower. The old tower probably had a one-handed, stone clock, the face of which is now on the wall of the ringing-room. It is assumed that the single hand moved over quarter-hour divisions and that the clock struck the hours. A 'skeleton clock' was installed in the new tower of 1733, but when a new clock was installed in 1856, it was placed in a turret above the stables at Bowden Hall. It is still in working order.

The clock of 1856, which is still in place, was made by T. Hammond of Manchester (successor to Peter Clare, of whom it was said, 'Peter Clare, that cunning old fox, who keeps the sun right by the time of his clocks') and was provided at the sole expense of Mrs Slack of Bowden Hall – the cost of installation being borne by the parishioners. Quarter-hour chimes were added in 1897, the cost being met by Mrs Bayley of Broughton Park, Manchester, in memory of her parents, Henry Constantine Renshaw JP and his wife Lucy, who had resided in the parish at Bank Hall. The chimes ring the quarter hours cumulatively, the full hour giving music to the verse:

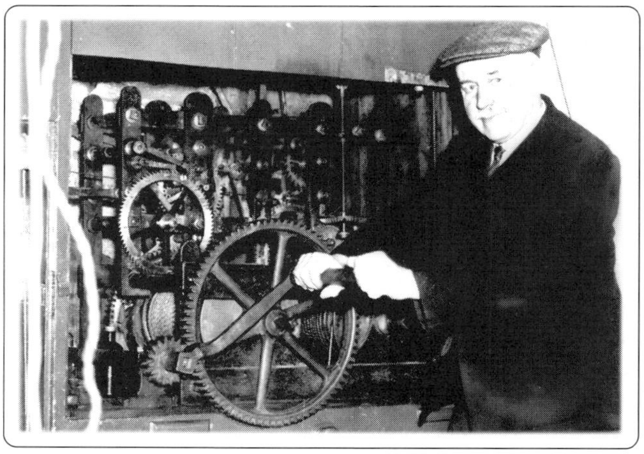

William Henry Hibbert winding the clock mechanism in 1950.

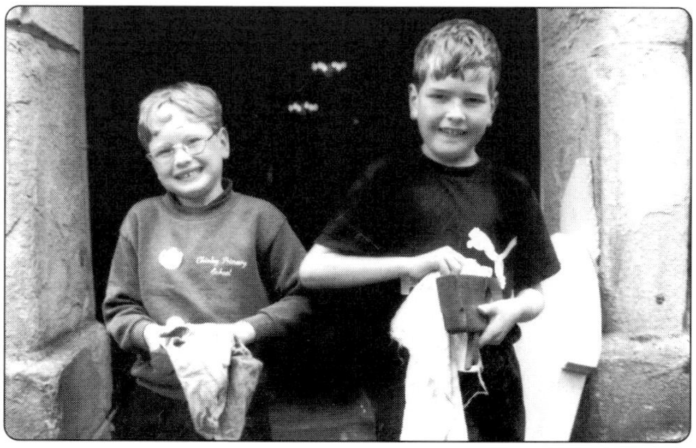

James and Peter Hibbert polishing their grandfather's tools. Peter is now the winder of the clock.

Lord by the Power,
Our footsteps guide,
So in the hour,
No foot shall slide.

The clock is in need of refurbishment, particularly with regard to the fingers and dials, and expert advice is being sought at the time of writing from John Smith & Sons of Derby. The clock has been cared for by the Hibbert family ever since its installation: William, 1856–1900; William Henry, 1900–50; Arthur, 1950–89; and now Peter Hibbert. Electric winding has replaced twice-weekly hand winding.

The Organ

The church has a fine organ, parts of which date back to the 1770s. The organ was originally on a loft under the chancel arch – a similar gallery was constructed at the west end. The galleries and the organ were completed in 1778. The galleries cost £30 and the organ, built by Richard Parker of Manchester, cost £150. The installation was celebrated on 13 and 14 July 1778 by the performance of two oratorios: Handel's *Messiah* and *Judas Maccabeus*.

In the early-nineteenth century, the east gallery was demolished and the organ was moved to the west gallery. When the west gallery was demolished in 1894, a new organ chamber was built at the eastern end of the south aisle. The organ was converted to electrical blowers in 1933 and completely rebuilt in 1998, utilising parts of an organ obtained from a church which was being demolished in Manchester.

The Churchyard

The churchyard was enlarged in 1940 and has been expanded twice since that time. Graves from most of the burials carried out since 1925 are on the slope below the original graveyard, making maintenance difficult. As there is no cemetery in the area, the church now has a cremation plot to cater for burials of ashes.

When the Becket Room was constructed, alterations had to be made to the graveyard on the west side of the church. The Saxon cross, which had been found in a wall at Ollerenshaw Hall, was moved from the Hodgson family grave, where it had been put for safe keeping in 1926, to a new site north-west of the tower.

The churchyard also contains a stone slab inscribed with the initials P.L. and a crude drawing of an axe. It is said that this simple tombstone marks the grave of a forester from the days of the Royal Forest. The claim may not be true, but it can be said with confidence that a church has stood on this high ground ever since 1225, when the foresters were first given permission to build a chapel in the forest.

A Brief History of the Methodist Church in Chapel-en-le-Frith

Written in 1974 by the late Gordon Helps for inclusion in the centenary souvenir programme, Gordon's text, in a slightly edited version, is reproduced here by kind permission of Revd David Youngs (the present minister of the church) and Gordon's son, Peter Helps.

Although we at Town End Methodist Church are celebrating [in 1974] the centenary of the opening of the present church building on 9 April 1874, the history of Methodism (or Wesleyan Methodism as it was then known) in Chapel-en-le-Frith goes back to John Wesley's first recorded visit to the area on 28 May 1745. This was the famous occasion when the miller at Mill Town (Chapel Milton) where Wesley was preaching in the open air, tried unsuccessfully to drown out Wesley's voice by opening the sluice of the millpond. As the preacher recorded, 'It was labour lost; for my strength was so increased, that I was heard to the very skirts of the congregation.'

Wesley paid further visits to the area, on 15 April 1766 and 1 April 1782, when he reported struggling through wind, snow and rain to the chapel built in 1780. This was on land on the west side of Warmbrook Lane, owned by Thomas Oliver of Longnor, which is also the site of the present chapel. He obviously felt his struggle against the elements to be worthwhile, for he reported: 'I soon forgot my labour, finding a large congregation that were all athirst for God.'

On 3 April 1786, he paid his last recorded visit:

> *... to preach to a crowded congregation in the new house near Chapel-en-le-Frith. Many of these lively people came from among the mountains, reminding me of the verse which says, 'The hills are a refuge for wild goats, and so are stoney rocks for the conies!'*

In his book on the history of Chapel-en-le-Frith and its people, William Braylesford Bunting notes that services were held in a building behind the Shoulder of Mutton Inn, before the chapel was built in 1780. An old stone building was recently exposed to view by demolition preceding the construction of the new Shoulder of Mutton, and it is thought that this may have been the old meeting-place.

By 1811 the church was flourishing and Thomas Oliver sold land containing 299 square yards, 'including a Chapel or Meeting House for use by people called Methodists' to Henry Merrill and ten other trustees for five guineas. In January 1832 Henry Kirk sold to the trustees an adjacent plot containing 252.5 square yards for the augmentation of the Chapel yard and in May 1852 John and Thomas Slack sold a further plot, containing three dwelling houses, to the trustees so they could erect a Sunday school. The three houses were demolished and the new Sunday school was built (on the eastern side of the then

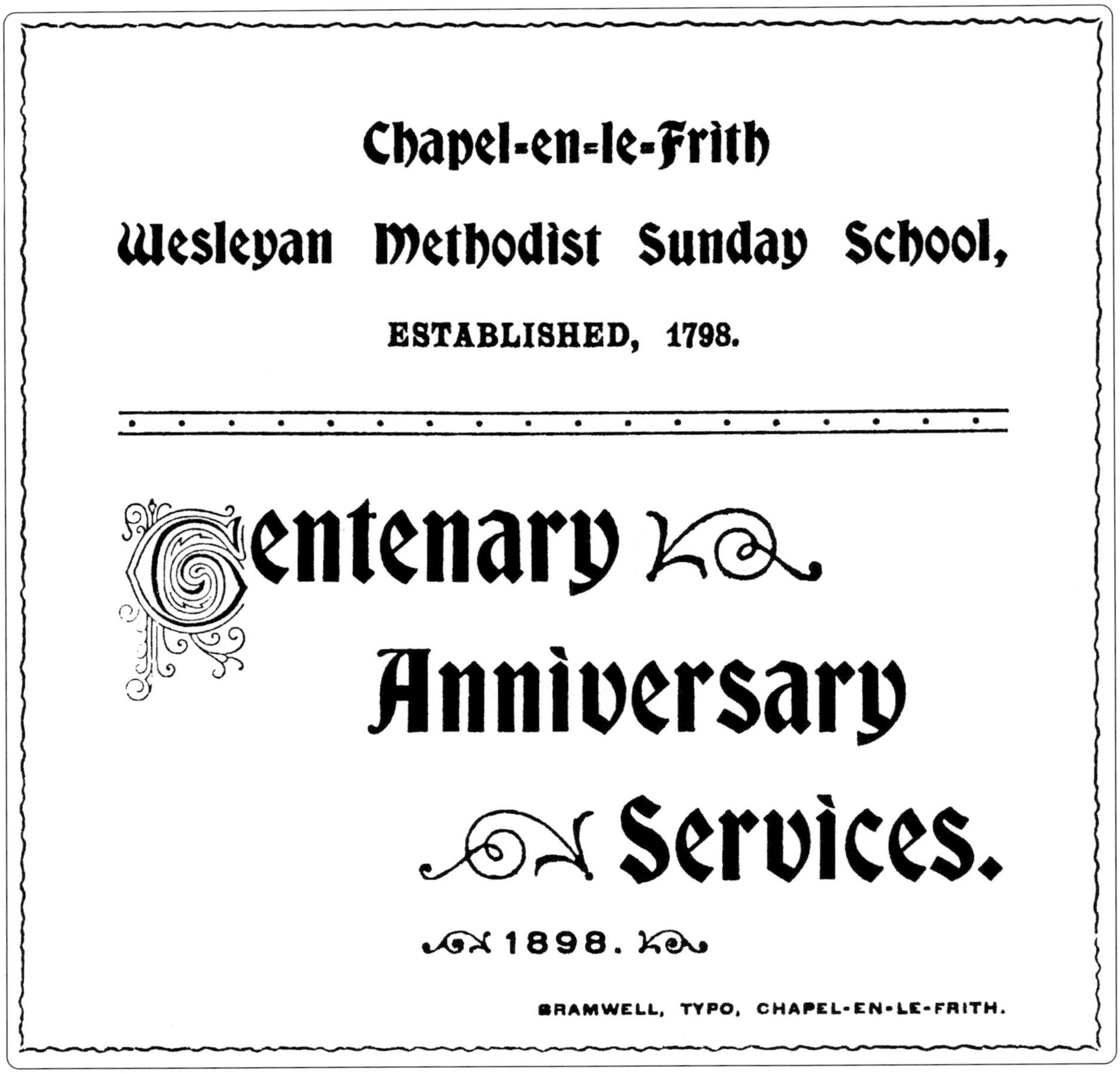
Chapel-en-le-Frith

Wesleyan Methodist Sunday School,

ESTABLISHED, 1798.

Centenary Anniversary Services.

1898.

BRAMWELL, TYPO, CHAPEL-EN-LE-FRITH.

Warmbrook Lane, now School Yard) in 1853. The cost of the land and the building amounted to £661.

The congregation grew progressively and in 1871 it was decided to demolish the 90-year-old chapel and build a much larger one. Negotiations to purchase 4,800 square yards of land from Joseph and Ebenezer Hyde took place and Messrs Goddard and Hadfield were able to start the construction of a new chapel designed by C.W. Johnson.

The foundation-stone was laid on 9 October 1872 by D. Holland of Macclesfield, S. Turnbull of Manchester, Thomas Barker of Stockport, Eli Atkin and Norman Bennett. The new building cost £2,450 and was opened for worship on Thursday 9 April 1874 by Revd George T. Perks. It is reported that collections at this and the four succeeding special services amounted to £350!

The land purchase was finally completed in October 1874 and the plot was large enough to enable a minister's house to be built adjacent to the new chapel. The house was constructed in 1885, thanks to a donation by Miss Heald of Chapel Milton of £1,000 towards the total (furnished) cost of £1,200.

With a growing population, a day school was added to the Sunday school in 1870, but the need for larger school premises was soon felt. An extension was duly built in 1877, concluding five years of concentrated growth. There are no more recorded land acquisitions until 1921, when the trustees began to think seriously of expanding the school premises once again. They bought a plot of 260 square yards on the south side of the school for £500 from the executors of Miss J.E. Williamson, one of whom was John Sidebottom, who will be remembered by older residents as the town's jeweller, as well as a benefactor and a devout Wesleyan.

In 1876, a new organ, built by James Cole of Manchester, was dedicated at the Easter anniversary service. Further enhancements to the church were carried out in 1890, when panelled screens were erected at the entrance and in the choir gallery. The work cost £450.

The next milestone in the church's history was the golden jubilee, celebrated in April 1924. Without

Right: *The opening of the new buildings at the Methodist Church in 1994. The group includes: Revd Colin Smith (the minister in 1994), Revd Malcolm Willey (previous minister) and High Peak Mayor, John Francis.*

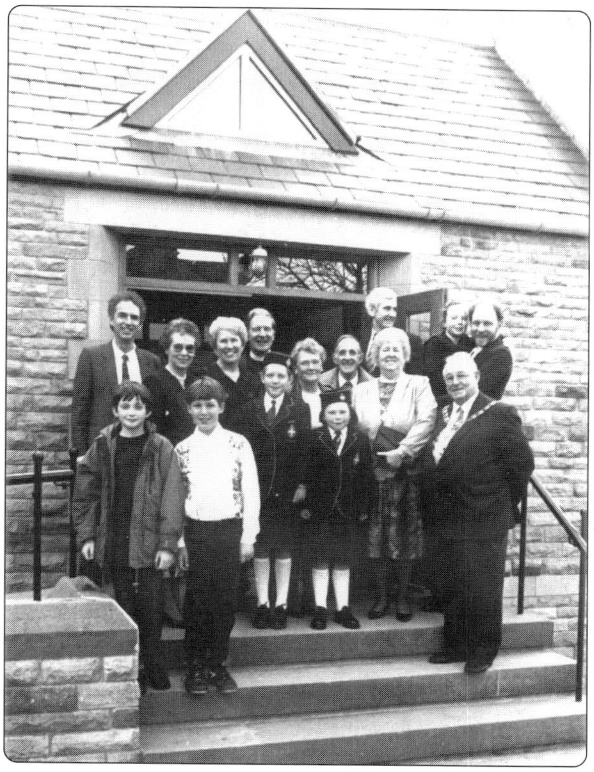

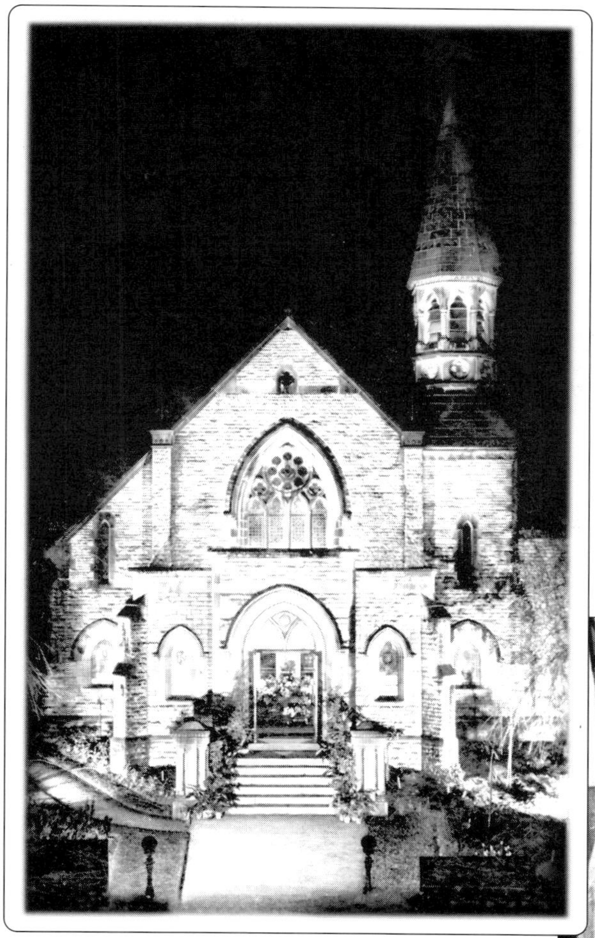

The Methodist Church floodlit for the coronation of George V on 12 May 1937.

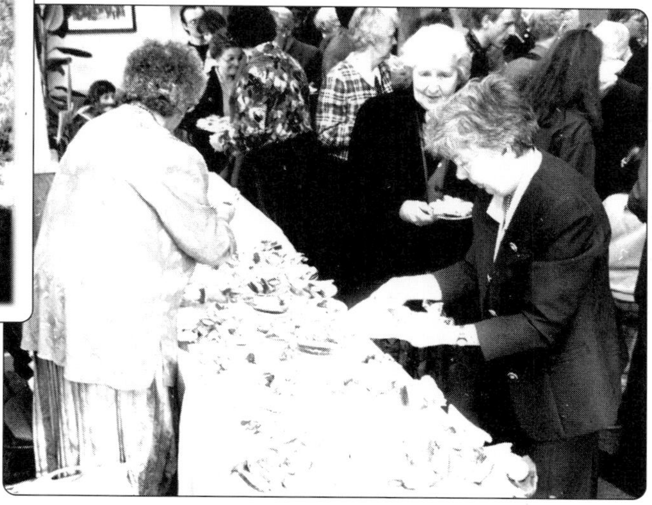

Bun fight at the opening of the coffee bar facility at the Methodist Church.

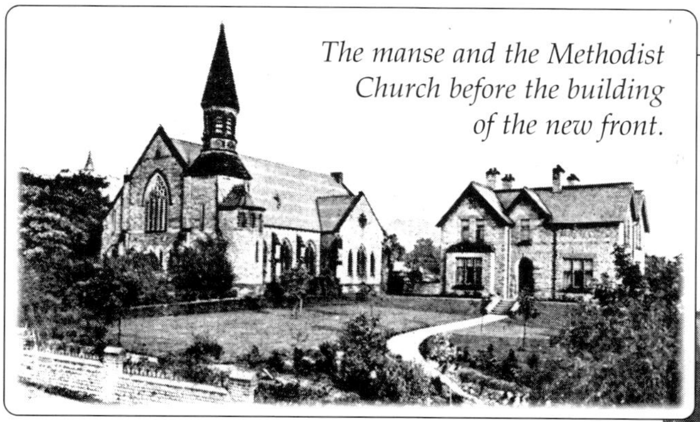

The manse and the Methodist Church before the building of the new front.

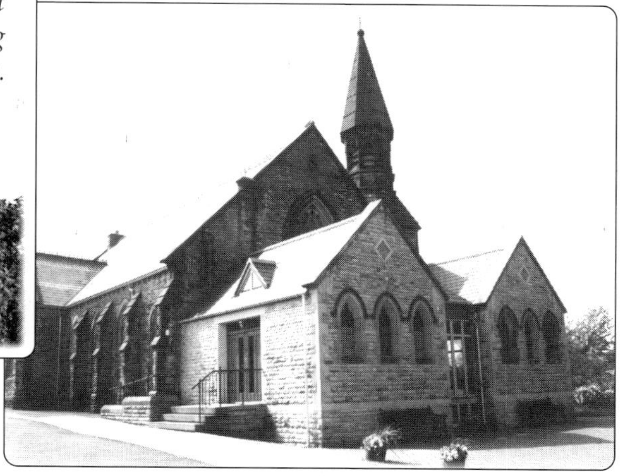

The Methodist Church after the building of the new front.

a copy of the brochure from that occasion, kindly loaned by Miss G. Carrington, some of the information contained in this historical sketch would not have been found. As at all good Methodist occasions, the opportunity was taken to give thanks to God in several services, gatherings and reunion meetings, and we sincerely hope that our centenary celebrations will likewise be an uplifting occasion as we give thanks for all the worthy people, some of whom are our closely related forefathers, who had the vision and will to provide us with our spiritual home.

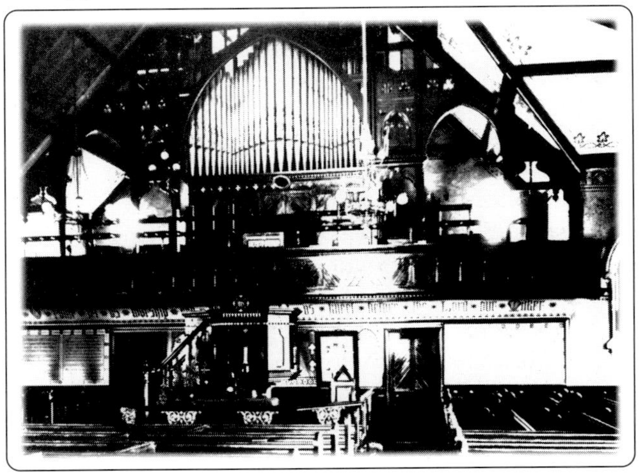

The interior of the Methodist Church in about 1920.

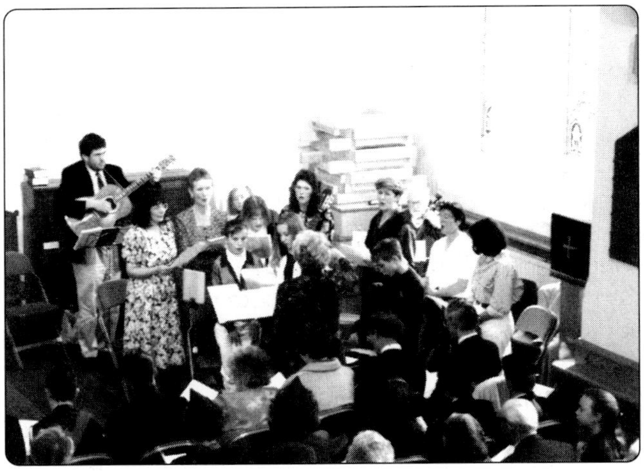

Gathering at the opening of the extension in 1994, with John Bamford on guitar.

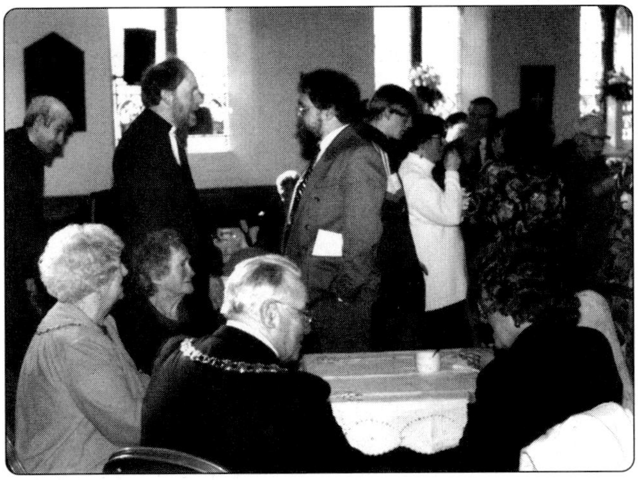

Celebrating the completion of the extension in 1994. Revd Colin Smith is in conversation with Cllr Malcolm Cawthorn, and Mayor Francis is in conversation with Cllr Ann Young.

Soon after the jubilee celebrations, it was recognised once again that there was an urgent need to expand the school premises. In 1929, three plots of land at the southern end of the school building were acquired from Joseph Bridge, Charles Lyall and Joseph Burdekin. In 1932, a garden between the school and the main road was purchased from Charles Lyall.

The extension to the school premises was finished in 1929 and officially opened on 22 January by Councillor Mrs Spencer. In 1931 the Hadfield family enhanced the beauty of the chapel by the gift of the front porch in memory of Mrs Heald, Mrs Hadfield's mother. There must be many photograph albums with pictures of radiant and shy brides and grooms framed by the lovely stone doorway of the porch, which always made an ideal setting for wedding photographs!

During the war years, 1939–45, the chapel and school continued to play a vital role in the spiritual and educational welfare of the people, and the school cellar was also used as a post for air-raid wardens. Thankfully, the only recorded attack was made by beetles who ate into the organ and the choir gallery, making it necessary to demolish and reconstruct the front section of the church, and so completely change its internal appearance. A rebuilt organ was installed in 1942, but the constraints of the war years meant that a temporary reconstruction of the front of the chapel had to be tolerated until 1952, when a great reopening ceremony was performed by Mrs Hadfield on 6 September in the presence of many notables, including His Grace, the Duke of Devonshire, who presided over the meeting. We are delighted that Revd A. Williams-Boote, who played such a large part in leading the church through the reconstruction period, will be taking part in our centenary celebrations.

With increasing fuel costs and the disappearance of resident domestic help, running a huge house like the manse had become too great a burden for the resident minister and his wife to bear. In 1959 they moved to a bungalow in Warmbrook, which had been kindly leased to the trustees by Sam Longson, and later to a house on Rowton Grange Road, bought by the Whaley Bridge Circuit Manses Fund.

The last land purchase took place in December 1960, when 3,340 square yards of land on Warmbrook, to the south of the graveyard, was purchased from the High Peak Manufacturing Co. Ltd.

The old manse was used for Sunday school and other church activities until the day school was transferred to the new Warmbrook School in 1968.

This move meant that the trustees had to face the entire maintenance and running costs of the school premises, five-sevenths of which had previously been met by Derbyshire Education Committee. With the school premises becoming available for church and Sunday school activities, the manse was no longer required and was sold in November 1970. The proceeds of the sale made it possible for the trustees to modernise the Sunday school's toilet accommodation and to provide a much-needed kitchen and toilet annex to the choir vestry. These were completed in October 1971 and bring our historical sketch to a close.

We hope that this story has stimulated your interest and has emphasised the great need for us to follow the example of our forefathers who made certain that we should have suitable premises in which to learn about and give thanks for the love of God. We too should try to ensure that our children's children will be able to enjoy the same privileges.

Postscript

By Peter Helps.

By the mid-1980s the congregation of Town End Methodist Church was struggling to maintain two under-used buildings, both of which required major expenditure because they were literally coming apart at the seams. At the church, the 1920s porch was cracking away from the main body of the building, and at the Sunday school the extension was cracking away from the rest of the structure.

An imaginative scheme was hatched to sell the schoolrooms to a housing developer and convert the church into a multi-purpose building by using revenue from this sale supplemented by money obtained from grants and a prolonged and sustained series of fund-raising events. The church was transformed into a flexible space by removing the fixed pews and levelling the floor, and the frontage of the building was extended by the addition of a new entrance and a meeting-room, complete with serving facilities and coffee lounge.

In addition to being used for Sunday services, the church building can be used by the Boys' and Girls' Brigades and many other church groups. Valuable income can also be generated by letting the building to keep-fit groups, dance classes and choirs.

High Peak's Mayor, John Francis, and Revd Malcolm Willey, who served at the Town End church from 1984 to 1990, were the special guests of Revd Colin Smith, the minister of the time, at the opening ceremony in 1994.

The transformation and extension of the church and the renovation and conversion of the schoolrooms were both carried out so sensitively that the architectural integrity of the original buildings was retained – the imaginative scheme earned a Chapel Amenity Society Gold Award.

John Wesley & Grace Bennett

Mike Smith traces the story of Grace Bennett, long-time resident of Chapel.

In 1748, John Wesley proposed to Grace Murray, who had nursed him through an illness in Newcastle-upon-Tyne. Grace joined Wesley on his travels and the pair were inseparable for five months. It is said that John and Grace even underwent a form of marriage ceremony in Ireland. However, Charles Wesley objected to his brother's liaison and Grace then turned to John Bennett, whom she had also nursed in Newcastle. She subsequently married Bennet, who was not only Wesley's rival in love, but also one of his leading preachers. When her new husband died at the age of 45, Grace moved to Chapel-en-le-Frith, where she lived until her death in 1803, at the age of 85. She is buried in the churchyard of Chinley Independent Chapel, a beautiful little Nonconformist church erected near Chapel Milton in 1662.

Primitive Methodism in Chapel-en-le-Frith

The Primitive Methodists, who originated in Burslem, held their first camp meetings in the early-nineteenth century at Mow Cop, near Stoke-on-Trent and the breakaway movement soon gained a considerable following in the High Peak. According to Bunting, Thomas Potts, Thomas Shepley and John Walton were pioneers of the Primitive Methodism in Chapel-en-le-Frith. The Primitive Methodist bethel was erected on Market Street in 1852 and a schoolroom, located across the road, was added in 1910. The bethel is now used as a joinery workshop by John Kelly, who has worked hard to preserve and renovate the simple, but highly attractive gabled building. Unfortunately, the schoolroom has been heavily corrupted by the addition of an extension. Until recently, it was used as a tyre services depot, but there are now hopes that the structure may be restored to its original form as part of a comprehensive redevelopment of the site.

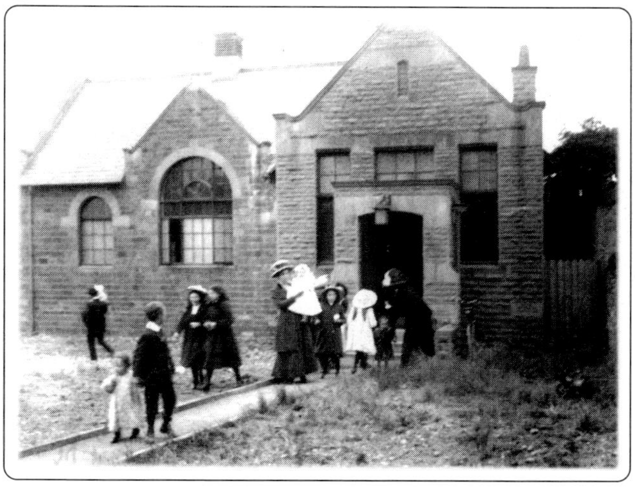

The Primitive Methodist Sunday school.

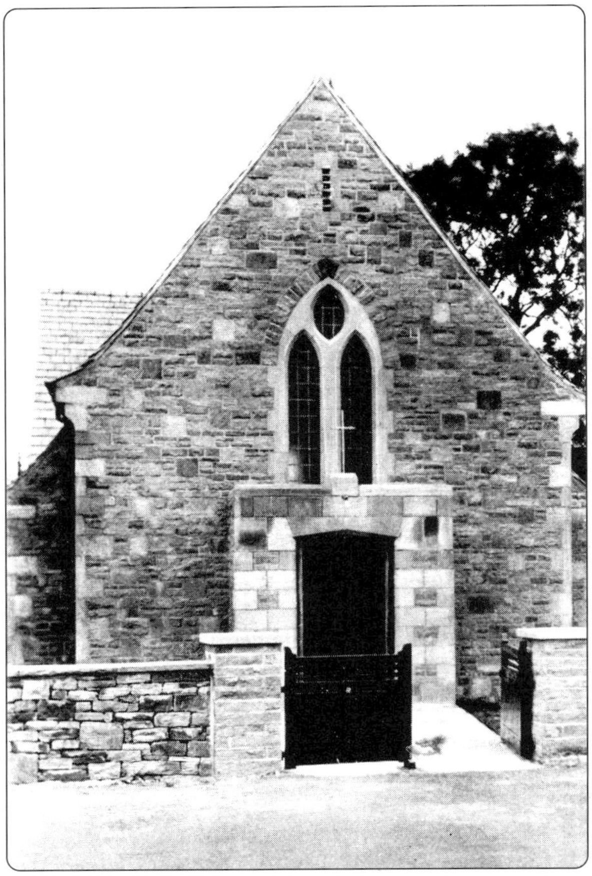

Chapel's Roman Catholic church.

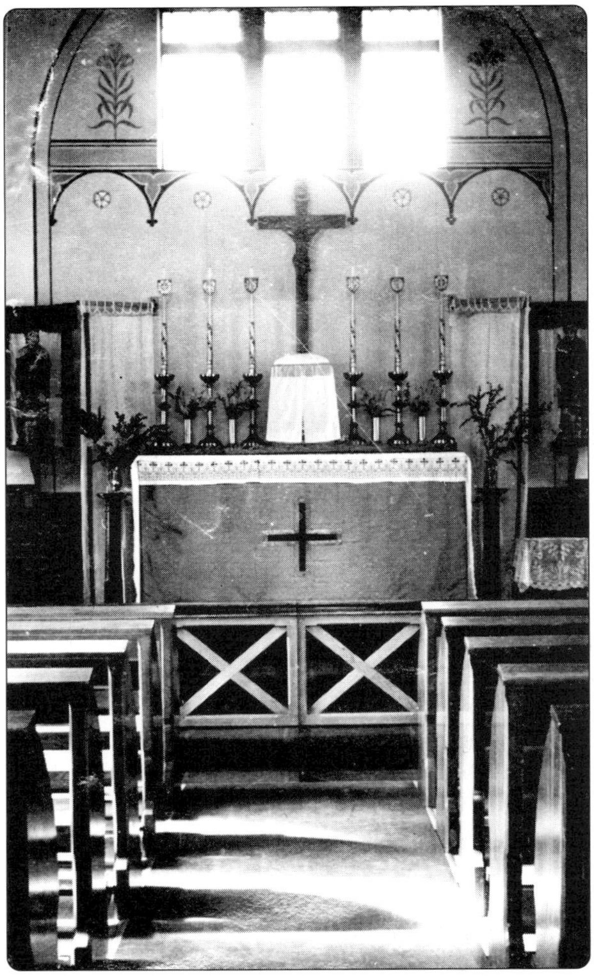

The altar of the Catholic church before the new altar was put in place.

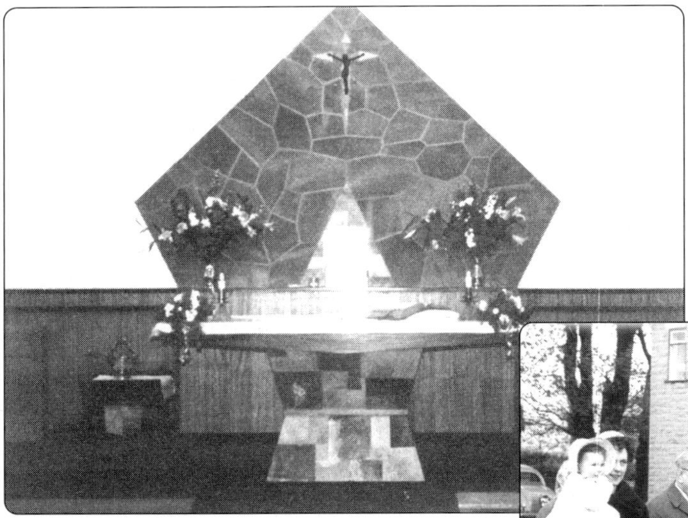

The altar, designed by Patrick McNicholas.

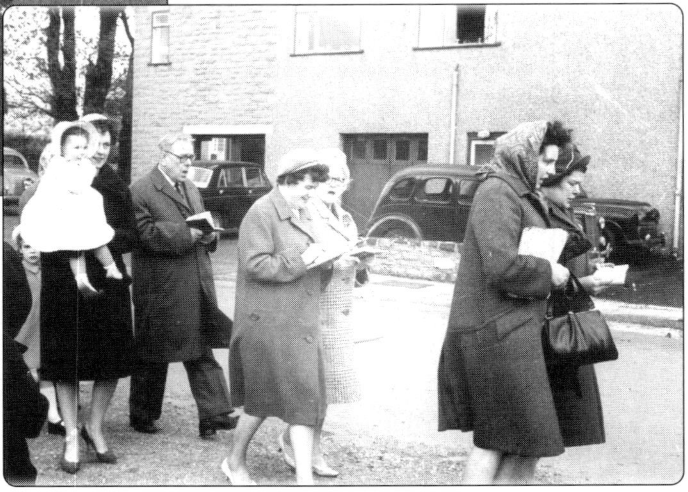

A procession of Chapel Catholics, including Fred Heather, Stella and Diane Allen, Winnie Barker, Jean Bushby, Eileen Evans and Donna Kadzewska in 1958.

The Roman Catholic Church of St John Fisher & St Thomas More

Based on press cuttings from the late 1930s and the recollections of Mrs Donna Kadzewska (née Heather).

Until 1937, the Roman Catholics of Chapel-en-le-Frith had no permanent place of worship, although Mass was held in the town on a number of occasions, either at the Constitutional Hall or the Town Hall – chairs would often move about during Sunday services at the Town Hall because the floor had been left slippery after Saturday-night dances.

Some Chapel residents made regular trips to Tideswell in order to attend Mass at the little church of the Immaculate Heart of Mary, where Father Cafferky presided, but the real wish of the town's Catholics was to have a church of their own. With this aim in mind, they established an account, known as St Anthony's Building Fund, and organised a host of money-raising events, including bring-and-buy sales, raffles and whist drives. Some functions were held in private houses, others in the upper room of Mrs Riley's fish-and-chip shop. The industrious band of Chapel Catholics included John Mone, Mr and Mrs Jansen, Mr and Mrs Bagshawe, Mr and Mrs Cox, Mr and Mrs Heather, Mr and Mrs O'Brien, Mrs Riley, Mr and Mrs McKenna, Mrs Lomas, Mrs Barker, Mrs Brick, Mrs Bushby and the three Imberry sisters. Dr Cogan (a local GP) and his wife made substantial contributions and Mr and Mrs Carter, who lived in the Hope Valley and were known for Carter's Little Liver Pills, were also major benefactors.

Eventually, enough money was raised to build a church on a plot of land on Horderns Road, which had been acquired from the Bagshawes of Ford Hall. As the site was located in the heart of a residential area, permission for the building of a church was granted on the strict condition that no bells be installed. Mrs Kadzewska's mother, Ada Heather, who had not been converted to Catholicism at the time, played the organ in the open air during the ceremony to mark the laying of the foundation-stone.

Father Cafferky spent two years making a carved-oak altar for the new church, which was to be dedicated to St John Fisher and St Thomas More. The famous Hunstone carvers of Tideswell produced two oak screens, as well as carved figures of the two martyrs. Thomas Hobson, a local blacksmith, made a wrought-iron cross to be placed over the main entrance and the Ferodo company contributed a durable floor covering for use in the aisles.

The church, which was designed by A. Lacock of Bakewell and built by Green & Sons, was consecrated on 1 October 1937 by the Rt Revd John McNulty, Bishop of Nottingham. The new building, which cost £2,000 and had seating for 150, was described in the local press as having an appearance that was 'pretty, as well as smart'. The church was largely designed in

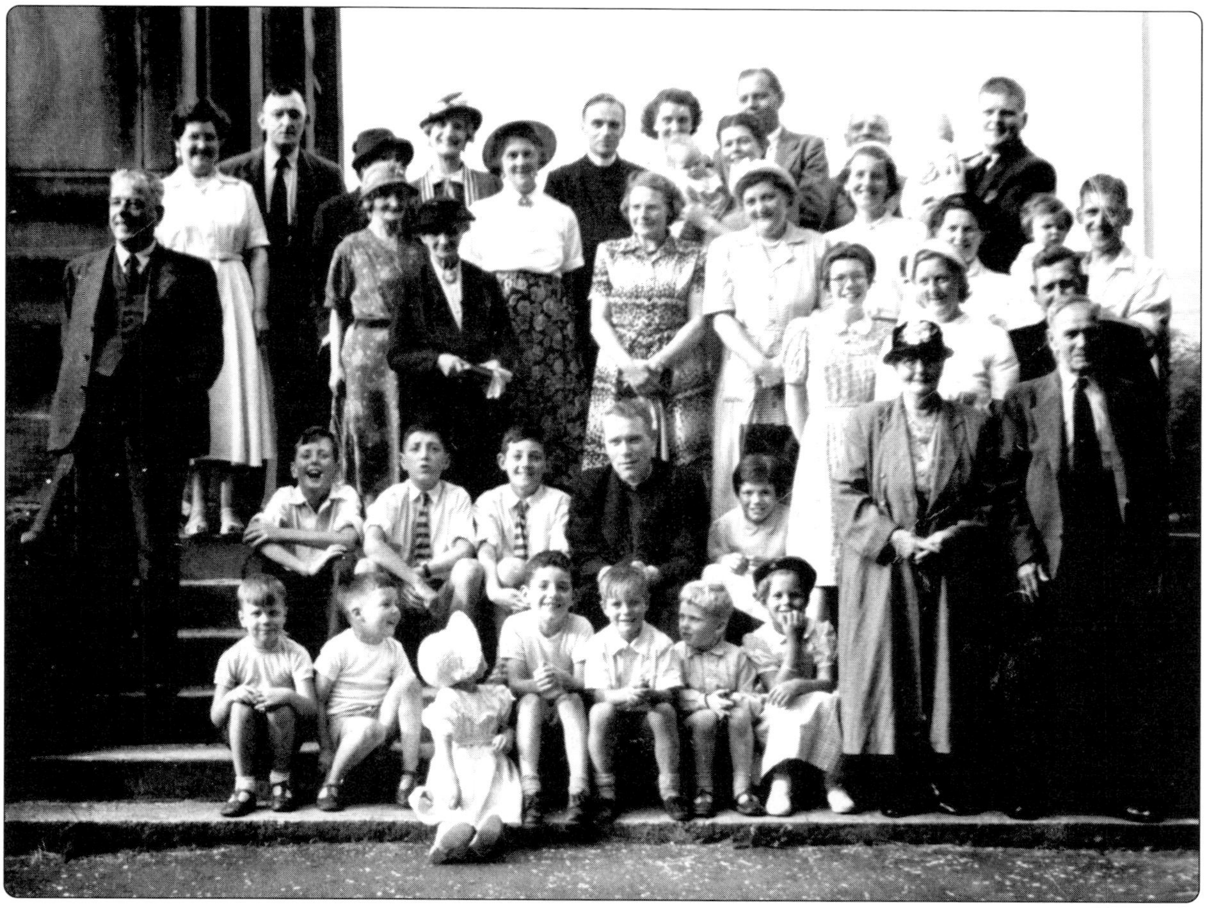

Gathering of Chapel Catholics for a trip in 1956.

a traditional style, but was given a few modern touches, including a particularly attractive tripartite window on the simple, symmetrical façade. There was no electricity supply in the original building but Mr O'Brien, who worked for the Trent Valley and High Peak Electricity Company, wired up the building, helped by a team of volunteers.

Father Cafferky had responsibility for the church at Chapel-en-le-Frith as well as the church of the Immaculate Heart of Mary in Tideswell. Fred Heather, who drove the local mail van, was delegated by the Chapel Catholics to call on the priest during his postal round and ask him if he would be able to take Mass in Chapel on a regular basis. When Fred arrived at the house, he was greeted by the housekeeper, because Father Cafferky was ill in bed at the time. She told the postman how she had to take jobs in Tideswell to help support the priest, who had no stipend and was living in near poverty. The Chapel Catholics responded to this news by raising money to buy a car for Father Cafferky, who duly learned to drive and agreed to motor over to Chapel to conduct weekly services.

Father Cafferky died in March 1944, at the age of just 59. He was succeeded by Father Andrew Murdoch, who lodged for three years with the Heather family, until sufficient money could be raised to build a house adjacent to the church for use by the priest. Father Murdoch also carried responsibility for the church at Tideswell, but he served the Chapel Catholics well and he was often assisted by Monsignor Docherty from the Salford Diocese, who became known as 'Father Tom'.

The Catholic people of Chapel-en-le-Frith, who had worked so hard to create their own church, remained close-knit and active. After Mass on Bank Holidays, the priest would lead members of his flock on expeditions to local beauty spots, such as the Goyt Valley, Millers Dale and Monsal Dale, where picnics would be enjoyed. Father Murdoch was succeeded by Father Whitehouse, who had begun training as a Methodist minister before joining a Catholic seminary.

During the late 1960s, when Father Ambrose Steen was the priest, the church owned two houses adjacent to the church, one of which was used for a short time as a nursery school. This venture was short-lived and the school house was sold. Father Steen was succeeded by Father McDermott, who commissioned Patrick McNicholas to make new furnishings for the church. Patrick used a mixture of wood, metal, slate from a quarry near Chesterfield and some Cheshire sandstone, which he had salvaged from damaged bridges, to produce an altar, a lectern, a seat, a table, a candle holder, two flower holders and decorations around the tabernacle. All these fittings were produced as a matching set, in designs which took their inspiration from the shapes of a chalice and a mitre.

Some other significant additions have been made to the church over the years: Father Duggan was responsible for the installation of a stained-glass window and Father Moynihan put in new stations of the Cross. Father Peter Wade is the priest in 2003 and will be looking to make his own modifications, one of which is likely to be improved access for disabled people.

The little church on Horderns Road continues to serve a small, but committed congregation, who are rightly proud that their place of worship was built as a result of a tremendous fund-raising effort by the Roman Catholics of Chapel-en-le-Frith.

Chapter 3

Venerable Institutions

Half way along Market Street, there is a cluster of Victorian buildings: the Town Hall, an austere Gothic structure completed in 1851; the Memorial Institute, erected in 1891; and the little Hearse House, built in 1818 to house the parish hearse. The Town Hall and the Institute remained at the heart of Chapel life throughout the twentieth century. The Town Hall was once the venue for sittings of the Magistrates' Court and later became the home of the Parish Council, the Registrar and the public library. The Institute, originally established for educational improvement and recreation, still houses a thriving social club and, until recently, was also home to the British Legion.

The austere Gothic façade of Chapel Town Hall.

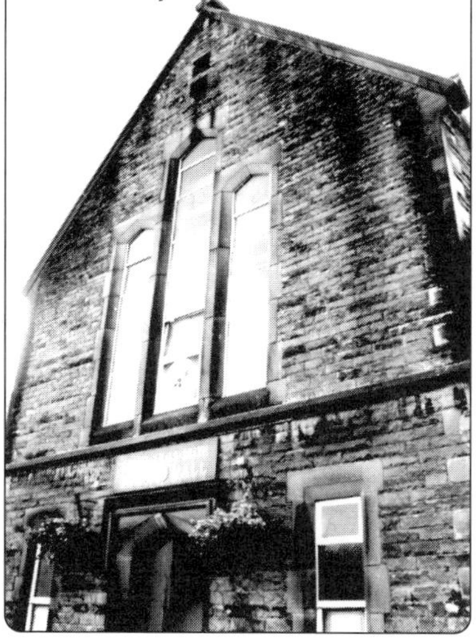

Both the Town Hall and the Memorial Institute have accommodated a host of whist drives, concerts and social functions over the years, and many of the participants in the dances held there learned their skills at Michael and Jackie's Saturday-morning dance classes, which have been held at the Town Hall since 1969.

The Hearse House was neglected for many years until it was renovated by the Chapel-en-le-Frith Amenity Society and opened as a visitor and heritage centre in 1992. The members of the Amenity Society, who have not only worked hard to preserve the natural and architectural heritage of the town, but have also added new attractions, use the upper room as their headquarters.

Up the Town Hall Steps

The 150th anniversary of Chapel-en-le-Frith Town Hall was marked by a grand four-day celebration in 2001, which included concerts given by Kinder Children's Choir and Chapel Male Voice Choir, traditional dancing by Chapel Morris Men and displays by members of Michael Hough's hugely popular Saturday-morning dance school, which has operated in the building for the past 34 years. Warmbrook Junior School's recorder group played to the assembled dignitaries at the commencement of the celebrations and Councillor Margaret Dyson organised a four-day exhibition which was opened by the Duke of Devonshire. It included displays of artefacts, documents and old maps from the Parish-Council archives, exhibits from the many local groups and organisations which have used the building over the years, copies of census returns dating back to the nineteenth century, press cuttings tracing the history of the parish over the last century and a half, and a large display of photographs of old Chapel from the extensive collection of local historian Alan Watson. The pupils of Chapel High School put their tapestry of the town on show, there was a display to publicise the Peak National Park, whose 542 square miles surround the town, and another large exhibit which celebrated the history of Chapel's largest and most famous employer, the Ferodo brake-lining firm. More than 500 people visited the exhibition and both concerts played to full houses.

The Town Hall, an austere church-like structure that still dominates the streetscape of Chapel's main thoroughfare, began life as a new home for the Magistrates' Court, and 92-year-old Ada Hitchens remembers that there was always great excitement in the town on the third Thursday of the month, when the court was held, especially if the defendants being led up the Town Hall steps were locals. However, the building was never simply a venue for the local court; Dr John Slacke, who paid for its construction, wanted the Town Hall to be used for the benefit of the public and it has been a focal point of town life throughout its existence.

The Town Hall once housed a branch of the Trustee Savings Bank and is now home to the Parish Council, the Parish Office, the local library, the Registrar for the area, and the Citizens' Advice Bureau. It has also been used over the years by organisations such as the Townswomen's Guild, the Women's Institute, the Ladies' Choir, St John Ambulance, the Over 60s, the High Peak Lodge of the Freemasons, Chapel Amenity Society and various pre-school groups. The building was once a popular

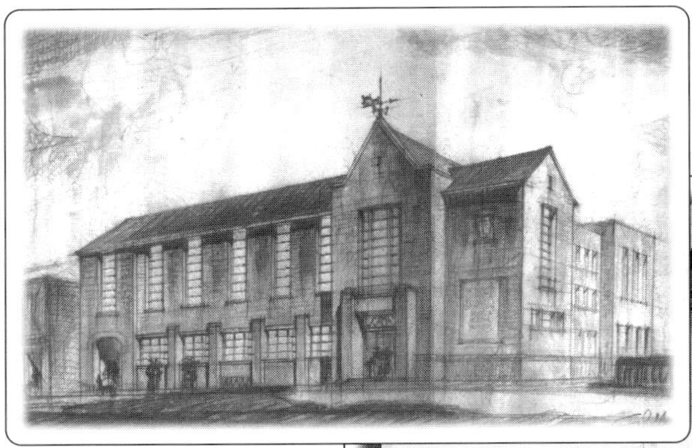

Left: *How the Town Hall could have looked if proposals for a rebuild after the Second World War had gone ahead.*

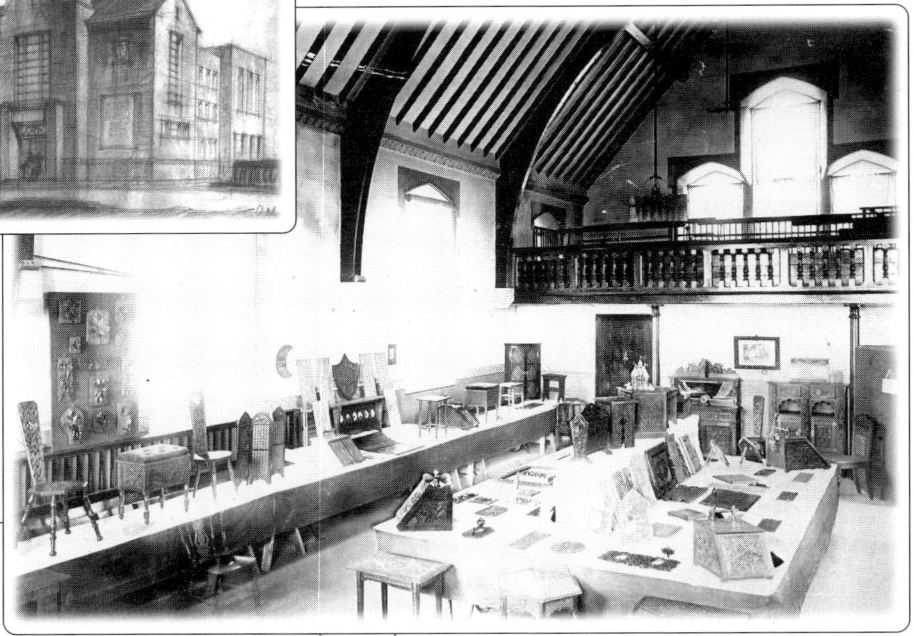

Right: *The main hall of the Town Hall in use for an antique fair.*

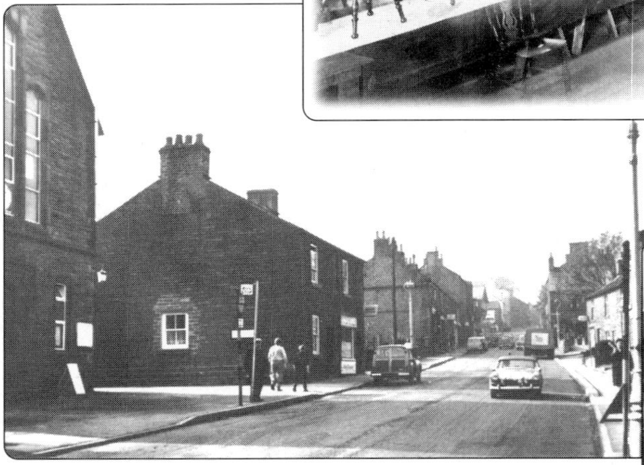

Left: *Market Street in the 1960s, with the Town Hall on the left.*

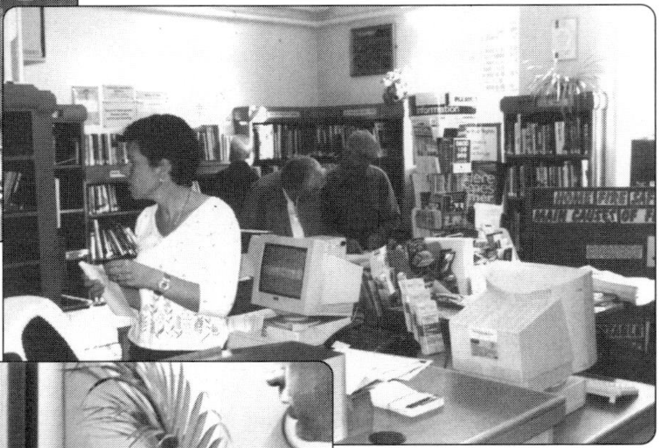

Right: *The library, on the ground floor of the Town Hall as it is in 2003.*

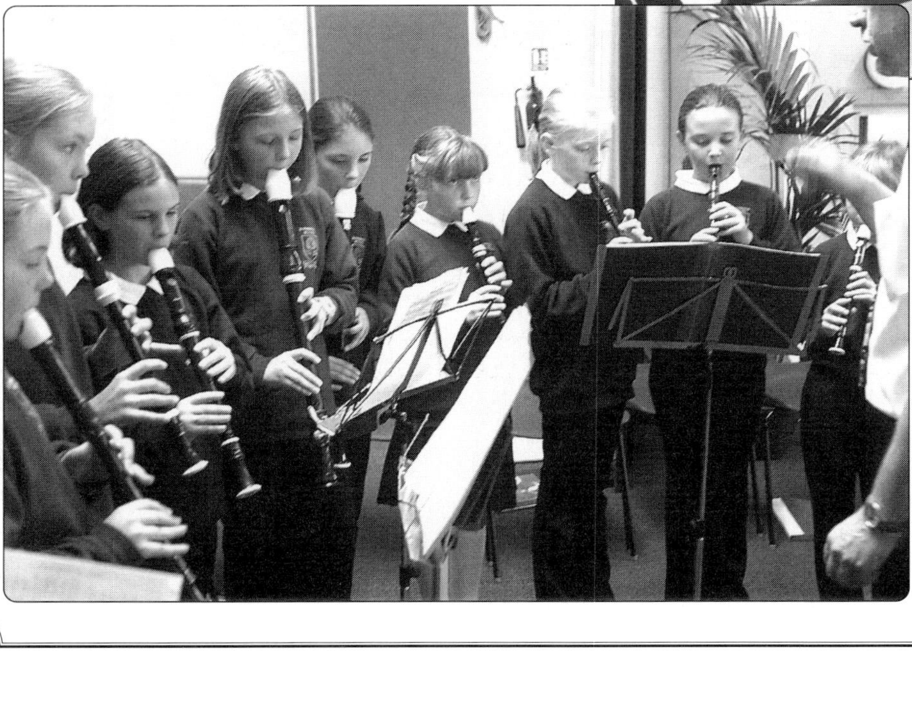

Left: *Warmbrook Junior School's recorder group performing at the 150th anniversary of the Town Hall in 2001.*

venue for whist drives and almost all Chapel people have attended concerts and dances at the Town Hall. Various martial arts, aerobics and keep-fit clubs now have weekly meetings in the building.

The cellar of the Town Hall was put to good use during the Second World War, when it was used as a base for a St John Ambulance ARP unit. The base was manned both day and night, but the unit was very rarely called out to an emergency. Merrill Bowdon, who was a St John cadet during the war and later became caretaker for the Town Hall, remembers that the ARP team won most of the local darts tournaments, presumably because they had plenty of time to hone their skills on the cellar's dartboard!

In the immediate postwar years, ambitious proposals were put forward to extend the Town Hall and convert it into a War Memorial Hall. One scheme even involved a complete rebuild in an incongruous Modernist style, but money was in short supply and it was 23 years before any structural alterations to the building actually took place, and these only involved the addition of a modest first-floor annex.

The staging of choir concerts to commemorate the 150th anniversary of the Town Hall is very apt, because the High Peak has a strong musical tradition. The Kinder Children's Choir is one of the newer choral societies, having been formed in the 1990s by Joyce Ellis, a former opera and concert singer. Nevertheless, it has already established a huge reputation; it has featured in a number of television and radio programmes and has won many prizes, including first prize in the children's section of the International Eisteddfod in 1997. The Chapel Male Voice Choir has a much longer history, having been formed by ex-servicemen returning from the First World War. The choir has given concerts every year since 1919. It would be nice to think that it will also be performing at the bicentenary celebrations in 2051.

Let's Dance

Michael Hough, from Reddish in Stockport, and Jackie Ensor, from Arnold in Nottingham, were rival Old Tyme Dance Champions when they met. After marrying in Nottingham in 1969, they came to live in Chapel-en-le-Frith and decided to set up a children's dance class in the town.

Michael and Jackie's first class was held in the Town Hall on 1 May 1969 and attracted just one pupil, Catherine Hulley. However, numbers soon grew and Mr and Mrs Hough, who had no car at the time, were to be seen each week pushing all their equipment down Market Street on a trolley in preparation for the weekly dance session.

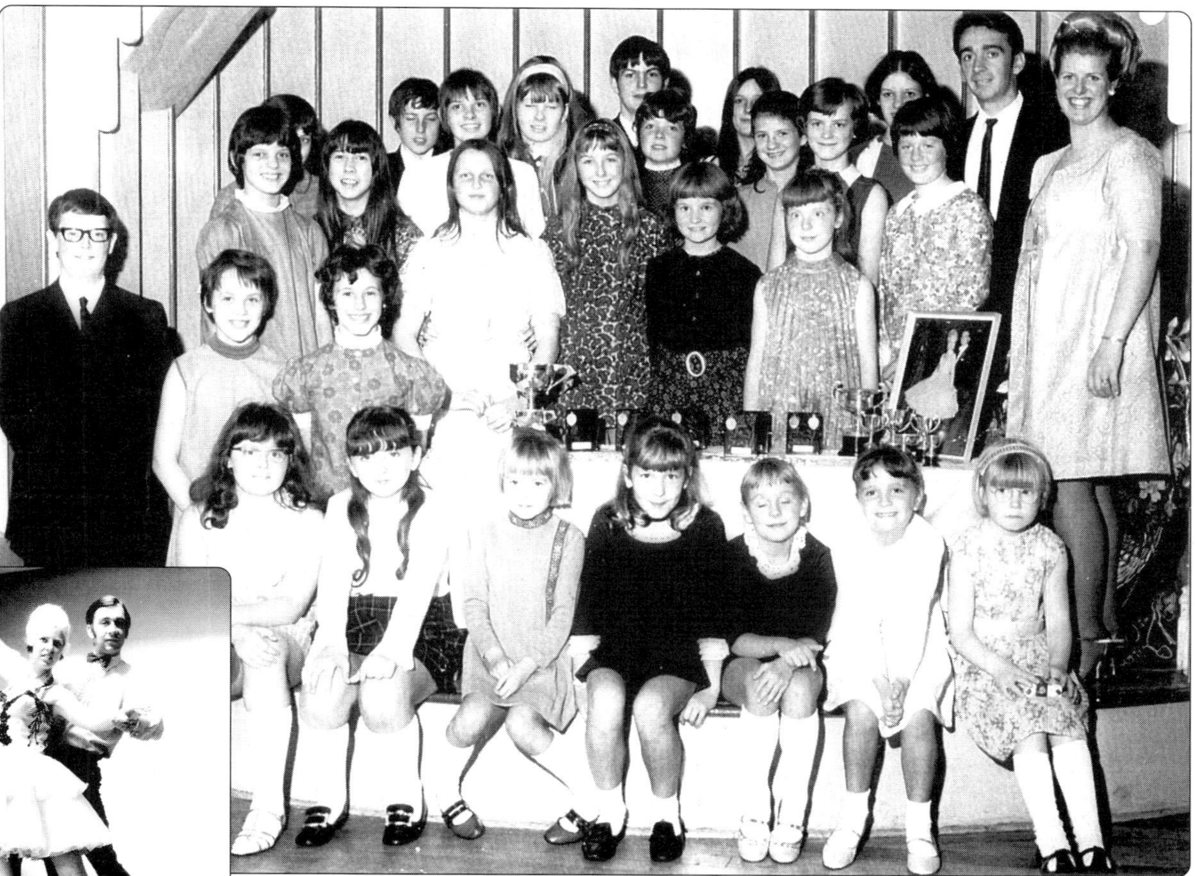

The very first presentation of dance medals to Michael and Jackie's pupils at St Ann's Hotel, Buxton, in 1969.

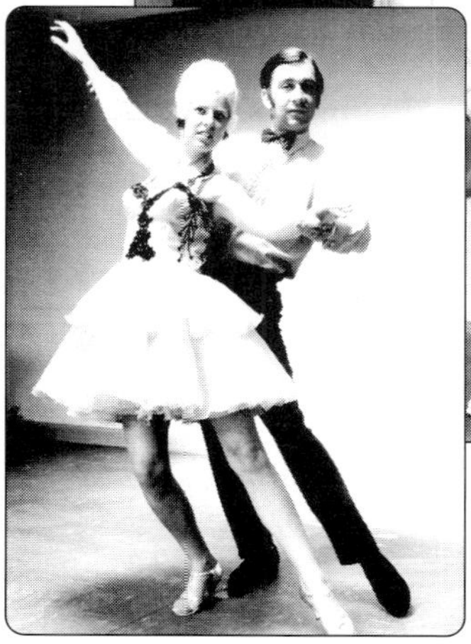

Michael and Jackie Hough, dance teachers.

After a few months, they added an adult class, which attracted 15 or 16 members, including Mr and Mrs Peach, Mr and Mrs Cottrill, Beryl Fletcher, Mary Bellany and Tom King. Michael and Jackie then set up further classes in Buxton and Whaley Bridge. In the early days, the annual presentation of medals was held in Buxton, at the Pavilion Gardens or the St Ann's Hotel, often with the Mayor of the High Peak in attendance. The twice-yearly presentations for Chapel students are now held in Chapel Town Hall and are always accompanied by dance displays by all the students for the entertainment of parents and friends.

Jackie has left the tuition at the Chapel class to Michael since the late 1970s, when the couple started a family, but the class has continued without interruption for 34 years. Hundreds of Chapel people took their first steps on the dance floor at Michael and Jackie's classes, although it has to be said that the vast majority of students have always been female. At any one time, the class attracts no more than half a dozen boys, so the girls and ladies of Chapel are always likely to be struggling for partners of the opposite sex!

At the start of 2003 the class had 65 members from the age of three-and-a-half upwards. Given the numbers and the range of ages, Michael is fortunate to have the weekly help of Beryl Stafford, Kelly Nadin, Mandy Elliott and Jennifer Etchells. The Medal Tests on offer range from Rosettes or Social Awards through Bronze, Silver, Gold, Gold Bars and Stars to the coveted International Awards.

Michael believes that dancing is not only an enjoyable and rewarding hobby, but also a social asset that remains with people throughout their lives.

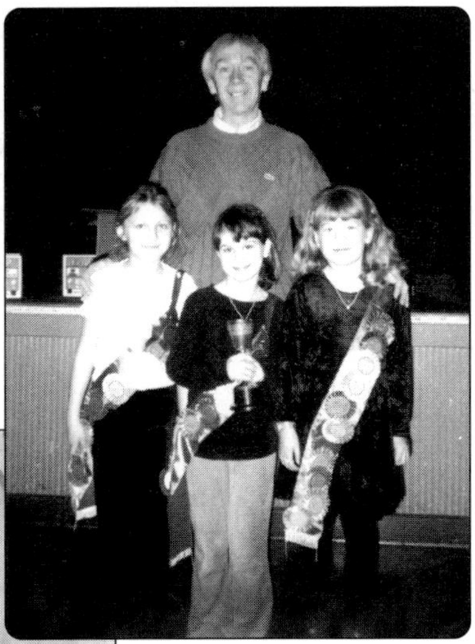

Michael Hough with rosette winners in 1997 Charlotte Smith, Emma Bennett and Hannah Lord.

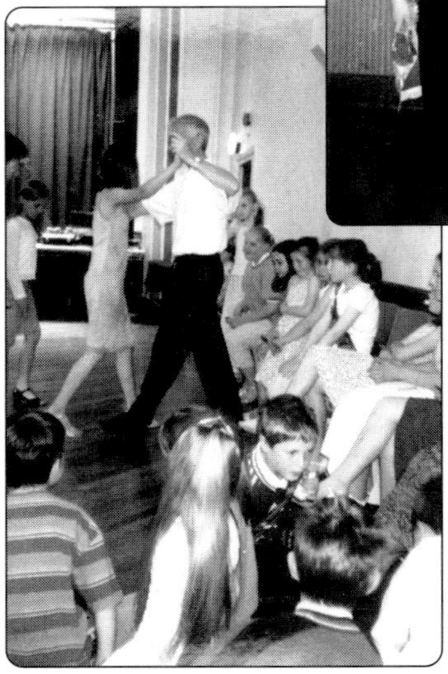

Michael and Jackie's dancing class in operation.

The Institute

Based on committee-meeting minutes, which are included in archive material kindly loaned by Norman Prime.

Chapel-en-le-Frith's Institute, which was erected and furnished at a cost of £1,000, was opened on 21 January 1891 by Professor Boyd Dawkins, the noted geologist and prehistorian. The Institute, whose facilities included a reading-room, a library, a billiards-room and a smoking-room, had as its object:

> *The supplying of every class of the community with increased means of instruction in the various branches of art, science, literature and useful knowledge, and such recreation as the governing body shall deem of an innocent character and not connected with gambling. Party politics and controversial theology shall be excluded.*

The members of the Institute's committee took their brief seriously, arranging lectures on geology and astronomy and setting up classes in drawing, shorthand, woodcarving, botany, mathematics, fruit growing, gardening and even bee-keeping! Professor Boyd Dawkins presented two parcels of books to the Institute, while other books were donated or purchased and a regular order was placed for a wide selection of newspapers and periodicals. Ladies were allowed to use the library for an annual fee and the Ladies' Sewing Committee was given permission to use the committee room on a number of specified occasions, but the club had an exclusively male membership and was largely a male preserve.

In their efforts to ensure that 'young men had a comfortable place to derive pleasure and amusement without any connection with drink or gambling', the Recreation Committee had to impose rules and sanctions from the very outset. In the first year of opening, they received:

> *... a report of disreputable conduct at the billiard-room windows, the window of the landing and also in the backyard by certain members of the Institute whose names are known.*

There were also frequent problems with newspapers being taken from the reading-room and with members failing to pay their subscriptions or billiards payments on time. The committee exercised firm control and even made one member retract his criticism of their decision to close the Institute on the occasion of the annual concert.

In 1897 the Institute purchased 15 volumes of works by Alexander Dumas and six volumes by Victor Hugo, arranged to borrow 200 books annually from the Lancashire and Cheshire Circulating Library and received donations of books from various benefactors. For example, Mr Bagshawe of Ford Hall donated *Tales of English Life*, Miss Goodman of Eccles

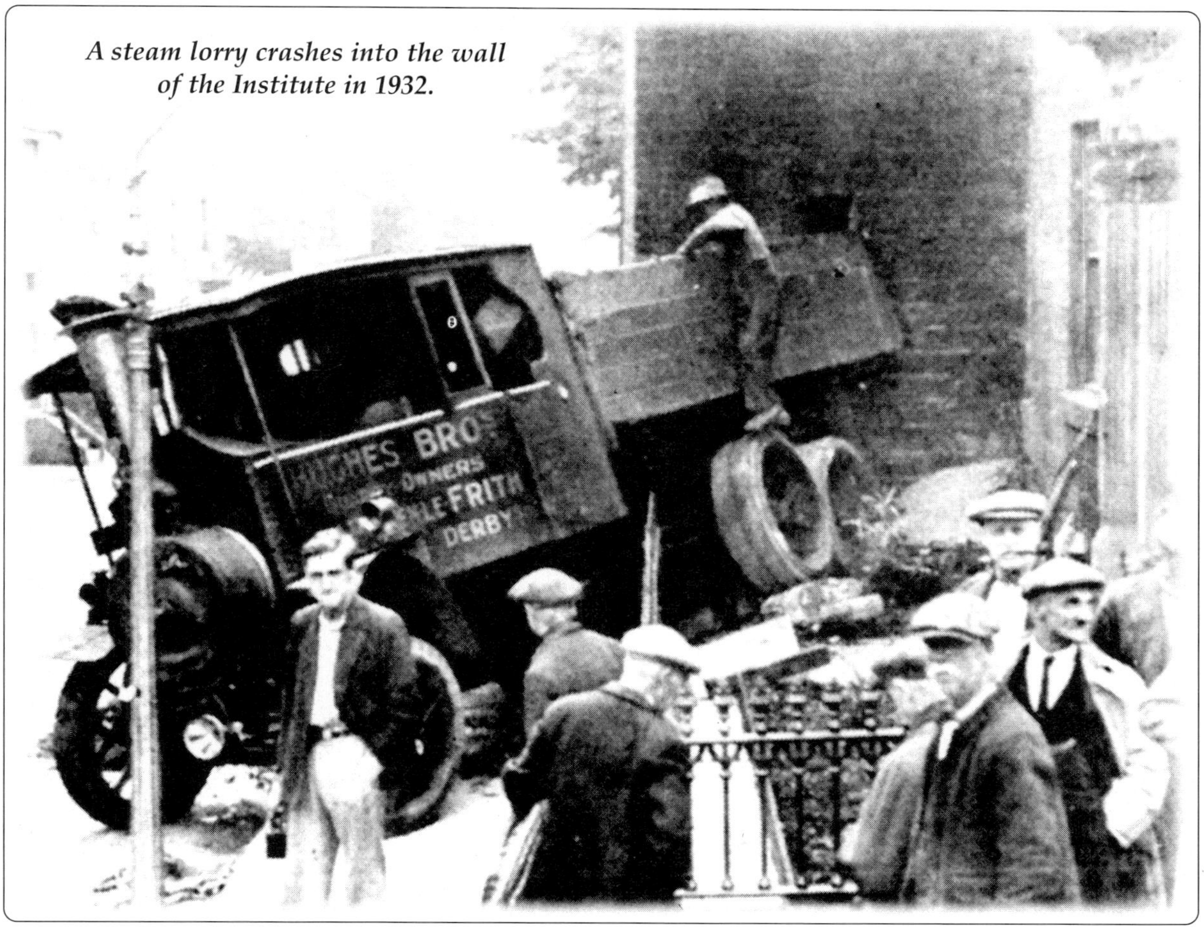

A steam lorry crashes into the wall of the Institute in 1932.

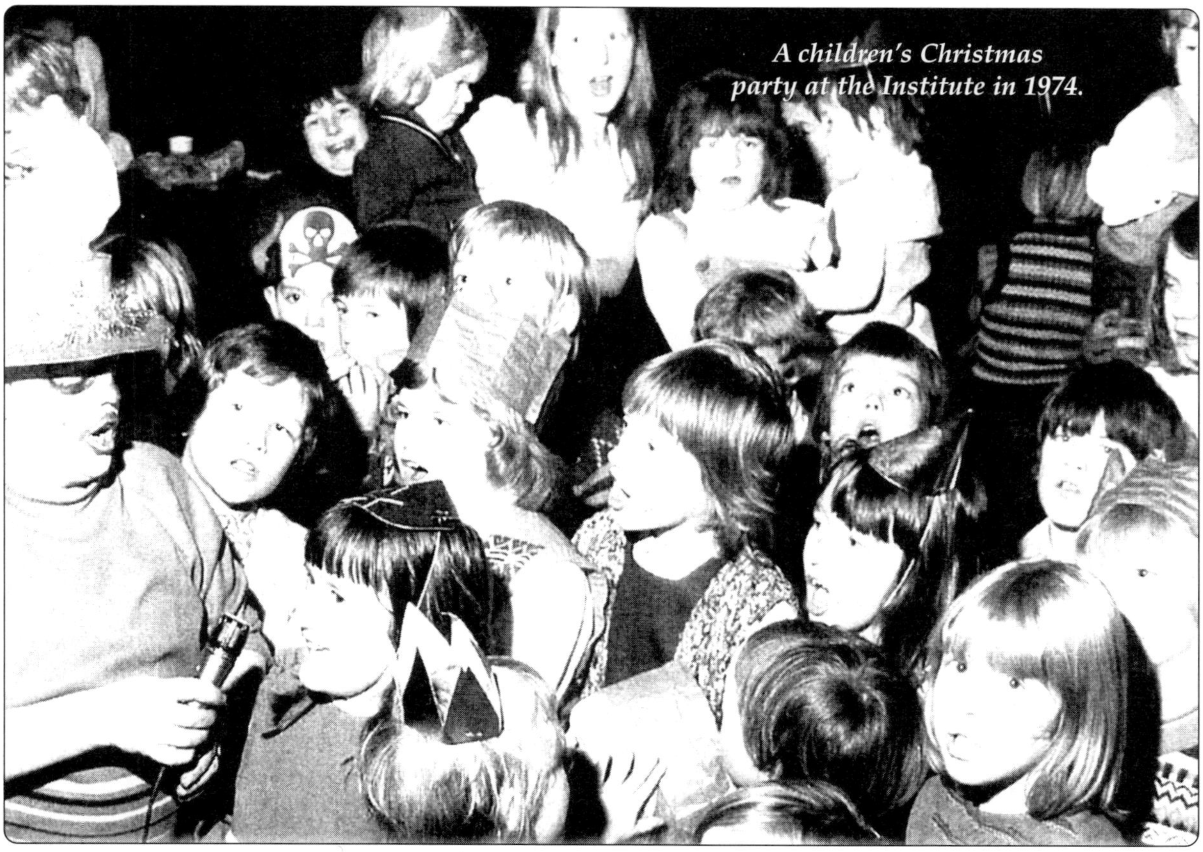

A children's Christmas party at the Institute in 1974.

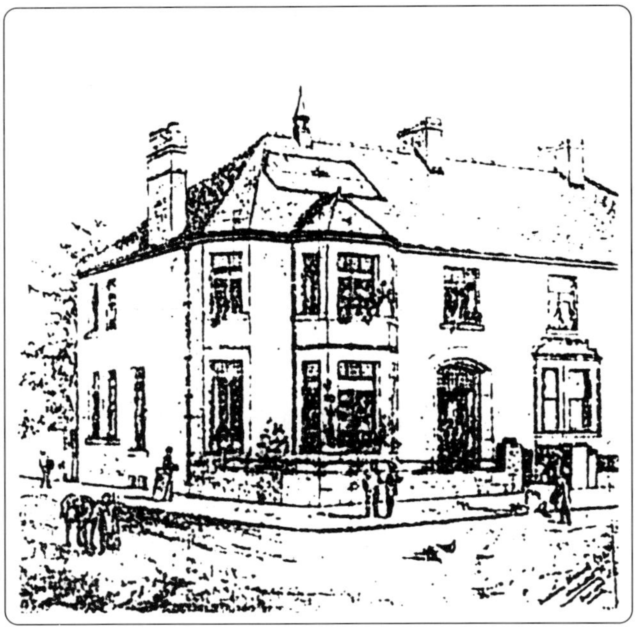

The Institute featured in a Chapel guide book shortly after opening.

House gave the Institute a copy of *One Hundred Years Ago* and Miss Tallent Bateman kindly donated *The History of Manchester Waterworks*. Just how much these worthy volumes were appreciated by members is not recorded, but it is known that some of the education classes were not well attended. However, billiards proved to be immensely popular and, in 1895, members were even treated to a demonstration by Mr Lonsdale, the billiards champion of England. A Christmas billiards handicap was instituted in 1904, with Mr Pink offering a goose as first prize and Mr Partridge a couple of rabbits as second prize. Members took advantage of the hot baths that were available in the Institute and the committee organised 'smoking concerts' and annual trips; Liverpool and Scarborough were favoured venues.

The committee continued to exercise its authority, with members being cautioned for offences such as throwing billiards balls around the room, striking matches on the wall, taking part in billiards tournaments while being in arrears with their account and allowing dogs on the premises. In 1911 the librarian threatened resignation after a firework had been discharged in the reading-room.

In 1910, the committee was faced with some financial difficulties and embarked on a series of cost-cutting and money-raising measures, including a reduction in the number of magazines purchased for the reading-room and the termination of the post of billiards manager. The Institute's rooms were let out to various groups and whist drives were started, which soon proved to be a good money-spinner.

By 1916, the membership had increased to 152 ordinary members and ten honorary members. During the First World War, the committee gave permission for the Institute to be used as an ambulance clearing station in case of an air raid or invasion. Gifts were posted to members serving in the Forces and food parcels were sent to prisoners of war in Germany. In that same year, a resolution was passed to 'allow smoking and conversation in the Reading Room after 6.30p.m. and the Library be thrown open to members who object to smoking.'

The roll-of-honour board erected in 1919 contained the names of 60 club members who had served in the war, nine of whom were killed. In deference to wartime sacrifices, the committee bought a Union Jack in 1919 and purchased a seat for the Memorial Park in 1921.

Membership in the immediate postwar years exceeded 180 and the main income was derived from whist drives, billiards and the hire of rooms. In 1921, for example, the receipts from billiards were £57.7s.4d. and the receipts from whist drives were £31.7s.6d. Rooms were hired in that year by the Literary Society, Derbyshire Education Committee, the Hospital Sunday Committee, Buxton and District Football League, Chapel Football Club and Chapel Cricket Club.

During the 1920s library membership dwindled until only Miss Anderson and Mrs Fuzzard were taking advantage of the facility, but overall club membership rose to over 200. Despite buoyant membership figures and healthy receipts from billiards and whist drives, the Institute ran up debts, largely because the adjacent premises had been acquired and considerable sums had been spent on extensions. Further expenses included a new boiler, purchased because the heating system was 'in a state of collapse', and the installation of electricity in 1929. It is interesting to note that the committee decided to lock up the main electric switch and place a key in the hands of the steward.

When membership figures took a dive in the early 1930s, the committee responded by cutting membership fees, issuing cards to allow subscriptions to be paid by instalments, introducing 'country membership' for people living within a two-mile radius of the town and reducing the number of magazines which came into the club. An even more crucial decision was taken in 1935, when the Institute was registered as a licensed club and the reading-room was converted into a games room and lounge. From this moment on, the Institute became a very different club.

In 1938, the Townswomen's Guild hired the upstairs room and the British Legion began their association with the club by requesting use of the upstairs room on two evenings per week.

During the Second World War, supplies of beer had to come in by rail, owing to petrol shortages, and the Ministry of Food commandeered the upstairs room as a Food Control Office. Membership figures were quite high during the years of conflict but the committee often had to chase overdue subscriptions and employ the sanction of refusing bar service to people who were in arrears. The new steward's wife gave help behind the bar and various ladies' groups, including lady members of the British Legion, made use of the club's rooms, but the minutes show that the committee decided to reject a proposal that ladies should be admitted as spectators at a snooker match. When the war ended, ex-servicemen were given three months' free membership and the name of the club was changed to Chapel-en-le-Frith Memorial Institute and Club. It was decided that three out of the seven trustees should be representatives of ex-servicemen's organisations and half the committee should be ex-servicemen. Ladies became integrated into the club by a process of very slow erosion, which began when the Ministry of Food vacated the upstairs rooms in 1950. A mixed social club for members and their wives was instituted, but located 'strictly in the upstairs rooms' and a stamp on whist score cards was introduced to allow ladies into social events. However, a proposal for 'Ladies' Admittance Cards' was firmly rejected.

In 1951 the committee was in self-congratulatory mood. W. Green was thanked for his good work in organising whist drives; W. Poulson and J. Hibbert were thanked for planning successful Christmas handicaps; F. Bramwell was congratulated on his care and efficiency, which had helped raise profits, and F. Firth, the chairman, was thanked for his 'good work and interest'.

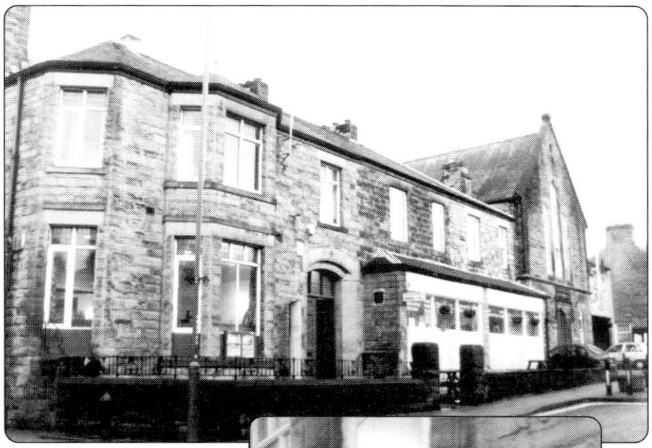

Chapel-en-le-Frith Memorial Club (the Institute) and the Town Hall.

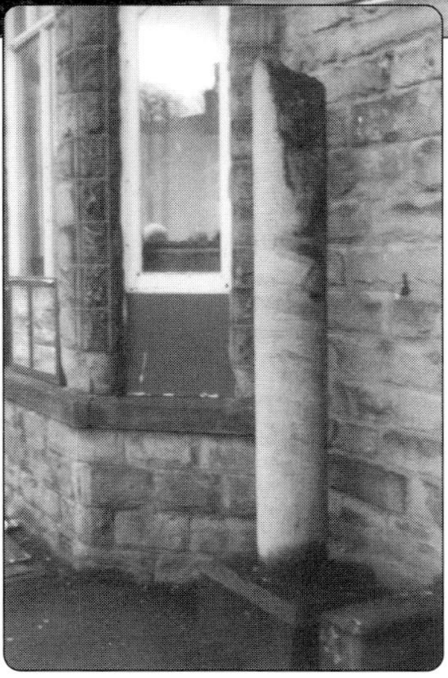

The limestone column at the entrance to the Institute.

Despite all this the loss of rental income with the departure of the Ministry of Food in 1950 soon took its toll on the club's finances. The rooms vacated by the Ministry were let for a time to a firm of accountants as well as to the gas board whilst alterations were carried out at their Market-Place premises. However, the committee really wanted the rooms to be at the disposal of members. Consequently, by halving the membership fee, more people were encouraged to join the club, which in turn increased bar takings.

In 1954, when Fred Winterbottom became chairman, it was decided to allow the British Legion, who were looking for a new headquarters, to base themselves in the premises on an initial 12-months' trial. Six years later, the reading-room was officially designated as the British Legion Room. In 1955 Sam Longson became president and arranged some high-profile events, such as a snooker-and-billiards demonstration by Fred Davis and Sidney Lee. Another crucial change to the club took place in 1958 when a fruit machine was installed and a tombola and Christmas draw were introduced. An application was also made for a theatrical licence and the Belper Revellers were booked as the first act.

The club owned a house at Town End for use as accommodation for the steward and his family, but the property became a financial handicap in the late 1950s because work had to be carried out in response to persistent complaints by the occupants that they were being plagued by rats and by the leakage of sewage. When it became clear that the club was living beyond its income, membership fees were restored to their original level.

The question of admitting lady members had been raised on a number of occasions in the 1950s, but meaningful discussion of the matter had been deferred time and time again. In 1958 it was agreed that 'lady friends' and wives could be brought into the club on one night per week 'as a trial' but full membership for ladies was not granted until 1961, when their fees were fixed at half those for men. Another fundamental change came about in 1961, when the decision was taken to apply for a seven-day licence. Although this move brought a resignation from the committee by W. Lomas, a Sunday Entertainments Committee was soon hard at work. The nature of entertainment at the club changed dramatically in the 1960s: a Miss Harp Lager Competition caused great excitement, several stag nights were held and bingo and quiz nights found their way onto the agenda; another fruit machine was purchased in 1961, a record player in 1962 and a juke box in 1970. A more traditional purchase came in the form of an organ in 1975. Despite all these changes, the committee was still trying to preserve standards, passing a resolution in 1973 that 'lights in the front room must be on at all times and that people must be told this if they are using the room for courting.'

Surprisingly, a Ladies Committee was not formed until 1975, but its members soon made their presence felt and Mrs Newton even asked for a place on the main committee. The male members emphatically rejected this application on the grounds that the new equal-opportunities legislation did not apply to private clubs. However, the ladies helped the committee to organise various events, including Christmas parties, for both young people and senior citizens, and Jean Ingram was even co-opted onto the Entertainments Committee in 1978. Road shows and discos were proving to be very popular in the 1970s and groups like The Generation Gap and Top Country Sound were hired. However, the committee still had its limits: suggestions that a male stripper and a heavy rock band be invited were both rejected!

The changing nature of the entertainment on offer and the greater affluence of the townspeople produced higher expenditure at the bar and much healthier club finances, but also gave rise to some bad behaviour. During the 1970s and early 1980s, the committee ordered a number of members, including ladies, to appear before them to explain disorderly conduct, bad language and even vandalism. Some people were expelled from the club, but some of the barred members responded by gatecrashing.

In 1981 the committee agreed to purchase the adjacent chemist shop, extend the club's premises and expand its frontage on Market Street. A wide range of entertainment was offered, from pop groups and discos to 'Slow Melody Contests' staged by Chapel Town Band and a charity night to raise money to purchase a wheelchair for a member's child.

During the 1980s, the committee concentrated their efforts on the provision of gaming machines and an adequate range of beers, a far cry from the anti-gambling and alcohol-free early days of the club. The purchase of daily newspapers, which had been a club tradition since 1891, was suspended for financial reasons in 1985.

When Norman Prime took over as secretary in 1992 the club was at a financial low, but Norman successfully negotiated interest-free loans from the brewery linked to a threshold guarantee of sales. The Institute is now financially sound; new furniture has been obtained from the Ferodo company and the bar, concert room, games room and lounge have all been redecorated.

The present committee comprises nine men and three women, and club membership has reached 400. The twentieth century ended with improvements being carried out on the Market Street façade with the support of a grant from the Heritage Economic Regeneration Scheme. However, the front of the building still features a prominent free-standing limestone column, which is actually the bottom bore of a deep-well borehole from Barmoor Clough and was donated to the Institute over 80 years ago by Mr Chaloner.

The atmosphere of today's Institute is very different from that of the club that was established in 1891, but more than a century after its foundation, the social function of the Institute and the recreational facilities which it provides are still very much appreciated by the people of Chapel-en-le-Frith.

Over 60s' Club

It is thought that Chapel-en-le-Frith's Over 60s' Club was formed in the late 1950s. By the 1960s, members were meeting in the Town Hall on a regular basis and enjoying two trips per year to the seaside. Cliff Johnson, who ran the chip shop at Town End, would generously supply members with a free potato-pie supper each Christmas.

As a meeting-place, the upper room of the Town Hall had the distinct disadvantage of being at the head of a steep flight of stairs. In 1983, a lift was installed in the building by the Parish Council, specifically to facilitate access for the members of the club. The installation was made possible by a grant from the Victor Burdekin Trust.

Some 20 years ago, the club moved to the Memorial Institute, which remains its home to this day. Club members have the use of a room every Tuesday afternoon and they automatically qualify as members of the Institute. Weekly activities include whist, dominoes, scrabble and an intriguing game called 'What?' which masquerades as an exchange of news, but is actually a wonderful vehicle for gossip.

A bingo session is held every month; the Christmas meal is an annual fixture and there are four subsidised trips each year – recent destinations have included York, Southport, Llandudno and Blackpool. These activities are funded by the proceeds from an annual Autumn Fair, when goods supplied by local shopkeepers and townspeople are put on sale.

Leaders in past years have included Mr Strong, Mr Halford, Ernest Belfield, Denis Longden and Peggy Fletcher as well as Charles Leach, who bequeathed £500 to the club.

Membership has been as high as 80, but the weekly attendance had dropped to about two-dozen stalwarts when a new committee was formed four years ago. Thanks to their drive and energy, membership is up to 60 in 2003 and the club is thriving. The committee comprises Ann Yates (chairman), John Baldwin (secretary), Jan Fernie (treasurer), Jean Baldwin, Grace Briggs, Mary Dakin, Keith Ball, Margaret Joule and Eunice Cundy.

The members clearly enjoy their weekly get-together, but they would much prefer their group to be known as the 'Tuesday Club' rather than the 'Over 60s'. One member even suggests that the 'Recycled Teenagers' Club' might be a more appropriate name!

Members of the Chapel Over 60s' Club on holiday in the 1950s.

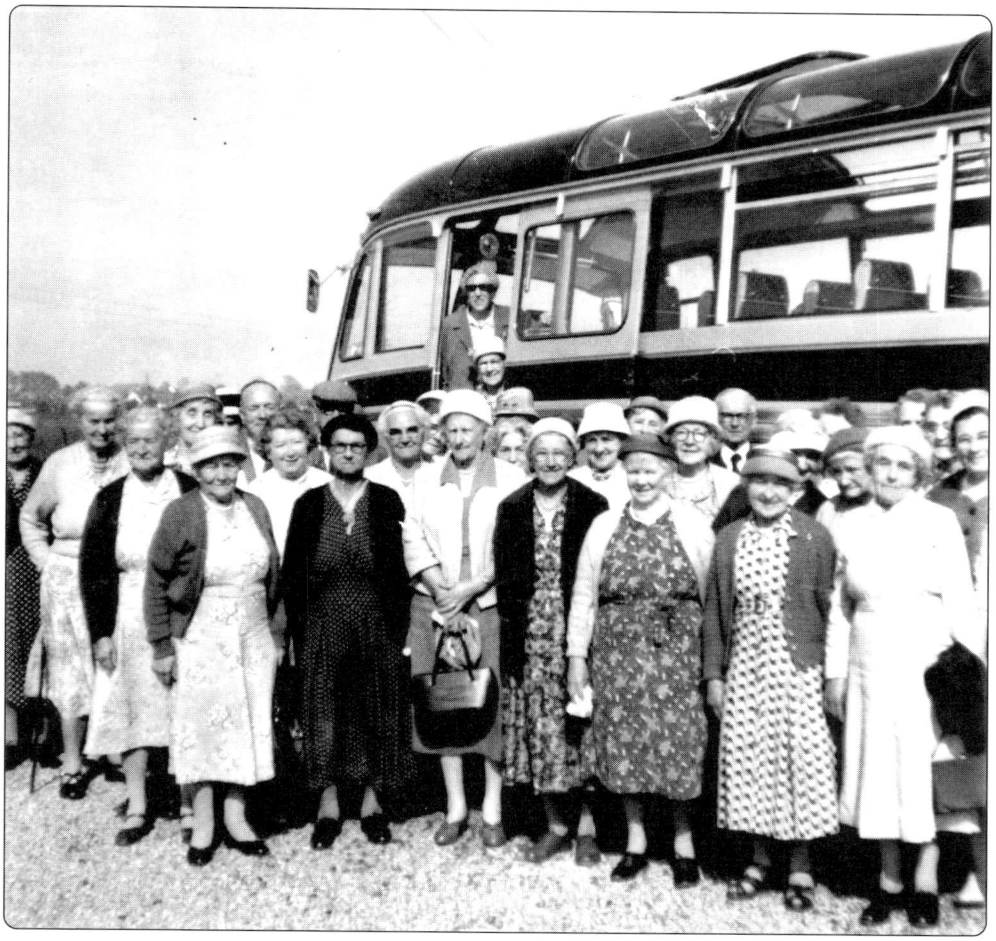

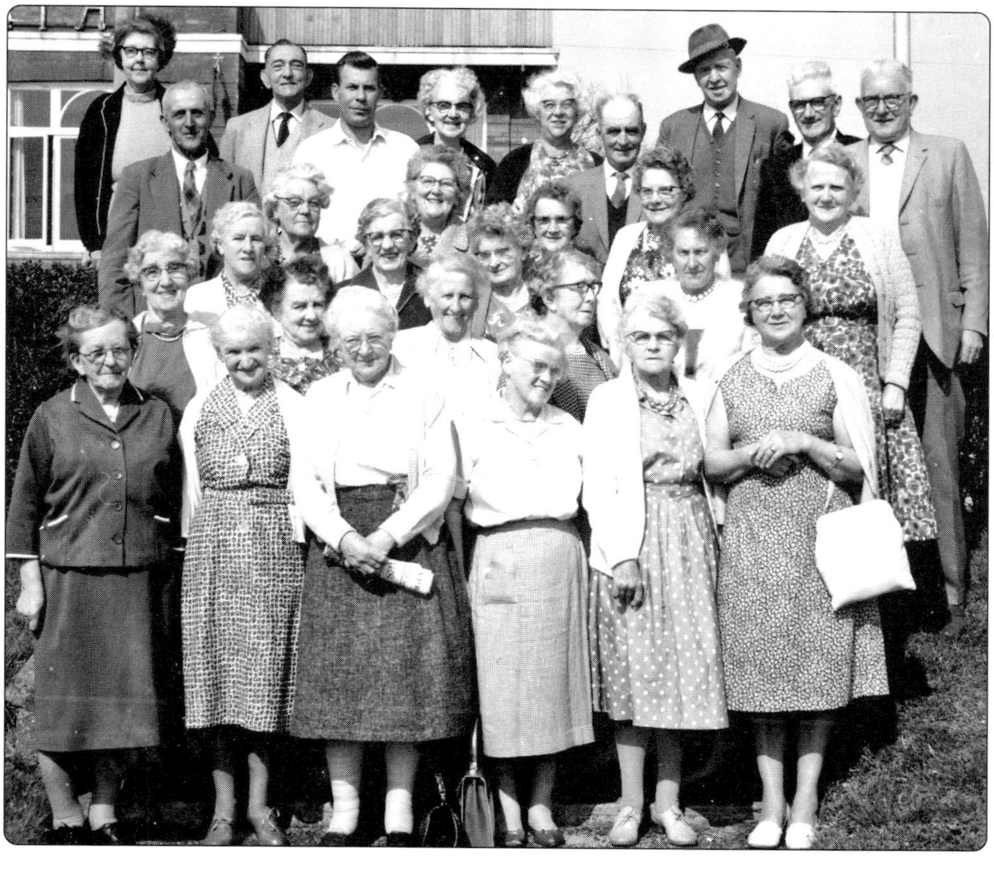

The Chapel Over 60s' Club on holiday on the South Coast in the 1960s. Members present are thought to include: Miss Ricketts, Mr Hoyle, Mr Liston, Ted the coach driver, Mrs Bennett, Mrs Ogan, Mrs Cottrill, Mrs Phillips, Mrs Ibbotson, Mrs Hobson, Mrs Hoyle, Mrs Hill.

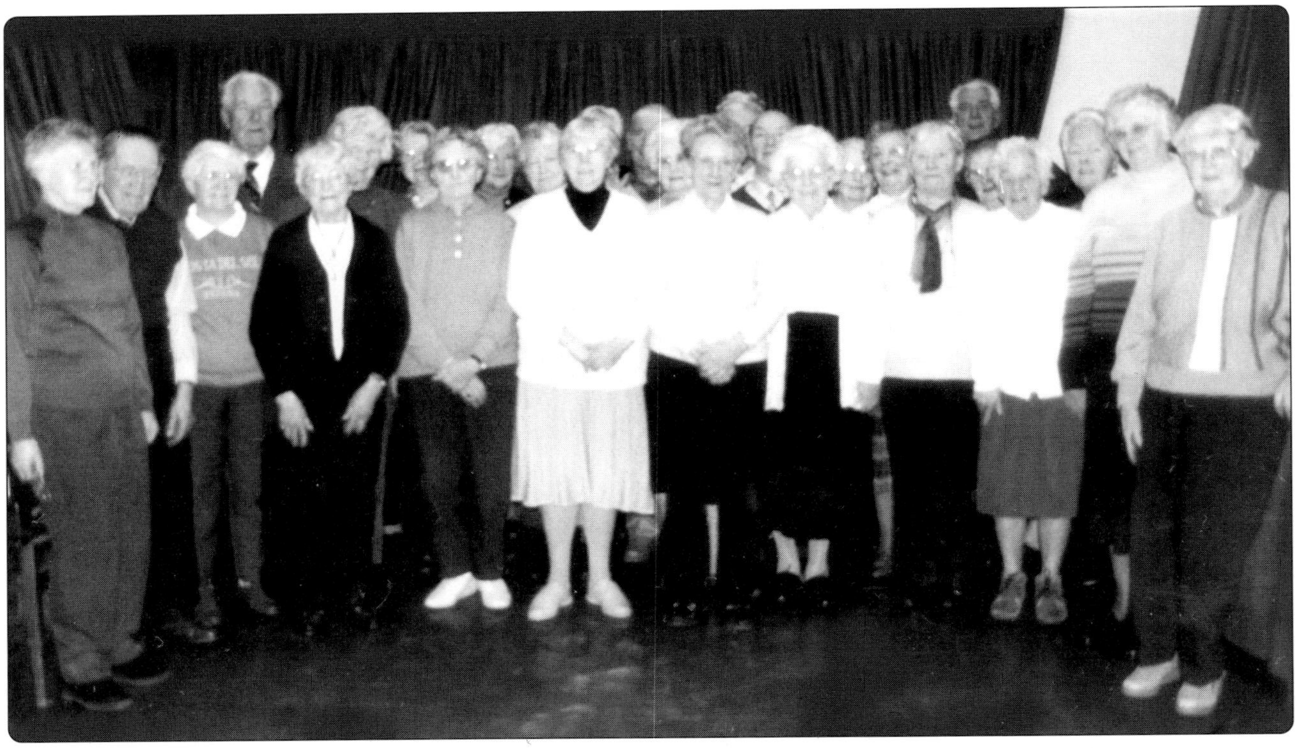

Chapel-en-le-Frith Over 60s' Club, 2003. Left to right: *Edith Fell, Horace Wilson, Sheila Tideswell, Syd Richardson, Lyn Richardson, Ruth Johnson, Anne Myers, Mavis Howe, Grace Briggs, Phyllis Nadin, Margaret Garner, Anne Yates, Joyce Bradley, Arnold Bradley, Mary Burrows, Jean Fernie, Doreen Reidpath, Eric Burrows, Jean Element, Ivy Davies, Ada Hudson, John Baldwin, Doreen Rowland, Margaret Holme, Connie Limer, Jean Baldwin, Cicely Stafford, Freda Lill.*

Chapel-en-le-Frith Amenity Society

By Brian Aries, chairman of the Amenity Society.

The origins of Chapel-en-le-Frith Amenity Society date back to 1977, when three people had the idea of forming a group which would concentrate on preserving our cultural heritage. The founding members were Jessie and Reg Jeffcock and Mike Mirams. Jessie and Reg were also members of the Rural England Society, which had very similar aims at a national level.

After the idea of a local society was born, the three founders set about getting other people round to their way of thinking. They booked the Town Hall at their own expense, organised a meeting with the chairman of the Rural England Society as guest speaker and placed posters around the town to advertise the meeting. On the evening of the event, just four people were present – the speaker and the three founder members!

Undaunted, the team pursued their dream of a local preservation society and by 1980 a committee of 11 people had been formed to run what had evolved into the Chapel-en-le-Frith Amenity Society. Committee meetings were held on a monthly basis at the Royal Oak.

A typical meeting in the 1980s would involve discussing all the local planning applications, particularly those submitted by Barratts, a major local developer, and representations would then be made to the local authority. The group decided to produce a Chapel Street Plan, which is still published to this day. In addition, a prototype walkabout leaflet was drawn up, which evolved into eight separate walk leaflets covering the parish.

The waymarking of the parish footpaths was undertaken and letters were sent to local landowners requesting that the paths be kept open for public use. On Sunday afternoons and Thursday evenings, the society led walks within the parish boundaries to acquaint people with the footpaths. The society also put forward a list of historical treasures to be placed on the Peak National Park register. In July 1984, the Amenity Society made strong representations to the Post Office authorities about the proposed closure of Town End Post Office; the closure was shelved and the facility remains as an asset for the people of Chapel.

In 1987 the society decided to progress a long-held hope of founder member, Reg Jeffcock, that the Old Hearse House in Market Street be turned into a visitor/heritage centre (some years earlier, Reg had seen a similar building in Tewkesbury which had been converted into such a centre). The group had just co-opted a local architect, John Bishop, on to their committee and John's contribution to the scheme proved invaluable. He felt that grants could be obtained from various sources to

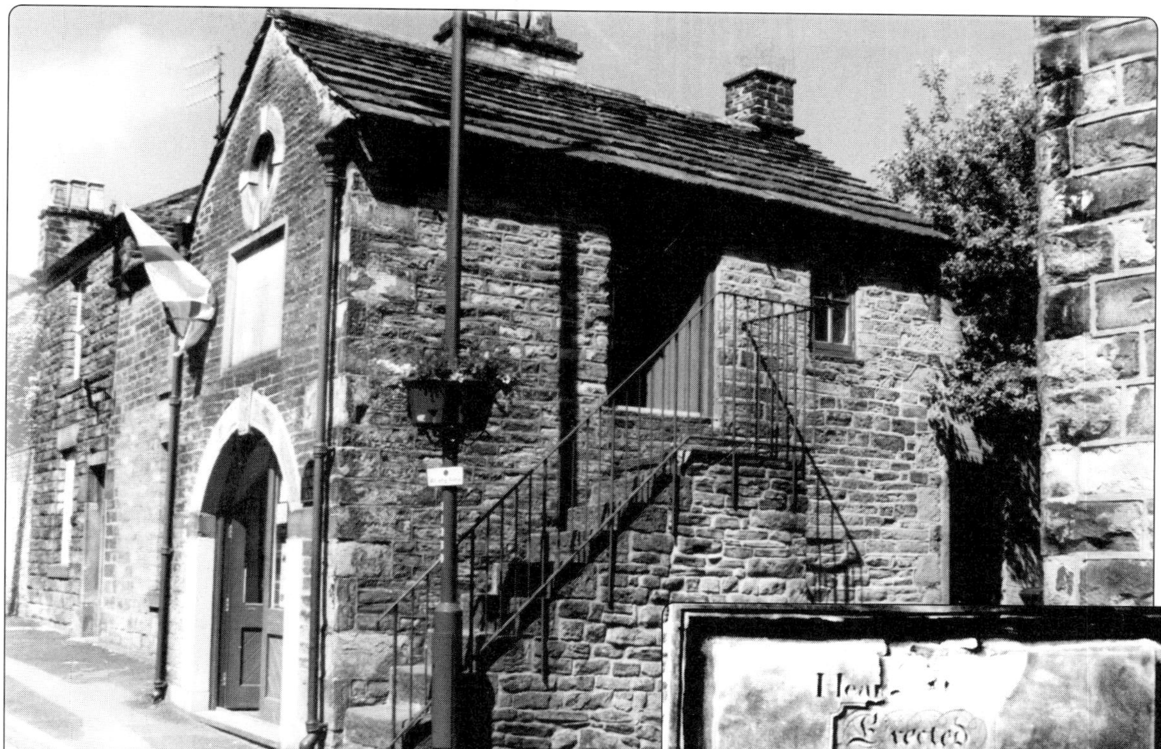

The Hearse House visitor centre.

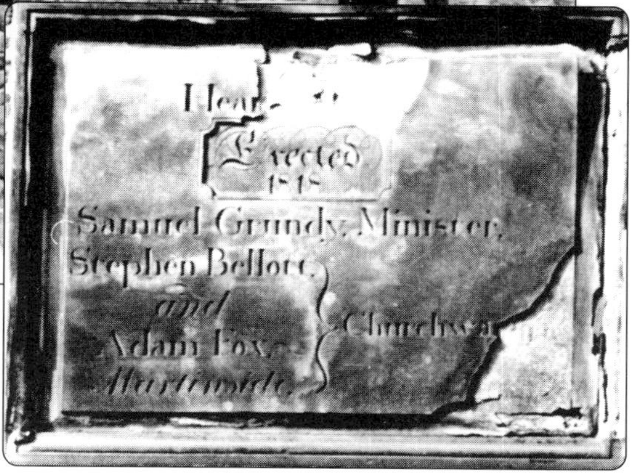

The crumbling plaque of churchwardens' names before renovation.

Below: *Close-up of the topograph on Eccles Pike.*

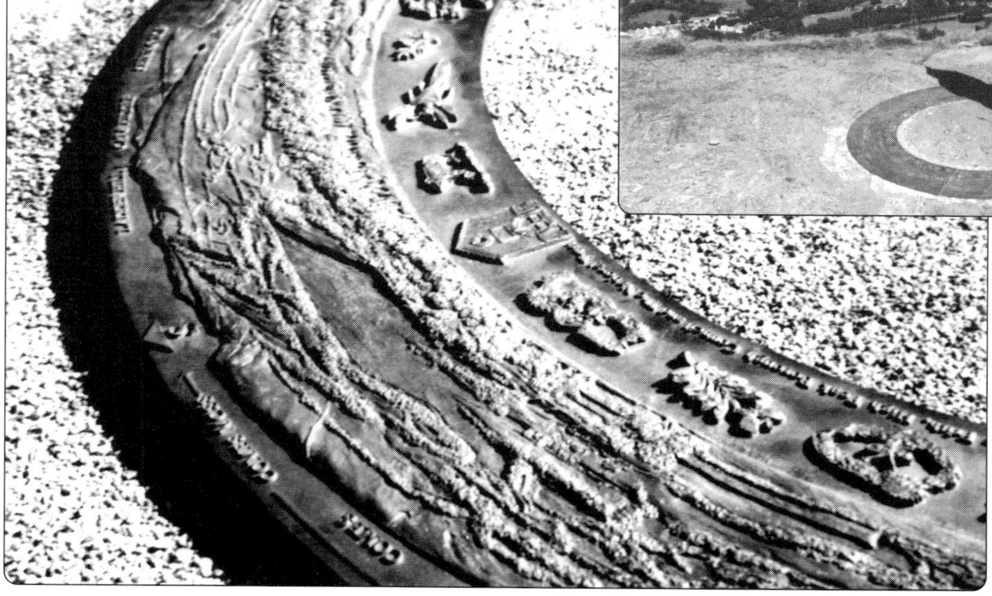

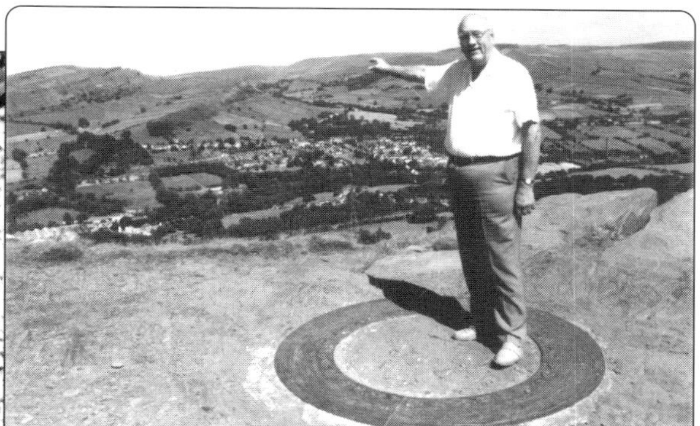

Amenity Society member Albert Goddard, who first proposed the construction of a topograph on Eccles Pike, points to the landmarks visible from the summit.

Below: *Celebrating the securing of funds for the Hearse House conversion, 1990. Presentation of a cheque from the Civic Trust (Community Pride Award). Picture includes: Elsie Stansfield, Ian Galloway, Jessie Jeffcock, Enid Phillips, Muriel Ross-Sharp, Reg Jeffcock, Anne Young (chair of Parish Council), Margaret Aries, John Bishop, Bill Stansfield, Bob Spurr.*

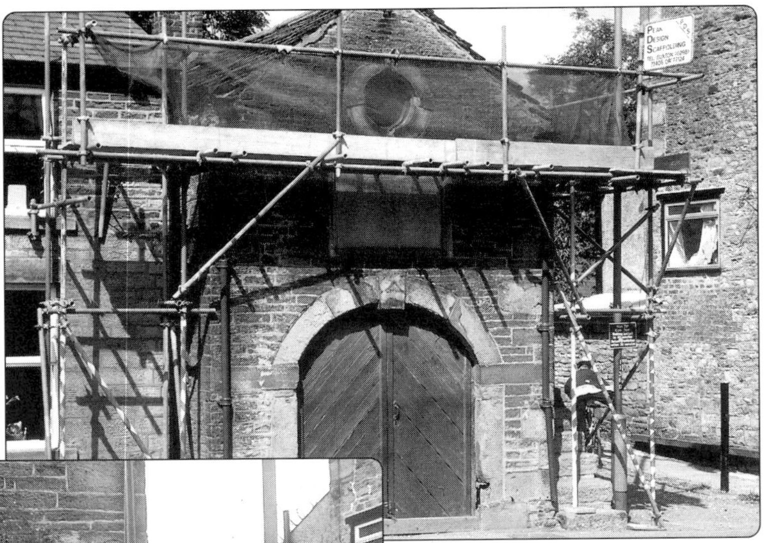

Above: *The Old Hearse House under renovation.*

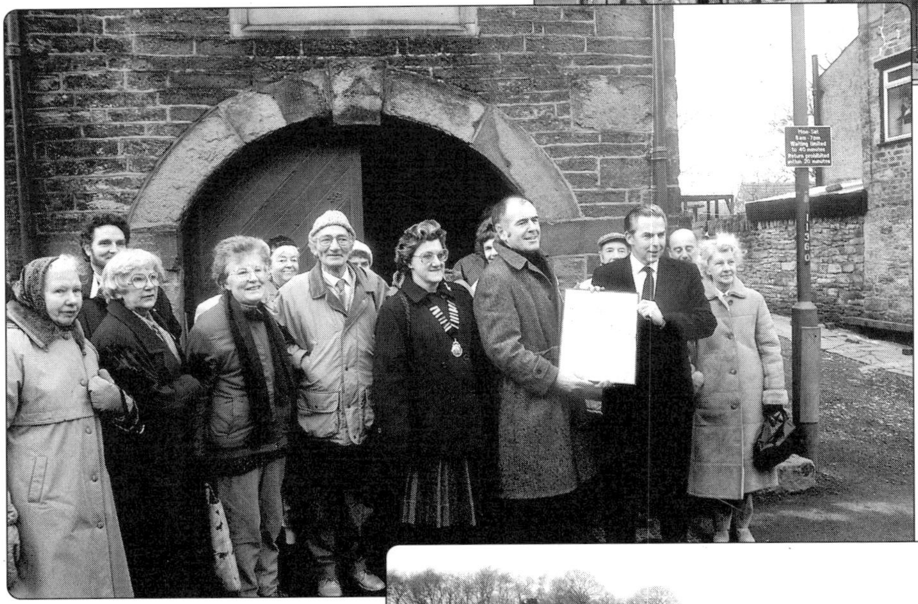

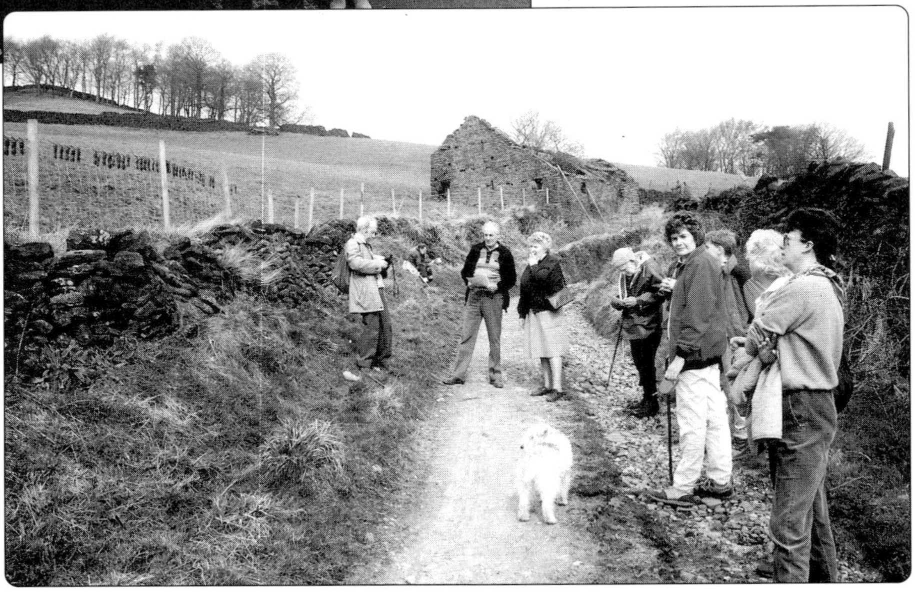

Amenity Society May-Day walk on Ladder Hill.

fund the project and, at the 1988 Annual General Meeting, he persuaded the society to go ahead with the conversion of the old building, despite fears expressed by some members that the scheme was rather an ambitious one for a small society and that wider support would be needed because the project leaders might be faced with a wall of apathy. John was to be the driving force behind the project over the next four years.

The Old Hearse House is a Grade II listed building, which was built in 1818 to house the parish hearse and was owned by St Thomas Becket Church. By 1987, it was being used as a storage point by the Parish Council and was in a neglected state. Over the following four years, the Amenity Society pushed the project forward while also continuing with their normal business. A lease was arranged with the Parish Church and restoration and refurbishment costs were estimated to be £7,500. The society received a £3,000 grant from the Civic Trust in 1990, but other funds were needed, especially when estimated costs rose dramatically to £14,000!

In order to apply for funding, the society became a registered charity and made many applications for support. By 1991, sufficient funds were in place to allow building work to go ahead and the centre was completed and opened by the Duchess of Devonshire in March 1992. Since the opening day, the centre has been run as a heritage and information centre by volunteers from the society, who open the building as often as possible.

Shortly after the opening of the centre, the Amenity Society committee decided to launch a gold-award scheme, which would be used to give recognition to any renovations or new buildings in the town which were of outstanding quality or enhanced the environment. The award takes the form of a framed gold certificate and a number of these now adorn the walls of Chapel buildings which have been deemed by the society as worthy of recognition.

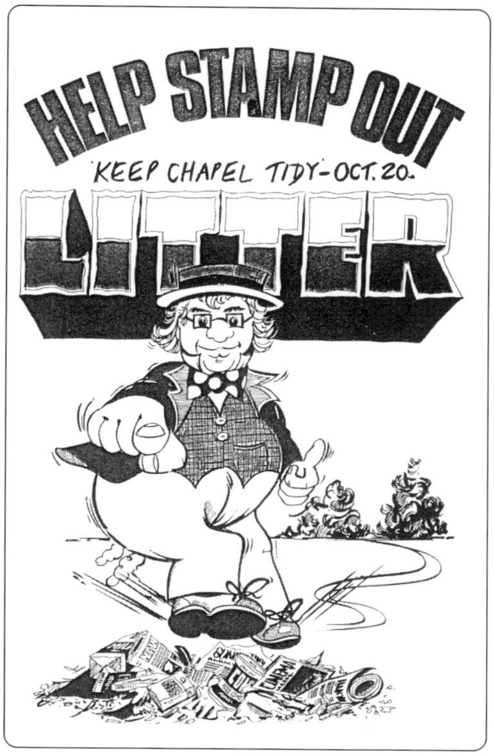

Chapel Amenity Society's 1984 campaign to 'Keep Chapel Tidy'.

In 1993 Mike Smith suggested that the society should revive the custom of well dressing in the town. After much discussion and planning over the following two years, the society produced their first well dressing in July 1995. By July 2002 there were no fewer than seven well dressings in the parish, all under the auspices of the Amenity Society. The well dressing has become a much anticipated annual event, which attracts many visitors to the town.

In 1966 the Parish Paths Partnership was unveiled by the Countryside Commission. The Parish Council agreed to take part in the scheme and invited the Amenity Society to join them. Over the following three years, Brian Aries (chairman of the Amenity Society), Alan Taylor (treasurer) and John Bailey (Chapel Ramblers) surveyed all the footpaths in the parish and made a comprehensive list of problems, such as a lack of signposts, broken stiles and blocked paths. Using money granted under the scheme, the Parish Council has undertaken work on behalf of the County Council to rectify any deficiencies. A Parish Paths Committee, formed under the chairmanship of Brian Aries, ensured that 90 per cent of work needed on the paths was carried out within the three-year duration of the Parish Paths Partnership. The work of the society on the parish paths continues, even though the 3Ps scheme has officially ended. Under the auspices of the scheme, the society has also completely updated the original walkabout leaflets and reprinted them in full colour on laminated cards. The walkabout packet, which also contains a new Parish Paths map, was the only publication to be given an award by the Sheffield and Peak District branch of the CPRE in 2001.

During the millennium year, the society instigated a project to place a viewpoint indicator (topograph) on the summit of Eccles Pike, a conical hill which provides a 360° view of all the major hills of the High Peak. The scheme was jointly funded by the Amenity Society, High Peak Borough Council, the Parish Council and the National Trust, who own the land at Eccles Pike. The scheme was driven to a successful conclusion by the society and a bronze ring is now in place on Eccles Pike. The ring, which has a circumference of 20ft, contains motifs designed by local schoolchildren and a detailed relief profile, fashioned by Amanda Cirrillo, of all the elements in the view from the summit.

The society still leads summer walks in the parish and arranges illustrated monthly talks on a variety of topics in the winter months. For the foreseeable future, Chapel's Amenity Society will continue the work begun in 1977 for the benefit of the community.

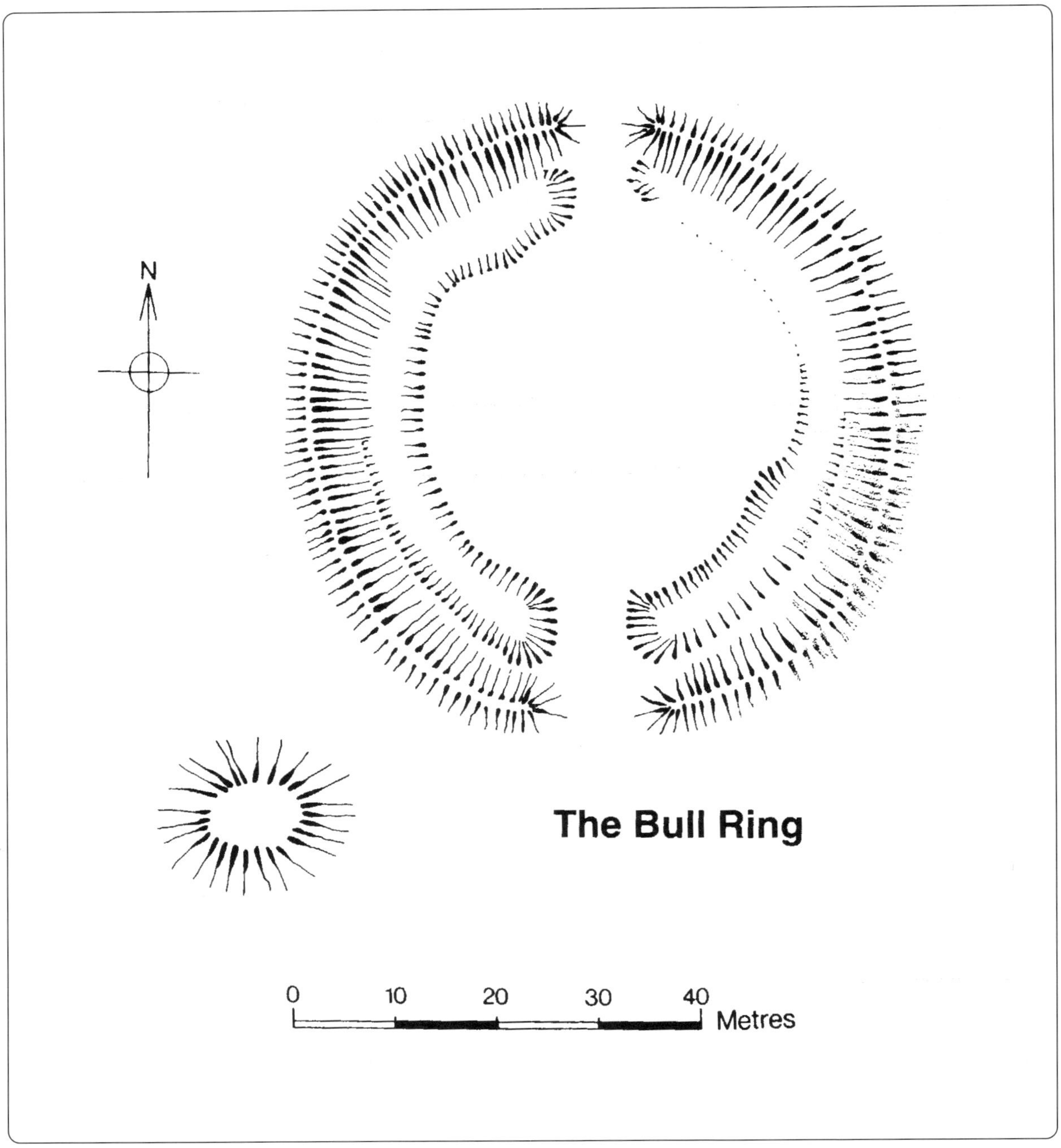

The Bull Ring, a neolithic earthwork.

Chapter 4

FROM DARK PEAK TO WHITE PEAK

The village of Dove Holes is situated immediately beyond the high gritstone ridge which runs along the southern boundary of Chapel-en-le-Frith. The settlement's southern boundary interfaces with the White Peak, an extensive plateau of almost pure limestone. This rock, which is in great demand for use in the chemical industry and in the making of roads, has been the making and breaking of Dove Holes. The vast quarries of the area have long provided the main source of work for local people, but they have also left great scars on the landscape. Much of the stone is now carried away by train, but scores of lorries still spew out of the quarries on a daily basis and leave noise and dust in their wake. The village narrowly escaped catastrophe 70 years ago when a spoil heap from one of the quarries began to slide.

In a recent poll conducted in 2001 by BBC Radio Five Live, Dove Holes was voted the Ugliest Village in Britain. It has to be admitted that the place would not win any prizes in a conventional beauty contest, but it would rank very highly in a poll which judged the quality of a place in terms of its community spirit. Jenny Nicholson's account tells of a vibrant village with fine musical and sporting traditions and of a people who have faced adversity and hardship with fortitude and humour.

Jenny's story also gives fascinating insights into a way of life which has now passed into history. She records the experiences of a German prisoner of war who served time and made lasting relationships in this friendliest of villages.

DOVE HOLES

By Jenny Nicholson, author of *When Heather Blooms on Ladylow – the Story of Dove Holes Village*, available from local shops, priced £9.99.

The village of Dove Holes is situated high in the hills to the south of Chapel-en-le-Frith. The earliest beginnings of the settlement are shrouded in the mists of time, connected as they are with a neolithic henge monument, known locally as the Bull Ring.

Accounts written by various visitors to the Bull Ring offer a range of theories as to its origins. In 1950 local author, Chrichton Porteus, wrote:

Beyond the churchyard wall is the oldest man-made feature of Dove Holes, the Bull Ring. All that remains is a grass-covered, circular ring of earth, 5 feet above ground level and 90 yards in diameter, with the remains of an annular ditch between them; there are openings or entrances at the northern and southern points of the ring, and an isolated mound in another field, 80 yards from the centre. Some archaeologists associate it with the early Bronze Age, c.1800BC, and couple it with Arbor Low.

In 1986 John Deardon wrote in *The Tale of the Backbone*:

At Dove Holes, near St Paul's Church, is an ancient stone circle, similar to that at Arbor Low, but known as the Bull Ring. It is believed to have been made [around] *2000BC, about the same time as the Arbor Low stone circle and Stonehenge, but it has been much spoiled by stone having been taken away to build a farmhouse nearby, and for gateposts and shippon door posts. It is said that when excavations for more stone were made in 1840, two skeletons were dug up. They were shown to a local surgeon, who said they suggested to him men nearly 7 feet tall. Arbor Low lies about 11 miles away and some people believe that an old track once ran between the two circles.*

As to the two skeletons, with their supposed tremendous height, I have been unable to find any evidence to support human remains ever being found in the Bull Ring. However, the North Derbyshire Archaeological Survey of 1984 dates the Bull Ring 'henge' as being of the neolithic period, meaning late Stone Age, an era traditionally associated with the origins of farming and a settled way of life. The period saw the rise of the first true villages, the cultivation of crops and the beginnings of the domestication of animals. Metals had not yet been smelted from their ores; tools were made of stone, bone, antler or wood. It would seem that Dove Holes may have had its origins as a village settlement at this time.

Evidence of early animal occupation of the area was found in 1901. Chrichton Porteus wrote:

At Victory quarry, Dove Holes, men at work in 1901 suddenly broke into a previously unsuspected cave, about 90 feet long, 4 feet broad and 15 feet high, with bones and teeth all over the floor. These were found to be the remains of mastodons, sabre-toothed tigers, elephants, rhinoceroses, horse, deer and hyenas. Never before in England had remains of such variety and completeness been found.

These remains are stored in Buxton Museum; they are not on display but they may be viewed by appointment.

Village Development

There is no record of the village in the Domesday Book, but the site of the present village was part of the Royal Forest of the Peak, a hunting forest of the Norman kings. In a local leaflet published in 1993, R.A. Young wrote:

Local people of this period would have been Celtic tribespeople. It is probable that the name Dove Holes originated from this period of time. Dove derived from the Celtic/Welsh name for black 'daube', that is 'black hole' or 'black water holes'. This refers to the area around Beech Lane and the Wheatsheaf Inn, where streams from Black Edge flow underground into limestone caverns or 'shacks', as they are known locally. During this period, the local Saxon people used the forest as grazing for their animals. Evidence for this can be found in place-names in the area, for example Hallsteads was a holding place for cattle or sheep, belonging to a man named Harald. At this time, Dove Holes was in the common or waste area of the Manor of the High Peak. During Medieval times the manor was split into townships or parishes.

We cannot tell whether the inhabitants of the royal hunting forest had begun to burn lime, but the Romans certainly did so. Jewitt suggests:

Burning limestone to produce lime has been practised since the time of the Greeks and Romans. A Roman bath excavated at Buxton was found to have been constructed of limestone blocks with lime mortar and faced with a lime cement.

The first reference to lime burning in Dove Holes is found in the General Survey of the Manor of the High Peak, which was carried out in 1650 to assess the value of the property of the late King Charles. The survey reported:

All those quarries or pits of Lymestone lyeing in ye crofts by ye Dove Holes, near Chapell Frith within the waste grounds of the Manor aforesaid for the burning whereof, there are at present 14 kilns at work or thereabouts, the kilns being set up ordinarily and taken down by the people at their pleasure without licence.

The Peak Forest Tramway

The Industrial Revolution initiated a revolution in transport systems. Goods were manufactured on a large scale for the first time, creating a need for movement of products to all parts of the country and to the ports. The roads, where they existed, were poorly surfaced and often impassable for months at a time. The introduction of turnpike roads in about 1760 brought about a vast improvement, but neither the turnpike or packhorse system was adequate for moving large amounts of raw materials and manufactured goods. Canals provided an answer.

An Act of Parliament authorising the construction of the Peak-Forest canal was passed in 1794 and work started in the same year. At the same time, the canal

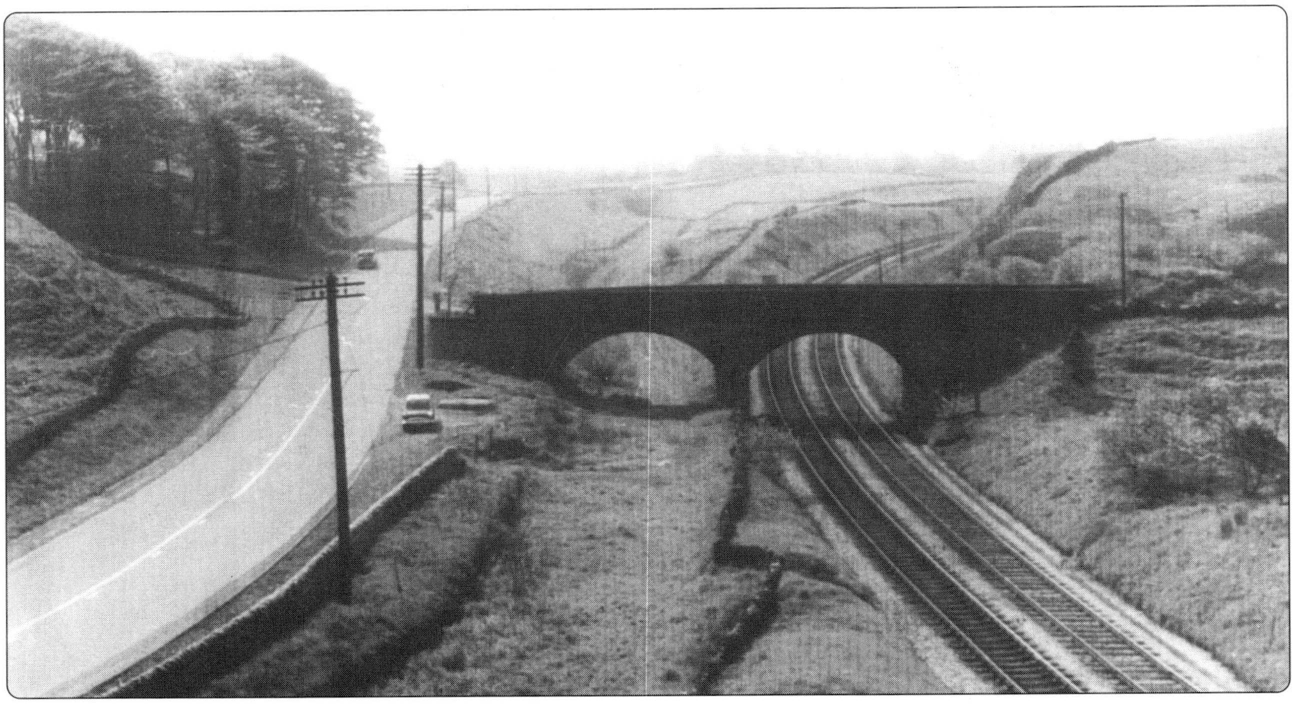

The route of the High Peak Tramway, running close to the railway.

company leased land at Dove Holes and opened a quarry to produce stone for the construction of the canal. In 1795, work started on a tramway to link the quarries to Bugsworth, where a canal basin was created. The tramway was completed in 1799 as a single-track line with passing places, but the line was converted into double track in 1830, with the exception of stretches running through tunnels. The tramway covered 6.5 miles from Loads Knowl at Dove Holes to Bugsworth, dropping over 500ft in the process.

Bill Hudson reported in *Through Limestone Hills*:

Loaded with stone (from 2 to 3 tons each) a train of up to 40 wagons was allowed to run downhill for six miles to the Bugsworth Canal Basin. Hundreds of tons of 6-inch stone sets for the cobbled streets of many Lancashire towns came down the Peak Forest Tramway.

In 1800, the line was extended from Barmoor Clough to the quarries at Dove Holes Dale. According to *More Than Just Dust*, published by the Peak Dale History Society:

In October 1800, the canal company wished to increase the number of quarrymen employed at their quarries in Dove Holes to 200. As the local supply of labour had been exhausted, they advertised in the Derby Mercury *for men, offering high wages, a quart of ale per day and a flannel waistcoat and trousers to those who would contract for working by piece.*

Although the expanding chemical industry and the invention of the 'basic' process of steel-making in 1879 led to a growing demand for limestone, the industry became fraught with problems. No single producer was big enough to satisfy demand, so 13 local companies merged in 1891 to form Buxton Lime Firms Co. Ltd. The companies owned by Samuel Taylor and Samuel Bibbington remained outside this federation.

Continuing Growth of the Village

The Chapel-en-le-Frith Tithe Schedule of 1836 shows seven buildings in Beech Lane, the house known as Meadow Lane Farm, three buildings opposite the farm and seven buildings at Higher Hallsteads. This seems to be the total number of dwellings in the village of Dove Holes at that time. However, the 1841 census lists 18 dwellings and 157 souls; the villagers were mainly occupied in farming and labouring, but the population included three shoemakers, one carpenter, one dressmaker, one wheelwright and one beer seller. Five servants were also listed, the youngest being 11 years old.

For some unknown reason, the 1851 census shows a drop in population: ten dwellings are itemised along with 83 souls. Interestingly, one scholar is listed (although the village did not have a school), as well as an Irish lodger, a beerhouse keeper and a wagoner on the railway (probably on the tramway, as the railway had not arrived by this time).

By the time of the 1881 census, there were 43 dwellings (one in Cross Cottages being uninhabited) and 225 souls. The number of occupants per house had dropped noticeably and there was a much wider range of occupations. The listing of station houses shows that the railway had arrived; there was also a schoolmaster, an American named Frederick Smith and his wife Mary (née Jones) who came from Conway, in north Wales. Frederick was a cordwainer (leather worker).

The Village School

The 1870 Education Act gave local school boards the power to establish elementary schools. In 1880, education was made compulsory for all children aged between five and ten. The school-leaving age was raised to 11 in 1893 and to 12 in 1899. A school building was not erected in Dove Holes until 1883, but the school may have met initially in the Gospel Hall, which was constructed in 1877.

Records show that plans for a school building were drawn up in 1881; the school was built at a cost of £800, designed to take 176 children in two classes and endowed by the Church of England. Average attendance was 149 children and the headmaster was Mr J. Hicks. In 1894, the school was enlarged at

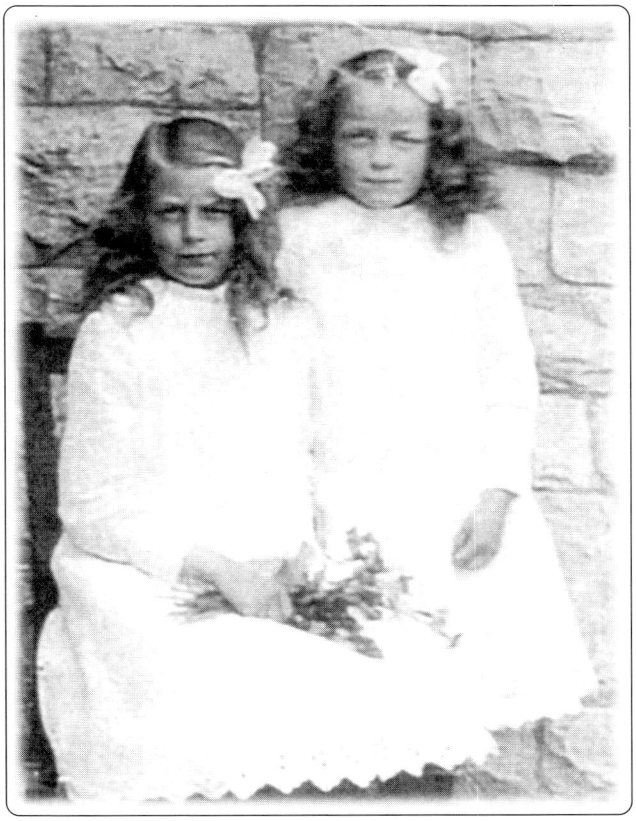

Mary and Florie Heathcote at school.

a further cost of £400. The school log of that year contains the following entry:

Commenced evening continuation classes (for adults); had 48 present. I arranged them as far as possible according to their attainments and took Arithmetic, Drawing and Reading as per timetable.

As time went by, the evening classes covered a greater variety of subjects, including vulgar fractions, elementary science, drawing, vocal music, letter writing and essays on subjects such as 'railways'. The classes were taken by the school's headmaster, who was assisted by Miss Wilshaw. Numbers enrolling had fallen to just 19 by 1911. Mr Hicks wrote:

A serious drawback to getting the young lads who have just left school is that most of them go to lime drawing which necessitates their being at work by 5a.m. or soon after, as the lime has to be ready for the railway soon after noon.

Two young men who were admitted quickly left; the mother of one of them excused her son on the grounds that he had to be up so early that it was necessary for him to be in bed early. Mrs Hettie Marchington recalls the conditions under which the lime drawers worked. She remembers:

When my brother went to pick lime for Ben Goddard he used to come for him at 3a.m. We used to think it was a shame. My mother had a side oven next to the fire and she used to put his shirt and things into it so that they would be warm for him to put on.

Entries for the evening classes finished on 26 March 1912, while entries in the school log-books from 1904 onwards show that the school often had to close for periods during January and February 'because of the very severe weather'. There were also regular epidemics of scarlet fever, whooping cough, diphtheria, mumps and chickenpox. On 31 January 1911 the school was closed by order of Chapel Rural District Council because there was an epidemic of measles in the district. The school was also shut for 19 days in January 1937 because 57 children were registered with influenza. In 1938, a death from diphtheria was recorded, only three days after the registration of the disease.

During the First World War, the schoolchildren sent chocolate and cigarettes to wounded soldiers. Mary Beswick of Peak Dale possesses two letters of thanks, which she received from Corporal James Howie Petrie, who served with the Gordon Highlanders. The first letter, sent from Skiddaw Grove Hospital in Penrith, reads:

My Dear Little Mary,
You don't mind me calling you by your name, do you? Though I have never seen you yet, I feel I almost know you. You and your little chums are too good to us. We all send best thanks for the latest gift of cigarettes. I am not a real soldier; I am only a Territorial, but we have to do the fighting same as the rest. I am sending you a

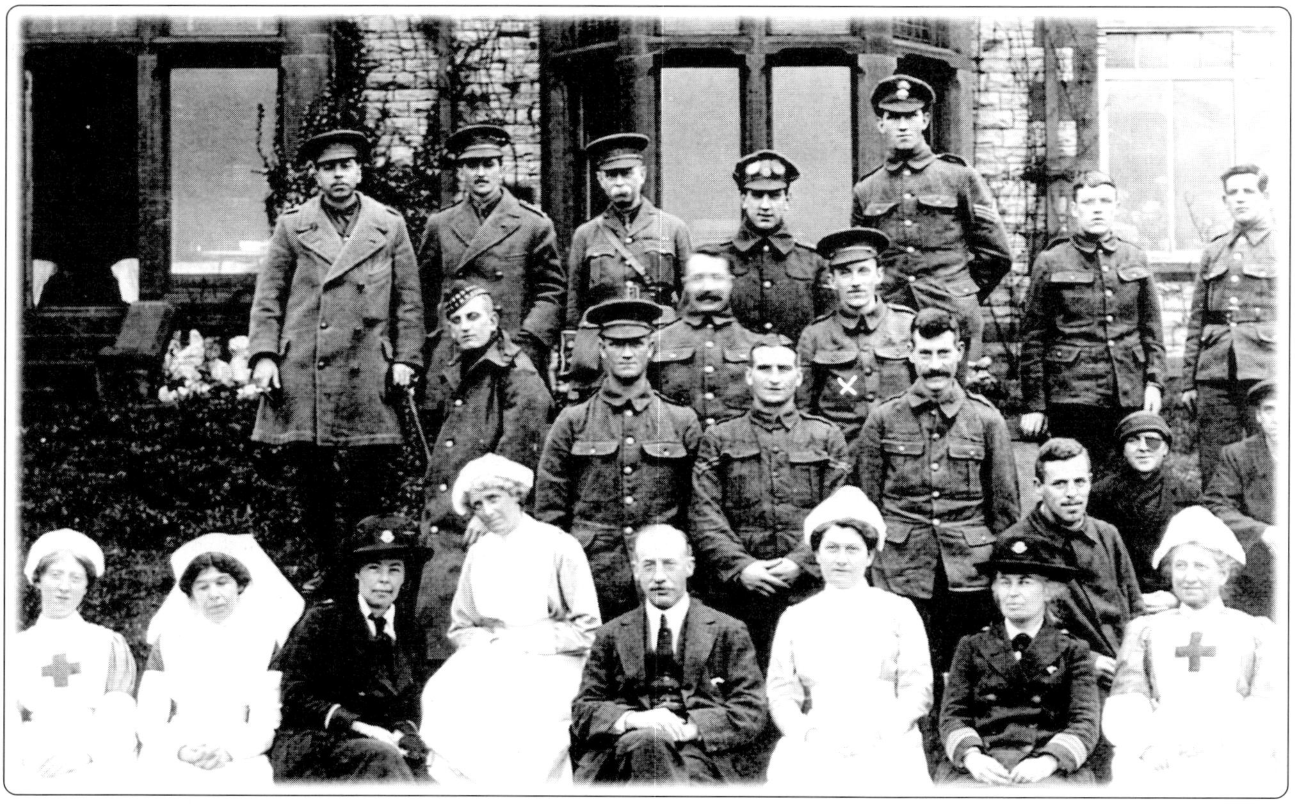

A group of convalescents. Howie Petrie is in the second row from the back, first on the right, wearing a cap.

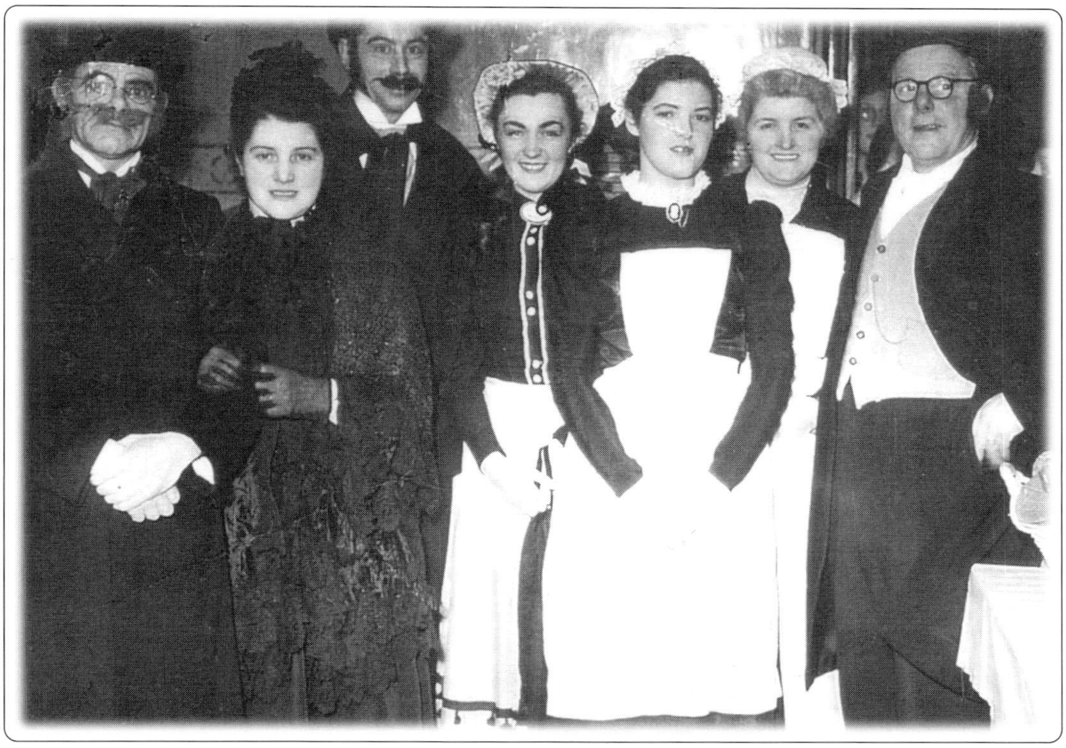

Chapel concert party, c.1950. Left to right: *Jim Naden, Hettie Marchington, Roy Forsey, Irene Vernon, Glenys Gregory, Freda Davidson, Vince Oldham.*

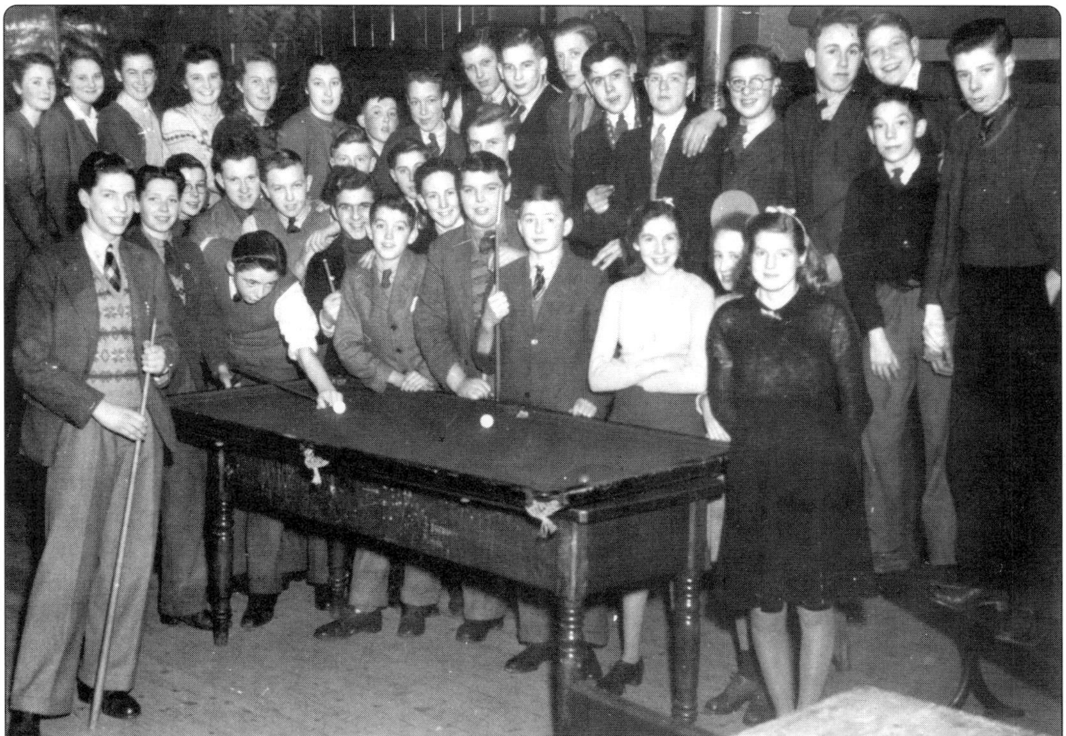

The Youth Club in 1947. Left to right, back row: *Norah Fletcher, June Proudlove, Margaret Fletcher, Phylis Wildgoose, Ruth Holland, Jean Tomlinson, David Jackson, Neville Hulley, Leslie Proudlove, Jack Bamford, Bernard Howe, Gerald White, George Fletcher, Norman Fletcher, Reg Spencer, Harry Hall, Jim Sherrett, John Cooper;* front row: *Ken Howe, Keith Spencer, Jim Goddard, Harry Hill, Fred Green, Denis Vernon, Donald Buckley, Arthur Coley, Eric Storer, Frank Marchington, Ted Cartledge, Jack Burton, Denis Hill, Gloria Bradley, Margaret Gould, Joyce Mannering;* at the table: *Peter Fletcher.*

picture of a group of some of us. I have made a small mark showing where I am.

I am a Highlander and should wear a kilt, but in hospital in France it was taken from me, so you see I am not in my usual uniform. My kilt was such a mess that it was really unfit to be worn because I lay for hours amongst the mud and water. I was struck with shrapnel on the left thigh and with a bullet on the right one. It did not hurt too much.

Howie's second letter contained the following promise:

My home is in the north-east of Scotland, near Aberdeen, so if teacher will show you on the map you will see that I stay a long way from Stockport, therefore I shall not have time to come to Dove Holes at present, but when the war is over and I get a holiday I shall come and see you.

Howie, who came from Kemnay in Aberdeenshire and was a banker by profession, never managed to visit Mary. He returned to fight in France and was killed in action on Tuesday 26 March 1918 at the age of 28.

The Methodist Chapel

Early records of Methodism in Dove Holes are sketchy, but there is evidence of preaching in 1789 at 'Flatt Doveholes'. By 1858, the Dove Holes Methodist Society had its own Preaching House, in what is now 13 Beech Lane – the gable-end of this building still bears the inscription, '1858 Primitive Methodist Chapel'. It is known that a Sunday school was also held there. A plan produced in 1870 lists four preachers, W. Howe, E. Vernon, R. Bray and E. Morton, plus one auxiliary, H. Brassington, together with the rubric, 'No preacher to be over 20 minutes'.

The foundation-stone for the existing Methodist Chapel was laid in 1871 by Samuel Bibbington, who also lent money to the trustees at an annual rate of 4 per cent. The land cost £121 and the church opened in May 1876. Members of the congregation had to pay rent for pews, but the rental was reduced in 1892 to 4½d. per quarter for side pews and 6d. for middle ones. Pews were declared free in 1896, but a quarterly collection was introduced. The chapel was lit by oil-lamps until electricity was installed in 1931.

Social events at the chapel were the highlight of many people's lives. The *Buxton Advertiser and High Peak News* of 1913 contained the following account of the Christmas concerts:

Part songs and Christmas carols were sung by the choir. Mr Harry Naden contributed a comic selection, Mr Ward and Mr George Hoyle rendered trombone items and two amusing dialogues were presented by members of the chapel. The outstanding items of the programme were an entertaining little ditty by the Sunday school girls, entitled 'Madcap Months', and a short performance by the boys, called 'An Hour with the Jacks'. There was a large attendance on both evenings and the proceeds, which were in aid of the Installation Fund, amounted to over £12.

In the latter half of the 1940s, the chapel had a thriving youth club. The club represented virtually the only opportunity in the village for youths to socialise and several marriages came out of friendships made there.

St Paul's Church

In 1878, the vicar of Chapel-en-le-Frith, Revd Hall, produced a document entitled, 'Proposed Church at Dove Holes'. He wrote:

The district of Dove Holes, the main portion of which is in the parish of Chapel-en-le-Frith, contains a population of 1,000, chiefly quarrymen and lime burners, who have come from distant parts of the kingdom and settled in the locality within the past few years, and the number of inhabitants is rapidly increasing. A site has been generously given by Henry Kirk, Esq., Barrister-at-Law, late of the Eaves, Chapel-en-le-Frith, and now resident of Essequibo, British Guiana. Plans have been drawn up for a free and open church capable of accommodating 250 worshippers, and it is estimated that the sum of at least £1,500 will be required for the erection and completion of the building.

The actual cost of the church, which was completed in 1879, was £1,976. The foundation-stone was laid by Samuel Bibbington, owner of Victory Quarry, on 17 August 1878, but construction was hampered by bad weather and by problems of subsidence, which necessitated the use of supporting buttresses. The church was originally intended to serve as a chapel of ease, with no clergy of its own. However, licence for Divine Worship was granted in 1879 and a parsonage was finally added in 1893.

In its first two years of operation the church did not have a burial-ground, so all internments took place at the Methodist Chapel. The situation is now reversed as the graveyard at the Methodist Chapel is full. Some years ago, unmarked graves of stillborn children were discovered on a site adjacent to the school which had been earmarked as the location of a portable classroom.

Sunday school days in the 1920s are remembered by Mrs Ada Fox:

Every Sunday, my Sunday school teacher, Miss Daw, walked up from Chapel-en-le-Frith to teach us. I used to watch out for her and walk to Sunday school with her. Yes, I learned all the books of the Bible during those walks and I remember them still! She was a strict teacher; all her class were girls. I can remember when we did a concert in the school for the church funds.

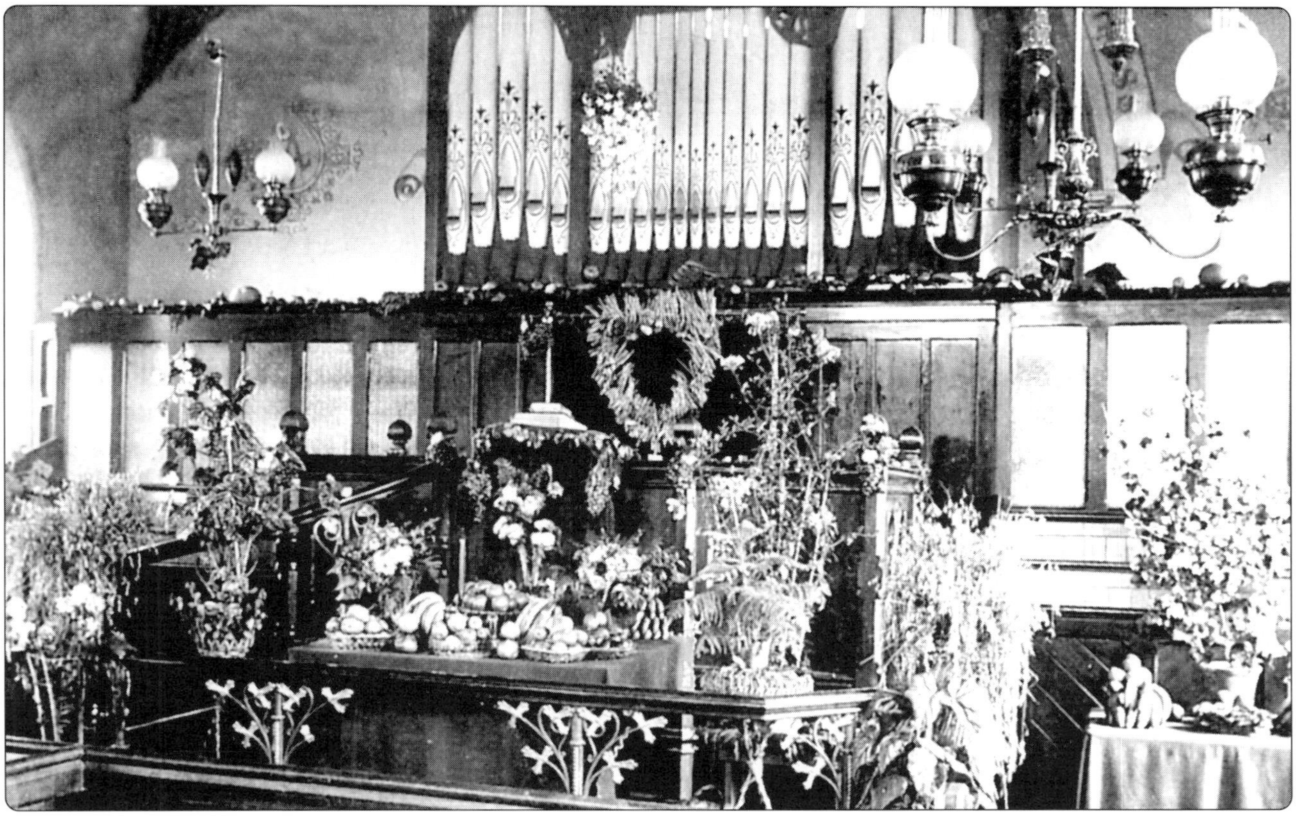

Harvest thanksgiving, 1965.

Miss Daw came and sat near the front. In we came, all blacked up and wearing trousers. One of the songs was 'Coming Through the Rye'; Miss Daw got up and walked out. Next Sunday, she made us all sign the pledge not to drink, and to promise her we would never wear trousers again. We had no choice; we had to promise. What would she think if she were about now, I often wonder. Of course, you went to Sunday school until you were married in those days – I did!

The First World War

At the outbreak of the First World War, Dove Holes sent its share of men to fight. Three local men were awarded the Military Medal; their citations read:

Nephi Cottrill: *Awarded Military Medal October 19th 1918 for an act of gallantry and for exceptional coolness and valour at Lebeaucourt on September 28th 1918 when his platoon came under heavy fire from a hostile battery and machine guns. He went out with great dash and gallantry, rushed the guns and killed or captured the teams.*

John Henry Marchington: *During the Austrian attack on June 15th 1918, when the bombardment was at its height, Gnr Marchington was sent to HQ with important letters. He had to go about three miles along roads that were heavily shelled with HE8 gas. In the course of his first journeys, a shell burst alongside, wrecked his motor cycle and threw him off. He continued on foot, and during the remainder of the day*

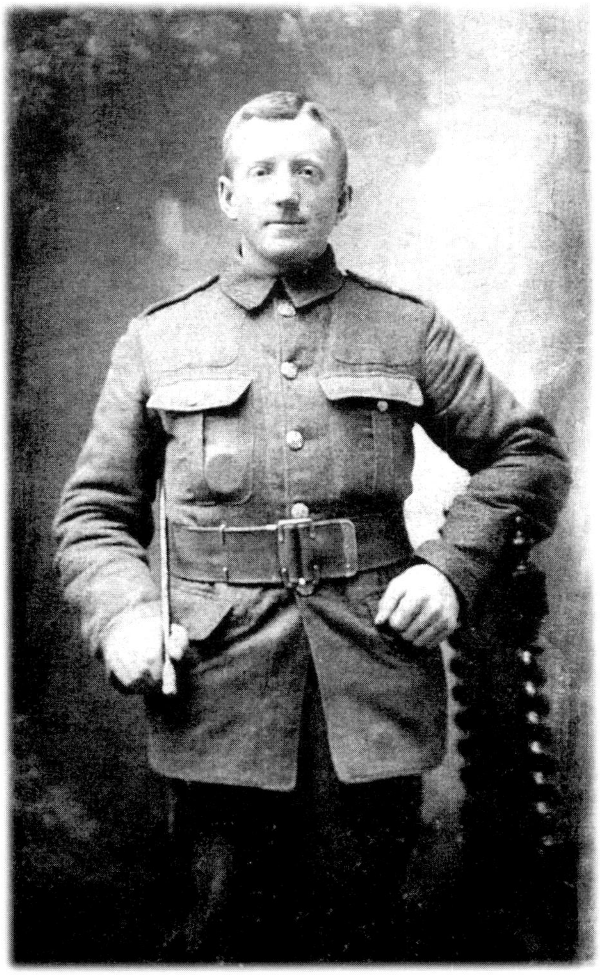

Nephi Cottrill.

made four journeys between Battery and HQ on foot whilst the bombardment was still proceeding.

William Clough: *Near Lens, July 1st 1917, for conspicuous gallantry and devotion. This man brought his Lewis gun with great courage and skill and materially assisted in driving back several hostile bombing attacks. He covered his flanks and finally succeeded in withdrawing his gun in spite of heavy machine gun fire and rifle fire.*

Those local men who died in the First World War were drawn from a variety of occupations, and included quarrymen, tailors, grocers' assistants, an apprentice printer, a farm worker and an engine driver. Their military occupations were: troopers, drivers, gunners, sappers, a trumpeter and a shoeing smith. A total of 44 men from the village were killed. One man attended a concert party at 46th HQ, six had been prewar Territorials, one was discharged through illness, two were discharged to civil work, three were discharged to serve at home, one died as a result of an accident in England while training and one was held as a prisoner of war from August 1917 to December 1918 at Ohrdurf, Germany.

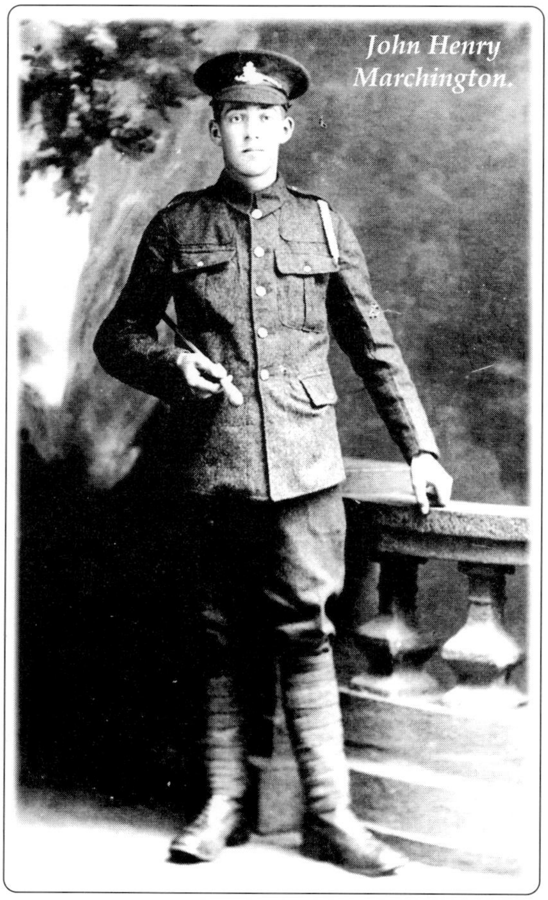
John Henry Marchington.

The cost to families can be gauged from the following recollection by Kathy Needham:

I had five brothers in the First World War. Three came back but two, George and Jack, were killed. When Jack got killed, they were in the trenches in those times, Jack and George were together. The bombs went off and they were shot – well, Jack was – in his head and he went to hospital. I think my brother George jumped up and he got hit. There was a big rush on and he got buried as an unknown soldier. I can remember it so well; I was 15. I can remember my mother praying for Jack, 'We cannot Lord thy purpose see, but all is well that's done by thee', because he'd gone, you see. When I think about my poor mother, what a time she had. I can remember the word coming through that George had got killed. It was on a Monday, the day of Jack's funeral and Abe Jackson, the postmaster, kept it away from my mother. Yes, he kept it away from her 'til a few days had gone. Yes, he wouldn't bring it to her at first. My poor mother.

The Second World War

With the Second World War looming, changes began to take place in the village. A petrol dump was placed on a site now occupied by Horseshoe Avenue and this was connected to a storage site on Dale Road. When the invasion of Normandy took place, a pipeline link, known as Pluto, was constructed to take the fuel from Dove Holes to the coast and then under the Channel to service the invasion fleet.

The village had its own section of the Home Guard, originally known as the Local Defence Volunteers (LDV) and sometimes disparagingly referred to as 'Look, Duck and Vanish'. There was also an auxiliary fire service, which had a fire tender that could be pulled by car!

In the early hours of 24 December 1944, the village was rocked by an explosion on the edge of the moors near Ladylow, followed by a fire. Although this event has been referred to as the crashing of a Doodle Bug, records show the craft was an unmanned VI flying bomb.

Many of the local people who served in the Second World War returned to their families, but six lost their lives and are remembered on the village war memorial.

The Prisoner-of-War Camp

The prisoner-of-war camp stood on the site now occupied by the car showrooms and the Trent bus depot. The following are excerpts from an account of life as a prisoner of war in Dove Holes, written by Herr Karl Lohkamp, who was 19 when he was captured. I am still in touch with Karl and proud to call him a friend.

In November 1944, I was taken prisoner by Canadians in the Nederlands. In March 1945, we were brought on a liberty ship from Ostend to Harwich and then by railway to Hampton Park, near London. There we had the first possibility after four months to wash ourselves and change our clothes. Our first impression of England

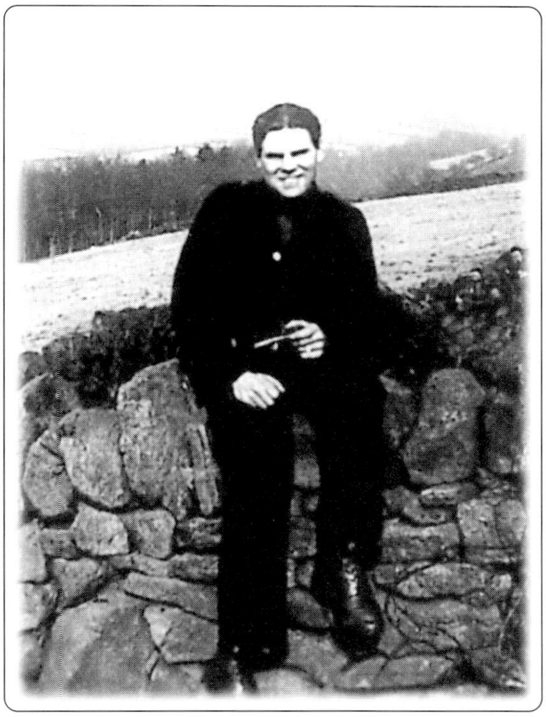

Karl Lohkamp.

– the railway wagons are so comfortable and now we get sandwiches and cake. Before, in the German Army, we had only heavy bread and heavy meals. At Hampton Park, we were registered by answering a lot of questions.

The next station was a camp of Army tents (each for five persons) near Chesterfield, with about 1,000 POWs, until May 1945. One day, we were asked if we wanted to work in a quarry – of course, we wanted. So we came to Nottingham in Nissen huts and had to go to work by bus (nearly 40km) to Dove Holes, with only a driver having responsibility. But where should a POW go?

We worked at Taylor Frith at Dove Holes, two groups of nearly 20 men. After welcoming us, the foreman, George Fletcher, gave us a 23lb hammer, a shovel and a fork, and we had to go to the big wall of the quarry, beat big stones into small ones, put them into lorries and fork clay and mud and put that into special lorries.

The first weeks were terrible, the muscles of arms and legs hurt. But the English workmen showed us how to do it and we got accustomed to the work and liked to do it – five to seven lorries a day. That was much better than to sit at camp for a whole day. At that time, English civil persons were not allowed to speak to us, give cigarettes or chocolate, or fraternise. But there were people who did not obey, so we had a good relationship with the quarrymen. The heavy work made hungry men and often we did not have enough to eat, so some POWs sold their cigarettes to the quarrymen and the driver of the bus brought white bread for us. That was the beginning of my learning English – we could borrow English teaching books, so I learned eagerly in the bus. Three months later, my English was good enough to allow me to be interpreter with George Fletcher, when he was arranging working groups – I got 4s. a week. The camp was staffed by just three soldiers.

Christmas 1947 was the first time of getting invited by English families and going out. Of course, we were happy. I got friendly with Jack Clapton, who was the blacksmith with Taylor Frith. My family and his daughter's family are still friends. Winter 1948 was a very cold one, lasting until March/April. We had to get the snow off the streets from Buxton to Chapel-en-le-Frith.

In January 1948, the officials at Taylor Firth trusted us so much that they let five of us work filling sacks with lime powder during the night without any guardianship, so that the lime could be delivered at 7 o'clock in the morning. I did the job until March 1948, when I went home. We got £1.10s. per week.

When his son returned home, Karl's father wrote a letter of thanks to Jack Clapton, expressing gratitude for their 'kindness, hospitality and care' and articulating the:

... hope that the captivity of my son has contributed to form a lovely relationship. Moreover, when the wounds of that terrible war have healed, our two nations will get together for a peaceful task.

Life & Times

The late Mrs Mary Beswick, who lived in Station Road, recalled the weekly routine of housework in the days when she was a child:

Monday: wash day, all day, rubbing clothes on the washing board, dolly pegging and mangling. It was all really hard work. In time, we progressed from dolly pegging to a copper posser in the dolly tub. We had a set boiler built into a corner of the kitchen, like most folk. You had to be up early to light the fire under it, to heat your water. When you had boiled the clothes and rinsed them, they had to be blued. You had to put a bit of starch in with the blue. It was all day of a job, you know, washing.

Tuesday: ironing. The clothes that you didn't iron were put through the mangle again. Of course, you used a flat iron, which had to be warmed on the hob.

Wednesday: upstairs cleaning. It was a day's job as well, mopping and polishing everywhere. Most folk had children at home and meals to look to as well.

Thursday: baking day. My mother did all her cooking on a large range – most folk did. Mother always made her own bread, pastry, cakes and everything. She would be baking all day on Thursday. She used to make tea cakes as well. I loved coming home from school on baking days – the house was full of wonderful smells and often her tea cakes would still be rising on the hearth. Of course, I did the same when I got married, but I could never get my tea cakes as light as my mother's. Our toilet was outside. It was next to the coal place; you had to go down the back yard to it – we'd no water toilet then.

Friday: downstairs cleaning day; everything shined and polished for the weekend. We had an order from the Co-op; it came on Fridays, so the order had to be put away.

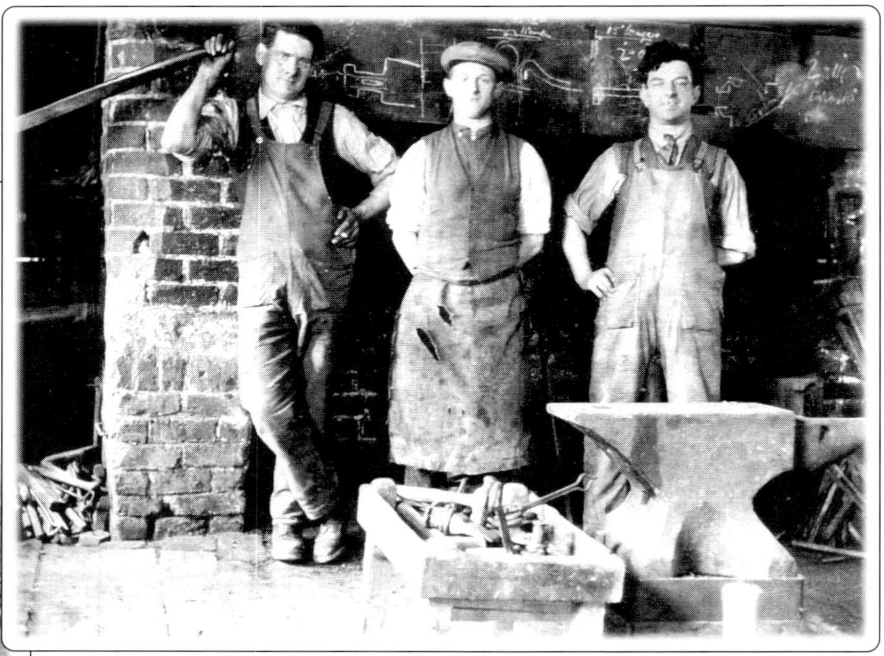

The blacksmith's shop, 1933, with (left to right) *Jack Clapton, Arthur Ford and Charlie Hallam.*

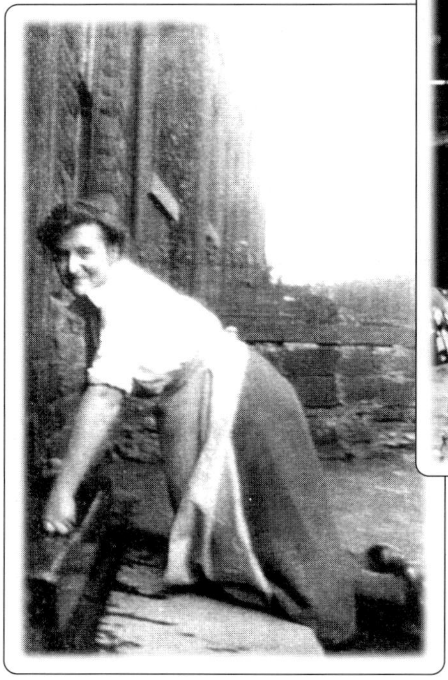

Fanny Heathcote, scrubbing her step.

Saturdays: we got everything ready for Sundays. Sundays: church and chapel.

As the late Mrs Fletcher recalled, the wives of quarrymen had to struggle to survive on the poor wages of the time:

It was awful in the quarry when we were first married in the late '30s. If the weather was bad the men would have to sit in the cabin, so they wouldn't earn anything. In those days, your man could be in the quarry all hours and come home at the end of the week with very little wages. Trying to keep food on the table and make ends meet was a big worry.

The Wakes & Carnival

The word 'wake' is said to originate from the wake or vigil-watch night service, which was held on the eve of the saint's day appropriate to the name of the village church. However, wakes changed from a sacred event to a secular festival – an annual holiday for working people, when the mills and workshops closed down and the fair came to town.

The date of the first wakes in Dove Holes is uncertain, but local people can remember Wakes Weeks in the early years of the twentieth century. The annual fairground attractions were set up in a field in front of Burton's Farm on Beech Lane. Arthur Hibbert's fair visited for many years and was followed by Morley's fair.

Mrs Kathy Needham recalls:

The most exciting time of year was Whitsuntide; the Wakes came up Beech Lane on Burton's Field. Lots of people were selling things as well. It all seemed dead when they stopped coming. They had donkey rides up Beech Lane – it was a happy life.

COMMUNITY LIFE & LEISURE ACTIVITIES

The Village Band

The first Dove Holes Public Prize Band was established in 1877 and soon thrived. The band provided tuition for new members and musical entertainment and accompaniment for concerts, carnivals, parades and religious functions, not only locally but also in the surrounding area.

The band declined for a while, but was revived in 1912 by Fred Goodwin, who retrieved the instruments from the Post Office, where they had been stored. The band became less active again during the First World War, but grew in the 1920s and '30s, when it not only supported local functions, but also competed successfully in many contests, including twice-yearly contests at Belle Vue, Manchester.

Dove Holes still has a brass band in 2003 and its members continue to train young players and entertain at community events.

The Jazz & Beer Festival

For the past 11 years, Dove Holes has been the unlikely venue for an International Jazz and Beer Festival. Begun in 1992 by Roger Marshall, who is continuing a long family tradition of music making in the village, the festival has gone from strength to strength. Enthusiasts

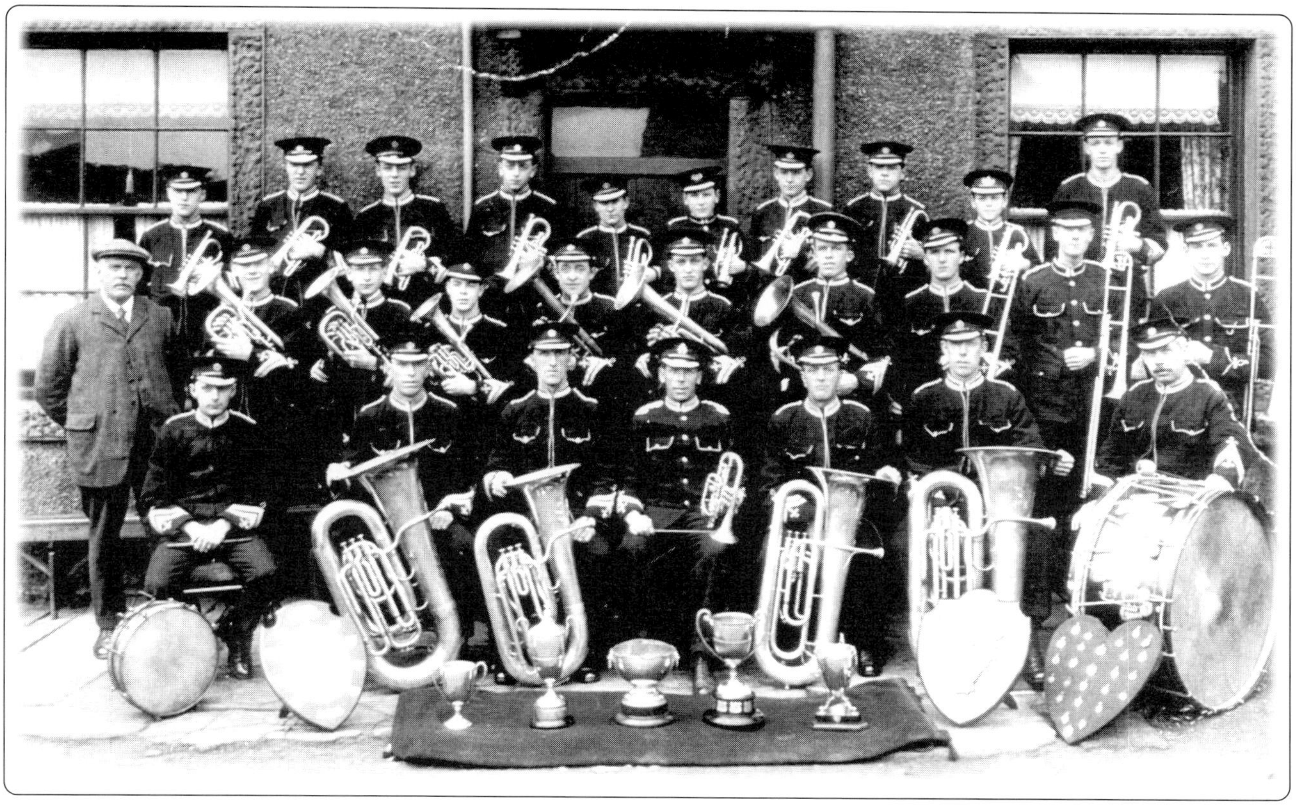

The Band in 1926, with Charlie Marshall standing on the left wearing a flat cap.

from far and wide descend on Dove Holes annually for a three-day extravaganza of real ale and jazz. A traditional feature of the event is Saturday's Grand Parade, which makes its way from the village's two pubs to the community centre. Gaudily decorated umbrellas, fancy waistcoats and sequinned skirts are much in evidence.

Jazz bands from all over the world come to perform at the annual event, which has earned a good reputation among jazz enthusiasts.

Over 60s' Club

The Over 60s' Club was formed in 1953, with Frank Frith as its first patron. The aim was to give senior citizens a meeting-place and provide them with a range of services, including haircutting for men and chiropody. Newspapers were delivered to the club on a daily basis, beetle drives and whist drives were held and talks were given by visiting speakers.

Thanks to a grant from Derbyshire County Council and funds from Help the Aged, a bus was hired to collect members from Peak Forest and Sparrowpit. Dancing was added to the list of activities and annual holidays were arranged to destinations including North Wales, the South Coast and Scotland.

The Cricket Club

Regular competitive cricket has been played in Dove Holes since the 1920s, although there is some evidence that cricket was played prior to this on a flat field opposite Bibbington Hall, close to Peace Farm. There is a record of a match against Chapel in 1883, when Chapel scored 70 runs and Dove Holes scored 42. Prior to the 1930s, there seems to have been three teams: Dove Holes, Dove Holes St Paul's and Dove Holes North End.

During the 1930s, the village team performed well: the First XI won the Second Division Championship in 1935 and, in 1936, Dove Holes became the first club to win the Second and Third Division titles in the same year. In 1937, Hyde (population 30,000) was relegated and Dove Holes (population 650) was promoted to the First Division. The local newspaper said of the team: 'They would play in a snowstorm and the villagers are as keen about their cricket as those of Hayfield.'

The club won the First Division Championship in 1970; were runners-up in 1971; reached four Bissenden Cup finals, winning the trophy in 1972 and 1975; and reached three Thompson Trophy finals, winning in 1971. Star players of the 1970s were bowler Harry Hall and all-rounder Brian Milner.

The Football Club

There have been various football teams and football pitches in the village since the beginning of the twentieth century. It is known that football was played at the back of the railway station, immediately below the old allotments, but the first football pitch in regular use was on the flat field between Lower Bibbington and Victory Quarry, where the local team played their home games in the Buxton and District

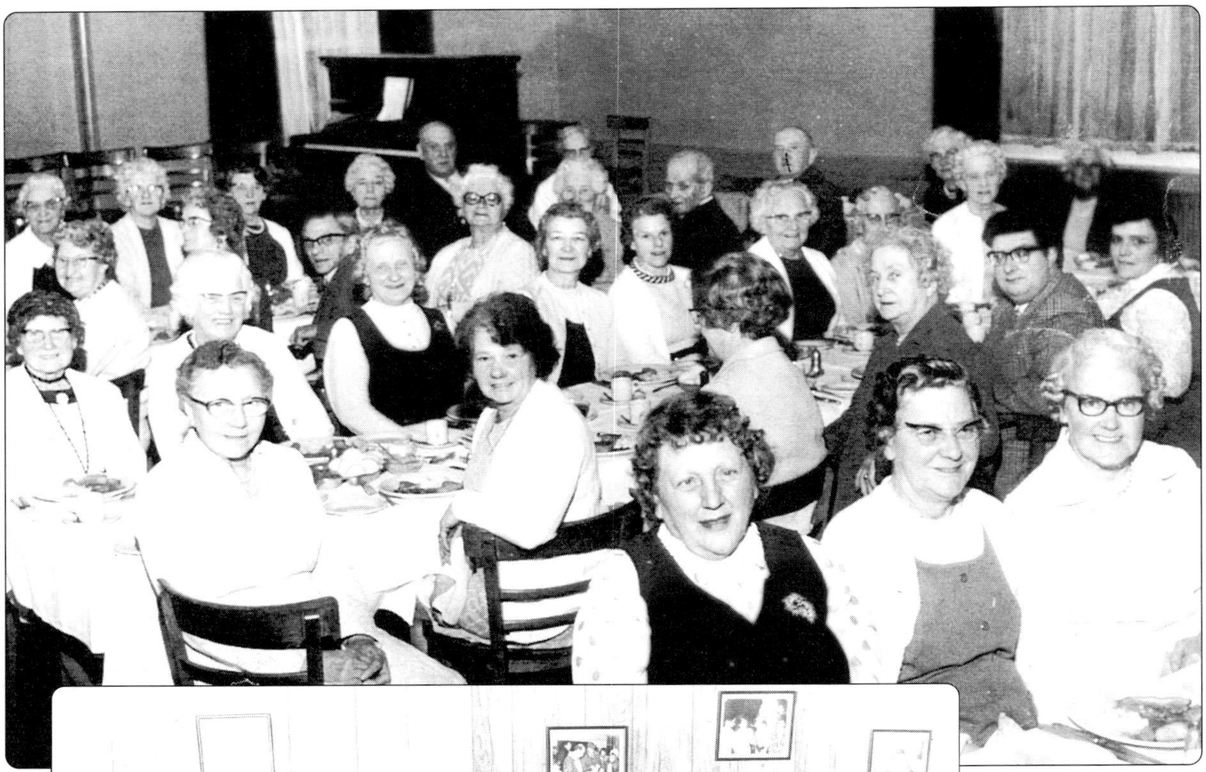

The Over 60s' Club, c.1960.

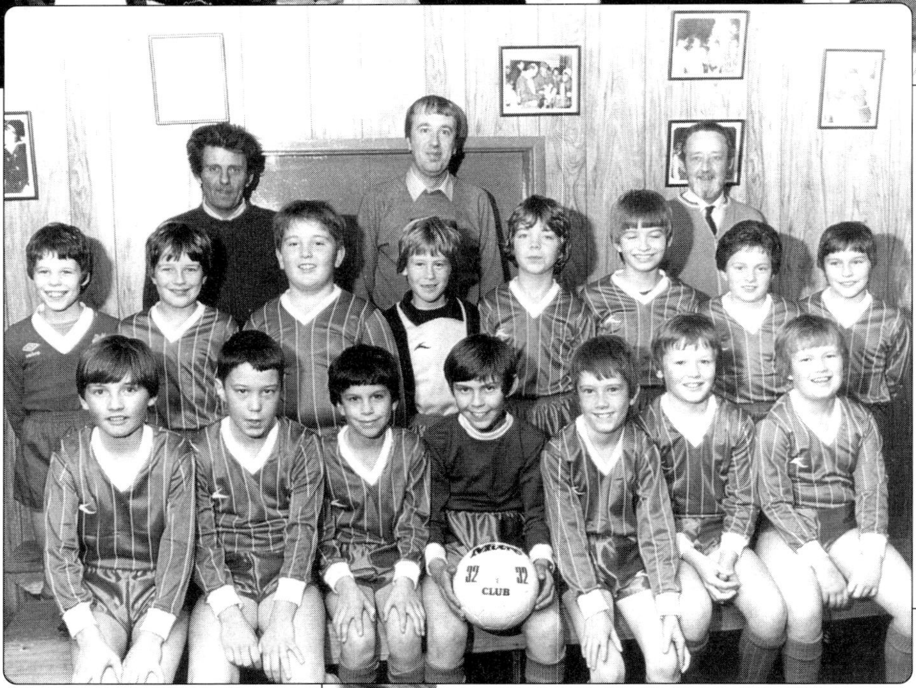

The football team in 1982 with their trainers. Left to right, back row: *Ernest Goodwin, Ken Gibson, Granville Neal;* middle row: *?, Stuart Millner, Marcus Jones, ?, Mark Canal, Paul Atkin, John Nicholson, Sean Moss;* front row: *Philip Burns, ? Mitchell, Stephen Crews, Paul Barber, Darren Gibson, Shane Simpson, Ian Gyte.*

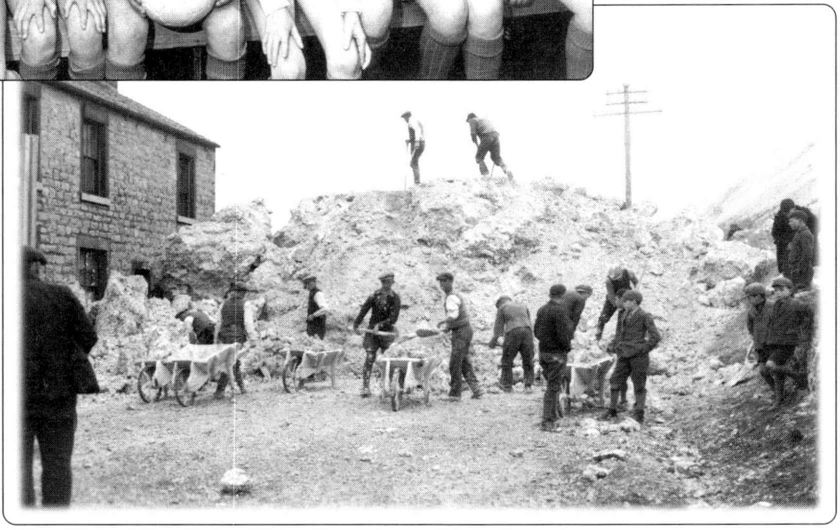

The day the earth moved – the Bibbington tip slip of 1933.

League during the 1920s and '30s. The team played for a time in the 1950s and was re-formed in 1970 by a few local teenagers. For about two years, the club played friendly matches against local teams.

In 1981, the ground was purchased by the Community Association and a junior side was formed in addition to the senior side. In December 1982, the local paper reported:

Junior football is flourishing in Dove Holes, as the youngsters are set to prove. And they have been prepared to work hard in the community to back their ambitions. They began training in August and at the first session about 30 children, some as young as five, turned up. Twice-weekly training nights continued until the winter closed in and the squad (age group five to 11) has taken shape.

The Day the Bibbington Tip Moved

In April 1933, the spoil heap from the Victory Quarry, which towered over the houses at Lower Bibbington, began to move. The *Buxton Advertiser* carried the following report:

Between 400 and 500 tons of limestone slag from the large deposit from the works of Messrs Bibbington, quarry owners of Dove Holes, became dislodged at about five o'clock yesterday morning and fell into the main road within a few inches of a row of cottages known as Lower Bibbington. The debris, which reached the height level with the eaves of the cottages, completely blocked the road and traffic had to be diverted by way of Peak Dale. The occupiers of the cottages had an alarming experience; most of them were fast asleep at the time and were awakened by a loud rumble as the debris rolled down the slope. This was quickly followed by a deafening crash as it fell into the road. Some of the slag actually piled itself up against two doors, but fortunately no damage was done, not even a window being cracked.

A short while after the crash, Mr Fanshaw of Buxton, the driver of the Post Office mail van on his way to Dove Holes, only just pulled up in time to avoid running into the debris.

Throughout the day, men were endeavouring to make a road through the debris, and it was found necessary to blast some of the huge boulders. Mr S.W. Bibbington, a member of the firm of Messrs Bibbington, owners of the slag, told our reporter, 'There must have been a hidden fissure'.

The quick thinking of one of the occupants was responsible for the lucky escape of the driver of the Post Office mail van. This lady had the presence of mind to wave a lantern from her bedroom window to attract his attention.

Had the tip been nearer the centre of the village or adjacent to the school, Dove Holes could well have suffered a disaster similar to that at Aberfan in 1966.

The Community Association

The Community Association came into being in the early 1970s after the village football club and the Parent Teacher Association of the school combined their resources to arrange a village bonfire. Early committee meetings were held at the Railway Inn and fund-raising events were soon organised.

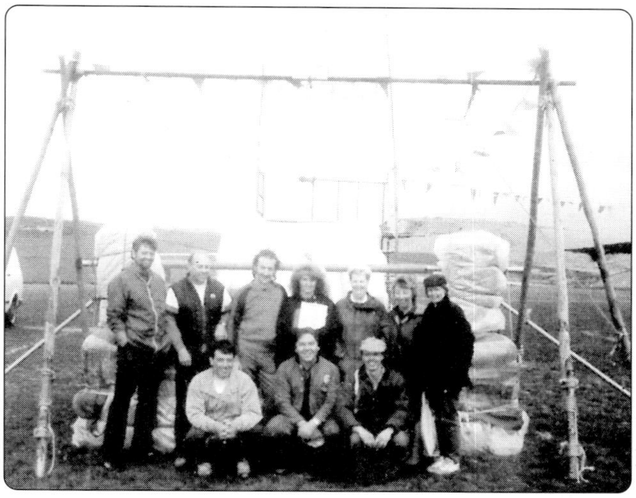

The Community Association's 'It's a Knockout' Committee, 1998: Left to right, back row: *Neville Atkin, David Scowen, Edward Cartledge, Margaret Cartledge, Rita Baldwin, Elaine Atkin, Helen Jackson;* front row: *Jason Lomas, Jim Pickford, John Jackson.*

In 1981, the Community Association bought 16.4 acres of land in the centre of the village from ICI for recreational use. The land already contained cricket and football pitches, which had been rented from the chemical company on a yearly basis. In 1984, the association began building a community hall on the site; everything except brick work was carried out by a team of volunteers. The hall opened for use in December 1985, but the official opening was held on 5 May 1986. The building was extended the following year, with the addition of a stage and a storeroom.

Events organised by the Community Association over the years include: 'It's a Knockout' competitions with teams from local firms and pubs; the annual bonfire and firework display, some of which have been lit by celebrities, including Bobby Charlton; an annual fête; dances; jumble sales; market stalls; car-boot sales; and Ho-Down nights. The association's logo is a dove with wings outstretched, which is surrounded by the motto, 'Make a Bold Venture and Persevere to Victory', a slogan which cleverly incorporates the names of three of the older local quarries. The Community Association still thrives to this day and is always keen to welcome new members.

As we enter the new millennium, the appearance of the village is greatly improved; many unsightly features, which are a by-product of quarrying activities, have been removed and landscaping has enhanced the general appearance of many areas.

Roger Marshall, guest Bobby Charlton, Phil Storer and Dennis Millner at the Dove Holes bonfire in 1982.

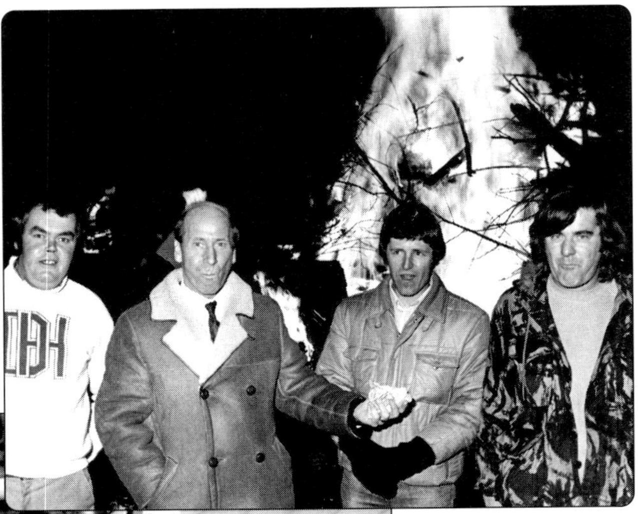

Princess Diana opening the Mountain Rescue Post in 1990.

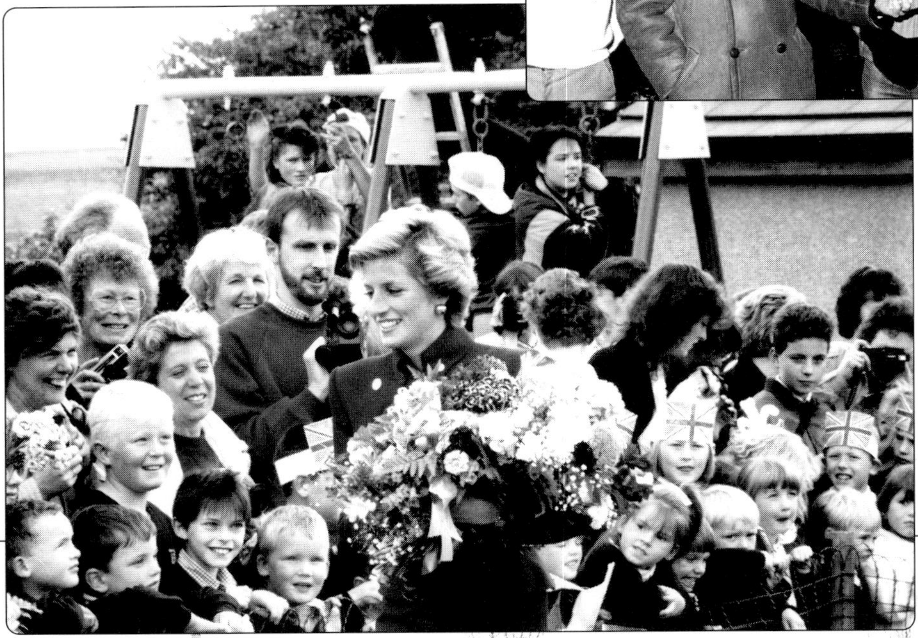

The next generation: the class of 2000 at Dove Holes School.

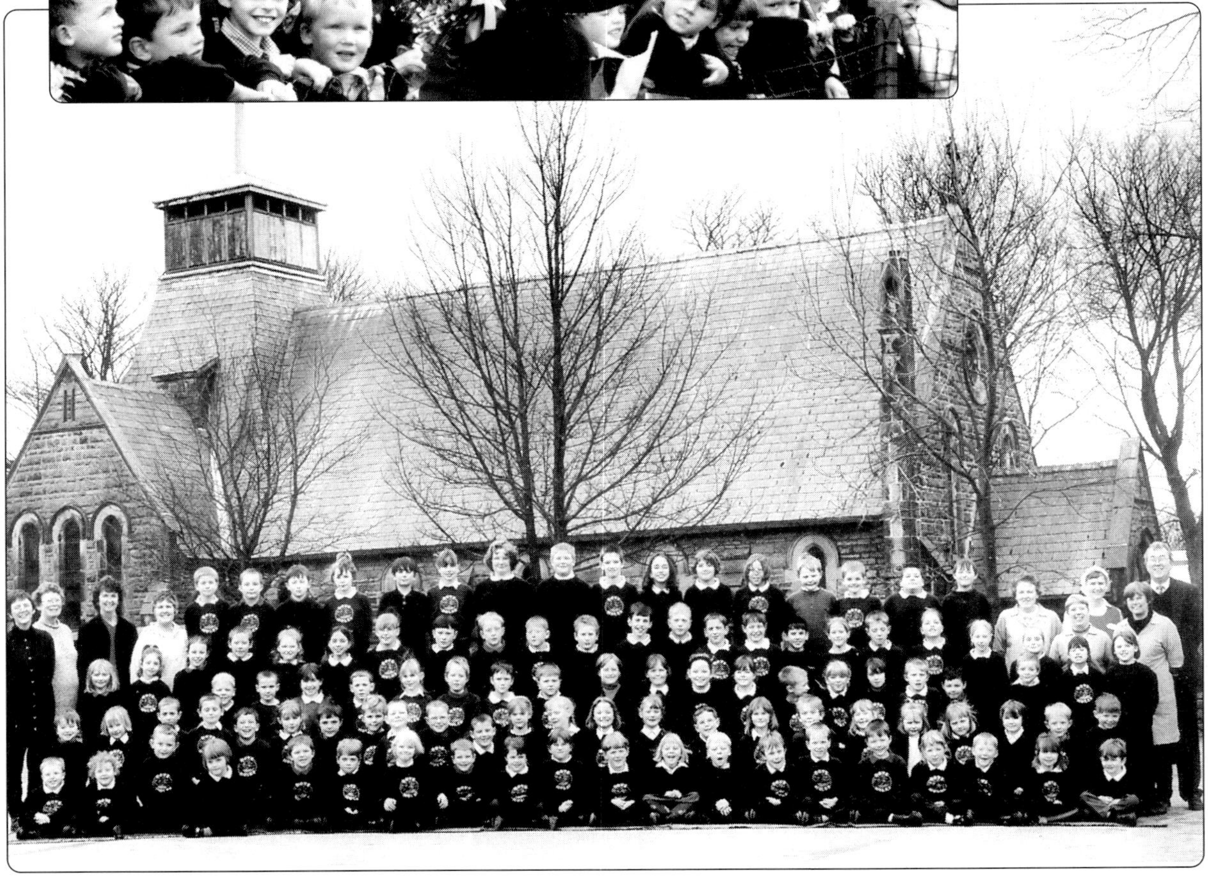

Chapter 5

Hamlets in the Hills

As well as the town of Chapel and the village of Dove Holes, the parish of Chapel-en-le-Frith contains the small hamlets of Combs, Whitehough, Blackbrook, Bagshaw and Sparrowpit. All of these settlements are in spectacular locations, some in exposed places in the hills, others tucked into cosy valleys, and all are picturesque places in themselves.

Bagshaw

The little hamlet of Bagshaw, which was first documented as Baggessawes in 1251, is situated in the high gritstone hills to the east of Chapel-en-le-Frith. In 2000 the entire village was designated as a conservation area, after a survey conducted by the Peak Park Planning Board noted that 'the village sits within the landscape, following the fall of land along its length, with individual buildings set either side of a sinuous road.' The report also commented on 'the strong visual link with the surrounding landscape, which cocoons the settlement on all sides.'

Bagshaw is a modern rarity; there has been almost no structural development during the last century, there is no pub, no street lighting, and there are no shops, no pavements, no yellow lines, no road markings, no street furniture and no formal parking places.

The hamlet's little Methodist Chapel was built in 1833 to serve a large High Peak farming community. The local farms are surrounded by irregular enclosures, which stem from earlier medieval cultivation, and the Peak Park is keen to maintain the 'loose and open character' of the hamlet.

The village is a linear settlement whose single street follows a steep incline to Bagshaw Hall, at the head of the settlement – there is no through road beyond this point. Many inhabitants are members of families which have been here for countless generations and eeked a living from grazing their animals on the exposed hills. Most of the gritstone houses and farm buildings date from the eighteenth and nineteenth centuries, and many have attractive names, such as Peartree Cottage, Appletree Cottage, Rose Cottage, Ivy Cottage and Hawthorn Cottage.

This little-known gritstone hamlet is a gem that fits easily and deferentially into its setting of the grey and green hills of the High Peak.

Sparrowpit

Sparrowpit is described by Humphrey Partington in *English Villages and Hamlets* as 'a mere handful of grey houses, which has a certain picturesqueness as it stands stolidly facing the winds of heaven.' This lyrical description is more than merited by the village, which stands some 1,200ft above sea level and is a linear settlement with almost all its dwellings on one side of the steep village street. On the approach to the village from either Chapel-en-le-Frith or Castleton, Sparrowpit's long terrace of gritstone cottages forms the profile of a prominent ridge.

The name of the village is possibly a corruption of Spar Row, the name of the terrace of lead miners' cottages which make up most of the settlement, but seventeenth-century records contain a reference to Sparrowpitte Yatte. Yatte is an Old English term used to describe a boundary or a pass in a hilly district.

Remains of old lead workings are to be found to the north and east of the village – some are covered by characteristic Derbyshire copses, planted to prevent cattle feeding on lead-polluted land. It is said that some of the men who worked the old lead rakes came here from the Cornish tin mines.

Sparrowpit's single village street drops from Peaslows to its junction with the A623 Chapel to Chesterfield road. There are no numbers on the

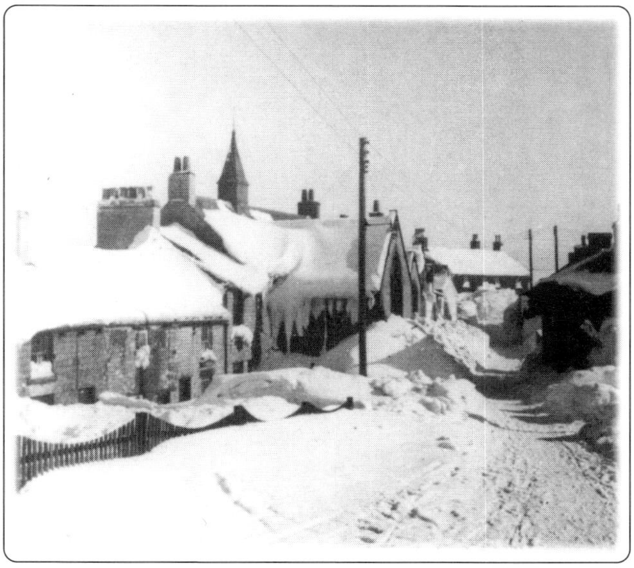

Sparrowpit under snow in 1947.

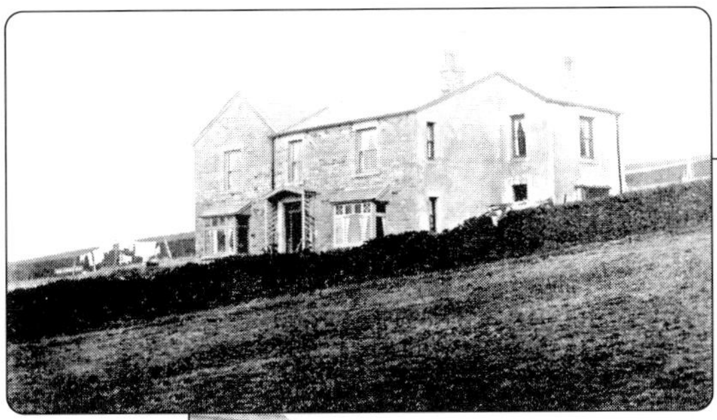

Rose Lea, Bagshaw.

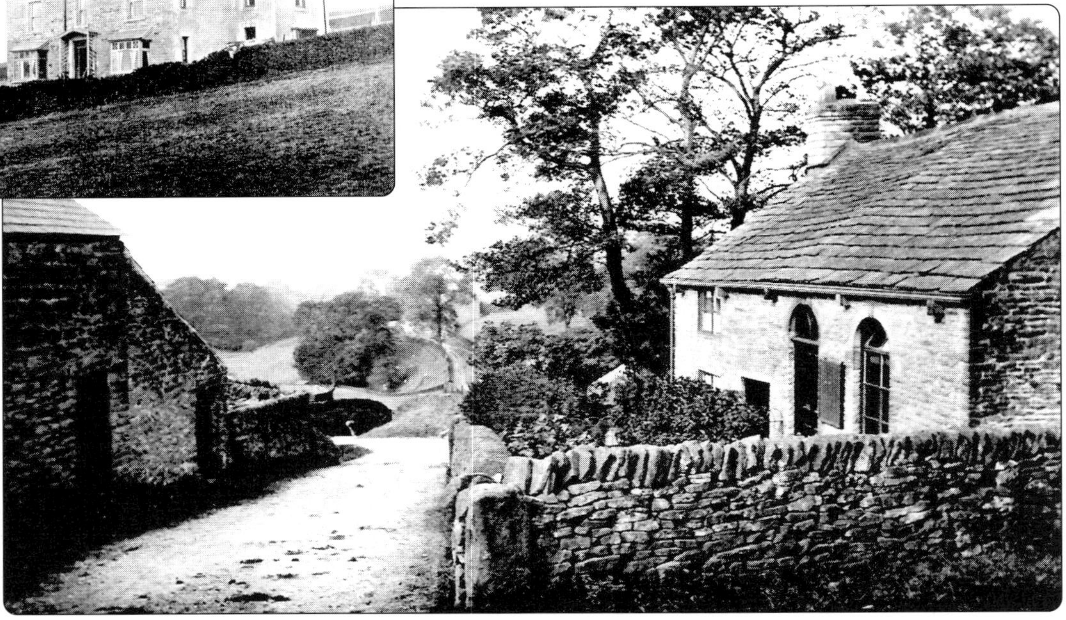

Wesleyan chapel, Bagshaw.

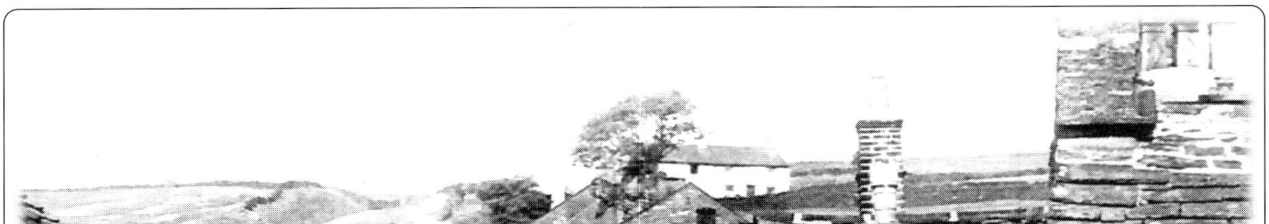

Sparrowpit's single street in years gone by.

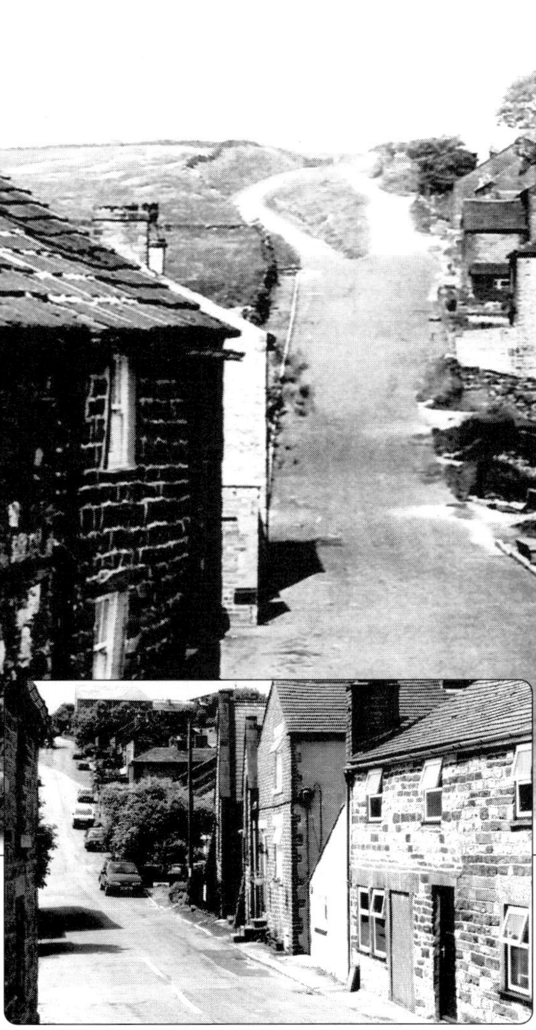

Sparrowpit's single street today.

cottages, but every house has a name. The junction is overlooked by an inn which was once known as the Devonshire Arms and was one of three pubs in the village, but its name was changed to the Wanted Inn when it was bought after it had been left empty and unwanted for a long period. The son of Mr and Mrs Buswell, who once ran the pub, played the part of Ray Langton in 'Coronation Street'. The inn is often surrounded by snowdrifts, the most spectacular of which reached the first-floor windows in 1901. The locals constructed a tunnel through the snow to gain access to their ale!

A man called Shotter once kept a bear at Sparrowpit. The unfortunate animal was used for bear-baiting and was regularly taken to Chapel-en-le-Frith's Market Place, where it was made to perform. The poor creature is remembered in the local expression, 'Rough as a Shotter's bear'.

A Methodist Church was first established at Sparrowpit in 1738, making it one of the earliest Methodist communities in England. The present building, which was erected in the nineteenth century, has a cellar which once housed the village smithy. Several houses in the village have wells in their cellars.

The Village Institute is a thriving centre of social life and home to the Sparrowpit Women's Institute, whose activities are described later in this book.

Blackbrook

By Bryan McGee, who, in 2003, is the owner of Blackbrook House, along with his wife. Historical information has been supplied by Bill Wilson, the previous owner of the property.

Blackbrook is a hamlet of seven households to the east of Chapel-en-le-Frith, through which the old Buxton road passed. This route was bypassed and became a loop when the Jolly Carter pub was built and an early form of weighbridge was used for every vehicle taking the new road.

Blackbrook takes its name from the brook that rises in the hills behind the hamlet. The stream follows a course to Whaley Bridge, where it enters the Goyt, which eventually joins the Mersey. When the Chapel bypass was constructed in 1987 there were fears that half the hamlet would be swept away, but in the event only one cottage was lost. The brook was re-routed and the lane through the hamlet became a cul-de-sac. Since this time, the plantation which forms part of the landscaping on the embankment has matured to form an effective screen, thus returning the lower part of Blackbrook to something like its former state of privacy, although the houses in the upper part of the hamlet remain somewhat blighted by the inevitable noise and light pollution which results from proximity to a busy highway. The boundary of the Peak National Park runs along the brook, enclosing much of the settlement.

The origins of Blackbrook are not recorded, but the plentiful supply of water and its sheltered position from prevailing winds suggests human settlement from at least medieval times. Some of the present buildings date back in part to the Tudor period, since when there have been modifications, rebuildings and additions. A number of Roman coins have been found in a field near Peaslows Lane.

The estate passed from the Carringtons to Joseph Storer in 1787 and, 54 years later, was passed to Storer's son-in-law, Thomas Partington, whose family remained until 1897, the year of Queen Victoria's diamond jubilee. The Partington family was the landowner until the estate was sold off in lots from the 1930s onwards. The estate continued to hold the title Blackbrook House until 1963.

The Jolly Carter stood at the bottom of Blackbrook Lane until the early years of the twentieth century. It was near here that a woman, making her way home one evening from Chapel to Sparrowpit, became stuck in a snowdrift and allegedly survived by eating the candles she had purchased.

At the time of writing the seven households, together with two holiday cottages and a caravan, form a diverse community. There are two working farms and a garden nursery requiring full-time supervision; residents of the other properties include chartered engineers, a banker and a park warden, who commute to work outside the area, as well as people who are employed within the High Peak and send their children to local schools. As is the case in many hamlets which lack a shop, pub or community centre, the residents have little contact except in times of crisis, such as floods or snowstorms, when co-operative efforts normally bring people together. There was an exception in the year 2002, when the residents organised a street party to celebrate the Queen's golden jubilee. The party doubled the population of Blackbrook for a day and was deemed to be a great success, because it brought people of all ages together in a spirit of jollification and goodwill. This spirit has persisted and has resulted in increased personal contact and mutual support.

The properties in the hamlet are outlined in the text that follows.

Blackbrook House

The house dates from the seventeenth century and was a yeoman farmer's dwelling until the late-eighteenth century, when the entire front was rebuilt in the 'Derbyshire-Georgian' style, a coach-house was added and the famous copper-beech tree was planted. This tree, with its gnarled and twisted crown sprouting immense branches which cascade to the ground, is probably the finest *Fagus sylvatica purpurea* in the region.

In the grounds of Blackbrook House there is a mysterious race and a substantial stone culvert which channels all the water from a fold in the hillside right under the property for approximately 50 yards.

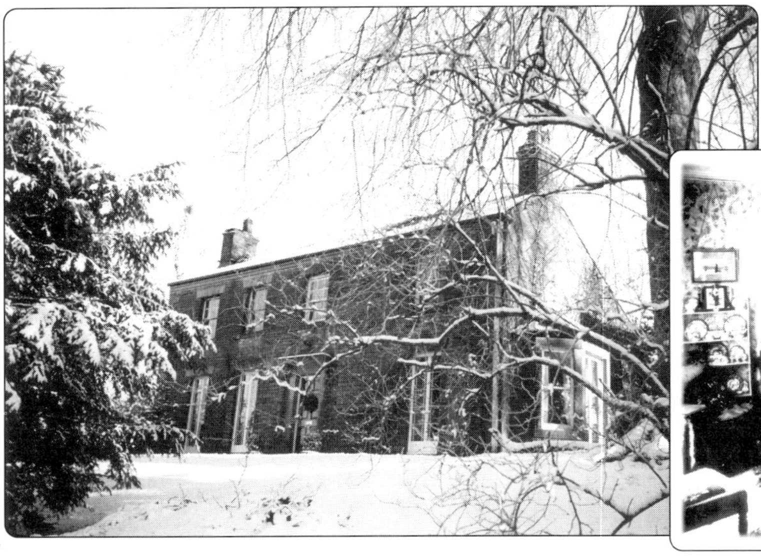

Blackbrook House in winter.

The interior of Blackbrook House in Victorian times.

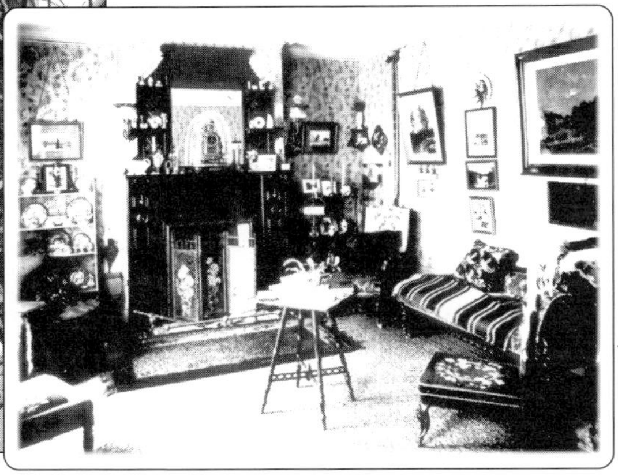

The village of Blackbrook.

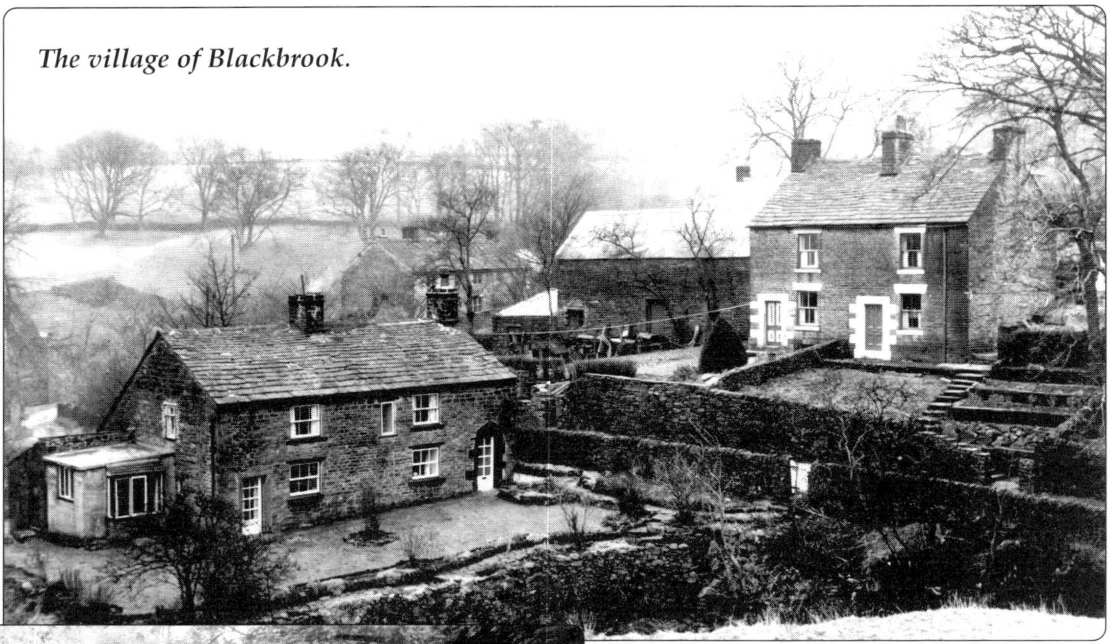

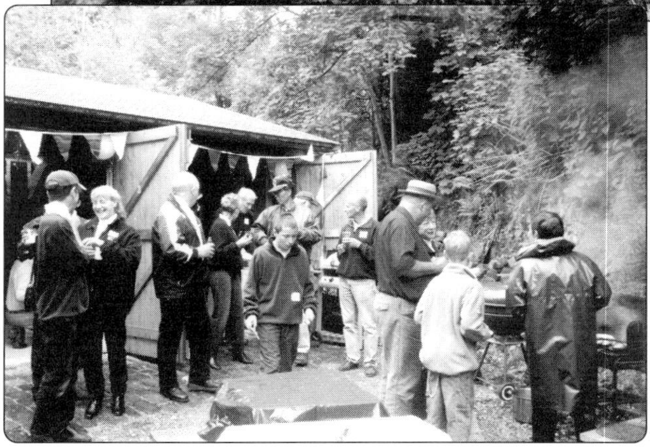

Golden jubilee party. Local people present include Lindsay Renton, Joan Green, Kay Jackson, Ken Aida (a visitor from Japan), Dennis Green, Alan Jackson, John Diggle, Callum Renton, Diana Blankley. Other people present are guests.

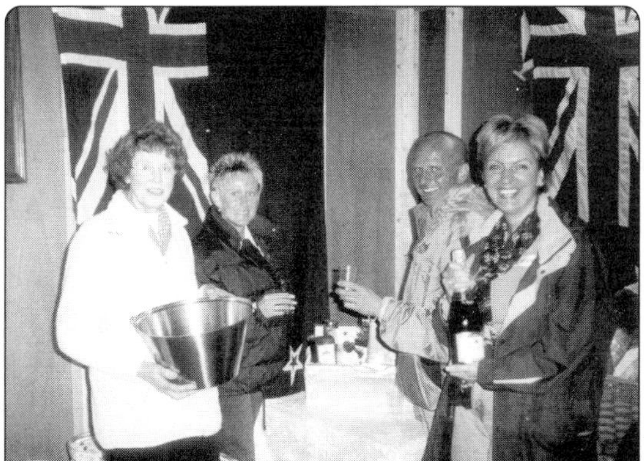

Golden jubilee party. Left to right: Myra Hearnshaw, Kay and Alan Jackson, Chris McConnell from Bagshaw.

Key dates in the history of Blackbrook House include:

1747 – Earliest deeds. Yeoman's house, possibly occupied by John Moult or John Cooper.
1787 – James Carrington sold the property to Joseph Storer.
Late-eighteenth century – Three front reception rooms and façade rebuilt. Copper-beech tree probably planted at this time.
1836 – Joseph Storer died and left the property to his wife Alice.
1841 – Property passed to Thomas Storer Partington, son of Robert Partington of Stockport, and Sally, daughter of Joseph and Alice Storer. Bay window added to the south end of the house.
1897 – Property was mortgaged by the Partingtons to Revd W.W. Stamper.
1930s – Breaking up of the estate began.
1939 – Owen Mytton Smith (solicitor of Bennett, Bunting and Smith) became the tenant of Partington of Sheffield.
1963 – Owen Mytton Smith purchased the freehold, possibly from Archibald Partington.
1970 – Death of Owen Smith.
1971 – Sale to Mr Clowes (architect/developer).
1972 – Sale to Mr W.L. Wilson.
1984 – Sale to Mr and Mrs Bryan McGee.

Blackbrook Farm

This farm of 55 acres is owned by John and Myra Hearnshaw, the longest-standing residents of Blackbrook. The deeds of the farm go back to about 1850, when the farmhouse could well have been the semi-detached cottages now owned by the Rentons and John Diggle and Diana Blakeley. Sam Warhurst built the present house for approximately £500 in 1939 and let the two cottages. The Hearnshaws bought the farm in 1952 and moved there in 1953; this year they are celebrating their own golden jubilee of occupation. They added an extension to the house in about 1980.

John Hearnshaw was born in Baslow, where his father was a tenant farmer on the Chatsworth estate and his grandfather was a butcher to Chatsworth House. John's wife Myra was born in Chesterfield and trained as a nurse, and met her husband through church activities in Baslow. John joined the Navy during the war and was en route to the Far East when hostilities ended.

Longdendale Nursery

A substantial gritstone barn was converted into a dwelling in 1977 by its first occupant, Alan Turner, who had bought the barn with planning permission from Eddie Haworth for £11,000. The current owners, John and Doreen Ranson, run their garden-nursery business from this site, bounded by the Blackbrook and the bypass embankment.

Rookery House

Rookery House is a farmhouse which probably dates back to the eighteenth century. The land is still farmed by the current occupants, Denis and Joan Green, who have a flock of pedigree sheep. They also organise equestrian events on the land behind their house.

The Homestead

Ian Stirling, who lives at the Homestead, is the owner of a chain-driven Frazer-Nash from the 1930s and a world authority on the classic sports car.

WHITEHOUGH

Adapted from Alan Watson's book, *Bygone Days of Whitehough and Bugsworth*, published here by kind permission of Alan Watson.

Crossing the route of the old tramway which ran between Dove Holes and Bugsworth from 1799 to 1926, we approach the village which was known as Whythelag in 1231, became Whitehalgh in 1303, and eventually came to be known as Whitehough in 1585. Passing the bungalow on our right, which is known as Sunrise and was built in 1934, we observe another bungalow on the left, which was the site of an old dwelling-house occupied by Sam Parker, a licensed hawker, and his wife Cilla. Revd Willie Simpson, the much-loved former minister of Chinley Independent Chapel, used to read the Bible to the couple when he was a resident of Whitehough as a young man.

The terrace known as Rock Cottages is a prominent feature of the Whitehough streetscape. Part of the terrace was the home of Alan Watson's grandparents, mother, uncle and aunts. The water for the cottages and the farm was obtained from a well situated in the rear yard, with a huge handle operating the pump. Adjoining Rock Cottages there is an old barn, built in 1623 by Arnold Kirke of Whitehough Old Hall. With the exception of the repaired roof, the building's outward appearance remains unaltered. A structure at the rear has been adapted for use as a garage and the former hayloft was once the headquarters of the First Chinley Scout Group.

The former Whitehough Primitive Methodist Chapel and Sunday School, which stands opposite Rock Cottages, was built by local craftsmen who would join together, after a day's toil in the quarries or fields, in a labour of love to erect Whitehough's first place of worship. Extra land was purchased in 1928 to build a new entrance at the side of the building, because the replacement of horses and carts by motor cars was making entry by the front rather hazardous. A new vestry was added in 1935, through the generosity of W. Hall of Oldham, and dedicated to the memory of his mother, an ex-scholar. The inside of the chapel was remodelled in 1965, with the plain

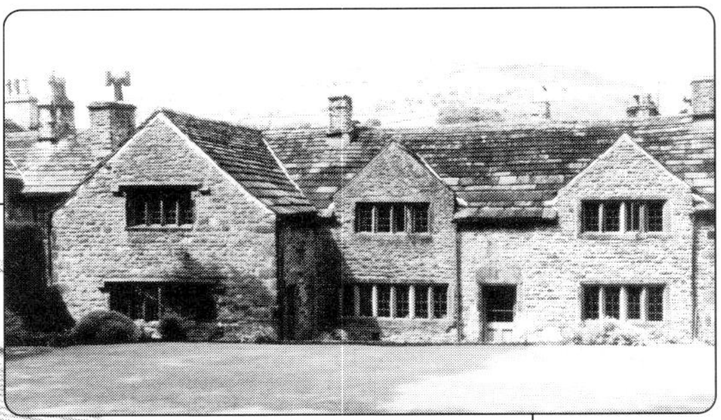

Whitehough Old Hall.

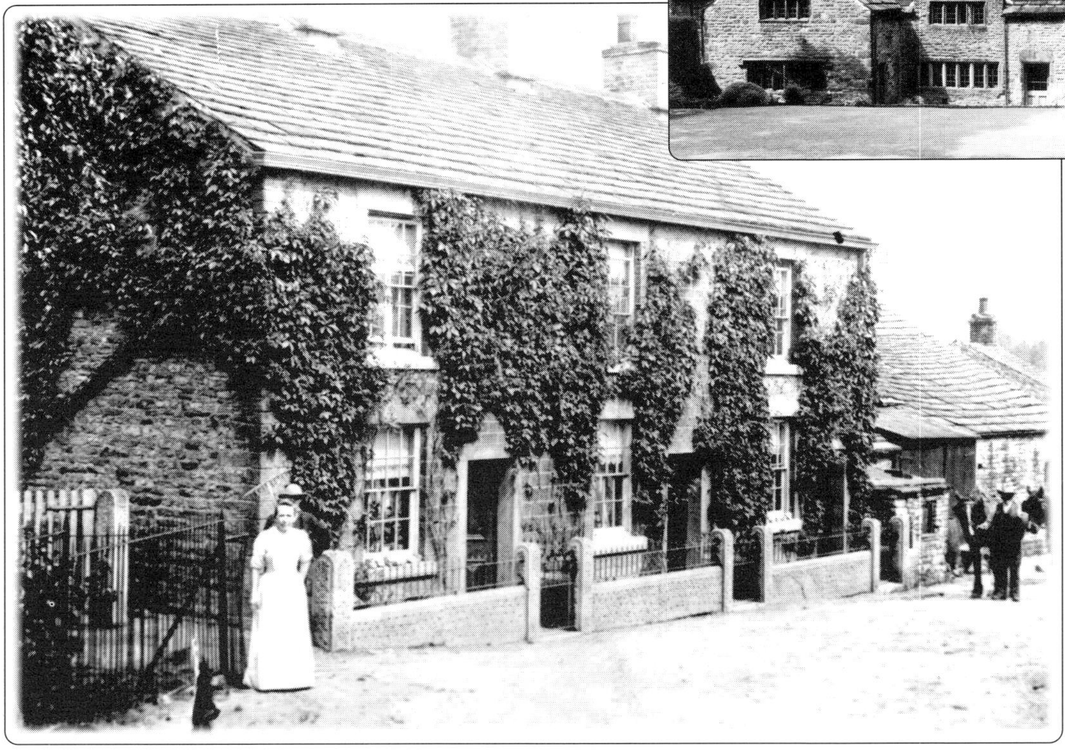

Rock Cottages.

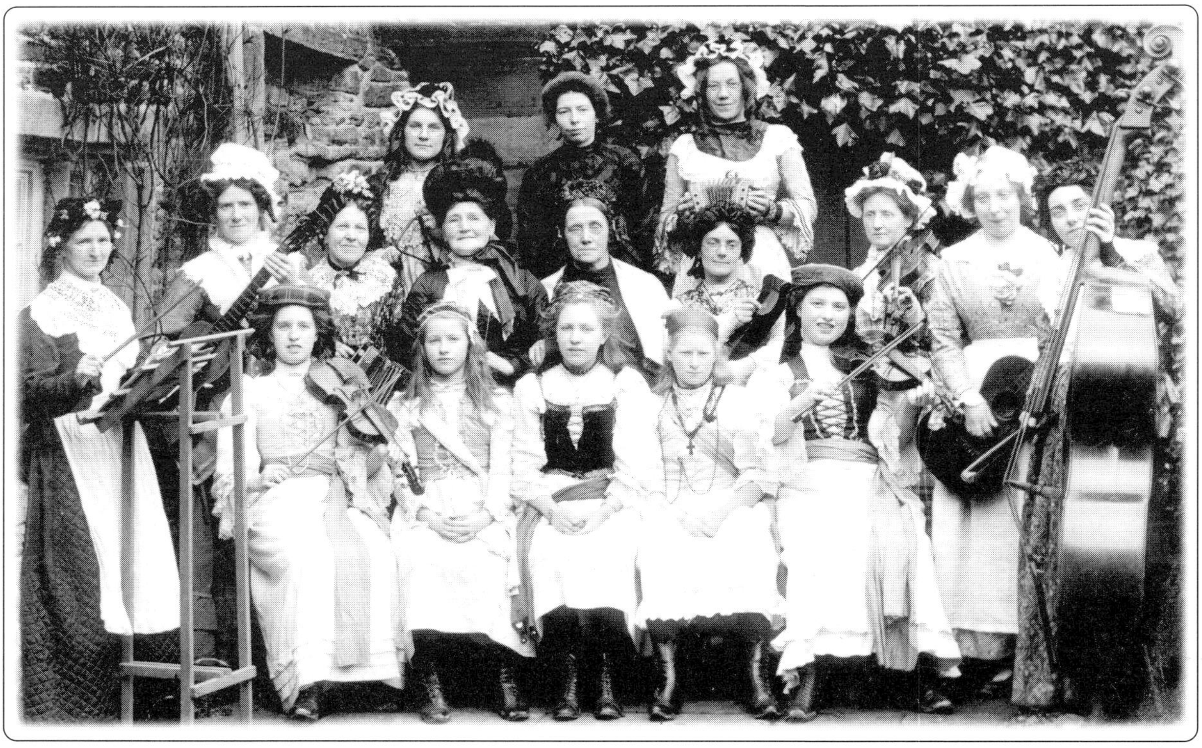

Orchestra and singers of the Methodist Chapel. Left to right, back row: *?, Annie Hulme, Mrs Cooke;* middle row: *Mrs Marsland (conductor), Mrs Horrox, ?, Mrs Horrox (senr), Mrs Hulme, Mrs Greenhalgh, Mrs Bradley, Joe Waterhouse, Mrs Smith;* seated: *Harriet Marsland, Anne Marsland, Clarissa Hallam, Ada Lily Simpson, Lily Marsland.*

walls, gallery, organ, communion table, rails, font, pulpit and stained-glass window all combining in their simplicity to give a peaceful atmosphere. The building was subsequently licensed for marriage ceremonies.

Throughout its history, the chapel was the venue for many happy occasions, not only in connection with Methodism and religious festivities, but also as a focus for the communal life of the village, with concerts, recitals, fêtes and many other events being held there.

St John's Church, which stands near the brook that forms the parish boundary, dates from 1905. In the previous year, the Church authorities of St Thomas Becket Church in Chapel-en-le-Frith, acting under the guidance of Revd Stredder, had bought two plots of land in Whitehough, with the intention of erecting a Sunday school and a chapel of ease for the convenience of people in this remote part of the parish. In the event, building costs proved to be beyond their financial resources and only a small building (the Sunday school section on the original plan) was erected. This little building served the community as a chapel from 1905 until 1927.

The church's alternating plain and decorative tiles and the gable parapet are uncommon sights in the Chinley area; the two dormer vents are also of interest. The outer walls are constructed of random stones. Looking inside, the principal roof members consist of three decorative collar trusses supporting an internal flat roof.

The church was unoccupied from 1927 to 1947, when a much-opposed plan was put forward to turn the building into a mortuary. Fortunately, it was never needed for this purpose and was handed over by the Hadfield family, who had acquired the building for the people of Whitehough. It was then re-christened Victory Hall and became a popular venue for social functions and meetings in connection with the village fête. In 1977 the Scout Association acquired the building.

One of the two public houses in the village is named the Oddfellows Arms, because it was the meeting-place of the Oddfellows Friendly Society from 1830 until 1970, when the organisation amalgamated with the Marple Society. Friendly societies came into being in 1795 to supplement the Poor Laws, whereby assistance was given to people who were deemed by the church as being in need of help. In 1808 the Chinley United Women's Charities were formed and operated under specific rules. Initially, persons between the ages of 18 and 38 were allowed to join, but, because there were so many claims for benefit, the upper age limit was reduced to 28. As a result, people only received help in their 'prime years'. Sickness benefits were 5s. per week for one month and 4s. per week afterwards. The Whitehough Victoria Lodge of Oddfellows was formed in 1830 and met at the Oddfellows Arms, which was then known as the Paper Mill.

James Smith's grocery shop once occupied premises adjacent to the Oddfellows Arms. James Smith was a nephew of the Misses Hollinshead of Wilshaw Farm, and he started his business as a young man. His shop became an institution in Whitehough and he grew to be a legend in his own right. He knew everyone and everyone knew him; his knowledge of the quality of bacon was unmatched and other commodities in his shop, including Danish cask butter, were much appreciated by his customers, who made their way to his premises from all parts of the High Peak.

Every side of bacon was washed in the little stream of spring water opposite the shop. Opinions were divided as to whether this exercise was designed to increase the weight of the bacon or to cleanse it. However, it has to be said that James Smith was the essence of cleanliness and honesty; every slice of bacon was cut by hand on the counter and time was regarded as unimportant. It was no use being in a hurry when shopping at Smith's – but life then was lived at a slower pace.

While cutting bacon one day, he overheard a customer saying that she'd got some new teeth. He responded to this news by saying, 'It would be better if you'd paid for the food which your old ones have eaten before you got any new ones.' When James Smith died, aged 87, he was remembered for his deep affection for his fellow men. His only book was the Bible – if offered other books, he would say, 'I have this good book; it is enough.'

Whitehough Old Hall stands at the heart of the hamlet. Although there have been earlier buildings on the site, the present structure dates back to Elizabethan times and is a very fine example of a sixteenth-century yeoman's dwelling. For several hundred years it was associated with the Kyrke family, whose noted members included David Kyrke, who was knighted in 1631, and his sister Mary, who was maid of honour to Queen Catherine, wife of Charles II. George Kirk (the spelling changed in the sixteenth century) was groom to the royal bedchamber of Charles I and was in attendance when the King was beheaded in 1649. Over the last century, the hall has been occupied by a number of professional people from the business community, who have taken refuge from the stresses and strains of everyday life by residing in this beautiful part of Derbyshire. Mr Becker, the first man to climb the Matterhorn from the Italian side, lived here with his family at one stage.

Structurally attached to the west side of the Old Hall is the Old Hall Hotel, which was formerly known as the Red Cow Inn and has been licensed for a period of some four centuries. In 1892 the inn was offered for sale by the executors of the will of Joseph Barnes of Daisy Bank. Joseph Barnes, nephew of the previous owner and Alan Watson's grandfather, became the proprietor for the sum of £500. Only a year after becoming landlord, he received a postcard from a

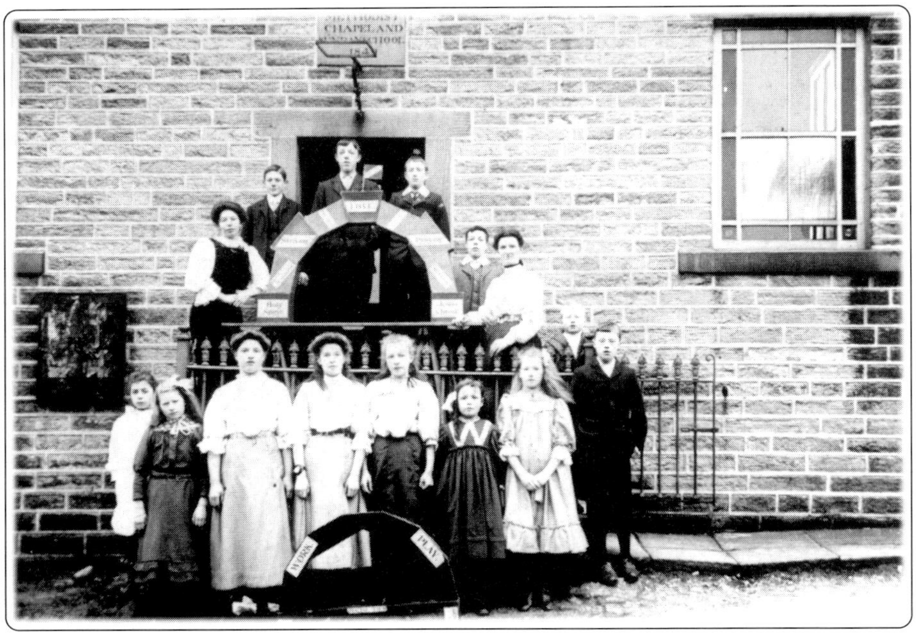

Outside the Methodist Chapel in 1912. Left to right, above the railing: *Anne Hulme, Harry Howe, George Shirt, ?, Harry Simpson, Mrs Marsland, Willie Simpson (now Revd Dr Simpson, aged 104 in 2003);* front: *Nellie Nunn, Ada Lily Simpson, Lily Marsland, Harriet Marsland, Clarissa Hallam, Ada Brocklehurst, Annie Marsland, Fred Ford.*

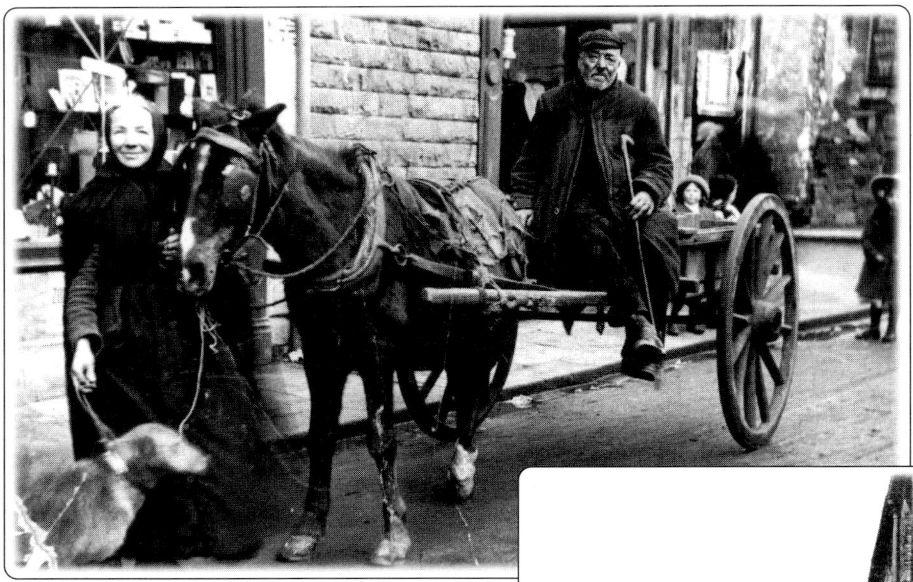

Sam Parker, a licensed hawker, and his wife Cilla in Chapel-en-le-Frith.

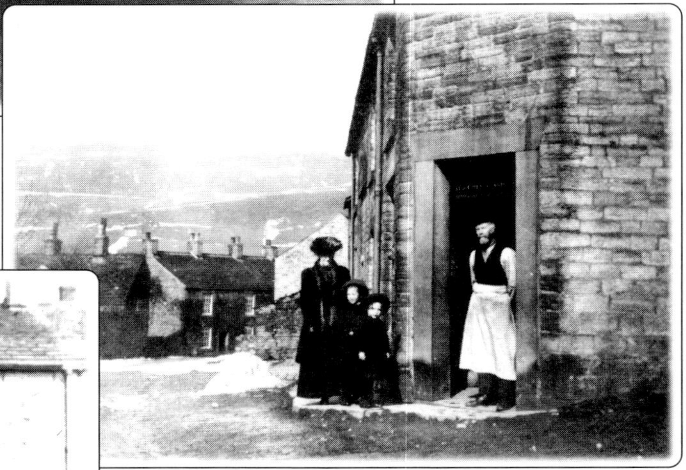

James Smith standing in his shop doorway, welcoming his prospective customers

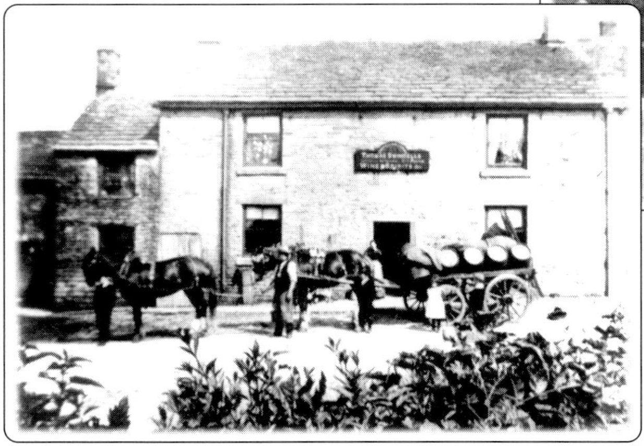

A delivery at the Oldfellows Arms.

resident of Hamilton, Canada, who expressed thanks for the hospitality shown by the inn to his daughter.

In 1926 J. Peatfield became the owner of both the public house and Whitehough Old Hall, and declared his intention to turn the entire premises into a combined hotel under the name Old Hall Hotel. Permission was refused, but the two premises were combined into one hotel by subsequent owners. However, they have now reverted to separate establishments.

Another well-known Whitehough property was the Co-op, which occupied Ivy Cottage in the centre of a terrace of three houses on Whitehough Lane. Evidence of the shop is still clear in the cellar of the well-preserved and attractive cottage, where hooks for the hanging of sides of bacon are still in position. Across the road from Ivy Cottage there is a well whose water never dries up. As trade increased, new premises were built; the local Co-op eventually amalgamated with the New Mills Co-operative Society and continued to operate as a business until 1956.

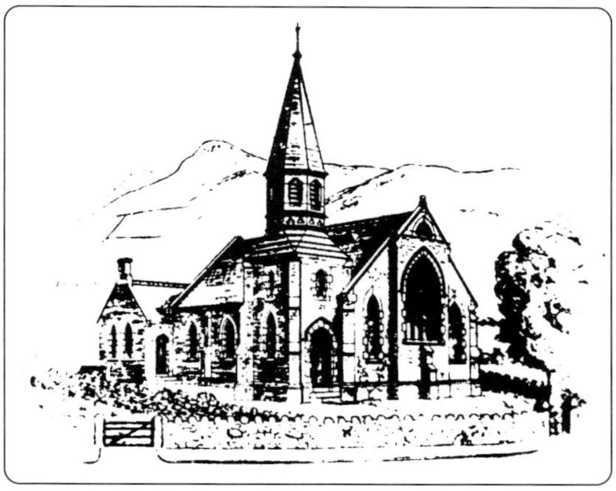

St John's Church as it was planned originally. Only the projection at the rear of the building was actually constructed.

The range of occupations available within the hamlet of Whitehough was always limited and many families augmented their income by operating farms and smallholdings. These included: Hall Hill Farm, Foxholes, Salt Pie, Whitehough Head Farm, Buxton House Farm, Moult Farm, Turn Farm, Barn Farm, Under Eccles, Wilshaw Farm and Harper Farm. Hall Hill Farm passed to the Vernons of Haddon Hall in 1534 and passed, a century later, into the hands of Dorothy Shirt of Disley. Dorothy was a staunch Royalist and her property was confiscated during the Civil War. Most of the lands changed hands several times in subsequent years and eventually became part of the Fleming estate. The house was occupied from the early-nineteenth century to the middle of the twentieth century by the Gregory family, who also owned Foxholes.

Whitehough Head Farm came into the hands of John and Richard Bennett of Little Hayfield in 1647. Dr Clegg, the minister of Chinley Independent Chapel, was a frequent visitor to the farm and formed a close friendship with the Bennett family. He used to hold services in the house for the benefit of family and friends. Wilshaw Farm used to be closely associated with Whitehough Head Farm, but the name probably dates back to the early-seventeenth century, when a Mr Wilshaw was resident. In 1840 the farm was owned by George Hollinshead, from whom the Primitive Methodists bought land for the erection of their chapel.

Under Eccles and Turn Farms both disappeared when the Chapel–Whaley bypass was constructed in 1987, and are now 'under the road'. Whitehough itself remains a quiet little hamlet, picturesquely snuggled in a valley below Chinley Churn and Eccles Pike.

Combs Village

By Mike Evanson, chairman of the Village Hall Trust.

Combs is a small village situated within the ancient parish boundaries of Chapel-en-le-Frith, which was historically divided into three geographical areas: Bowdon Edge, Bradshaw Edge and Combs Edge. The village of Combs lies within the boundary of Combs Edge.

The village is situated at an altitude of 700ft above sea level and is located in the three-sided valley of Combs, with Ladder Hill to the west, the high moor of Combs Moss to the south-east and the Iron-Age fort of Castle Naze to the east. The valley opens up to the north, where Combs Reservoir flanks the road to Chapel-en-le-Frith and Whaley Bridge.

History

Due to its landscape setting, the valley was able to offer security to early settlers, whose presence can be traced in the ancient trackways which cross the slopes of Combs Head, Castle Naze and Ladder Hill, and in the Iron-Age fort of Castle Naze. In addition to the fort, there is other evidence of prehistoric use of the valley. On the road between Dove Holes and Combs village there are two round barrows, known as Cow Low and Lady Low. A third barrow at Sitting Low has been disturbed by ploughing.

Following the Norman Conquest, Combs became part of the Royal Forest of the Peak, which was subdivided into three wards: Campana, Longendale and Hope Valley. Chapel-en-le-Frith and Combs were situated in the Campana ward, which covered the district between Kinder and the River Goyt. Records in existence from the days of the hunting forest date from 1216 and show occupancy, transactions, court judgments and tithes.

The High Peak area has close links with Nonconformism. One of the fields at Owlgreave Farm, in Combs, is named Gospel Brow, in commemoration of its use for preaching by William Bagshawe, the Apostle of the Peak. William, who resided at Ford Hall, was forced to resign his ministry in 1662 for refusing to accept and use the *Book of Common*

Prayer, but he carried on preaching in various secret venues in the area.

In the late-eighteenth century, the exploitation of the vast limestone deposits in the Peak District by industrial entrepreneurs brought about the construction of the Peak Forest canal, a major development project which had a marked influence on the geography of the valley. The main objective of the canal was to improve the transportation of manufactured goods and bulk materials, particularly limestone from the quarries at Dove Holes. The building of the canal was driven by the increasing demand for alkali by the expanding glass, soap and textile industries, which could no longer be supplied from natural sources, such as ash or seaweed. Benjamin Outram, an engineer from Alfreton, constructed the canal as well as Combs Brook Reservoir. The canal was completed in 1797, with the first delivery of lime being received on 31 July that year. The 16 locks at Marple, which were situated one and a half miles below Marple Lime Works, were designed by Thomas Brown and constructed by a contract company, James & Fox, and completed in 1805. The Combs Reservoir, covering some 80 acres, was designed initially as the sole feeder for the High Peak canal, with dam construction commencing in 1794. The field boundaries of five farms were affected and two farms were lost underneath the water.

The construction of the London North Western Railway (LNWR) was a huge project, involving the building of a section from Whaley Bridge to Buxton which cut the valley of Combs in half. Farmland had to be redistributed due to the inaccessibility caused. During the boom years of the construction, practically every available room in Combs was let to navvies, joiners and other individuals employed on the line.

The railway work also provided alternative employment for farmers and their families, some of whom never returned to the land to earn their living. The village inn, known as the Beehive, was rebuilt at this time with the money spent at the inn by the construction workers. The railway greatly improved access to centres of commerce, such as Manchester, and helped to attract new residents to the area.

Some Historic Figures who Lived in Combs

The Nightingale family

In 1840 William Nightingale (father of Florence) purchased Pyegreave, which lies on the east side of Combs valley and is reached via a long drive from Dyke Lane, the old road to Dove Holes. It is recorded in Peggy Bellhouse's book, *Combs, My Village*, that Miss Lomas of Ivy Cottage recalled seeing Florence and her father riding on horseback through Combs. Florence could boast of at least two firsts among her many achievements. She founded training schools for nurses and became the first woman to be elected as a Fellow of the Statistics Society (in recognition of her contribution to Army statistics).

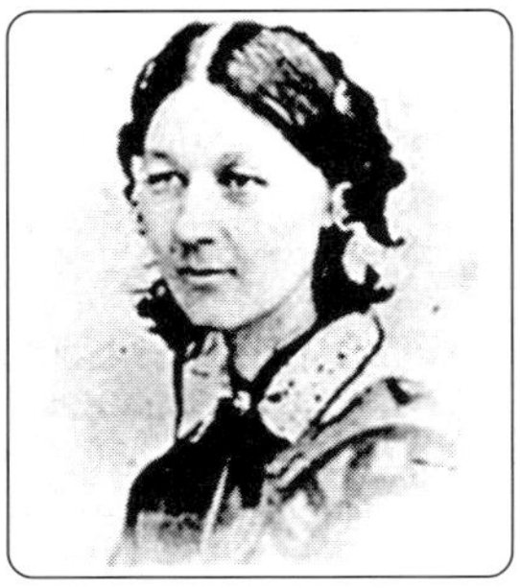

Famous Combs resident, Florence Nightingale.

Herbert Frood

In 1895 Herbert Frood moved with his family to Rye Flatts in Combs, from where he commuted by railway to his business in Manchester. Being an inventive character, he used some equipment found in his father-in-law's belting factory to experiment in friction materials in his wooden garden hut. The materials that Frood developed were applied to horse-drawn trucks and motor vehicles, and created the basis of Ferodo, which went on to sell its products worldwide and become the major source of employment in Chapel-en-le-Frith.

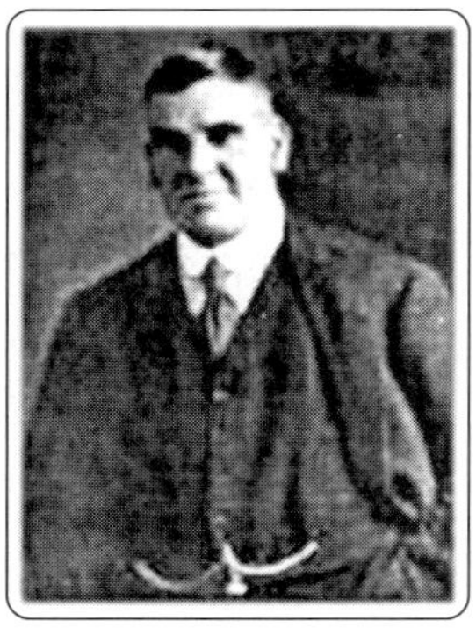

Famous Combs resident, Herbert Frood.

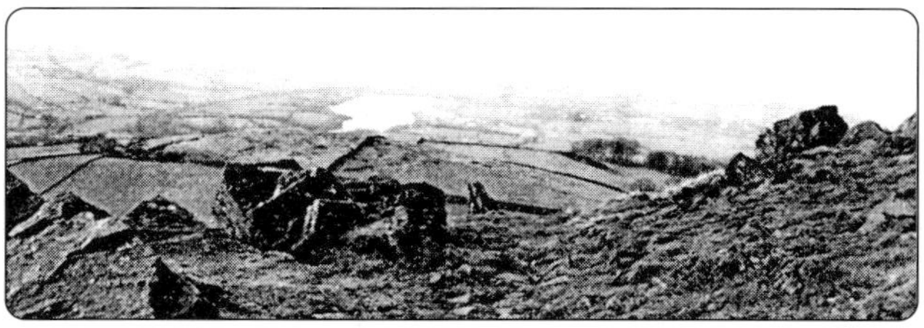

Combs valley and reservoir from the Iron-Age fort of Castle Naze.

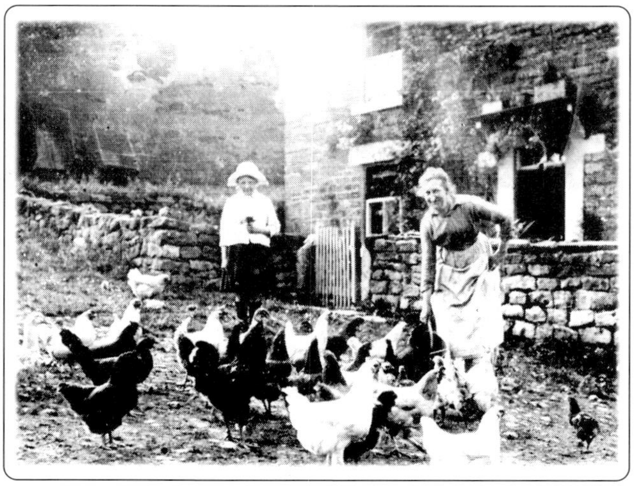

Villagers outside Hey Lee Farm in 1917. Sarah Thornley (née Lomas) is pictured with Ada Morten feeding the chickens.

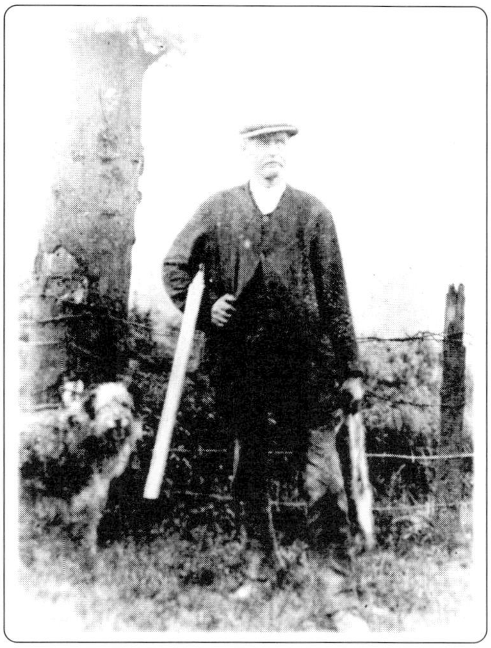

Joel Morton with his dog Rufus. Joel's daughter, Mrs Thornley, later became the village postmistress.

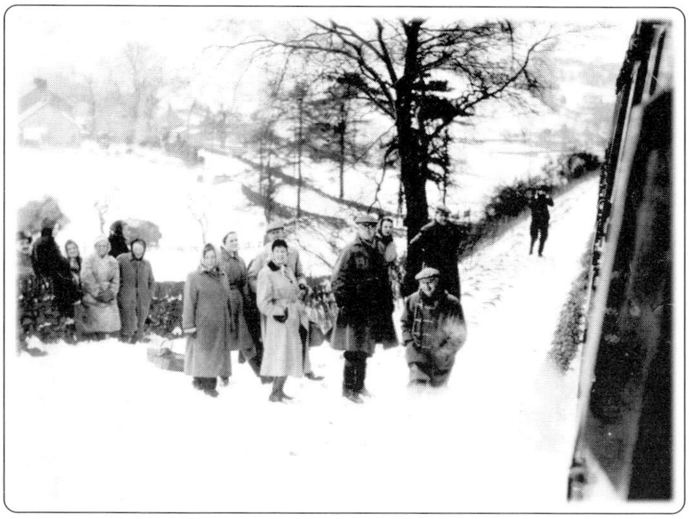

Combs villagers helping to unload relief supplies from the train during the winter of 1947.

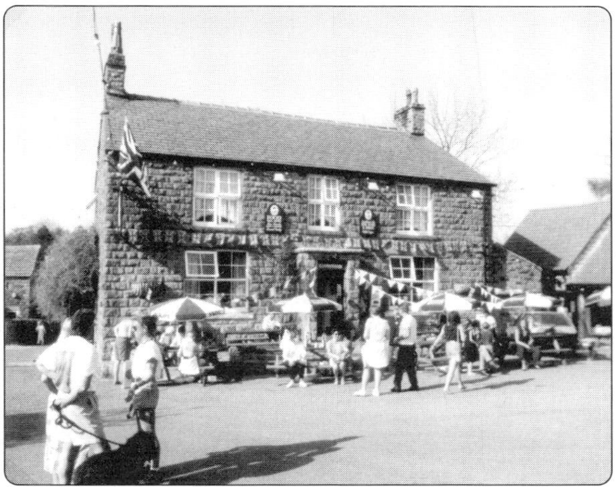

The Beehive Inn on the 50th anniversary of VE Day.

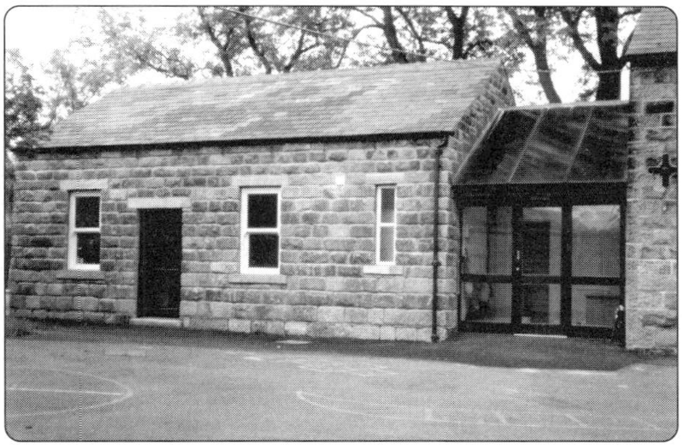

The Village Hall, which opened in 1998.

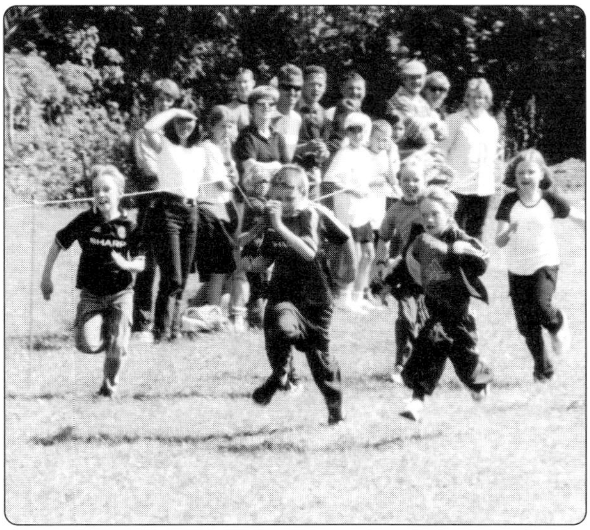

Fun Day at Combs.

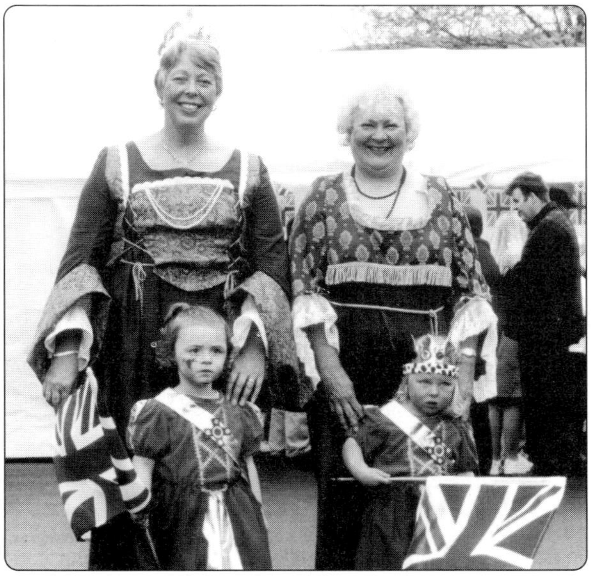

The Queen's golden jubilee celebrations. Jean Evanson is pictured with Liz Goodwin and Liz's grandchildren.

The New Village Hall & Village Fun Days

Combs villagers had been working for a number of decades to raise money for the construction of a Village Hall, which could be used to provide an additional meeting-place for the community. The project finally came to fruition on 4 July 1998, after a small project team had succeeded in raising the necessary funds. Each August a committee, headed by Jean Evanson and Liz Goodwin, organise a village Fun Day, which includes a full day of activities for young and old alike. Regular features include a produce stall, art and craft show, pet show, children's sports races, a fell race and a tug-of-war competition.

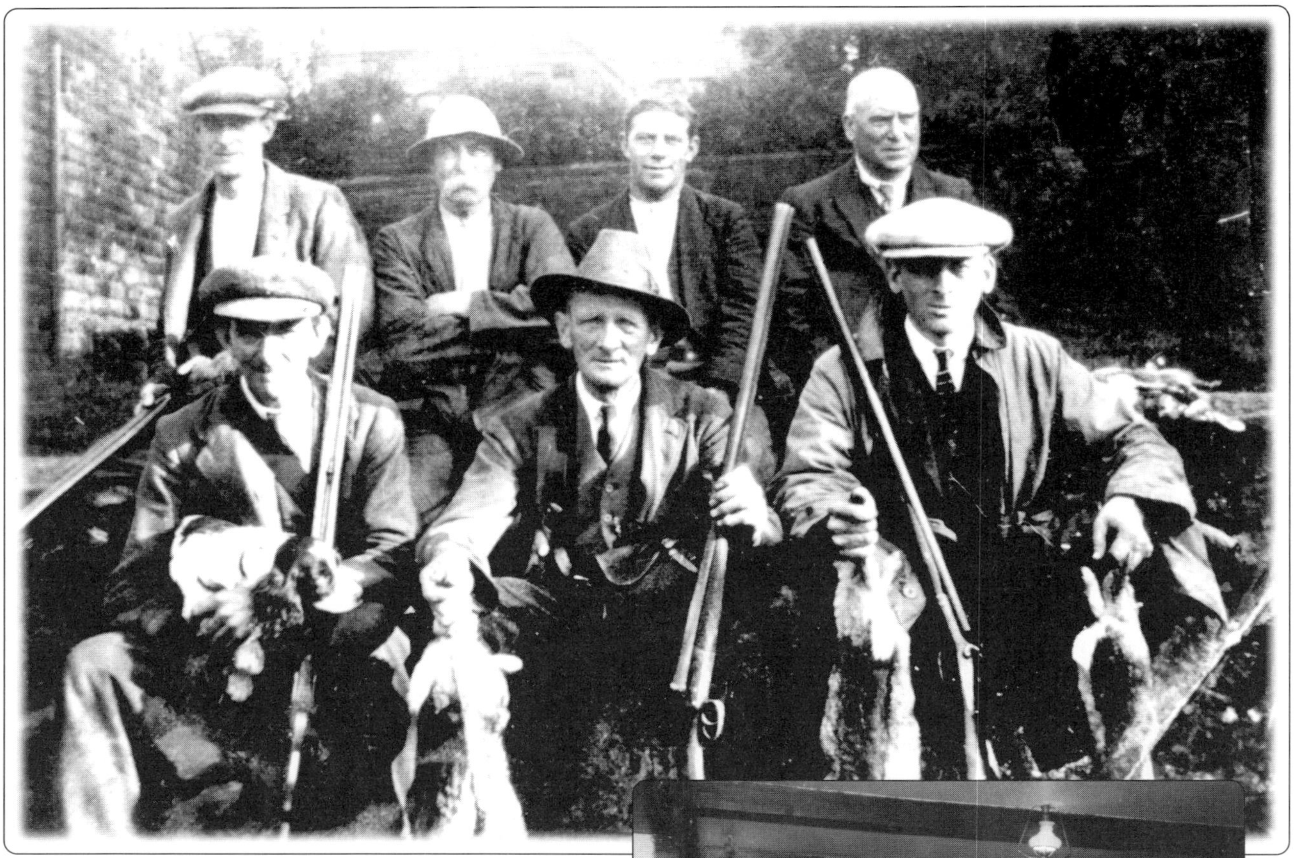

A shooting party which bagged 247 rabbits in a four-hour shoot. Left to right back row: *William Lomas (junr), William Lomas (senr), Ted Hartle, Jack Flint;* front row: *George Lomas, Jack Royle, Sam Jackson.*

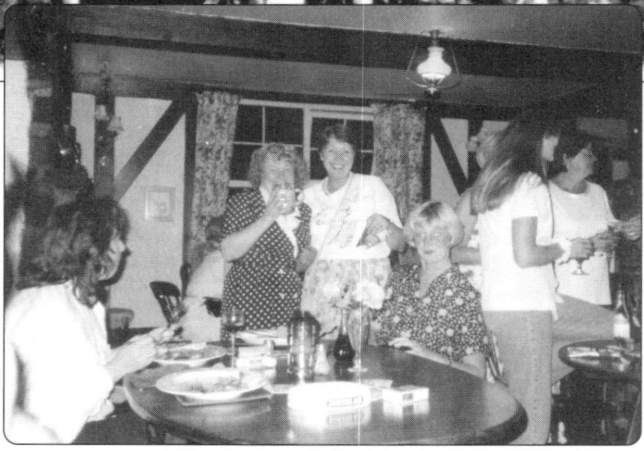

Right: *Fund-raising raffle in 1995. Picture includes Jean Evanson, Liz Goodwin and various locals of the Beehive Inn.*

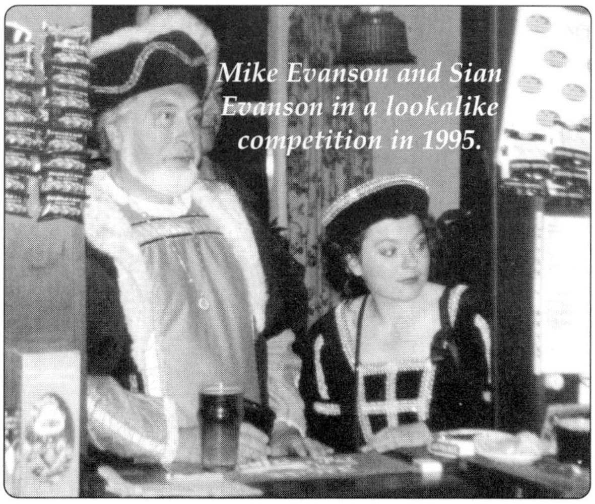

Mike Evanson and Sian Evanson in a lookalike competition in 1995.

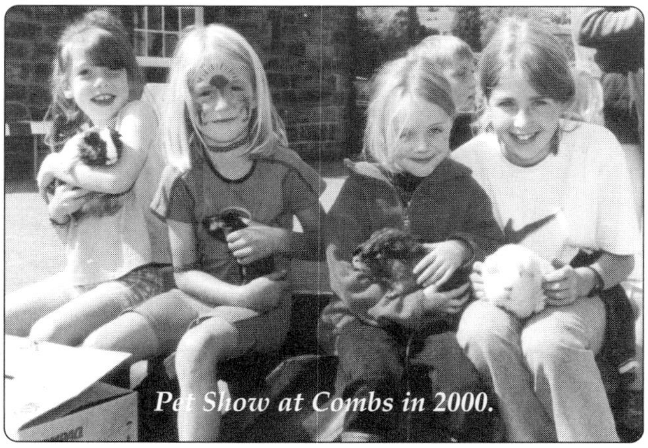

Pet Show at Combs in 2000.

Chapter 6

The Happiest Days of Your Life

In 2003, 'Education, Education, Education' is seen as a Government priority, but there was a time when the provision of education was left to the churches, benefactors and individuals who ran fee-paying schools. For most, education was a brief affair conducted in inadequate buildings. The State eventually stepped in to ensure elementary education for all, and later secondary education for all, but the effects of selection, fee-paying, varying physical provision and denominational priorities meant that children had widely differing experiences. The introduction of the comprehensive system and the later imposition of the National Curriculum attempted to combat these discrepencies, but the persistence of varying standards heralded the introduction of testing at all levels.

Chapel-en-le-Frith has witnessed all these changes over the years, but its young people have been well served throughout by some highly dedicated teachers, who have had to work in some woefully inadequate buildings, including leaking classrooms and prefabricated structure which vibrated from the rattle of passing trains.

The last four years have seen a revolution in provision. A brand new, state-of-the-art Infant School was opened in 1999 and is now part of the newly formed Chapel Primary School. In addition, in 2003, the town is about to have a new Secondary School, complete with a leisure centre, which will also be available for use by the townspeople. At long last, the teachers, pupils and parents of Chapel-en-le-Frith will have the buildings they deserve.

Memories of Gisborne School

In the 1930s and '40s, three sisters, Ethel, Edith and Madeleine Bateman, ran Gisborne School, a fee-paying establishment in Chapel-en-le-Frith, which was housed in just two rooms – one up, one down. There were toilets down the garden path, a bicycle shed, a yard and an orchard where the children played. When the air-raid sirens sounded, the children were taken to the cellar of a nearby house. Former pupils have very fond memories of this little school of no more than 25 pupils. Their reminiscences form a vivid portrait of school life 60 years ago and may well trigger memories of school-days, fond or otherwise, in readers.

By Beryl Pilkington (née Fletcher)

The school was run by Ethel Bateman, who was the headmistress and was known as 'Miss Bateman', while her sisters were known as 'Miss Madeleine' and 'Miss Edith'. The latter dressed in a brown, box-pleated gym-slip, like ours but bigger! She took gym, which involved shinnying up and down a climbing rope and playing in the park. Miss Bateman was strict – 'Children should be seen and not heard' was her motto. Although teaching methods were old-fashioned in many ways (we had a thorough grounding in the 3Rs and French) they were progressive in others. Boys and girls were taught to sew – I still have an apron I stitched and embroidered for myself. Miss Bateman would receive letters from ex-pupils serving in the Forces, thanking her for teaching them to sew, as they could stitch on buttons and do running repairs for their comrades. While I was at the school, she took on a mentally-handicapped girl who seemed to integrate well with the rest of us.

School lunch involved a crocodile procession to a local café. Miss Bateman would sit at the head of a long table and keep an eagle eye on our table manners. Once a year, we had a school treat and went for a walk and picnic in the countryside. Music lessons were taught by Miss Farthing and we sat on two forms at either side of the piano to sing. Drama productions were a feature of the school: one year, I played the pussy cat in 'The Owl and the Pussy Cat' and, on another occasion, I took the part of the child Jesus in our end-of-term play and concert. I don't know why I, being a girl, was chosen to play Jesus – perhaps I was the right size for the part. We also put on 'A Masque of Flowers' at the Town Hall.

The Bateman sisters lived in Chapel-en-le-Frith, close to their school. When the family wanted to visit Castleton, their donkey was harnessed to a cart which was only large enough to carry 'mother', so the girls had to walk at the side. After the cart was pulled to the first summit, the sisters had to release the donkey from the shafts so it could have a roll on the road before it undertook the next stretch of the journey down Winnats Pass!

My memories of the Batemans and my five-and-a-half years at their school are very happy ones.

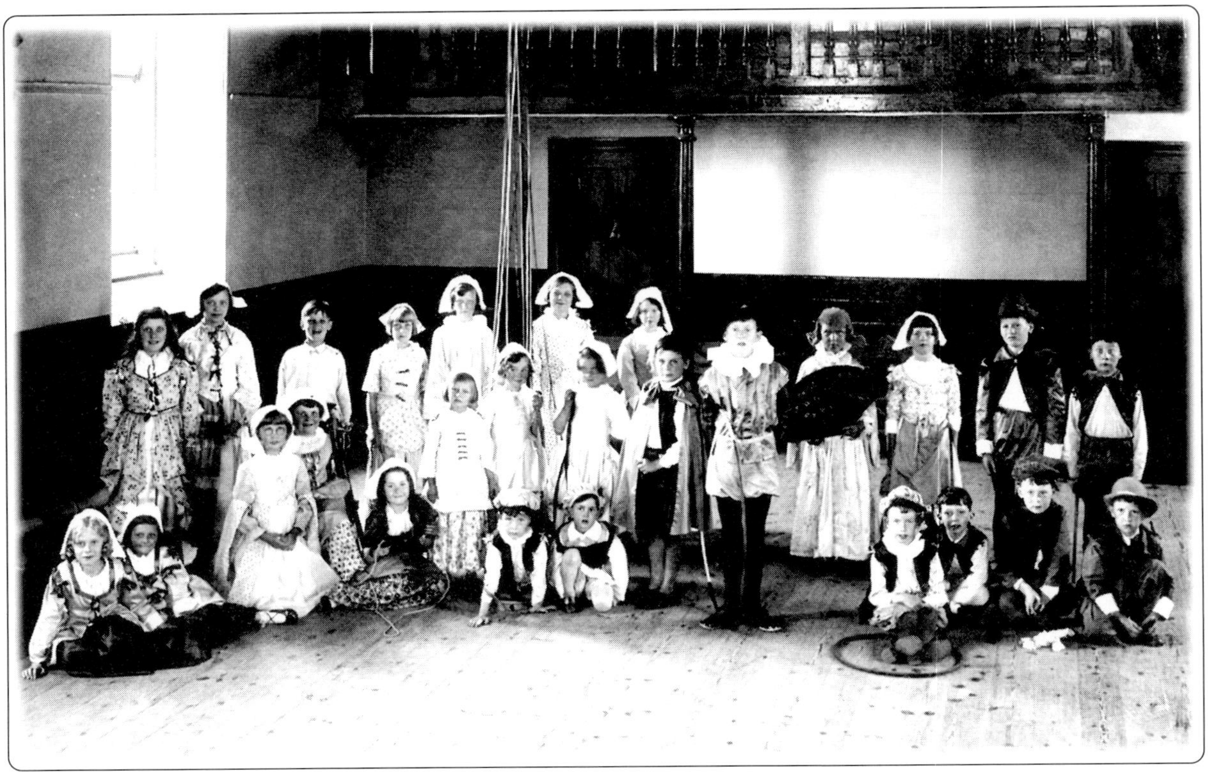

Gisborne School Elizabethan Pageant in the Town Hall, c.1932.

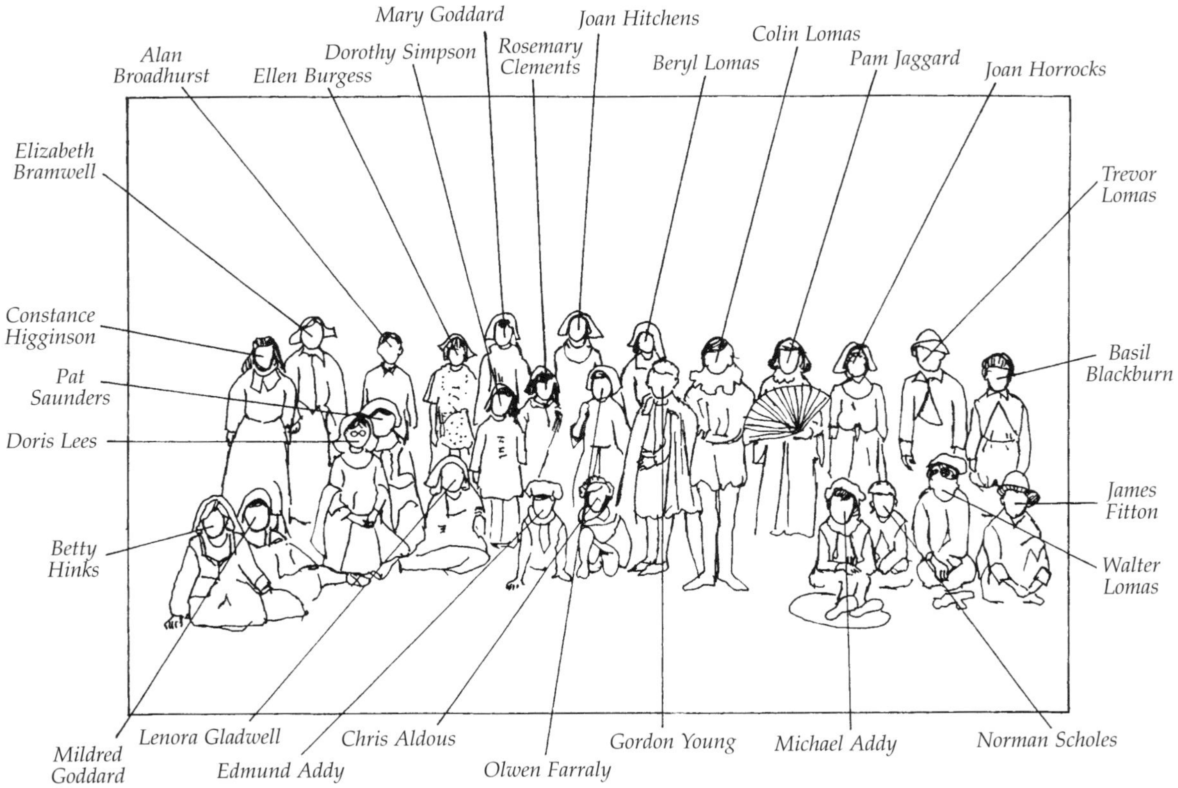

By Heather (Nona) Williams, now resident in Queensland, Australia.

I can still see the old stone building, the playground and the orchard, which collectively made up Gisborne School, and I have memories of a typical school day 60 years ago:

My brother and I run through the park carrying our gas masks in case they are needed for an air-raid drill. Children are walking and skipping along, others are riding bicycles, as they make their way to school. Miss Bateman ('Bakey') stands in the classroom close to the blackboard, looking rather stern, but with a touch of sadness in her eyes. She dresses in a long, straight skirt, wears spectacles and has greying, tied-back hair.

We sit at wooden desks and benches which are decorated with an assortment of initials carved into the wood by pupils past and present. We learn the alphabet by singing it, arithmetical tables by chanting them and study nature by drawing flowers and plants which we have brought to school. Writing begins with chalk on wooden-rimmed slates, then with pencil and paper (used with great economy) and finally with pen and ink – always so messy from the time it leaves the ink-wells. We have ink stains on our fingers, books and even our blouses and shirts.

Miss Madeleine, with her gentle, sometimes mischievous smile, teaches more arty subjects in her easy-going way. Six or seven of us are ushered into the front room of the Batemans' house on the other side of the road. We gather around a large table draped with a bobble-fringed cover and learn the mysteries of the French language and other interesting things, such as how to make ink out of candle smoke and quill pens from feathers.

Playtime now, and milk to drink out of little glass bottles with cardboard tops. On cold winter mornings, we struggle to suck the half-thawed milk through soggy paper straws. Now we're free to play games like 'Tick' and 'Walking in the Blackout' or we might just walk around sharing secrets with a friend.

One day, Miss Bateman takes the cane out of the cupboard. Suppressed smiles light our faces when the boy withdraws his hand and the cane snaps in two as it hits the desk. Then, stony silence.

By Patricia and Dorothy Simpson.

Although we attended Gisborne School at different times, the ethos remained the same: high moral values; a strong emphasis on courtesy and respect for others; endeavour and achievement; a broad and balanced curriculum; and an emphasis on basic skills.

The school was managed by Miss Ethel Bateman, who was assisted by her two sisters, Miss Edith and Miss Madeleine. The number on roll was approximately 40 and the colours of the uniform were brown and gold. School hours were from 9a.m. to 12 noon and 1.50p.m. to 3.50p.m. – children living locally usually went home for lunch. The day began with the customary short service of prayers and hymns – on Armistice Day this was held mid-morning to accommodate the two minutes' silence and the youngest pupil held the Union Jack as we sang God Save the King.

The open-plan design of the building lent itself to small-group teaching. The infants occupied the ground floor, where there were rib stalls, climbing ropes and an art area. The 'magic' witch hazel for treating grazed and cut knees was kept in the cupboard under the stairs.

As we grew older, we progressed to the upstairs room, where each pupil was allocated a desk in form sequence. Part of the room was used for our music sessions on Thursday afternoons and needlework lessons on Tuesdays. There was a blackboard, a piano, the desk used by Miss Bateman, which was loaded with hand-printed work cards, a stationery cupboard and a glass-fronted bookcase which housed the Museum Collection, comprising items collected by the Bateman sisters, schoolchildren and contacts over the years – these were our visual aids.

The rooms were heated by a coke-fired boiler, supplemented by additional heaters in extreme weather conditions. Miss Madeleine wore a thick, hand-knitted, navy-blue suit in winter. As the cold intensified, she exchanged this for an even thicker one in emerald green. In 'Arctic' conditions, which were prevalent at the time, she even wore both together!

The range of subjects taught included French and we received a sound grounding in core skills. Miss Ethel Bateman believed all children should be able to read by the age of seven and much emphasis was placed on developing clear, legible, joined-up handwriting from an early age. In order to achieve correct letter formation and orientation, we had to progress through a series of copy books. Spelling, composition and punctuation were given equal importance. As for mathematics, woe betide anyone who had not learnt their multiplication tables or the tables of length, capacity and weight.

A highlight of our week was the music afternoon, when we played simple percussion instruments in a group under the direction of Miss Farthing LRAM. Some of us had piano lessons after school and entered for the Royal School of Music examinations. Those who learnt the piano often had to play in the end-of-term concerts.

Formal examinations were unknown, but form positions and subject marks were displayed on the notice-board each month and detailed written reports were sent to parents at the end of each term. Form positions for the year were read out at the Annual Concert and Prize Giving, held at the Town Hall, where prizes were awarded for effort, good work and conduct.

It was usual to progress to secondary education outside the town, but a few pupils stayed on at the school until they reached the statutory leaving age.

Those were carefree days!

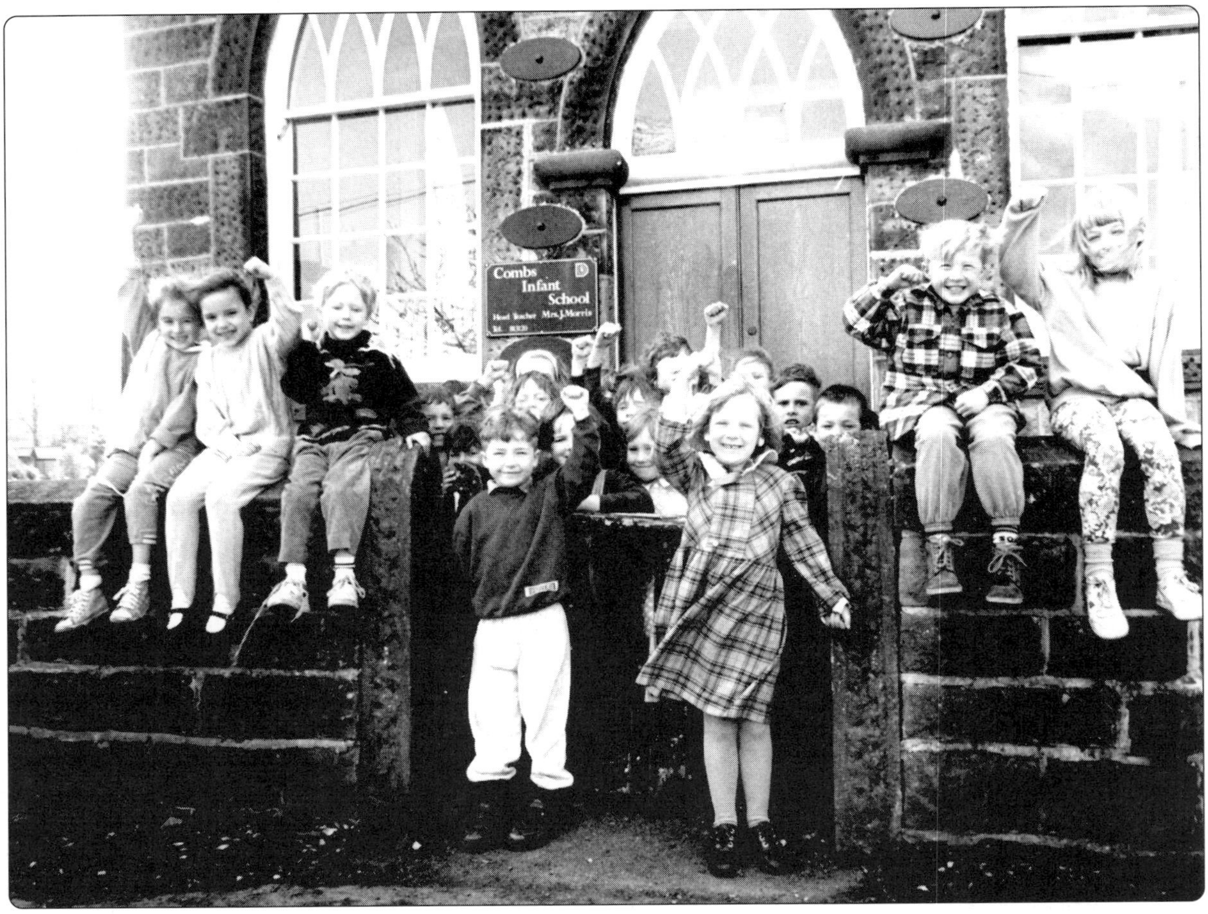

Combs School during the 1990s in pre-uniform days.

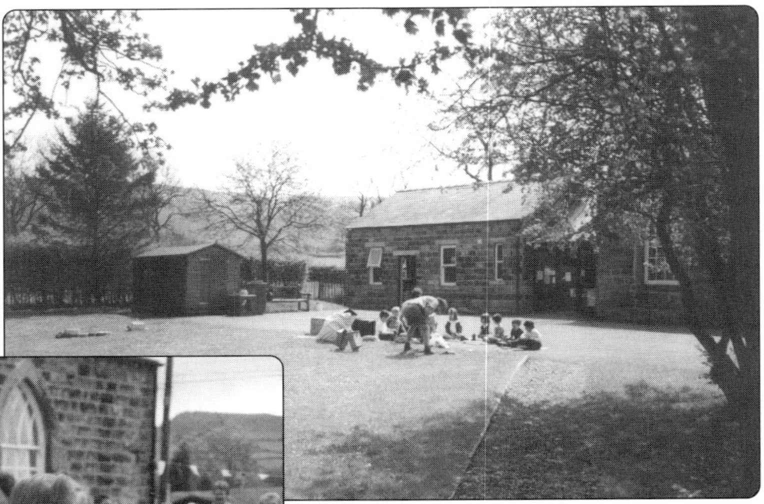

Children working with the Peak Park Ranger on the construction of nesting boxes.

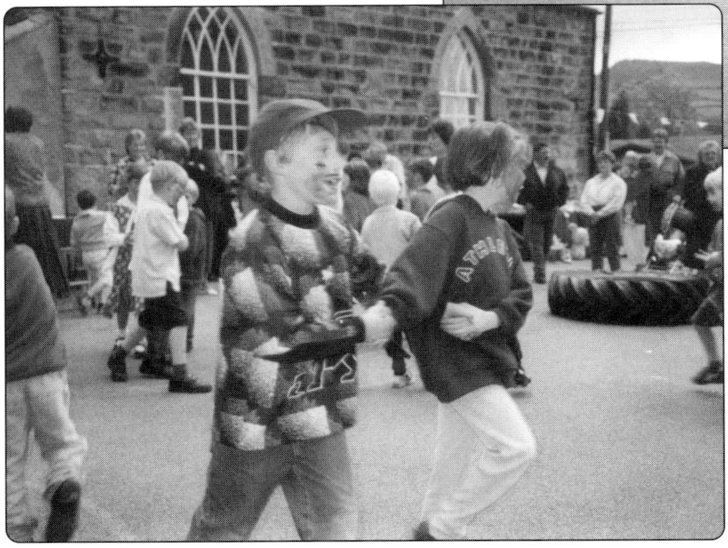

Practice for maypole dancing at Combs School.

Combs Infant School

The history of Combs School has been compiled from the school log-books, which form an unbroken record from the school's opening in 1881 to the present day. The story is related at some length because it not only gives a fascinating insight into the changing pattern of life in a small Peak-District community, but also exposes the enormous changes which have taken place in education over the last 120 years.

Combs Infant School is the idealised image of an English village school made real. The little school building, which also serves as a village hall and a Methodist Chapel, has a neat, symmetrical façade with three Gothick windows. The school has a delightful rural setting, at the edge of the hamlet of Combs and below the great bulk of Combs Moss.

Combs Infant School opened on 24 January 1881, with Miss Jackson as headmistress. After her first week in charge, she reported, 'The pupils are very backward, especially in orthography.' The poor educational attainment of the children probably resulted from a previous lack of adequate schooling in the village, but it was not helped by frequent absences due to bad weather and sickness. By February, the head teacher had resorted to keeping some children behind after school in order to give them extra tuition.

Miss Jackson remained at the school for only two terms and was replaced by Miss Bebbington, who was left to cope with the problems of poor attendance and low educational attainment. On her first day in charge, no boys turned up and fewer than half the 21 pupils on roll were present. The school-inspector reported, 'The children are, as yet, naturally backward, but the school has a prospect of future efficiency.' In attempting to meet the inspector's expectations, poor Miss Bebbington had to contend with frequent pupil absences due to roads being blocked by snow, pupils being required for haymaking and outbreaks of scarlet fever and measles. By the time of her departure in the summer of 1883, she was able to report, 'Exam results are satisfactory for those who have attended regularly.'

The school's third head teacher, Mary Alice Goldstraw, was determined to tackle the attendance problem. She visited the homes of absent pupils and promised prizes for regular attendance. Her campaign brought dividends: attendance figures improved dramatically, although there were the inevitable slumps due to influenza, mumps and chickenpox epidemics and severe snowstorms in the winters of both 1884 and 1885. Nevertheless she expressed some satisfaction with educational progress:

The infants are learning to associate meaning to what they read; the boys are learning sewing nicely and neatness is becoming general in all the standards.

By 1886, the school-inspector was able to report, 'This little school is conducted with much energy'. Indeed, his only criticism was an observation that, 'The children should answer and recite in a louder tone of voice.'

Unfortunately, the headmistress had a number of absences herself during 1886 and 1887, presumably due to ill health, and the children were often taught by stand-in teachers. In his report for 1887, the inspector noted, 'The change of teachers has affected the state of the school.'

A new headmistress, Miss White, was appointed in June 1887 and immediately restored some stability, despite disruption due to a severe diphtheria epidemic in the village, and brought about very noticeable improvements in educational attainment. In 1893, the inspector told the managers of the school that they 'should provide some assistance for Miss White, who is an earnest and painstaking teacher.' An assistant was duly appointed, but Miss White left in 1894. She was replaced by Marion Muir, who carried on the good work. In 1898, the inspector reported, 'In spite of much sickness, this little village school is making good progress and is in satisfactory discipline.' The managers tried to increase attendance and reduce health problems by granting half-day holidays for regular attendance and installing heating in the school for the first time. However, the stove proved temperamental, the winters in the early years of the new century were severe and even the headmistress had a number of absences due to sickness. Her assistant, Esther Morton, spent nine weeks in the scarlet-fever hospital.

Marion Muir retired in the summer of 1905 after a job well done. Unfortunately, the school then took several steps backwards. The managers had difficulty in finding a suitably qualified permanent replacement and a number of head teachers came and went, 'one pupil was taken away by death quite unexpectedly' and there were frequent complaints that the building was not being kept clean. Indeed, Grace Vowles, who was headmistress in September 1906, even refused to open the school for the autumn term because the schoolroom was in a 'disgraceful condition'.

The school was transferred from the control of the Methodist Church to the local authority in 1907 and a permanent, properly qualified headmistress was finally found in the shape of Gertrude Shilton in 1908. In the words of the inspector, 'During the last five years there have been five teachers in charge of this small and remote school. This has brought the school to a lamentable condition.'

The new head teacher quickly made an impression: attendance figures began to exceed 90 per cent and the inspector was soon reporting, 'A pleasing feature of the work is the attention given to nature study. This subject is being treated in a practical and intelligent way.' Gertrude Shilton felt that the children were learning to 'appreciate good books'. Hygiene was given priority, with the headmistress asking for an improvement in the toilet facilities and

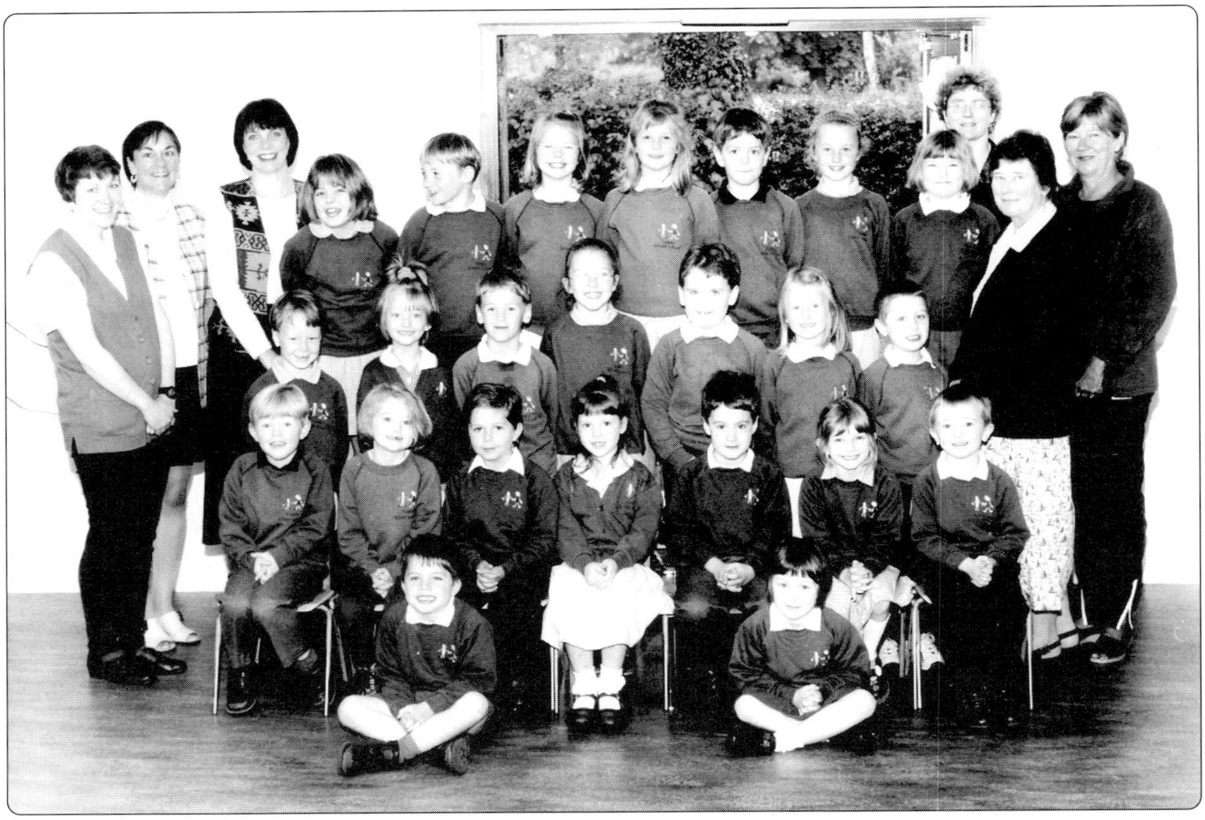

Combs Infant School – the class of 1998.

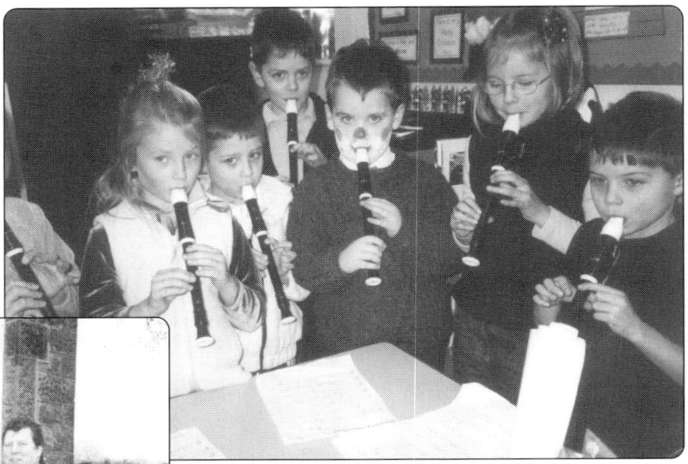

The 2001 recorder group.

Opening of the extension with Eric Stokes (architect), Mike Evanson (project manager), and Chris Pettett (chairman of the group).

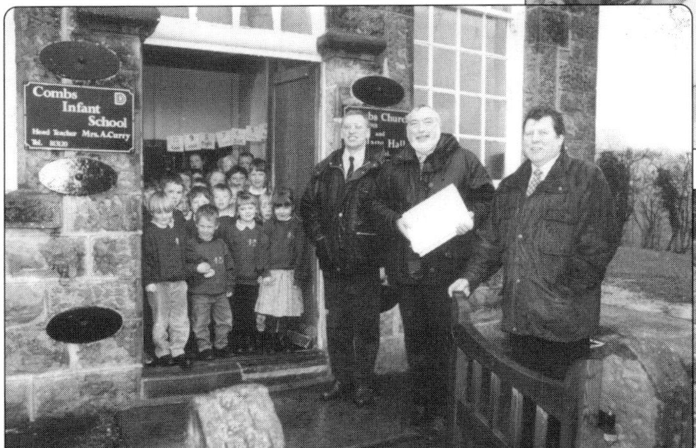

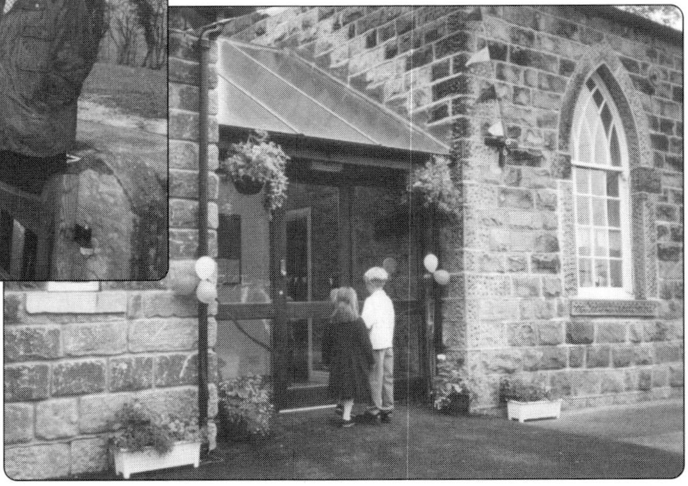

Children waiting to go in the new school entrance.

toothbrushes being sold to all the children, who were also given lessons on the care of teeth.

The school records conjure up a clear picture of country life before the Second World War. Children were allowed to leave school at the age of 13 'for agricultural purposes'; school holidays were often adjusted to allow for haymaking; one boy cut off a finger while working in the fields; there were frequent epidemics of measles, chickenpox, ringworm, influenza, whooping cough and diphtheria, and heavy snowfalls often made the Pennine lanes impassable.

Education had a highly patriotic flavour in those days. Empire Day (24 May) was always marked by the 'singing of appropriate songs' and lessons about Britain's pre-eminent role in the world, followed by a half-day holiday. On 12 December 1913, the children and teachers left school at 2.40p.m. to see her Majesty the Queen pass.

In 1914, Gertrude Shilton attempted to brighten up the building by buying the school's first framed print, Holman Hunt's *Light of the World*, with the proceeds from a school concert, but she faced some criticism from inspectors, who were becoming more demanding at this time. The inspector asked for more rigorous planning of work and the sanitary inspector closed the school for two weeks while cleanliness was improved.

Emily Coates took over as headmistress in July 1914 and instituted home-management lessons. Girls were taught how to wash and iron clothes and the school nurse brought a doll into school to demonstrate the dressing and undressing of a baby. The school had a rat plague in 1918 and the village was hit by an influenza epidemic in 1919; some pupils were absent for over a month.

Meanwhile, the inspector expressed satisfaction at the atmosphere of 'happy industry' in the school and Miss Coates used £1.8s.8d. from the Peace Committee to buy seven books, three games and some plasticine.

In the early 1920s, there were frequent problems with the operation of the stove and shortages of coal; there was a foot-and-mouth outbreak in the village, and Miss Coates began to have a number of lengthy absences due to illness. She was horrified on returning from a three-month absence to find that the term's syllabus had not been written, that the school was devoid of rubbers and plasticine and the pupil teacher had not been given a chance to observe lessons.

As Miss Coates' health improved, she was able to reintroduce her own high standards. In 1922, the inspector reported, 'This little country school continues in a quiet and pleasant manner to train its children in habits of courtesy and of industry.' It is interesting to note that the normal geography lesson was abandoned on 30 January 1922 and replaced by a lesson on Shackleton's life and his expedition.

Miss Coates was doing her best to expand the library, using proceeds from the Combs Agricultural Show, in order to widen the horizons of her pupils. In his report for 1926, the inspector acknowledged her efforts, but reported, 'The children's acquaintance with the outside world is very limited. Only three of them have seen the sea and they rarely go outside the bounds of the district.'

In the late 1920s, there was talk of closing the school because just a dozen pupils were in attendance. However, 16 pupils turned up on September 1929 and so the school was deemed to be viable. The school was not only saved, but was soon receiving a glowing report from the inspector:

This is a delightful little school nestling at the foot of a great coomb in the Peak District. It would be difficult to exaggerate the human and scholastic merits of the school.

The school records for the 1930s show signs of a changing world. The local authority began to lay on refresher courses for teachers and the headmistress duly attended a number of these, but the school had to close in her absence if a cover teacher could not be found. The pupils were taken to Chapel Town Hall in 1935 to see a film about electricity and two pupils had to leave in the same year because their homes had been commandeered for reservoir developments.

Bertha Raguley took over as headmistress in December 1938. War broke out in the following year and she was soon faced with the problem of accommodating the first influx of evacuees. The war years certainly had an impact on the life of the school. When the air-raid siren sounded in Whaley Bridge on 12 September 1940, children living nearby were sent home and pupils who remained in school were instructed to lie on the floor under their desks. In addition the pupils were fitted with gas masks in June 1941; £40 was raised in War Weapons Week in 1941; a collection was taken on Empire Day in the following year for the Overseas League Tobacco Fund; money was raised in 1943 for the Wings for Victory fund; the pupils entered a poster competition for Salute the Soldier Week; and a VI bomb landed in the nearby hills on 30 December 1945, killing a number of sheep at Castle Naze Farm. When VE Day finally came, every child was given a small Union Jack and a two-day holiday. Other wartime developments included: the introduction of school milk in November 1940; the setting up of a National Savings Bank in response to a request by the inspector in 1940; a garden which was started during the same year; the introduction in 1941 of injections to combat diphtheria; and the installation of a mains radio, thanks to donations from parents.

In 1946, Miss Raguley was one of three representatives from Chapel invited to Buckingham Palace in recognition of work done during National Service Week.

The winter of 1947–8 brought horrendous blizzards. The school was forced to close for three weeks and the head had to lodge locally because she was unable to reach her own home. The pipes burst, so the school had to close once again, but the headmistress resorted to opening the school in Mrs Williams' tea rooms, 'Quiet Ways'. The winter was so bad that dinners could not be delivered from Chapel until 20 March and pupils had to rely on sandwiches kindly provided by Mrs Williams.

Other notable developments in the late 1940s included the acquisition of PE equipment, the installation of a telephone, and an increase in the number of pupils taking examinations for entry into local grammar schools. In 1948, intelligence tests began to make an appearance; head teachers were also asked to invigilate in one another's schools in order to ensure there was no cheating. The new tests were soon being used to select pupils for secondary schools – two Combs' pupils, Roy Limer and Eunice Mosley, were allocated grammar-school places in 1951 on the basis of their 11+ results. Chapel's Secondary Modern School opened in 1952 and took pupils from Combs who had not been allocated grammar-school places.

Meanwhile, the range of educational and cultural opportunities at the school was widening: the children entered the Sunday Pictorial's National Exhibition of Children's Art; posters were designed for National Safety Week; visits were made to Arbor Low, Haddon Hall and Matlock and to an exhibition of modern art in Manchester. The children were taken to see the film 'Mudlark' at Buxton Opera House and a performance by the Scottish Children's Theatre at Chapel Town Hall. They even began to put on their own regular puppet shows in school.

Royal events impacted on school life in the early 1950s. On 6 February 1952, King George VI died. The children listened to the radio broadcast of his death and, a fortnight later, they went to Lower Lea, at the invitation of Mr and Mrs Maynard-Smith, to watch his funeral on television. On 24 March 1953 Queen Mary died and school opened with the singing of the National Anthem. In June, the children received coronation souvenirs and were given a coronation holiday.

The inspector's report for 1953 gave a fairly comprehensive picture of life at the school. He noted that there was a small playground and grass area and that all pupils were in the habit of staying for lunch. He reported that the headmistress had been at the school for ten years and that she had been helped by a full-time assistant until pupil numbers fell, but now received only intermittent assistance. The inspector found:

> *Most of the children are self assured and read well. Several radio broadcasts are listened to, providing a welcome and desirable additional voice. In general, this small school provides satisfactory instruction and is a contented community.*

He also noted, 'All signs of school life are cleared away at the weekend when the building reverts to its original role as a Methodist Chapel.'

Miss Raguley retired in the summer of 1953 and Miss Huss spent a 'very happy' autumn term temporarily in charge until Mrs Poole took up post in January 1954. Unfortunately, the new head teacher decided to resign after just three years, because her husband was taken ill. During her short term of office, she made parents particularly welcome in the school, inviting them to open days, when they could see lessons in progress and inspect work.

Phyllis Mackenzie was next in the post in September 1958 and was immediately faced with a plague of mice in the school. In October, the Duke of Edinburgh was scheduled to pass through Combs on his way from a visit to the Outdoor Pursuits Centre at Whitehall to the official opening of the new laboratory block at Ferodo. The three oldest pupils, Mary Ashbury, Roy Brocklehurst and Stephen Lomas, were given the honour of opening the gates for his car as it passed along the gated country road.

By 1959, the number on roll had increased to 25, a pupil number which merited the provision of two teachers. However, the head teacher expressed the view that those pupils aged 10 and 11 would be better served if they were to be transferred to Town End Methodist School, rather than remain in a school with two teachers in a single classroom space. Consequently the plan was enacted.

The school received some coverage in the *Daily Express* in 1961 because the authority refused to provide transport for a boy from an outlying farm. The head teacher experienced some transport difficulties of her own in the winter of 1963 when she had to walk to school along Combs Lane on top of a snowdrift.

The school was a happy place during Phyllis Mackenzie's headship. She not only arranged fun events, such as an annual Christmas party for pupils and parents, which included films, plays performed by the children, games and refreshments, but also kept herself informed about new educational developments, such as the Initial Teaching Alphabet method of teaching reading. The inspector reported:

> *This small school provides a pleasant and friendly environment in which educational foundations are soundly laid and boys and girls are encouraged and helped individually to develop their growing abilities to the full.*

The mid-1960s saw the repetition of two problems which had been faced in the early years of the school: 36 sheep wandered into the school yard during one day and there was a mumps epidemic in the village.

Phyllis Mackenzie left in the summer of 1966 after 'eight extremely happy years'. She had been greatly helped by Mr Thornley, who had acted as caretaker, midday supervisor and dinner helper and she was grateful to her assistant Mrs Lomas, who had been a loyal companion and had helped to relieve the loneliness that can be felt by anyone who is the only teacher in a school.

The departure of the head teacher heralded an important change. From September 1966, all the juniors transferred to Town End Methodist School and Combs School became a school for infants only.

Audrey Anderton was appointed to the headship of the 'new school' and the Parent Teacher Association became active at this time. The association raised funds to purchase a television in 1970 and ran a raffle to raise money to hire a coach for a school trip to Riber Castle. These PTA activities probably reflected the increasing affluence in the village, as did the growing number of pupils leaving to go to fee-paying schools.

In 1973, the head teacher had to suffer the loss of Mrs Lomas, known to children as Auntie Mollie, who retired after acting as caretaker, dinner supervisor and ancillary helper during 30 years' service at the school. Miss Anderton also had to cope with persistent problems with the school boiler, which led to the children being sent home on a number of occasions when the temperature dropped below 40°F!

The late 1970s and early 1980s saw the children involved in three major celebrations: the 750th anniversary of Chapel's Parish Church in 1975; the Queen's silver jubilee in 1977 (when a fun sports day was held involving such bizarre events as a needle-threading race and a mixed three-legged race, with married couples banned from forming a team) and school centenary celebrations in 1981, when the children dressed in Victorian costume, and later participated in Chapel carnival wearing the same outfits.

In the 1980s, the head teacher was given the support of a half-time teacher, which gave her time to effectively lead the school into the computer age. A microcomputer was used to log the school's contribution to the BBC's Domesday Project, which involved a great deal of research into the locality, visits to local farmsteads and work with the Peak Park Ranger. The success of the project prompted the *Buxton Advertiser* to report, 'When historians of the future look into the 1985 Domesday Book they will probably be impressed by the great work of a tiny village school.'

Other signs of the times were visits by the police with their film 'Don't Talk to Strangers' and school trips to the Buxton Micrarium and the radio telescope at Jodrell Bank.

The year 1988 saw the statutory introduction of annual reports to parents by governors and in-service training days for staff. The first INSET days at Combs were concerned with important educational developments of the time – the use of computers in the teaching of mathematics and the introduction of community education, which was a major initiative of Derbyshire LEA (until the funds dried up). Of course, the head teacher also had to deal with a number of other, rather more mundane matters, such as the increasingly unstable front boundary wall, which had to be rebuilt in 1988. After the renovation, Miss Anderton was pleased to report, 'It looks as if it will be good for the next 100 years.'

In 1989, the head teacher retired after steering the school through a period of enormous change. Mrs Judith Morris arrived in April 1989, just as moves were being made to introduce the National Curriculum at Key Stage 1 (infant years).

The school acquired a photocopier in 1990. Staff attended courses on AIDS and educational innovations continued unabated in the early 1990s. Governors were given powers to manage school budgets, head teachers had to produce a School Development Plan, Standard Attainment Tests (SATs) were introduced and so-called 'Cluster' meetings were set up with head teachers from other local schools, who were quick to use these gatherings to share their woes about inadequate budgets and the uncertain future of small schools.

Indeed, the future of Combs School looked uncertain in the early 1990s, not only because the budget was tight and pupil numbers had fallen, but because the future of the building itself had been placed in doubt by a growing bulge in the front wall. The educational future became even bleaker when the PE adviser suggested that the school was too small to effectively deliver the National Curriculum. However, the prospects for the building began to look brighter when Combs Village Hall Trust and the Parish Council entered into a series of meetings to plan the rebuilding of the schoolrooms. Major construction work began in 1993 and the pupils had to be moved to Chapel Infant School for more than a term until the work was completed.

Meanwhile, educational changes were still occurring. In 1993, the head teacher attended training in preparation for teacher appraisals and OFSTED school inspections. At the end of the summer term in 1994, Judith Morris made the following note in her log-book: 'A letter should be waiting on our return about an OFSTED inspection. Happy holidays!'

Judith left the school at the end of 1995 to take up an appointment as the head teacher of Buxton Infant School. The governors and parents appeared to have won their fight to save the school and the Village Hall Trust had even decided to build an extension on the schoolrooms.

Mrs Avis Curry was appointed in January 1996. Her first entry in the school log-book, written on New Year's Day, which was officially her first day in school, reads: 'Spent my first afternoon defrosting the toilets and getting them repaired.' However, she was soon attending to educational matters by preparing for an OFSTED inspection and advising the governors and parents not to break free of local authority control by applying for Grant Maintained Status (GMS).

The school had a splendid first set of SATs results and was developing a growing reputation for high standards. Combs School was seen by discerning parents as a popular choice; in 1996 the head teacher even received applications from two sets of parents for pupil entry in the millennium year.

The first OFSTED inspection took place in April 1997. Under the rules of the inspection, the head is not allowed to be present when the inspectors meet the parents, but Mrs Curry was told, 'The parents gave inspectors a run for their money'. When the inspectors arrived in school to begin their work, she found that 'it was not possible to prepare afternoon lessons adequately, because the inspectors insist on interviewing staff during the lunch break'. She need not have worried, because the school received a very favourable report.

These were hard times for head teachers, but Mrs Curry was able to rely on support in the classroom from Mary Birch, except for a period when Mary was fulfilling the role of acting head teacher at Bradwell.

The Village Hall Committee saw their plans for a greatly expanded Village Hall/school/church finally come to fruition in 1998, when builders knocked through to join the old and new buildings. A grand opening was held on 4 July 1998, which was attended by the great-grandson and great-niece of Gertrude Shilton, who had been head teacher in the early 1900s. The addition of a new hall on the back of the old schoolroom was closely followed by the construction of a storage gallery.

In 2003 the number of demands placed by modern educational requirements and Government initiatives on all schools is enormous. Head teacher Avis Curry stresses that she simply could not manage the school successfully without the support of a group of committed people who work as a strong team. They comprise: Mary Birch, a long-time teacher at the school; Jacky Buxton, a cleaner and senior dining-room assistant; Shirley Jackson, a senior midday assistant and teaching assistant; and Beverly Hodgson, clerk to the school and clerk to the governors. The school takes new Government initiatives, such as the Literacy Hour, in its stride and has collected a number of awards for excellence, including a Health Promoting School Award, a Basic Skills Agency Quality Mark and a School Achievement Award. Combs Infant School, in its remote valley in the High Peak, has even had the accolade of being listed in the *Sunday Times* as an OFSTED Gold Star school. It was also singled out as a 'particularly successful school' by the Government's Chief Inspector, Mike Tomlinson.

The Development of Primary Education in Chapel-en-le-Frith

In April 2002, Chapel-en-le-Frith acquired its very first primary school. The genesis of the new establishment, which is the largest primary school in Derbyshire, is a complex and revealing story of educational development over three centuries.

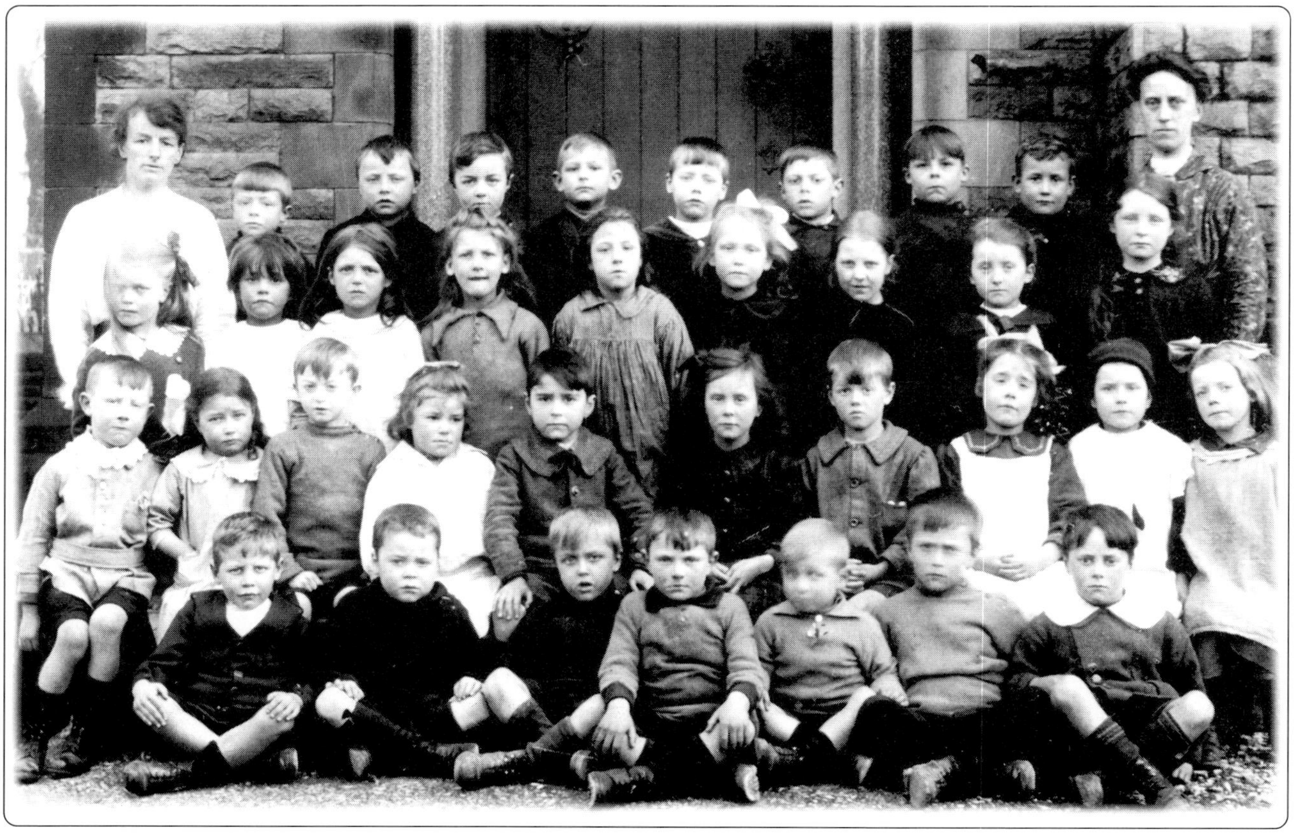

Town End Day School in 1915.

Before the mid-nineteenth century, the quality and extent of educational provision in any particular locality was largely determined by the generosity of philanthropic individuals. A bequest from Mary Dixon in 1696 enabled a rudimentary educational establishment to be founded in the Hordens area of Chapel. In the eighteenth century, the school was relocated to Cromwell Croft, on the area now occupied by Cromwell House. In 1785, a bequest by Mary Bagshawe, the wife of William Bagshawe of Ford Hall, together with money left by John Frith, was used to set up a little school at Bowden Head, which remained in use until 1927.

During the nineteenth century the churches became increasingly proactive in expanding educational opportunities. When Revd George Hall became vicar of St Thomas Becket Church in 1836, he began to campaign for the establishment of Church of England schools in the parish. By 1839, sufficient funds had been raised to set up a boys' school in a splendid building on High Street. The stone edifice, which has an impressive gabled façade with mullioned and transomed windows, is now Grade II listed. The Parish Church authorities also established schools at Bugsworth, in 1869, and Dove Holes, in 1881. A new wing was added to the Chapel school in 1889 in order to house girls and infants, and improvements carried out in 1927 included the addition of a new playground for the girls.

Meanwhile, the Wesleyan chapel at Town End was also providing education for some of the town's children. Chapel Methodists were among the early pioneers of the Sunday school movement, which had been initiated by Robert Raikes. A Sunday school operated at Town End in some rather dark and dingy cellars, before it was moved to a cottage in an enclosure now known as Old School Yard. In 1853, a new Sunday school was erected next to the old Wesleyan chapel on the south side of Market Street (the new chapel and the manse not being built until 1874).

Education provided by the Sunday school teachers went beyond instruction in the scriptures and included the fundamentals of the three Rs. Regulations for the Wesleyan Sunday school included the following:

This school is open for poor children of all description except those who are afflicted with any dangerous contagion or who are scholars of any other Sunday school in the town. It is required that children shall attend clean washed and hair combed by half-past eight in the morning from April to October, by nine from October to April, and a quarter before one in the afternoon. Those who have been scholars three months being able to read the Bible and say the Church Catechism, will be taught to write on providing their own pens and paper.

A day school was added to the Sunday school in 1870, the year in which a landmark Education Act made elementary education compulsory for both boys and girls. The day-school building was enlarged in 1887, but the Local Education Authority was beginning to express dissatisfaction with the premises by the early years of the twentieth century. After holding an enquiry, the authority decided that it would have to construct a new school for children at Town End. By 1914, plans had been drawn up for the building, but the outbreak of war put paid to the scheme.

In 1928, the managers of the school at Town End received final notice from the LEA that the school would not be recognised after 31 July of that year. In response, the trustees and managers submitted plans for a new extension at a cost of £2,500. The authority agreed to contribute £1,000, but the church was left to find the remainder through donations. The costs actually rose to £3,100, but the money was found and the extension was completed by January 1930. Writing in 1940, local historian William Braylesford Bunting described the extended Wesleyan school as 'a fine range of buildings meeting all the requirements of the Education Authority.'

Some private schools, such as Gisborne, sprang up in Chapel during the first half of the twentieth century, but all-age education in the town was largely in the hands of the two church schools – the Church of England school on High Street and the Methodist school at Town End. Needless to say, there was some rivalry between the two institutions, with the pupils at the Methodist school being known as 'Town End Skittlings' and those at the Church-of-England school being labelled 'Up Town Bulldogs'.

The surviving log-books from the Church of England establishment paint a revealing picture of school life in the early years of the twentieth century. The building was frequently very cold because of a lack of adequate heating, with the temperature inside the classrooms often falling well below 50°F. Attendance was often low, either because roads were blocked due to snow or because there were epidemics of diseases such as measles, chickenpox, whooping cough, scarlet fever and mumps. The attendance officer was sometimes called upon to visit the High Peak Shirt Factory to insist on the return to school of girls who were working there despite being under the school-leaving age. One boy was absent in 1926 after swallowing a lead pencil in its case. The head teacher reported, 'The case is two inches long and the pencil was projecting from it at least an inch further.'

Two particularly noteworthy entries in the log-book survive from the days of the First World War. An entry in October 1914 reads: 'A gentleman called this morning to inspect the school buildings. He said he was valuing the property for the Government.' In March 1918 the following entry was made:

The school staff will be employed at the local food office until the end of the week preparing food cards in

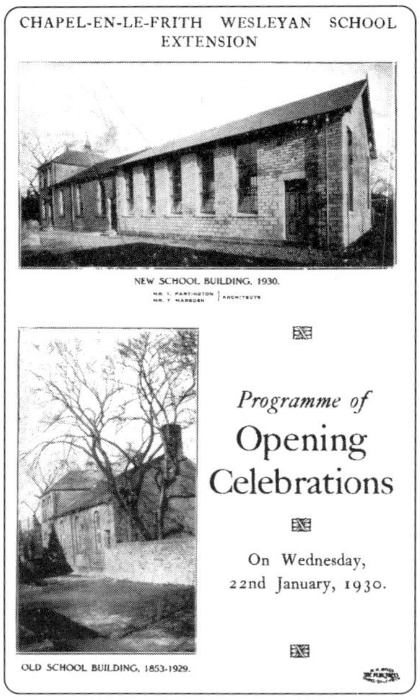
CHAPEL-EN-LE-FRITH WESLEYAN SCHOOL EXTENSION

NEW SCHOOL BUILDING, 1930.

Programme of

Opening Celebrations

On Wednesday, 22nd January, 1930.

OLD SCHOOL BUILDING, 1853-1929.

Cover of the programme for the opening of the extension at the Wesleyan school in 1930.

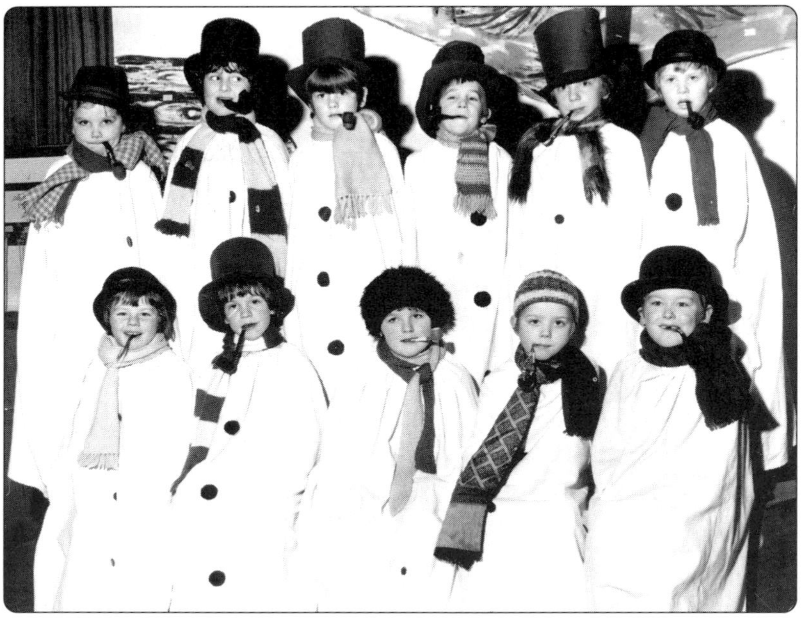

Pipe-smoking Christmas snowmen from 1974.

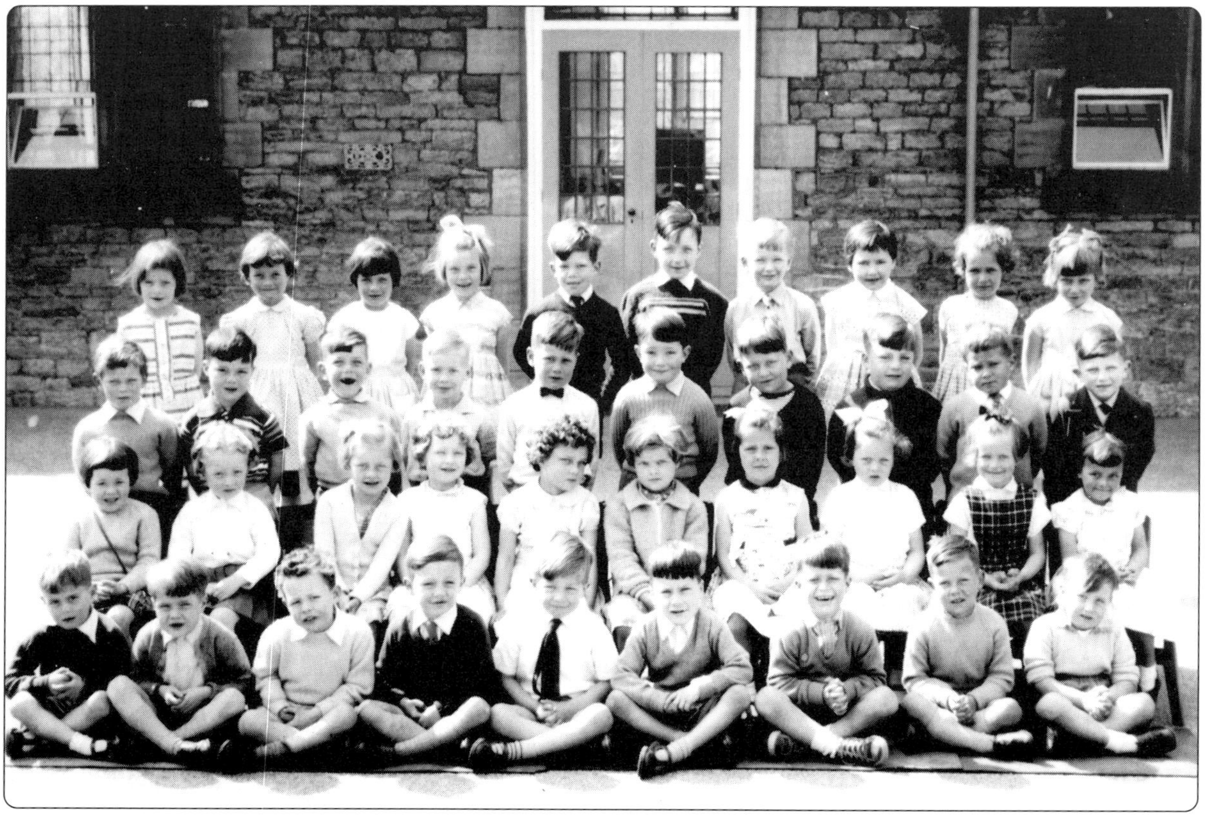

Group A of Chapel-en-le-Frith Infant School in the 1960s. Left to right, back row: *Susan Howarth, Jane Saunders, Christine Bridge, Christine Middleton, Clive Lomas, Nigel Ingram, John Broomhead, Anne Hibbs, Hilary Lomas, Diane Longden;* third row: *Timothy Scowcroft, Philip Anderson, Philip Critchlow, David Fuzzard, Anthony Marchington, Jason Lomas, Victor Nadin, Ian Stafford, David Lomas, Phillip Johnson;* second row: *Michelle Reynolds, Carol Beardsall, Susan Crane, Anne Allsop, Ann Mifflin, Gaynor Hoyle, Jill Mellor, Joanne Halford, Jane Bunting, Linda Hudson;* front row: *Shaun King, Kenneth Matthews, Ian Fell, Ian Cuson, Michael Travis, Robert Vernon, John Ashton, Christopher Hartle, Philip Osborne.*

connection with the national rationing scheme, so the school will be shut.

In the years before the Second World War, Empire Day was always celebrated in schools with a display of jingoistic fervour. The head teacher's report for Empire Day, 1920, included the following:

The girls of Class I gave a dramatic Geography lesson entitled 'Britannia and her Daughters'. Patriotic songs were sung, ending with the National Anthem. School closed at midday for the rest of the day.

With the introduction of free secondary education for all, as a result of the 1944 Education Act, and the raising of the school-leaving age to 15 in 1947, some rationalisation of educational provision in Chapel-en-le-Frith became necessary. All children of primary-school age that attended the Church of England school on High Street were transferred down the road to the Methodist school and all infant- and secondary-school pupils at Town End were moved up the road to the Church of England school.

By the early 1950s, psychologists and advocates of IQ tests had used research findings, which were later found to be very suspect, to convince educational strategists that a child's intelligence could be measured by the age of 11. The introduction of the 11+ examination saw successful candidates from Chapel moving to grammar schools in Buxton or New Mills for their secondary education, while examination failures were left to complete their compulsory education in the grossly inadequate buildings on High Street. Thankfully, this arrangement was an interim measure pending the construction of a new Secondary Modern School on Long Lane in 1952.

In 1968, the Junior School at Town End was moved from the old Methodist school into a new building on Warmbrook Road. The new school, which was christened Warmbrook Junior School, soon began to play an active role in the community. For example, elderly residents were invited to attend Christmas carol concerts in the school and maypole dancers would frequently entertain residents in local care homes. In addition, the children took up the custom of well dressing and participated in church and civic functions. Chapel's secondary pupils also got a new deal in 1973, when the Secondary Modern School on Long Lane took in its first fully comprehensive intake.

Meanwhile, the infant-school pupils and their teachers were having to make do with classrooms in the old Church of England school, supplemented by some additional teaching spaces in Horsa huts on the north side of High Street, where lessons were punctuated by periodic noise and vibration induced by the rattle of passing trains. Despite the poor physical provision, the Infant School maintained a wide curriculum and achieved high educational standards. It also gained a national reputation for supporting pupils with special needs in mainstream classes.

By the mid-1980s, the staff, parents and governors had decided that teaching in 50-year-old huts was no longer acceptable and they began a high-profile campaign for a new school. In 1986, a correspondent from *The Teacher*, the NUT's newspaper, visited the Horsa-hut site and reported:

Sandwiched between a railway line and the main A6 trunk road, the annexe of Chapel-en-le-Frith Infant School is shaken 12 times a day by the passage of enormous trains carrying quarry materials.

A journalist from the *Daily Mirror*, who visited the school in 1987, gave the situation some tabloid treatment when he reported: 'Caroline Brookfield was terrified and tearful on her first day at school, covering her ears to hide the deafening noise of passing trains.'

This unsatisfactory situation came to an end in 1999, when a state-of-the-art Infant and Nursery School was erected on a site adjacent to Warmbrook Junior School. Before leaving their old building, staff, pupils, parents and friends took part in a week of celebrations to commemorate 160 years of education in the school. Teachers and children dressed up in Victorian costume, took part in a traditional sports day, complete with egg-and-spoon races, sack races and three-legged races, and enjoyed a street party, with a traditional menu of ginger beer and sandwiches.

An exhibition, organised by teacher Ruth Mullis, used a series of illustrations and artefacts to record a century and a half of change. Examples of Victorian corsetry recalled the prim and restrictive nature of society at the time the boys' school first opened; old Army uniforms, a sketchbook from the Belgian battlefields and photographs of soldiers going 'over the top' graphically illustrated the carnage of the First World War; ration books were a reminder of the hard times during and after the Second World War; and Peter Blake's record sleeve from the Beatles' Sergeant Pepper album illustrated an era of unprecedented freedom and experimentation in the 1960s. Staff even acted as exhibits by dressing in a variety of fashions from the past and newspaper articles were used to recall notable landmarks in history, including Edward VIII's abdication, the first scaling of Everest and Neil Armstrong's 'giant leap for mankind'.

Ruth had also collected reminiscences from former pupils. Denise Wragg (née Angus) wrote:

I remember the little bottles of milk [we] *got at first break. In winter they froze and the bottle top ended up resting on an inch of frozen milk. We still drank it ice cold.*

Neil McKay recalled:

I remember when my friend and I were told off for talking too much in class. The head teacher told us to

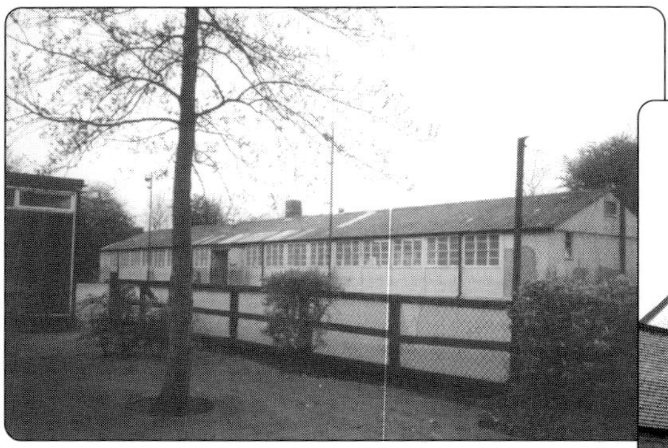

The infamous Horsa huts.

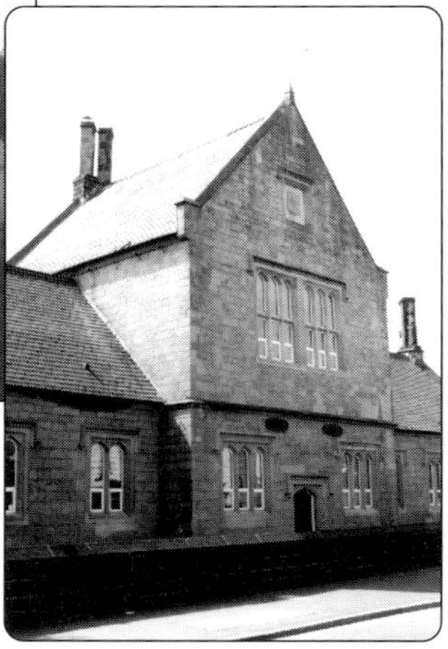

The Church of England Boys' School in High Street.

Centre picture: *Teaching staff at Chapel Infant School in 1994.* Left to right, back row: *Monica Townend, Jude Boyd, Ruth Mullis, Brioni Evans, Geoff Wharton, Debbie Barlow, Rosemary Easton, Beverley Bigham;* middle row: *Nikki Johnson, Joy Nash, David Bell, Carol Girling, Nina Hirst, Angela Foulkes, Linda Wilson;* front row: *Claire Ridgeway, Chris Flitcroft, Dot Oxley, Sue Taylor (head teacher), Sheena Lowe, Janet McNicol, Debbie Frith, Pam Moorcroft.*

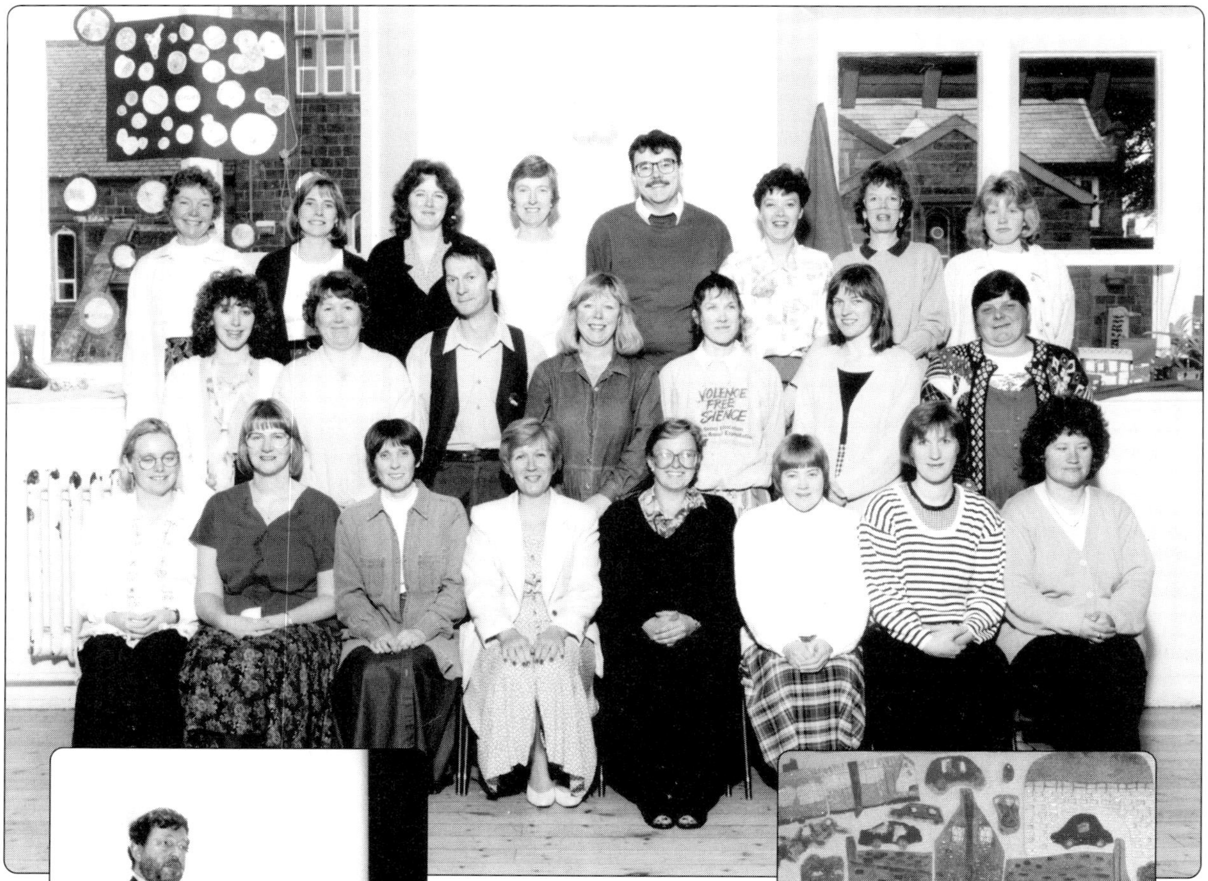

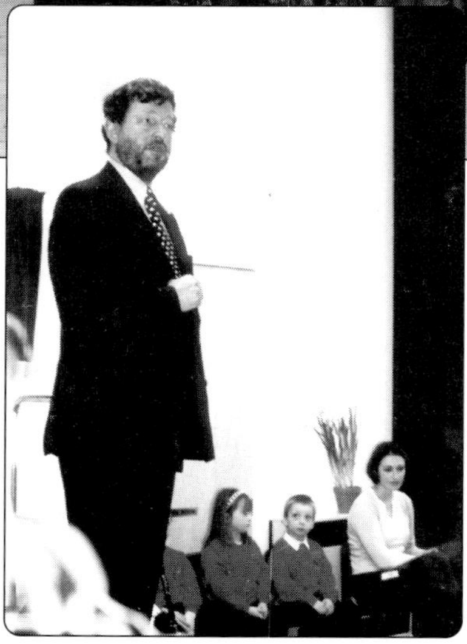

David Blunkett officially opening the new Chapel-en-le-Frith Infant and Nursery School on 27 March 2000.

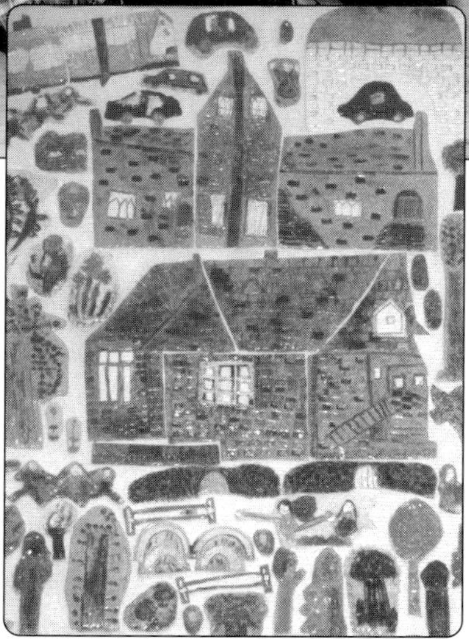

Millennium Mural in the new Infant and Nursery School.

go to the toilets and rinse our mouths out with soap and water – and we did!

Chris Hartle added his painful memory of school-days in the 1960s: 'I had four teeth knocked out at cricket. The batsman was the local butcher's boy.'

The new Infant and Nursery School on Warmbrook Road was dedicated on 29 September 1999 by the Bishop of Derby and officially opened on 27 March 2000 by David Blunkett, the Secretary of State for Education and Employment. The purpose-built classrooms, with up-to-the-minute provision for infant and nursery schoolchildren, are arranged around a landscaped courtyard and the playground includes areas designed to encourage imaginative play. There is even a sensory garden for physically and visually impaired children. The building contains scores of decorated bricks and brass plaques designed by the children as well as a Millennium Mural featuring pictures of Chapel, also produced by the pupils.

The slow evolution of mainstream educational provision in Chapel-en-le-Frith has been matched by a revolution in special-needs education. In the early 1980s, a 'special class' was located on the Horsa-hut site, but it was segregated from the rest of the school. However, by 1989, the Infant School had become an integrated special-needs resource for young children.

In the millennium year, John Smith retired as head teacher of Warmbrook Junior School. The LEA decided to amalgamate Warmbrook Junior School and Chapel's Church of England Infant and Nursery School, following extensive consultation with parents, staff and governors. In April 2002, Sue Taylor became head teacher of the new Chapel-en-le-Frith Church of England Controlled Primary School, which includes an integrated special needs resource for pupils aged 3 to 11. Primary education on one site had finally arrived in the town!

Secondary Education in Chapel-en-le-Frith, 1952–2003

By Tom James, former assistant head teacher at Chapel-en-le-Frith High School.

Prior to 1947, education for children of secondary-school age in Chapel-en-le-Frith had been provided by two all-age church schools in the town: the Church of England school on High Street and the Methodist school at Town End. In 1947, the older pupils at the Methodist school were transferred to the Church of England school, whose junior pupils, apart from those of infant age, were moved down the hill to the site at Town End. The two-way shuffle created a junior department at Town End as well as infant and secondary departments on the Church of England site. However, this was an interim measure as plans were being hatched for a new Secondary Modern School for Chapel-en-le-Frith.

The notion of Secondary Modern Schools arose out of the 1944 Education Act. These schools were designed to cater for children who had not been deemed academic on the basis of tests in English, mathematics and verbal reasoning taken at the age of 11+. The new Secondary Modern Schools were provided with many of the facilities found in grammar schools, such as laboratories, workshops and gymnasia, but the teachers and their pupils were freed from the pressure of examinations.

The first buildings of Chapel-en-le-Frith's Secondary Modern School were built on flat, marshy land off Long Lane in 1952. Dan Northall, a young, enthusiastic teacher from Sheffield, was designated as the first head teacher. He had already taken up appointment as head of the secondary unit at the Church of England school after a number of inspections by both HMI and the LEA had revealed deficiencies in provision. Only two of the existing secondary staff had been retained: Les Bell, who had joined the school after serving in the RAF, and Miss Wallace, a probationary teacher.

It was envisaged that the new buildings would be ready for use in September 1952, but it was not until 17 October that books, apparatus and equipment were finally moved into the new school. At 3.30p.m. on that day, the head teacher held a brief assembly in the new entrance hall for the 70 or more pupils. By 27 October, there were 83 pupils on roll and by the start of the new year four members of staff had been appointed, in addition to the head teacher. They were: Mr Bell, who taught class 4 (top class); Mrs Knox, class 3; Mrs Jones, class 2; and Miss Wallace, class 1. In September of that year, Miss Wallace was also given charge of the girls' welfare. The start of the spring term of 1953 saw the first pupils arriving from Chinley and Buxworth.

As flaws were being found in the research which suggested that 11+ failures were incapable of academic success, Dan Northall began to search for suitable examination courses for his pupils. By 1959, the school was offering a few youngsters a series of examination courses run by the University of Lancashire and the Cheshire Institute of Further Education. Initially, these were offered to pupils who had expressed an interest in taking up craft apprenticeships or commercial courses. Following on from the success of these first candidates and with the completion of all the new buildings, which coincided with the arrival of pupils from Whaley Bridge and Fernilee, other options became possible. Mr Northall had discovered that some Secondary Modern Schools in other parts of the country had begun to enter a few candidates for one or two key GCE O-level examinations, particularly mathematics and English. After determining with local employers which subjects they would deem to be worthwhile, the school decided to offer O levels in English, mathematics, physics and geography, along with engineering and

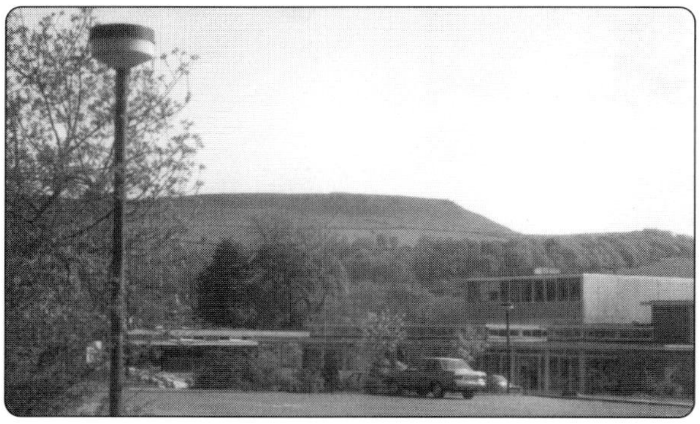

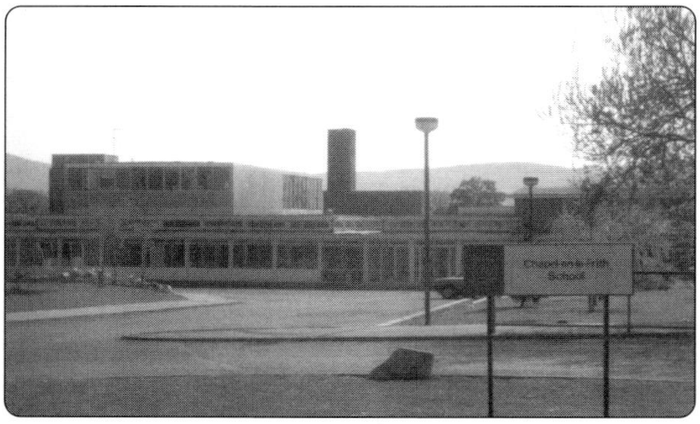

Above and above right: *Long Lane School in 1984.*

Right: *School ski trip to Schladming, Austria, in 1970, with the Ged Armitt, Pat Bailey and Kathleen Heyword.*

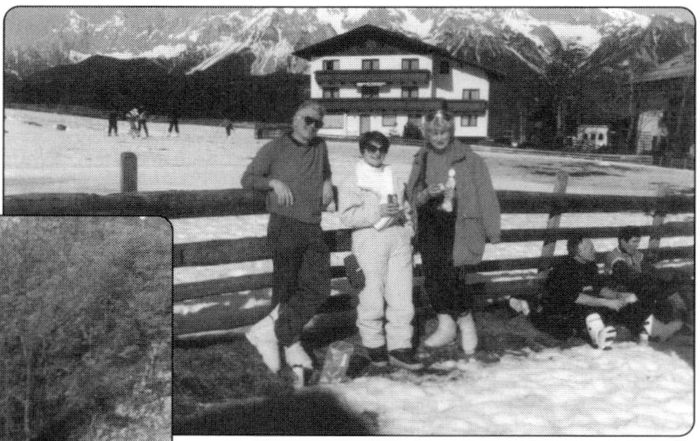

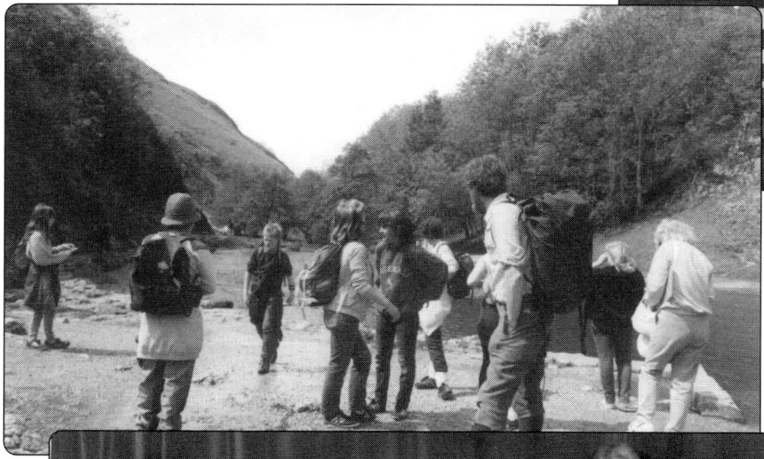

Left: *First-year pupils on a school trip to Dovedale in 1985.*

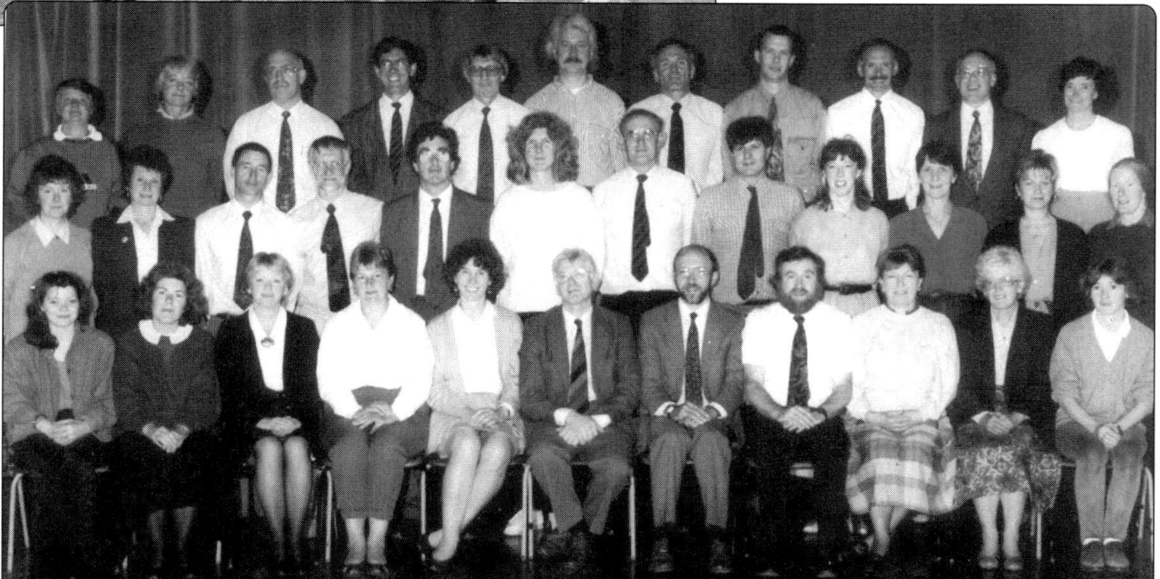

The school staff in 1984. Back row, left to right: *Margaret Middleton, Joyce Burton, John Tillett, Mick Mattia, Brian Smith, Doug Agnew, Mike Walker, Tony Sharpe, Ian Durham, Hugh Griffiths, Delia McCabe;* middle row: *Beryl Axell, Joy Fairy, Dave Allsopp, Barrie Creed, Al Westwood, Fran Boaler, Ged Armitt, Mike Jackson, Sue Smith, Pat Bailey, Lynne Colgrave, Janet Stott;* front row: *Betsan Lloyd, Jane Gettins, Jan Westwood, Cynthia Knight, Lynne Spedding, Ron Bedell, Zen Batowski, Tom James, Helen Conway, Alice Diack, Muriel York.*

technical drawing for boys and domestic science and needlecraft for girls.

Before embarking on this revolutionary path, the head teacher had to convince parents of the value of their children staying on at school for an extra year (until they were 16) in order to complete examination courses. In the event, 20 parents consented to his proposals and the courses went ahead successfully, with one candidate achieving six O-level passes and another five pupils each achieving five passes. At the time, such achievements were seen as remarkable and they were certainly a tribute to Mr Northall's foresight. From then on, O-level courses flourished at the school, with many pupils achieving creditable results. In the year prior to the introduction of the new CSE examination in 1967, 24 pupils achieved a total of 110 passes.

Meanwhile, the school had been encouraging the development of adult education. In 1959, the head teacher assumed responsibility for all evening adult-education classes in the school's catchment area. With the introduction of Posts of Special Responsibility, the governors were able to allocate a point for a teacher in charge of this area. As this aspect of the school grew, the local authority decided to create a purpose-built adult-education centre on the site.

In the 1950s, the newly developing school was plagued with building-related problems, not least those associated with water, a lot of which is frequently deposited on Chapel-en-le-Frith! The flat roofs of the building leaked rather badly and buckets and all manner of other receptacles capable of catching dripping water had to be placed strategically in corridors and classrooms. Strips of wood were placed across the doorways to classrooms, while sawdust was sprinkled liberally in a vain attempt to soak up the offending water.

In the early years of the school, there were no playing-fields and drystone walls marked the perimeter of the site. At times, the whole area was a sea of mud, with the only dry patches being the drive and a small service yard. Landscaping of the fields began in 1958: the drystone walls were dismantled and contractors began to dig out a cricket square. As they did so, two large springs were unearthed which supplied a stream running towards Combs Reservoir. Geologists from Sheffield University discovered that the school had been constructed on the site of an ancient lake! This news should not have come as a surprise, because the developers could have picked up some easy clues from the names of the neighbouring farms, such as Marsh Green and Marsh Hall.

In addition, water used to pour down the railway embankment and flood the site. A pump proved inadequate for the task and drastic measures had to be taken in the form of a 6ft-deep trench, which was dug around the whole site and then filled with limestone. On one occasion, Mr Bell informed the head teacher that he could smell gas. Gas-board officials were called to the scene, but they were unable to find a leak, until they discovered that the screw worm feeder at

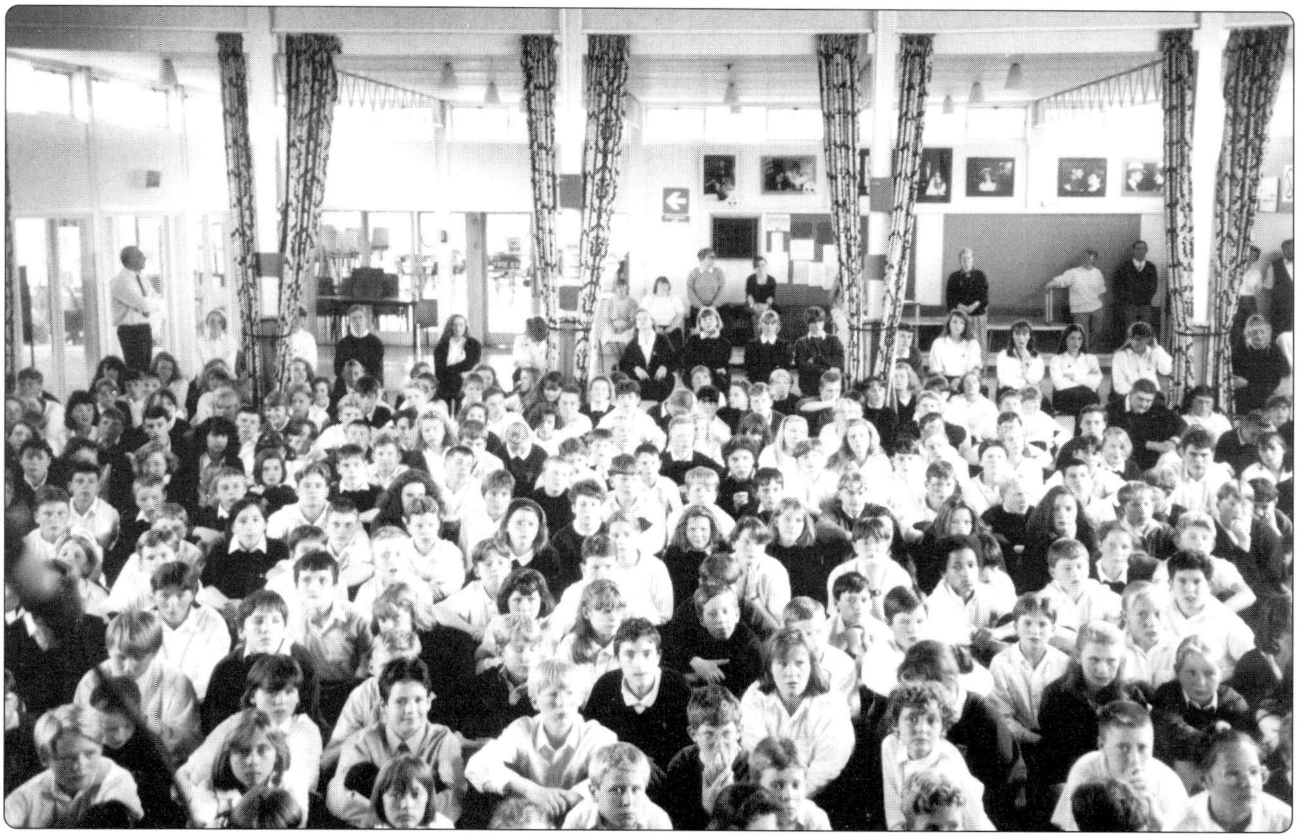

Dr Bedell's last assembly as head teacher, 1993.

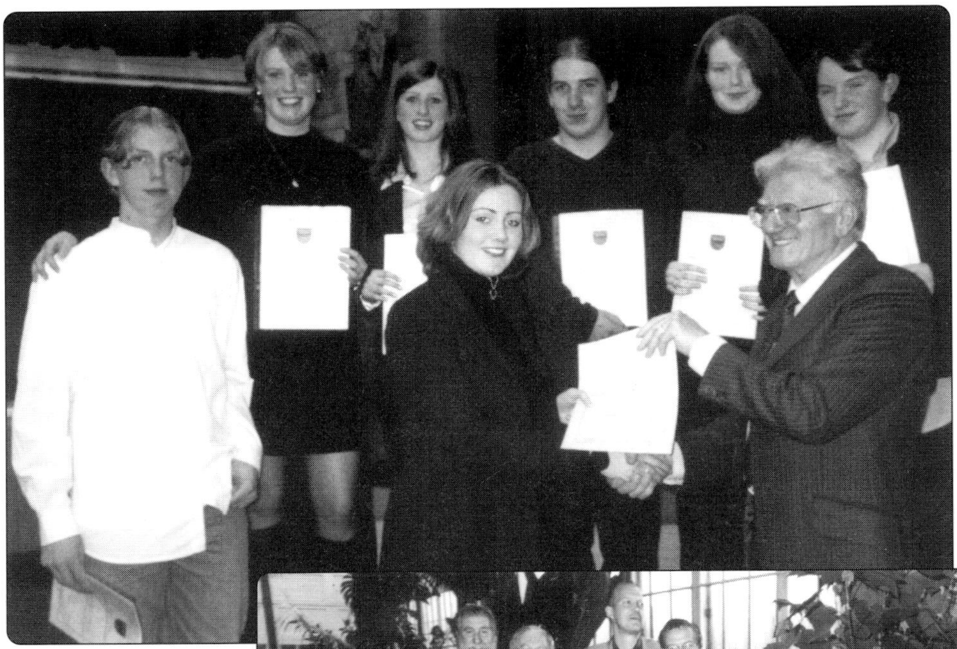

Dr Bedell returning to present certificates in 1996. Left to right: *Gareth Kirby, Emma Hudson, Suzanne MacMillan, Greg Davies, Sarah Bailey, Rachel Goy;* front: *Anna Beresford with Dr Ron Bebell.*

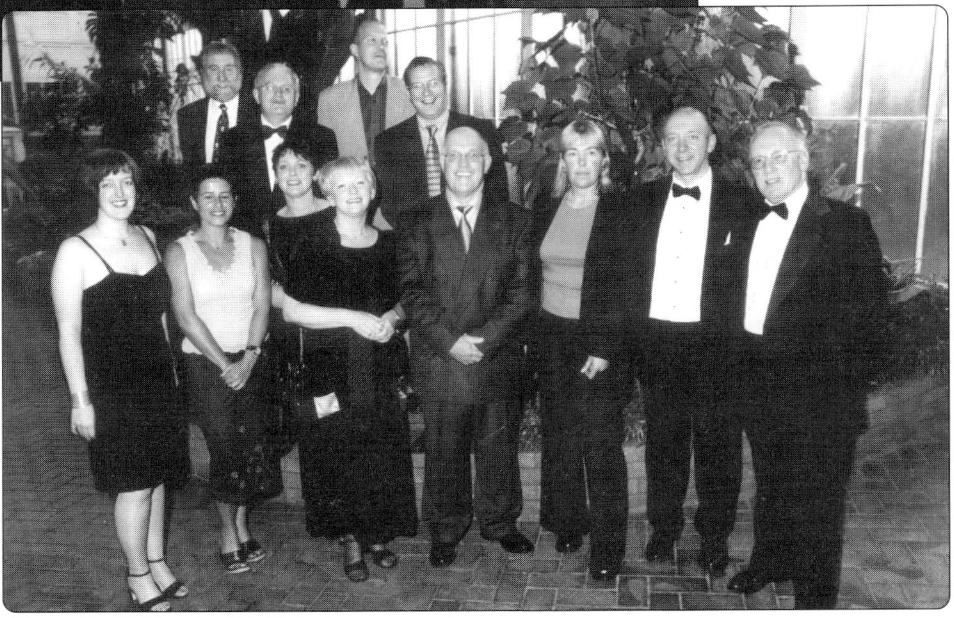

School staff attending a 'Prom' at the Pavilion Gardens, Buxton. Back, left to right: *Tom James, Stuart Ash, Tony Sharpe, Mark Jones;* front: *Linda Longhurst, Karen Todman, Pat Deery, Jan Westwood, John Tillett, Alison Massey, Zen Batowski, Hugh Griffiths.*

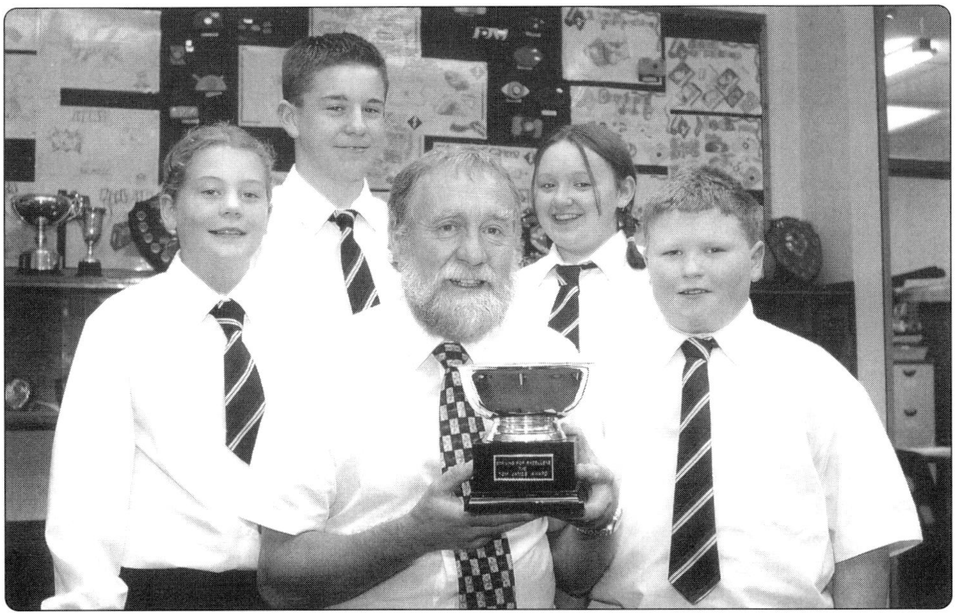

Tom James presenting a Rose Bowl trophy to the school on his retirement in 2002, after 37 years at the school.

the bottom of the coal bunker had become clogged with coal tar and had been producing coal gas throughout the previous winter by distilling the coal!

By the end of the 1950s, major building work had seen the addition of a gymnasium, an assembly hall, a stage, workshops for woodwork and metalwork and a three-storey block with domestic-science rooms and science laboratories. One former member of staff remembers the pride which the then caretaker, Mr Gibbons, took in his highly polished mahogany floor in the new hall. He even insisted that ladies at a prestigious dance attended by the Lord Lieutenant of Derbyshire should remove their stiletto-heeled shoes before dancing on 'his' floor!

By the commencement of the 1962–63 school year, there were 476 pupils on roll and 29 staff, plus the head teacher. Pupils were organised into ability groups, or 'streams', with three streams in each of the first three years and four classes in the fourth year. For the first time, pupils in the fourth year were given a choice between GCE, technical, commercial or practical courses. Mrs Knox, who had been deputy head since the school opened, was replaced by Eric Green, whose arrival coincided with the expansion of GCE courses.

Links were made between the school and Derbyshire's Outdoor Pursuits Centre at Whitehall, on Long Hill, which is still providing Chapel pupils with opportunities to enjoy a wide range of outdoor educational activities. During the 1960s, the school continued to give pupils a host of educational opportunities outside the classroom. Following on from their success at O-level, more and more pupils sought to continue their education beyond 16 and New Mills Grammar School became a popular choice for sixth-form education. One pupil, Ian Hawtin, who left Chapel School in 1964 and became a prefect at New Mills, went on to represent his county at both football and cricket before returning to take charge of PE at Long Lane School in 1971.

The school year 1965–66 was marred by the death in a car accident of PE teacher Pat Horrocks. Her death came as a tremendous shock to both colleagues and pupils. The death of staff in service is a relatively rare event in schools. However, in 1998, Helen Conway, who had served the school for over 25 years and who was in charge of biology, as well as being the school's examinations officer, also died in service.

By 1966–67, Long Lane School had over 500 pupils on roll and the number of GCE courses on offer had risen to 11 subjects, CSE French having been introduced for the first time. In light of recent events, it is worth noting that cross-country running had to be curtailed in 1967 because there had been an outbreak of foot-and-mouth disease in the area.

Towards the end of the year, the county received permission to build an adult-education centre on the existing site; it opened on 18 September 1970. The school was offered use of its modern facilities, including two small carpeted teaching areas, a lounge and coffee bar.

A Government circular issued in 1965 had outlined proposals for the raising of the school-leaving age to 16 and for the introduction of comprehensive education. A further building programme was required to cope with comprehensive reorganisation and this took place in two phases; one was completed for the first comprehensive intake in 1973 and the second for 1976, when the school was expected to have over 900 pupils on roll as the result of large-scale housing developments in Chapel-en-le-Frith and Whaley Bridge.

Courses in connection with the raising of the school-leaving age (ROSLA) began in September 1972. The early 1970s also saw the introduction of language laboratories in secondary schools as an aid to the teaching of modern languages. In line with this new thinking, Long Lane School embarked on the conversion of a French teaching room. However, the language laboratory did not stand the test of time and the room reverted back to a normal classroom after a short period. A rather more memorable experience for students of French was a trip to Brittany organised by the French and German departments. The party of pupils and staff arrived at their French hotel in a very sorry state after a prolonged crossing in a force-nine gale, only to be greeted with a meal of greasy chicken and chips. Needless to say, there were very few takers!

Fred Millward, who had taught woodwork in the old Horsa-hut site opposite the New Inn, even before Long Lane School had opened in 1952, retired in 1972. The following school year saw a period of intense building activity. The old library and staff room were demolished and temporarily replaced by a prefabricated building erected on the hard play area in front of the school – this later became the staff car park, which was required because teachers gradually became sufficiently affluent to join the age of the internal combustion engine! A constant stream of tractors and bulldozers and the persistent noise of circular saws cutting through building blocks and concrete slabs made conditions for both teaching and learning almost intolerable.

Older pupils helped to move furniture and equipment into the new buildings at the start of the autumn term of 1973. The school had a new staff room, new offices for the head teacher and two deputies, a library, a lecture theatre with tiered seating, a new suite of rooms for history and geography, a much larger gymnasium and changing rooms, plus a dining-room above the lecture theatre. There were new workshops for woodwork, metalwork and technical drawing, together with three new art rooms, which were joined to the existing adult-education centre. However, the new boiler house wasn't ready for the start of the new school year and wasn't handed over, in fact, until the last day of January 1974.

September 1973 saw the arrival of the first fully comprehensive intake – the school had evolved from being a Secondary Modern School into a comprehensive school, albeit one without a sixth form. Over the next few years, the lack of a sixth form became a major issue with some parents and governors, who set out to persuade the LEA that the school needed a sixth form if it was to have the same status as New Mills Grammar School. However, the LEA rejected the proposals, on the grounds that two 11–18 schools in such close proximity would have sixth forms which would not have sufficient numbers of students to enable them to offer an acceptable range of A-level studies. As New Mills already had a sixth form, it was decided that Long Lane School should remain as an 11–16 establishment.

Dan Northall retired at Easter 1975, having been head teacher at the school for 23 years. His successor was Dr Ron Bedell, who had previously been a deputy head teacher at a school in Sutton Coldfield. There was a short transition period from Easter until the start of the next term when Eric Green was acting head teacher.

During the late 1970s, the school continued to grow in size due to the effects of an increased birth rate and the extensive housing developments in the catchment area. By 1977, when the number on roll exceeded 900, there was an acute shortage of teaching space. The upper and lower dining-rooms had to be used as classrooms, often with two classes in each room, and even the stage had to be commandeered as a classroom on occasions.

By the late 1980s, numbers on roll had declined significantly. This was partly as a result of the fall in the birth rate, but was also because some parents decided to send their children to other schools in the area. Their reasons were varied, but the lack of a sixth form was frequently cited.

By 1988, the old GCE and CSE examinations at 16+ had been replaced by GCSEs. The Technical and Vocational Education Initiative (TVEI) had also been introduced as a result of the 1988 Education Act. Developments in careers education, the introduction of work experience for pupils and a thriving Parent Teacher Association were all features of this period. Trips to locations at home and abroad continued to grow in number, and many staff and pupils became involved in music and drama activities, including a number of fine drama productions inspired by Chris Bridge, deputy head.

Dr Bedell remained as head teacher until his retirement in the summer of 1993. He was succeeded by the head teacher at the time of writing, Stuart Ash, who had previously been a deputy head teacher at Wilmslow High School. Two of Stuart's early initiatives were the relabelling of the school as Chapel-en-le-Frith High School and the introduction of a school uniform. Despite the new name, there are many older people in the community who continue to refer to the school as Long Lane School.

May 1994 saw the Standard Attainment Tests (SATs) for 14-year-olds in English, Mathematics and Science completed for the first time. In the autumn of that same year, the first OFSTED inspection took place and the resulting report confirmed the good work being done at the school, which was granted 'Investors in People' status the following year. The 1996 GCSE results were the best of any Derbyshire local authority school in terms of the number of pupils achieving five or more A–C passes.

OFSTED made another inspection in December 1999 and again praised the work of staff and pupils. However, as in the previous inspection, there were critical comments about the state of the buildings, although this deficiency was no fault of the staff or governors. Indeed, during both the Dr Bedell era and the 1990s, a great deal of work had been undertaken to create new classrooms and administrative areas within the framework of the existing building. For example, the old lecture theatre had been converted into a modern and attractive ICT room, in order to service the increasing use of computer technology across the curriculum.

During the early part of the autumn term in the millennium year, consultation took place in relation to the planned closure of John Duncan Special School in Buxton. This resulted in a decision to replace the existing Chapel school with an enhanced-resource school, to cater for the needs of pupils who would have attended John Duncan School and in the process it will give the pupils of Chapel-en-le-Frith hugely improved facilities. The cost of this large new building, erected on a site immediately adjacent to the old school building, was met by a Private Funding Initiative (PFI) and on 12 May 2001 a contract was signed with Babcock & Brown, who had emerged as the preferred bidder. Construction began in the summer of 2001 and by January 2002 the first phase was completed, giving the school new tennis and netball courts and an all-weather pitch.

Not surprisingly, the contractors experienced a few drainage problems! Their report included the following observation:

Ground conditions are particularly poor on the site, which lies at the base of a bowl, and the site drains poorly. The area lies over an artesian basin, with a water head encountered at 10m. This unfortunately prevented the use of piled foundations (unless the intention was to create the 'Old Faithful of the Peak').

The second phase of the building operations (construction of the main building) began in September 2001 and was completed during the spring of 2003. The old school building was then demolished and the vacated area used to accommodate a car park and an outdoor sports area. Staff and pupils were enthusiastic about their move to the new school, which was designed to provide educational facilities of a very high standard, as well as give the people of Chapel-en-le-Frith access to much-needed community leisure facilities.

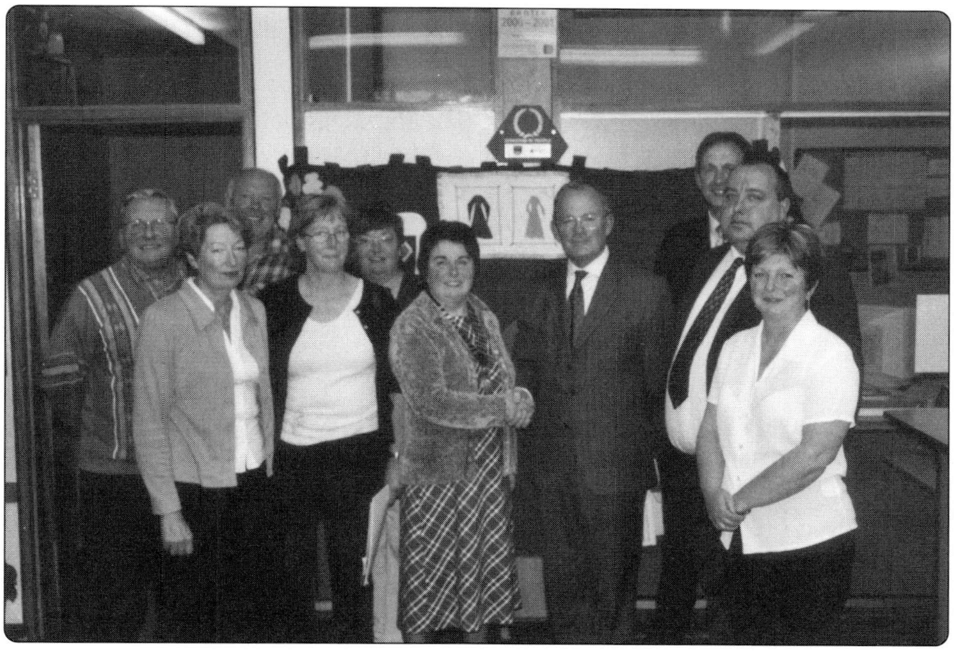

Members of the leisure centre committee meeting with representatives of City Centre Leisure in 2002 to discuss the make-up of the new leisure centre. Left to right: *Peter Harrison, Lynne Hartley, Robert Barratt, Sue Bamford, Margaret Bullen, Margaret Dyson (chair of Parish Council), Roger Bottomley (chairman of City Centre Leisure), David Swinburn, Tim Norton, Anne Western.*

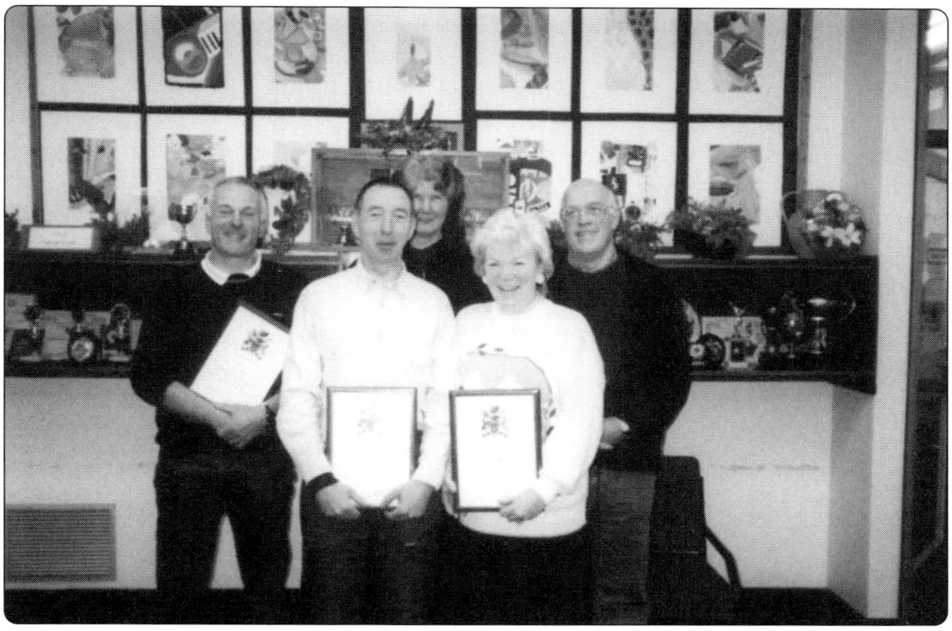

Celebrating 25 years' service with Derbyshire Education Authority are Mike Walker, David Allsopp, Frances Boaler, Mary Alger and John Tillett.

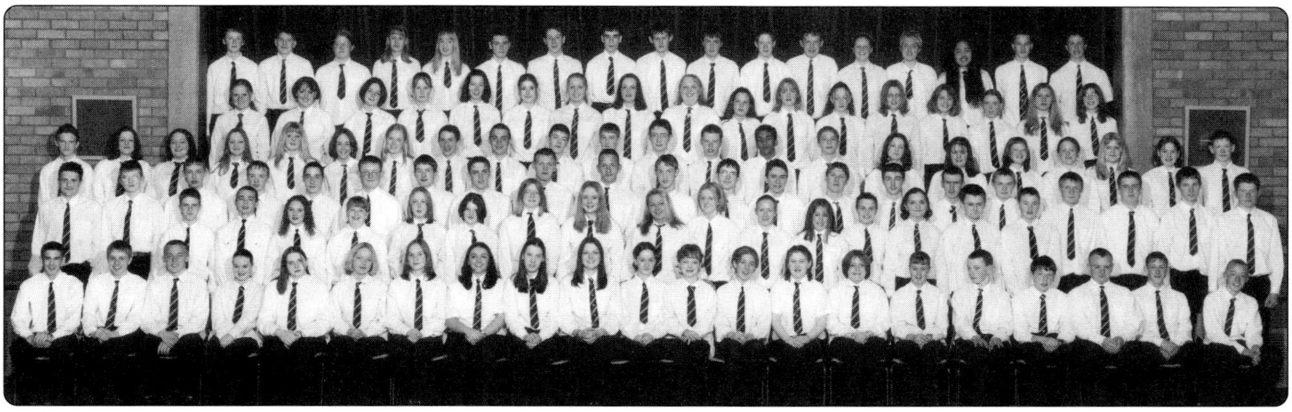

Chapel High School in 2002.

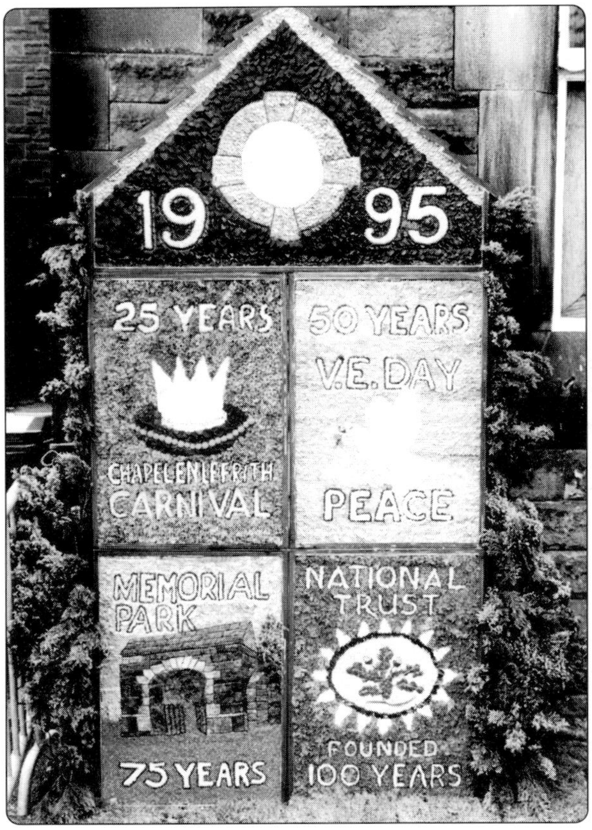

The Town Well, 1995 (first effort).

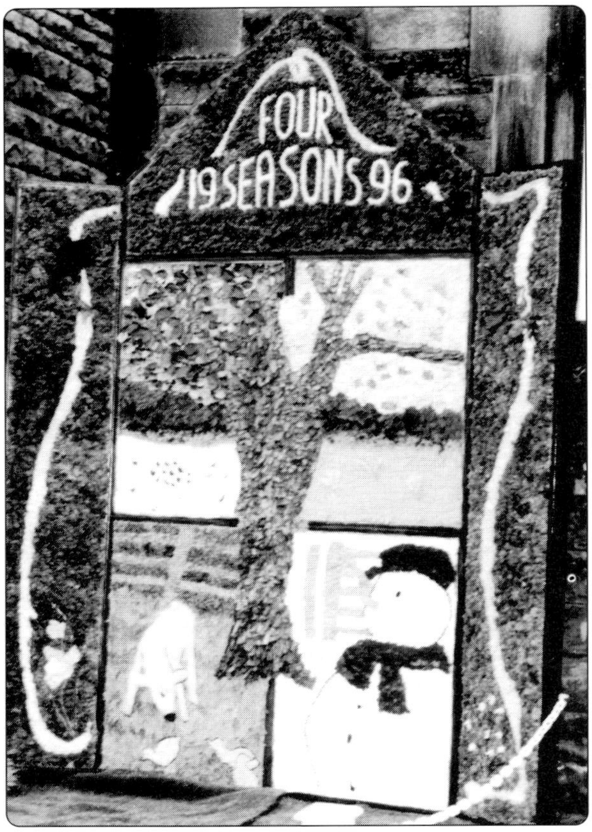

The Town Well, 1996 (still with the quadripartite arrangement).

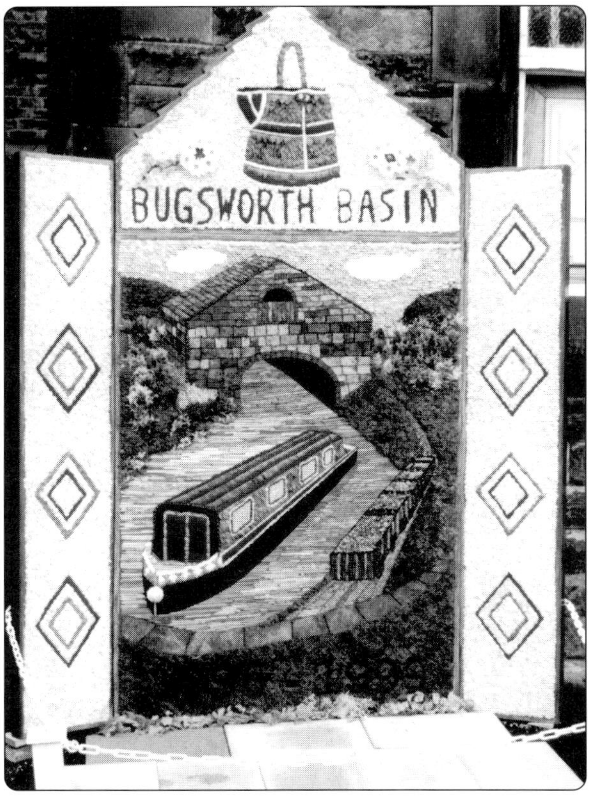

The Town Well, 1999 (commemorating the reopening of the Bugsworth Canal Basin).

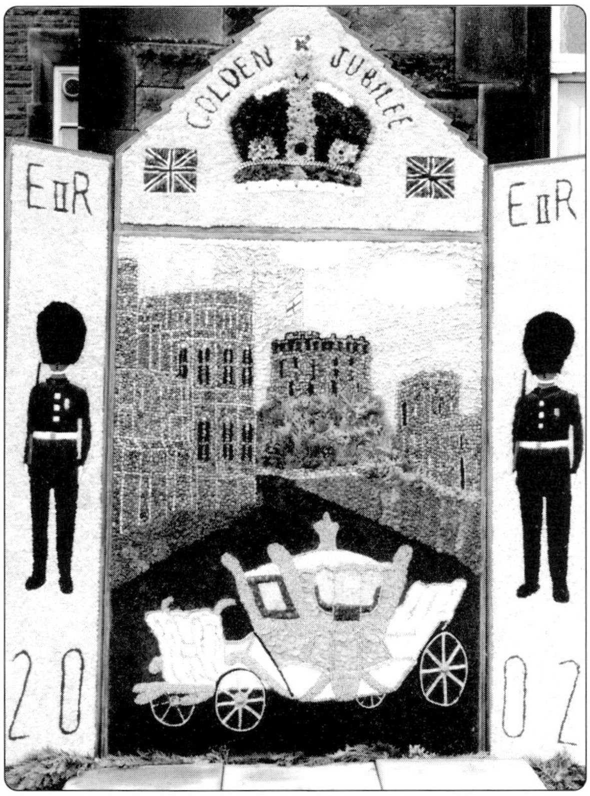

The Town Well, 2002 (commemorating the Queen's golden jubilee).

Chapter 7

Keeping up a Tradition

Three annual events are now firmly established in Chapel-en-le-Frith – the well dressing, the carnival and the Christmas lights. The carnival tradition dates back many years, but the custom lapsed for a time before being revived in 1970. The other customs are of more recent foundation: the annual display of illuminated Christmas trees was begun in the late 1960s and annual well dressings started in 1995.

The well-known English tradition of Morris dancing is also firmly established in the town. Church records show that Morris dancing was practised in Chapel-en-le-Frith in the eighteenth century, but lapsed before being revived in 1975.

Although particular individuals and organisations have been responsible for initiating or reviving these traditions, there is every reason to suppose that they will now continue indefinitely.

Well Dressed

By Mike Smith, chairman of the Well Dressing Committee.

Was it a thanksgiving for a supply of pure water during the Black Death? An expression of gratitude for a productive well in a period of drought? Or a pagan ceremony which was hijacked by Christians? The origin of the Peak District tradition of well dressing is uncertain, but the current popularity of the custom, which is now practised in over 70 towns and villages, can be explained very easily – well dressings are a great means of pulling in the tourists!

Well dressing, in the form of a Christian-sponsored event, is a White Peak tradition which began over 650 years ago in the village of Tissington, and then spread to other settlements on the limestone plateau. In recent years, Dark Peak villagers have shown a determination not to be left out and many places in the gritstone hills of the High Peak now have an annual dressing of the wells.

In 1995 members of Chapel-en-le-Frith's Amenity Society decided it was high time that Chapel joined in the summer round of dressings. Our decision was based on a simple sentiment: 'Everyone else does it, so why shouldn't we?' In many ways, our enthusiasm for the project was foolhardy. All of us knew about the strict rules governing the ancient custom, which demand that only natural products, such as petals, leaves, stones and bark, must be used to create the pictures, and we were all aware that the decorations are created by pressing the materials onto damp clay contained in large wooden boards, but not one of us had any experience whatsoever of the practicalities of well dressing.

Our first task was to consult the experts. We asked David Sanders, an experienced well dresser from the Hope Valley, to give us a demonstration. Thanks to David, we learned how to overlap petals on the clay in the manner of tiling a roof. We also spent an afternoon at Tissington and watched in awe as the dressers there produced pictures which seemed perfect in every way – fashioned with precision, appropriately coloured, realistic, and entirely correct in their perspective. All the members of our committee, which is a sub-group of the Amenity Society, spent much of the summer of 1994 visiting villages where wells are dressed. While other visitors stood back to admire the flowery compositions, we peered closely at the make-up of the pictures and examined them forensically.

It did not take us long to discover an important truth – every village has its own method of dressing. Some dressers use only flowers, others make liberal use of stone and bark; some pictures are made up of petals, whereas others feature whole flowers; some dressers prick out their entire pictures on the clay with pins or needles, others cut out their compositions in sections and work on one area at a time. There was also the vexed question of outlining. David Sanders had told us that it was not necessary to outline the shapes in our pictures, because borders could be created simply by tucking the petals into the clay. The dressers of Tissington were equally adamant that outlining was necessary in order to create definition. We also found that some villages had pictures with figures outlined in coffee beans, while others used wool.

Just as we were trying to reconcile these conflicting pieces of evidence and advice, we made an unexpected and important discovery: Chris Thomas, a teacher at Chapel's Warmbrook Junior School, had been producing little well dressings with pupils in her classes for almost a decade. The dressings had not been displayed in the street, but they had been constructed in the traditional manner, with a

Right: *Puddling the clay before it is placed in the boards.*

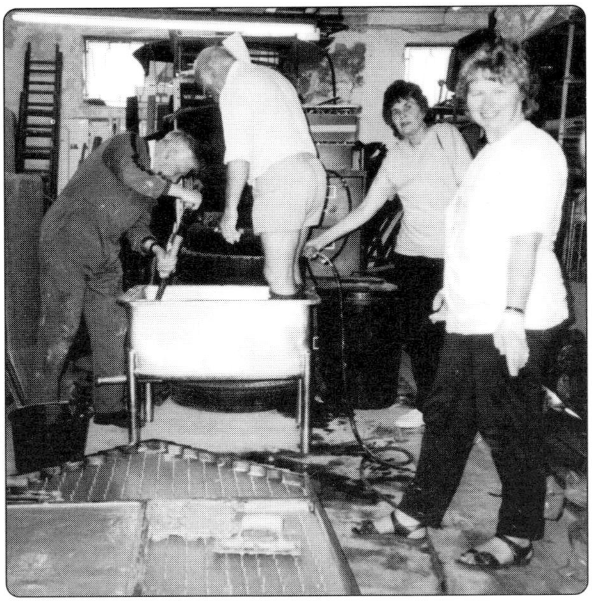

Bill Stevenson at the newly unearthed Windy Wall Well.

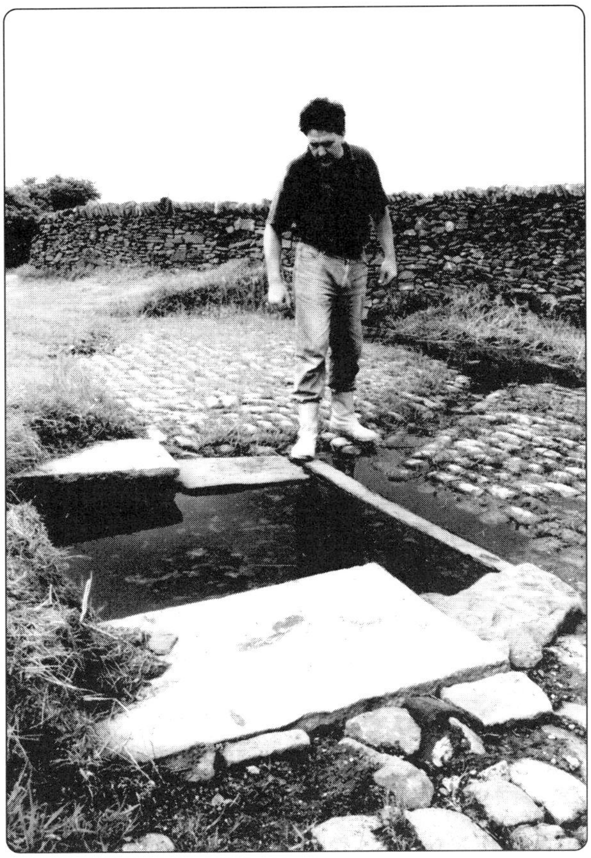

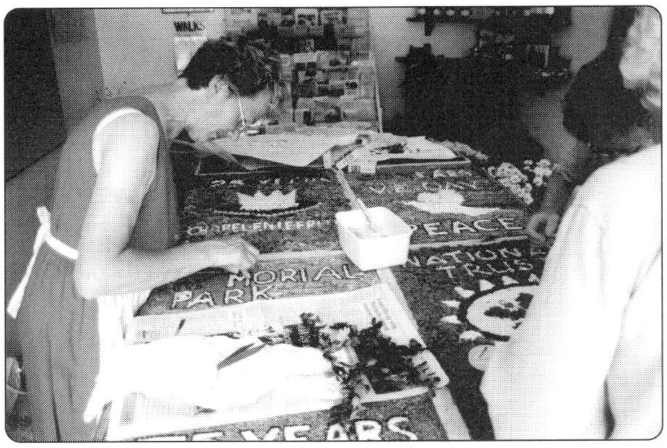

Dressing the clay.

Children from Warmbrook Junior School with their well at the blessing ceremony.

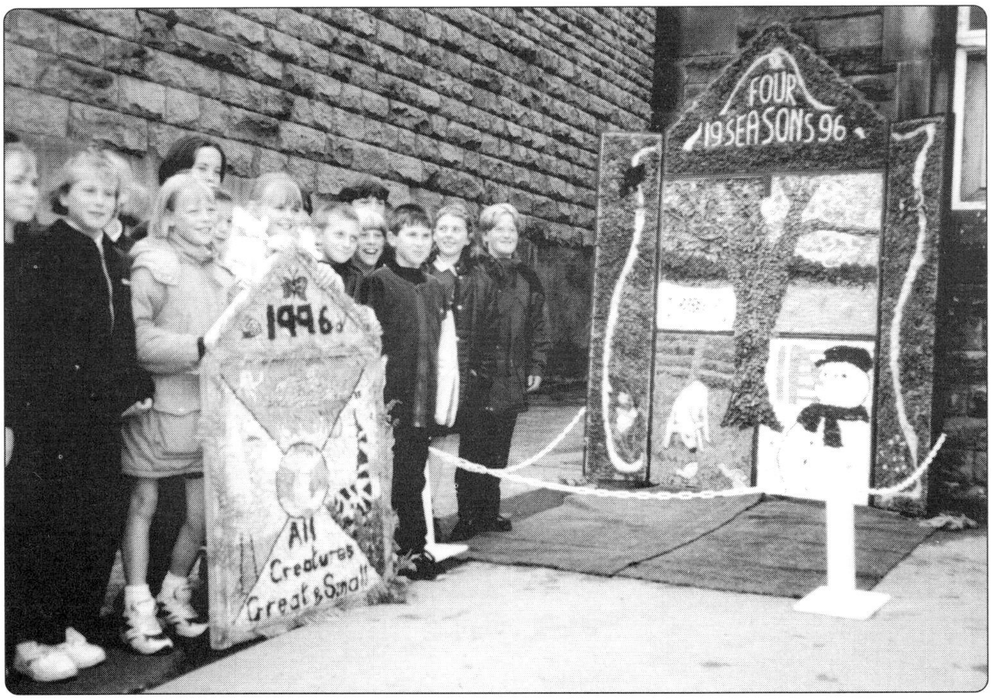

strict adherence to the ancient rubric. We needed Chris' expertise and she was quickly co-opted onto our committee.

By January 1995 the members felt brave enough to give the new venture a try. We decided that we would prepare our dressings for display during carnival week, when there would be lots of people in the town. We decided to add a novel touch by constructing a board with the same shape as the façade of our little visitor centre, a simple, symmetrical former Hearse House which has a porthole-like window in its apex. We also made the main frame of our board into a quadripartite arrangement, which would allow us to accommodate four pictures rather than the usual one.

The four-part arrangement was largely driven by our decision to use our first dressing to commemorate four key events – 25 years since the revival of the town's carnival, 50 years since VE Day, 75 years since the founding of the Memorial Park, and the 100th anniversary of the National Trust. We commissioned Neil Bennett, a local artist, to draw our pictures and we then added another novel touch by asking Richard Weedon to transfer the images to computer screen so that we could make adjustments to the sizes, colours and shapes featured in the composition.

Pleased with our creative and original thinking, we embarked on a six-month planning process, followed by two days of exhausting, messy, but enjoyable 'puddling' (trampling in the wet clay to give it the correct consistency) and three days of intensive 'dressing' (producing the picture by pressing the petals and other materials in the clay). We issued press releases stressing the uniqueness of our hi-tech, quadripartite dressing and, with foolish bravery, we invited members of the public to visit the Hearse House and watch the process of creating the pictures. In truth, we were novices posing as experts!

We did, of course, make horrendous mistakes. After much discussion, we had decided that we would outline some of the shapes in our pictures and we chose to use cloves for this purpose. On the second day of dressing, we turned up to find that oil from the cloves had run onto the neighbouring petals and badly discoloured them. After debating whether we could pass this off as a deliberate artistic device, we realised that we would have to unpick our work and start again!

The quadripartite structure of our board would also prove to be a problem. The arrangement was fine for our first chosen theme of four anniversaries, but it left us with the annual task of thinking up ideas that would lend themselves to four picture panels. In the fifth year of dressing, our creative quadripartite thinking dried up and we modified our board so that it could accommodate just one large picture, rather than a group of four.

But we did also have our successes. One of our members, Joyce Taylor, discovered that dried rhubarb leaves, when cut into squares, make a realistic representation of stonework on gritstone buildings; our two Brians (Brian Aries, chairman of the Amenity Society and Bryan Bywater, a local businessman) proved to have all the practical skills necessary for the constructional work; and all the dressers became incredibly enthusiastic and dedicated to their task, often spending six or more hours at a time working on their particular corner of the picture. It soon became obvious to us that well dressing provides a wonderful opportunity to harness talents and foster community spirit and pride.

It was my task to go around the village at 6a.m. on the big day and round up eight strong men to carry the dressed boards to the forecourt of the Town Hall, where they would be put on display for a week. After the main well was put in place and the Children's Well was put out for exhibition in the Hearse House Visitor Centre, all our dressers patted themselves on the back and rejoiced in the establishment of a new custom in Chapel-en-le-Frith.

We had asked the parish chaplain to conduct a blessing ceremony and he duly obliged by coming up with a suitably watery theme for his address and a selection of hymns which included 'The Water of Life'. With a little embarrassment we had to inform him that we had cheated a little. Chapel once possessed over 20 wells, but its main surviving well, Nanny's Well, is on the edge of town, and we wanted our display to be in a more central location. We had been pleased to discover that the Old Brewery Well once occupied a site close to the Town Hall, where our dressing would be displayed, but we were forced to admit that our well was rather unusual in having no water! The minister hastily altered the details of his blessing ceremony.

After the qualified success of our first venture, we resolved to make the event an annual one, but none of us could predict that our initiative would lead to a spectacular year-by-year growth of well dressing and even inspire some townspeople to uncover long-hidden wells. Bill Stevenson and his family uncovered and renovated an old well across the road from Windy Walls, their hilltop farmhouse, a mile or so south of the town, and the family and their helpers decided that they would produce an annual dressing there. Jonathan Danson uncovered an old well in the Town End area of Chapel and duly used his considerable artistic skills and enlisted a team of helpers to produce a dressing for it. His mother Emmy decided that she would produce a small dressing at the Bear Well, where an unfortunate performing bear was once given water on its way to be chastised on Chapel Market Place. Kath Bancroft, Ann Young and their team then resolved that they would produce a dressing at Nanny's Well, an old medicinal spring which is said to have enjoyed the protection of St Ann or St Ninnian (a name which became corrupted to Nanny).

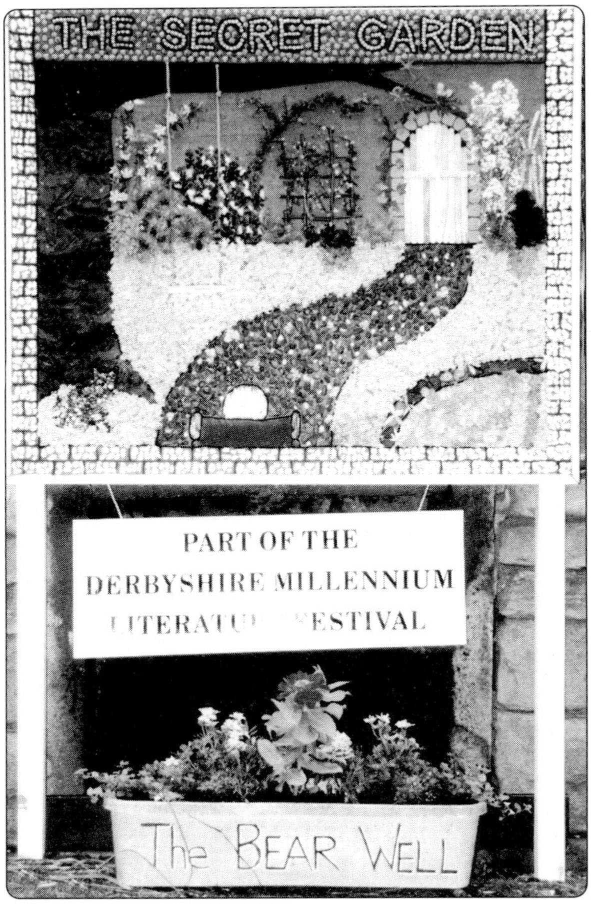

Bear Well.

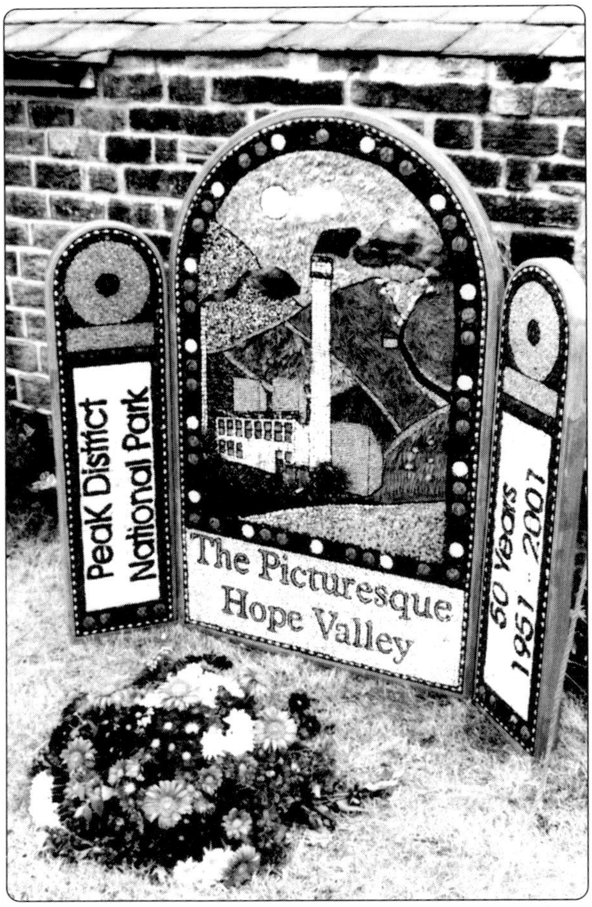

Bowden Lane Well (with a touch of irony).

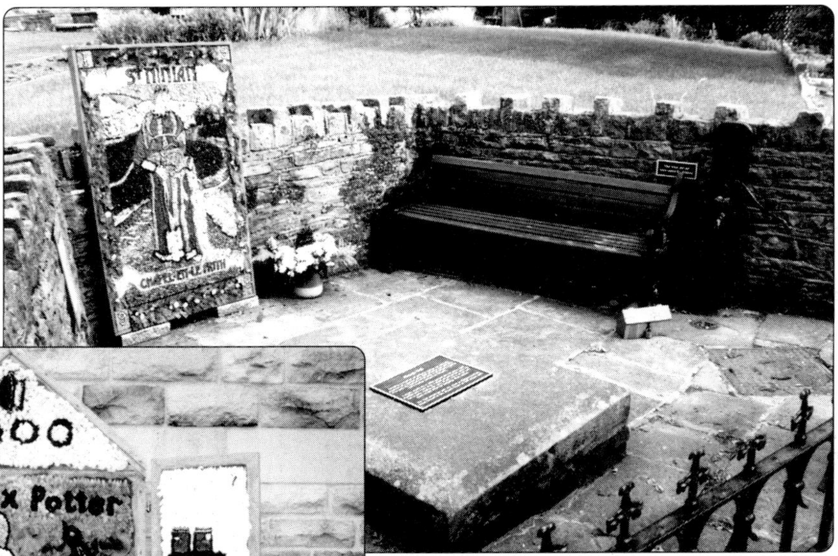

Nanny's Well,
a medicinal spring.

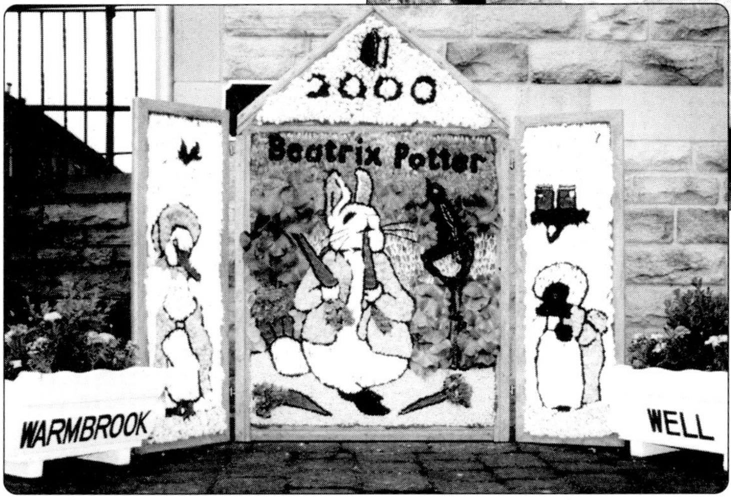

The Children's Well.

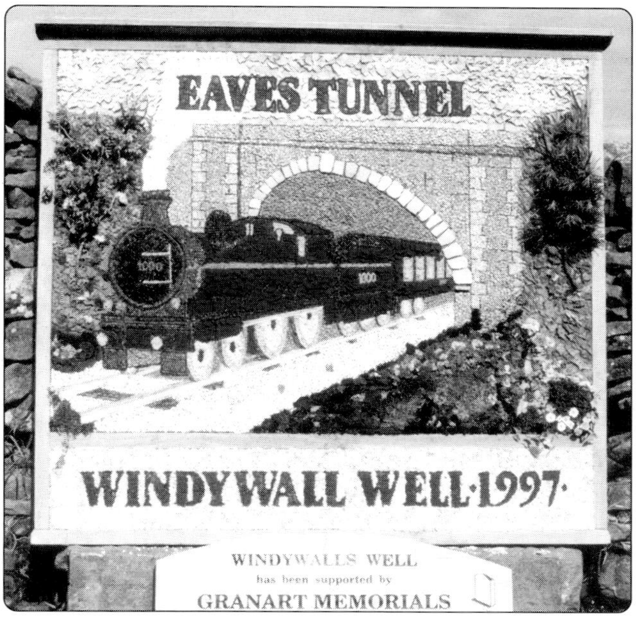

The Windy Wall Well.

Meanwhile, it was decided to place the Children's Well, which had grown two side panels by this stage, on public display each year outside the Methodist Church. All the children in Year Six at Chapel's primary school are given the chance to contribute to the making of the dressing. The experience they gain should enable some of them to make up the Well Dressing Committee of the future and so ensure the continuity of this ancient Peak District custom which is now so firmly established in Chapel-en-le-Frith.

Chapel Carnival

The 2003 Chapel-en-le-Frith carnival will be the 33rd to be held since the tradition of an annual procession and pageant in the town was revived. The carnival has its origins in the Hospital Gala Days, which were held in the early years of the last century on the nearest Saturday to 7 July, the Feast Day of St Thomas. Chapel's Parish Church, which is dedicated to St Thomas Becket, was first consecrated as a chapel of ease in 1225, exactly 55 years to the day after the saint was murdered in Canterbury Cathedral.

Proceeds from the Gala Day were always donated to the Hospital Fund and the festivities marked the beginning of the town's Wakes Week, when all the local factories shut down for the annual holidays, except for the Ferodo works, which remained open throughout the year in those early days.

During the 1930s the carnival procession ended in the football field on Park Road, where Commander Cook acted as Master of Ceremonies. According to tradition, the crowning of the Chapel carnival queen was followed by the entry of the Cotton Queen, who was sponsored by the *Daily Dispatch* and the Whitworth Doubling Company. On the evening of carnival day, a dance always took place in the Town Hall, with the queen in radiant attendance.

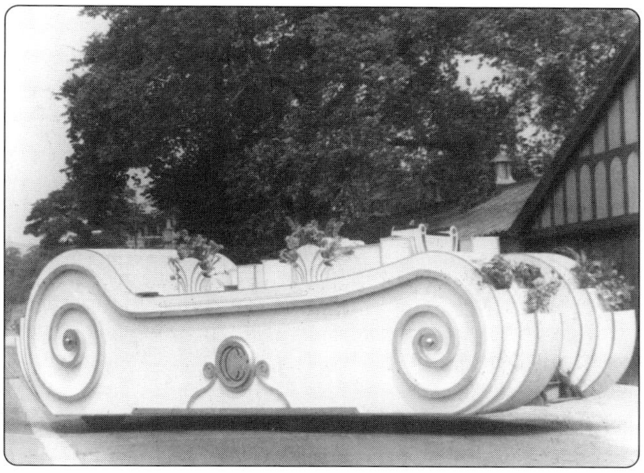

Streamlined float.

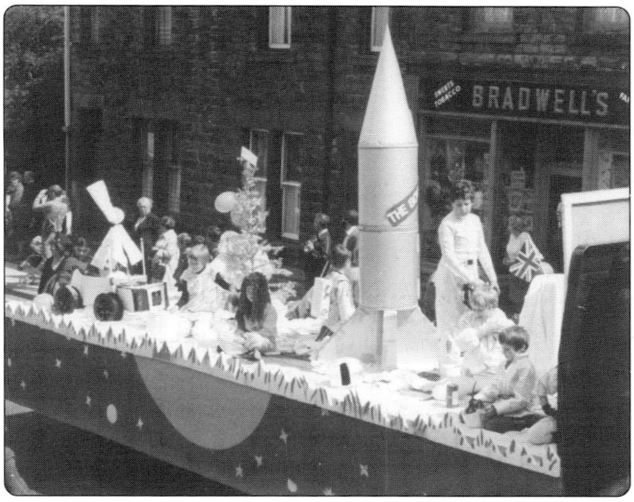

Rocket Science.

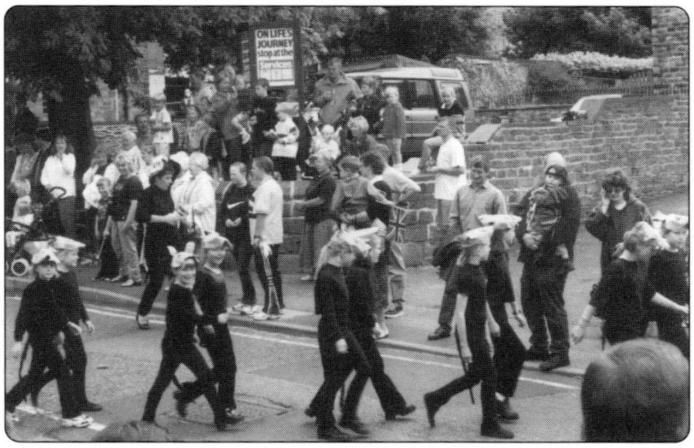

On foot in the carnival.

The procession took a long route from Blackbrook Lane to Cockyard and then on to the presentation arena. The famous 'Hazel Grove Twins', Mr Rowbotham and Mr Clough, who made regular appearances at Chapel carnival, gathered some £11,000 for charity in their galvanised buckets over the years.

Competitions for the best-dressed houses, shops, pubs, lampposts and windows have long been a feature of carnival week and local businesses have

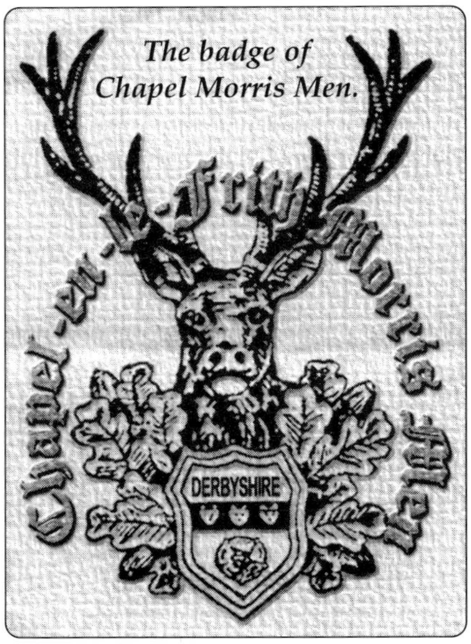

The badge of Chapel Morris Men.

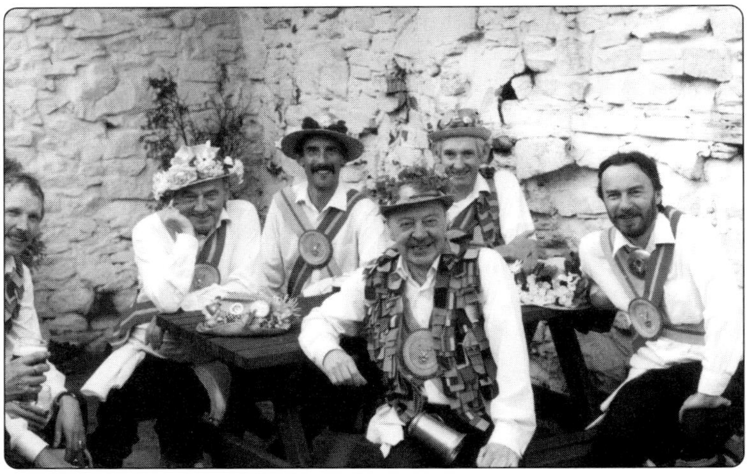

Left to right: *Will Newman, Alex Needham, Nigel Lloyd, Jim Hirst, Peter Helps and Robin Edwards at the Glossop Victorian Weekend, 1996.*

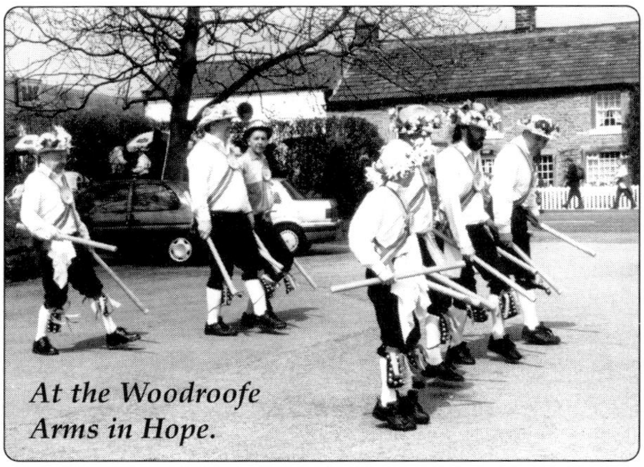

At the Woodroofe Arms in Hope.

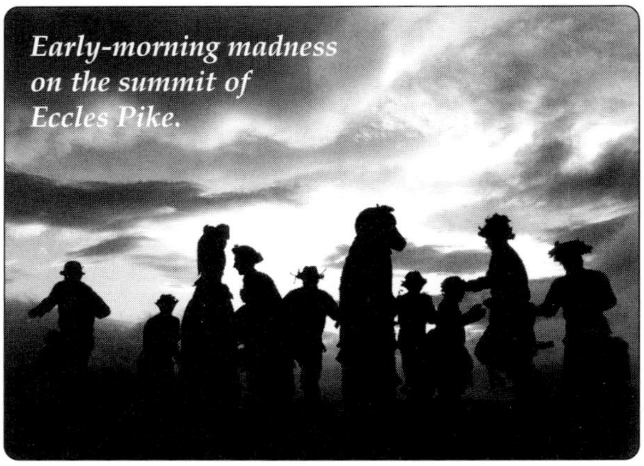

Early-morning madness on the summit of Eccles Pike.

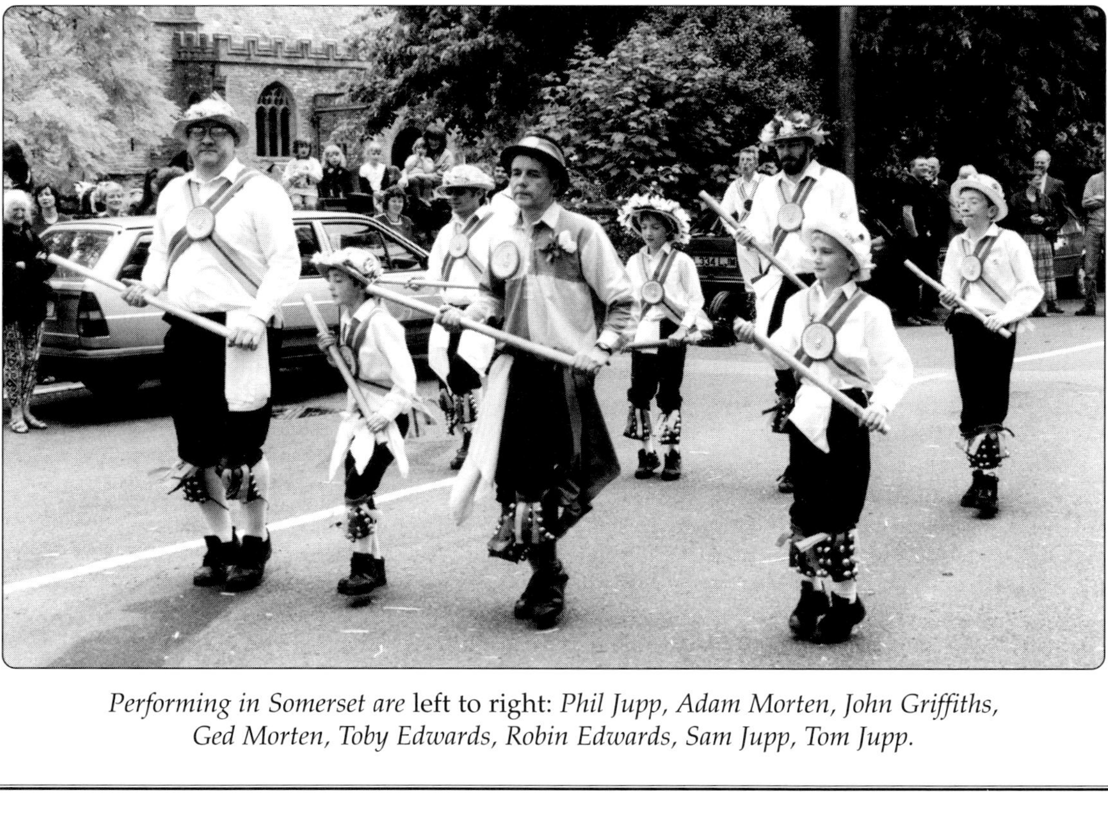

Performing in Somerset are left to right: *Phil Jupp, Adam Morten, John Griffiths, Ged Morten, Toby Edwards, Robin Edwards, Sam Jupp, Tom Jupp.*

always played an important part in the events. During the 1937 carnival week, Hardware Services offered a prize of one guinea to anyone who could name and give the function of 100 items on display in their shop window.

The carnival tradition lapsed during the Second World War, but was revived in the late 1940s when a group of local men constructed the artificial mound in the Memorial Park where the carnival queens are now presented. After another lapse, the carnival was revived in 1970 and has continued to this day.

Carnivals are held in many towns and villages throughout the Peak District and all of them require the presence in their procession of bands, dance troupes and queens from other villages. A few years ago, the organisers of Chapel carnival decided to make the date of their event one fortnight earlier than the traditional weekend, in order to avoid clashes with other local carnivals. The date may have changed, but the organisers and participants in Chapel-en-le-Frith's carnival continue to maintain a long-standing and much-cherished tradition.

Chapel Morris Dancers

Compiled from the collective recollections of Peter Helps, Jim Hirst, Randall Dawson, Will Newman, Nigel Lloyd and Julian Barber.

The origins of Morris dancing are uncertain, but probably date back thousands of years. What is certain is that the activity is very mystical and magical. The Morris is a ritual dance that has been passed down over the centuries; it began as a fertility rite performed at the time of seed sowing and was intended to bring good fortune to the crops. The dance was always a countryman's ritual, and the drift of population from the land to the cities during the eighteenth and nineteenth centuries led to many traditions dying out. However, a chance encounter between Headington Morris Men and Cecil Sharp, the folksong collector, led to a revival of the Morris.

After the First World War, and the death of so many men who had danced, the Morris could easily have been lost forever. Thankfully, there was a revival of interest and new sides were formed to replace those which had vanished – some sides were even established in areas where no traditions had been recorded. In 1934, six of the revival sides met to inaugurate the Morris Ring, with the purpose of preserving and promoting the traditions of the Morris. This organisation now boasts nearly 300 members and associate teams.

In his book, *The Parish Church of St Thomas Becket*, William Braylesford Bunting records that 3s. were paid to Morris dancers at rushbearing in 1758. It would seem that rushbearing was an annual ceremony in the town and that rushes were fetched from Rushop and Poors Piece by schoolchildren and others and carried in a procession, which included a band and a group of Morris dancers, to the church, where they were spread in the centre aisle and remained for a week. This ceremony may have persisted until the late-nineteenth century.

The origins of the current Morris side in Chapel date back to 1975, when Will Newman and Alan Wilson placed a letter in the local newspaper asking men who might be interested in forming a Morris side to contact them. The dozen brave souls who turned up to an inaugural meeting at the King's Arms in the autumn of 1975 included only one man, Jim Hirst, who had danced before. Undaunted, the group decided to form a side and take up the offer of a practice room at Chapel High School, where they would attempt to learn the art of Cotswold dancing under Jim's tuition. The group included an accordionist, Mike, whose wife had taken to grumbling about the persistent sound of the accordion in their home. Mike was more than pleased to offer his services to the dancers.

At the end of their first term, the new side, which had managed to put together a repertoire of six dances, had to face a stiff examination set by Jim Hirst's brother, Stuart, who invited the embryonic Chapel Morris Dancers to perform at a folk-dancing club which he had formed in Sandbach. Heartened by their survival at this event, the dancers went on to perform at the Whitestones and Elms care homes and outside the Dog Inn and the New Inn.

The members of the new side went for their Christmas dinner to the Chimes, at Taxal, where they had a stroke of luck in finding a second accordion player, Randall Dawson, who happened to be enjoying a Christmas dinner at the pub with his colleagues from the National Westminster Bank.

By Easter 1976 the members of Chapel Morris Men were confident enough to undertake a Peak District tour, which included Edale, Castleton and Buxton. The side had adopted a costume of white shirts and socks, black shoes and breeches, decorated straw hats and crossed baldricks in yellow and green, with a stag's head emblem in the centre to represent Chapel-en-le-Frith's historic links with the royal hunting forest that once covered the area.

In the same year, six members of the side went to a folk festival at Sidmouth, where they hired a cottage which turned out to be the former home of the Rodneys, of Admiral Rodney fame. During the course of the festival, they not only enjoyed the fellowship which is always engendered at any gathering of Morris Men, but also learned a great deal from attending workshops, watching other teams and even joining in as guests with some of the best teams in the country. However, as Morris dancing novices, they were somewhat taken aback and almost overcome with nerves when they inadvertently found themselves performing before the assembled experts after joining in a procession which ended up on the stage.

The side adopted a routine of practising on Monday nights in the winter months, initially in the upper room of the King's Arms and, more recently, at the Playhouse (formerly the Constitutional Hall) and performing in the summer months. Eventually, the side collected a repertoire of 26 dances and graduated, in 1980, from associate to full membership of the Morris Ring, after they had been proposed by the Morris Men of Stafford and Derby. Jim Hirst was presented with the white staff, which signifies full membership, at a ceremony in Ledbury.

The Chapel dancers tour Peak villages throughout the summer and make an annual appearance at the Buxton Festival, where they enjoy performing in the congenial surroundings of the Pavilion Gardens. They also have one or two weekends away each year, when they perform at festivals in various parts of the country, and they have even danced at Vaassen, in Holland, and Osnabrück, in Germany.

Robin Edwards, a one-time resident of Eccles Road, was responsible for initiating a very special annual event which involves the Chapel Morris Men performing on the summit of Eccles Pike at 5a.m. on May Day. This piece of madness is followed by breakfast at the King's Arms.

The Chapel Morris Men have three rather special claims to fame: they performed for the crowds when Princess Diana visited the High Peak in 1991; they appeared on Australian television, because a crew happened to be filming while they were dancing at Chatsworth House; and they even attracted coverage in the *News of the World* after performing in a local farmer's barren field. No crops grew as a result of their dance, but a bull escaped from the field a few days later and went on the rampage amongst a group of heifers!

Christmas Lights

Chapel-en-le-Frith's main street and Market Place become a blaze of light during the Christmas period. Illuminated Christmas trees are attached to the walls of most retail outlets and some other buildings. The Parish Council erects a large illuminated tree in Market Place and the Traders' Association erects a tree on the forecourt of Town End Methodist Church.

A carol service, involving all the ministers of the parish, is held at Town End, and the carnival queen switches on the lights of the Traders' tree. The townspeople, the ministers, the Town Band, the carnival queen and Father Christmas all walk up Market Street in procession to Market Place, where the ceremony is repeated in front of the Parish Council's tree. The Chairman of the Parish Council wishes everyone a merry Christmas, the children queue up for presents from Father Christmas, and the Traders, in the guise of Harry and Joyce Hall, Brian and Margaret Bywater and Jason Foster, add to the feeling of good cheer by providing everyone with punch and mince pies.

Alwyn Pickering and Ron Wragg started the tradition of Christmas lights in the late 1960s and Christine Francis, Mike Kirkby, Sandra Millner and Joyce and Harry Hall have continued the custom ever since. Councillor Malcolm Cawthorn brought unity to the display of trees by manufacturing a set of Christmas-tree holders for the walls of all the shops, and Steve Rumblelow fixes and wires up the trees each year.

The tradition of a Business Association tree at Town End was started in the late 1980s and has continued since that time, even in the year when building operations were taking place at the church.

Once traditions are established in Chapel-en-le-Frith, they are likely to remain in place for ever.

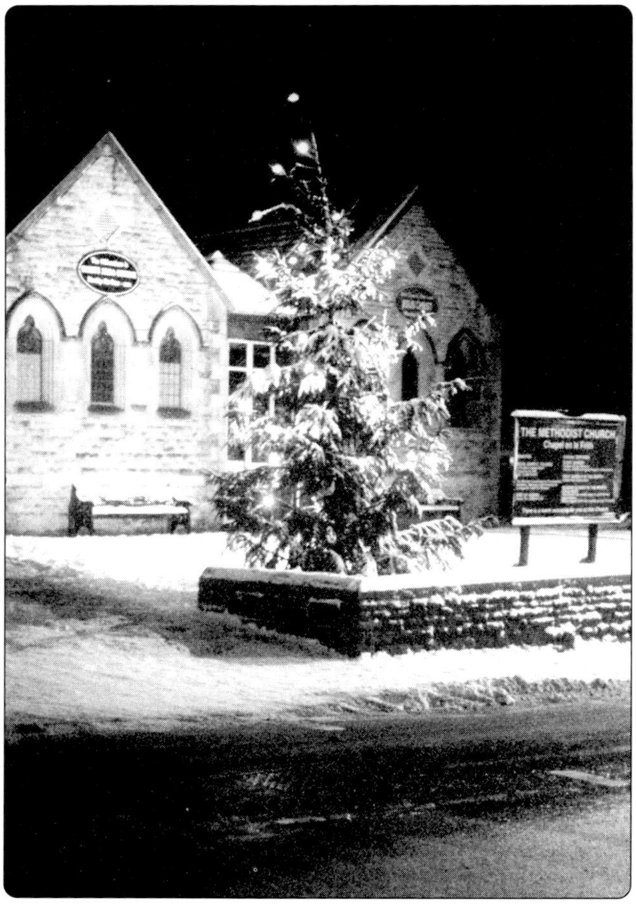

The Traders' Christmas tree at the Methodist Church.

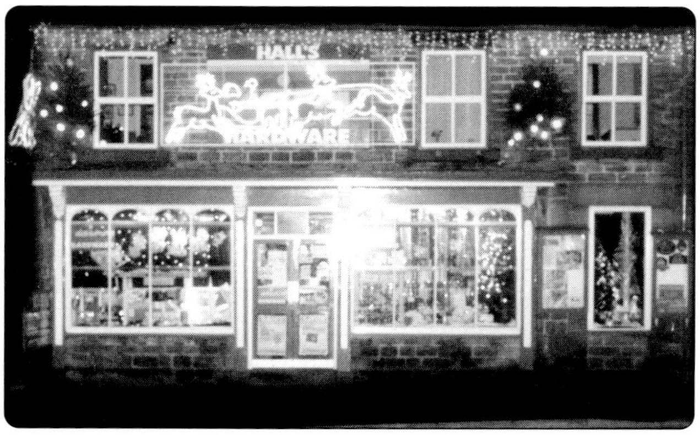

Christmas lights on Harry and Joyce Hall's shop.

Chapter 8

THIS SPORTING LIFE

Chapel-en-le-Frith is a town with very strong sporting traditions and its sports clubs have the good fortune to be sited in idyllic locations. The football and cricket clubs, which sit side-by-side on land between Willow Drive and Brookside Road, and the bowling club, which is located on the edge of the Memorial Park, all have the great ridge of Combs Moss as a backdrop. Combs Sailing Club operates on Combs Reservoir, at the very foot of the Moss, and the course of Chapel Golf Club is beautifully situated between Combs Moss and the conical peak of Eccles Pike.

Although the townspeople are fortunate in having such wonderful locations for their sport, they have fought long and hard for a comprehensive sports centre with indoor as well as outdoor facilities. In April 2003 their wish will be granted when a brand-new sports complex will open on land adjacent to the new High School. The centre and the school are products of an innovative private funding initiative (PFI) partnership scheme involving the Chapel Leisure Centre Committee, whose members have campaigned for almost 20 years, Derbyshire County Council, the Parish Council and developers Babcock & Brown. The facilities of the complex, which include badminton courts, areas for indoor bowls and cricket, community rooms and outdoor pitches, will be shared by pupils at the High School and members of the public. The sports centre will be run by City Centre Leisure.

CHAPEL-EN-LE-FRITH CRICKET CLUB

Compiled from material kindly loaned by Bryan Cooper and from a short summary written by the late Arnold Palmer.

There are many picturesque cricket grounds in England, but it would be hard to find one with a setting to match the idyllic location of Chapel-en-le-Frith Cricket Club, whose ground shelters below the long, high ridge of Combs Moss, in an upland bowl in the Dark Peak hills. The club was formed in 1884 by the amalgamation of the club at Town End and the Church Institute's club, and the playing surface was carved out of agricultural land, originally rented, but purchased outright in 1927, when 1,000 square yards of the pitch were re-turfed and re-drained. Further improvements were carried out in the 1950s, when extensive levelling of the outfield took place, using material excavated during the construction of the new Ferodo laboratory block on Hayfield Road. In 1969 a strip of land on the southern boundary was acquired to increase the drive area. Although the cricket ground is now ringed by housing developments, the surrounding hills remain untouched and the setting retains its rural charm.

A First World War Army hut was used as a pavilion for many years, but this was replaced in 1936 by a new building. The purchase of a second-hand, prefabricated structure in the 1970s allowed the club to provide a licensed social area for its members. By 1990 the members had not only raised sufficient funds to replace the two buildings with a brick pavilion, comprising changing rooms, showers, kitchen, toilets, bar and social area, but also managed to arrange a high-profile official opening by the BBC commentator and former Australian captain, Richie Benaud. Subsequent improvements have included the addition of a machinery store, permanent practice facilities, wicket covers and a new scorebox.

In 1904 the club became a founder member of the High Peak League and went on to win the First Division Championship on nine occasions, including the 1950–51 season, when the club left to become a founder member of the Derbyshire and Cheshire League. Alf Lomas and Les Barton were star performers in the '40s and both players represented the Derbyshire County side at 2nd XI level. On the day the new pavilion opened in 1936, Alf Lomas contributed 103 to a record stand of 180 with Stanley Bolton.

Throughout the 1940s the Chapel club was well supported by local people, both male and female, and even had a very successful ladies' team, ably captained by Connie Pink. The club made league history 40 years later by including a female player, Maureen Wild, in their 2nd XI. Maureen was a promising bowler in women's cricket.

The achievements of Alf Lomas and Les Barton were emulated in the '50s by Joe Lomas, who was not related to Alf, and Les Barton's son Ian, who both played for Derbyshire 2nd XI. During these years Bryan Cooper was the club's main fast bowler. In a match against Stockport in 1953 he placed eight fielders behind the bat and took eight for 43; in a game with Bredbury in 1956 he took four wickets in seven

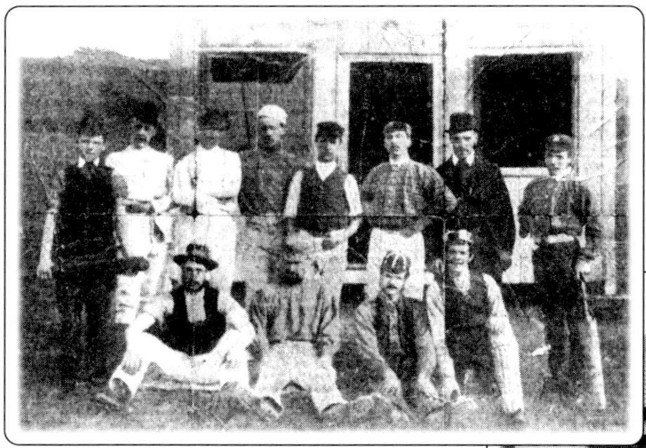

Above: *The Cricket Club in 1881.*

Below: *The Cricket Club in 1927.*
Left to right, back row: *League umpire, Messrs Crossland (scorer), Day, Pearson, McDonald, Holland, Duckmanton, Roe, Jagger, Longson, Heyworth and a league umpire;* front row: *Messrs Hitchens, Lomas, Horrocks (president), Hadfield, Hitchens.*

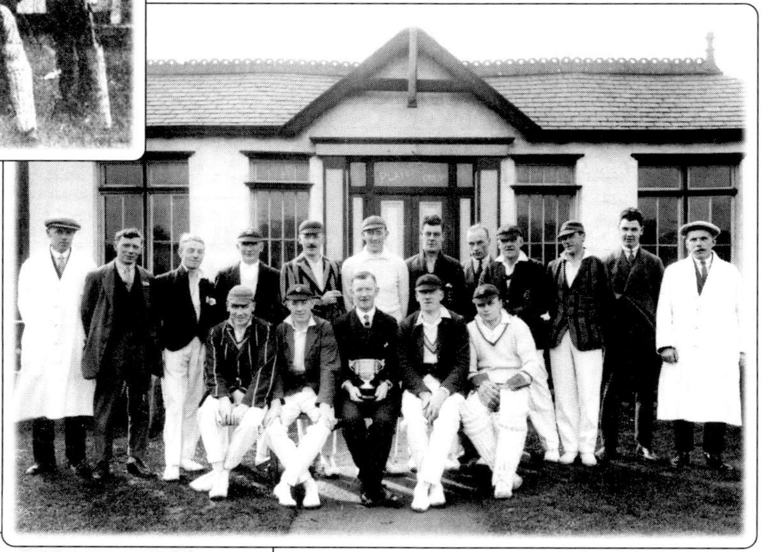

Below: *The team that won the league for the first time, 1964.*
Left to right, back row: *A. Brick, D. Page, N. Cooper, D. Belfield, B. Cooper, A. Bamford;* front row: *R. Maycock, R. Nadin, J. Lomas, F. Eaton (captain), K. Woodwiss, M. Cooper (scorer).*

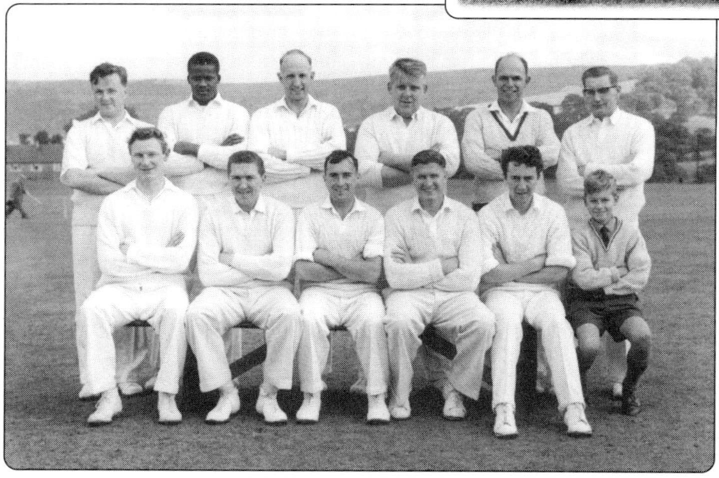

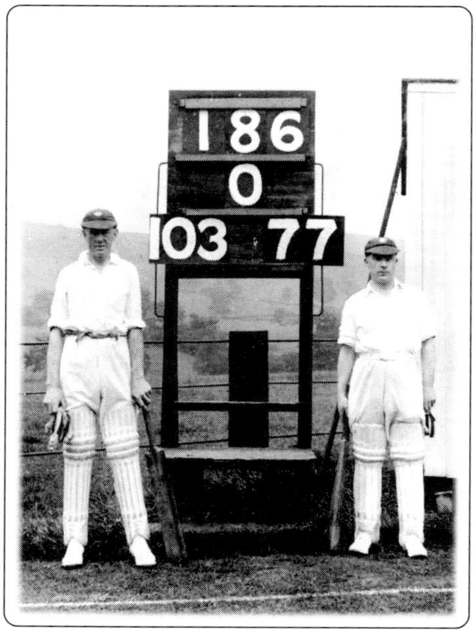

Above: *Alf Lomas and Stanley Bolton after their record-breaking stand in 1936 on the day the new pavilion opened.*

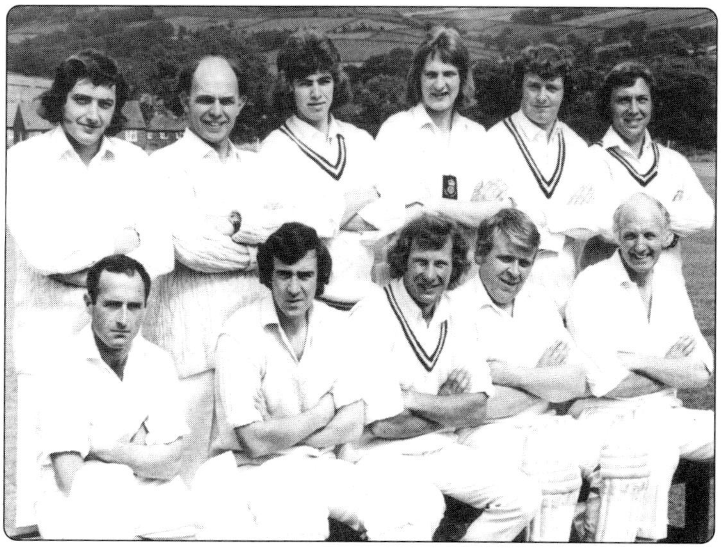

Left: *The double-winning team of 1974.*
Left to right, standing: *D. Morris, B. Cooper, M. Cooper, N. Hawtin, A. Johnson, D. Harding;* seated: *J. Lomas, K. Woodwiss, I. Hawtin (captain), D. Belfield, N. Cooper.*

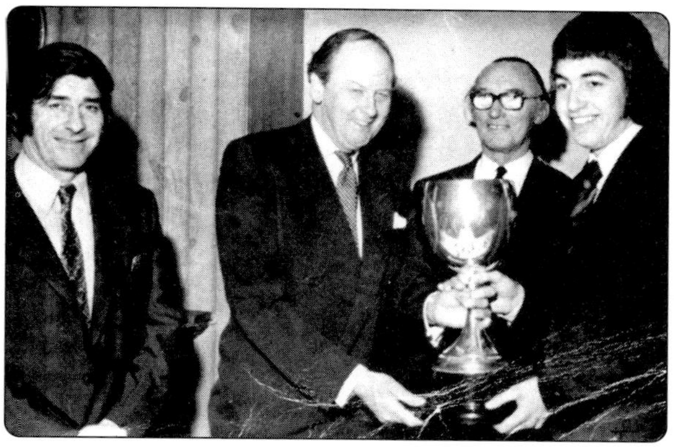

Freddie Trueman and the Duke of Devonshire present Captain Martin Cooper with Derbyshire's Under-19 trophy in 1971.

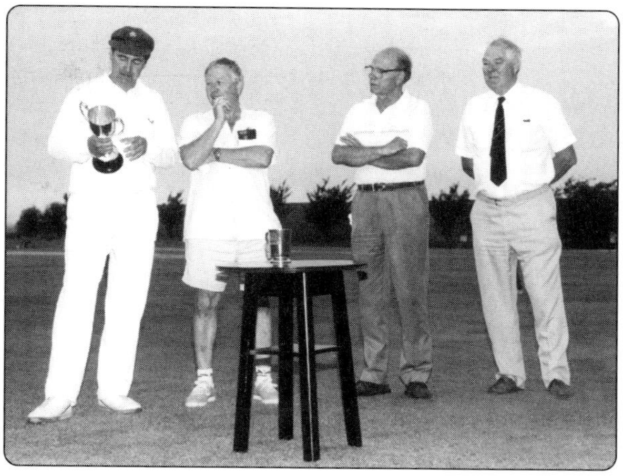

Presentation of the Bissenden Cup in 1997 – the day the match was won on the very last ball. Left to right: *Martin Cooper (captain), Roy Cartledge (league chairman), Bryan Cooper (league vice-chairman), Brian Whalley (league secretary).*

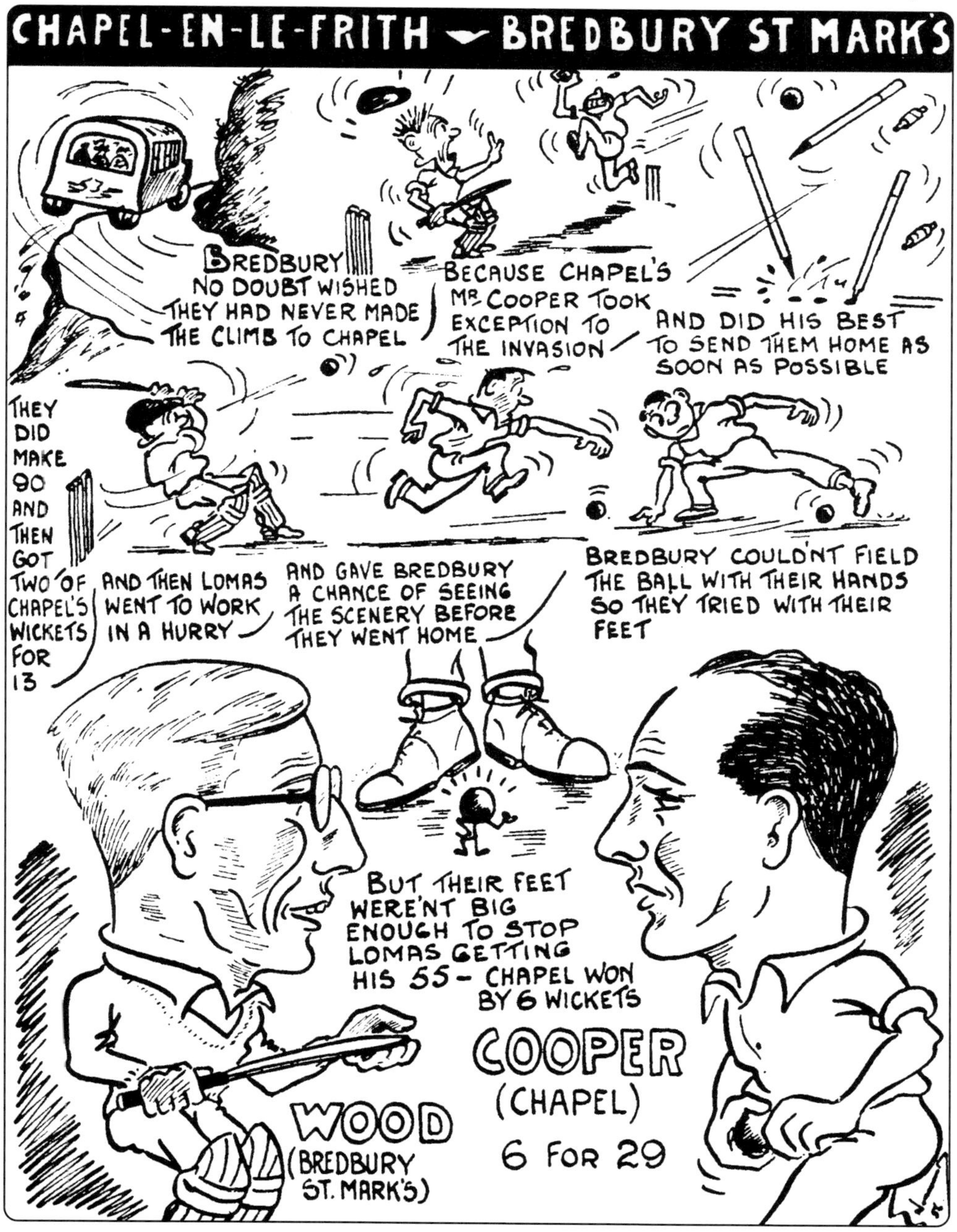

Press report from 1956.

balls, including a hat trick. The fast-bowling attack was an essential part of Chapel's armoury in the '50s – Bryan Cooper and Bill Mirfin, the cricketing policeman, once bowled unchanged for 35 overs. Despite these heroics, Chapel did not win the league until 1964, when the championship was clinched with a victory over Compstall, in which Joe Lomas scored 80 and David Bellfield hit 34.

Playing as the new champions, Chapel then defeated a side representing the rest of the league, with Joe Lomas and David Bellfield sharing a stand of 85 and Bryan Cooper taking 6 for 39. They went on to emphasise their class by winning the league title again in the following season. In 1966 Joe Lomas topped the batting averages of the Derbyshire and Cheshire League with 68.12 and Chapel's new fast bowler, David Page, headed the league's bowling averages with 8.77.

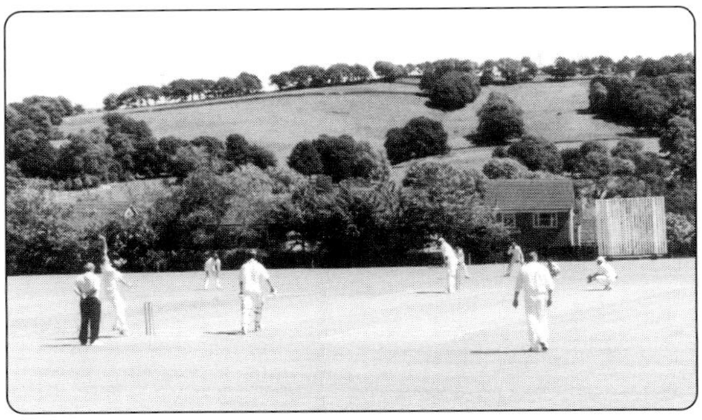

Cricket in an idyllic location.

Roy Buxton and David Page became the club's main opening bowlers in the late 1960s, but Bryan Cooper made a comeback in the '70s, when he opened the bowling with his son, Martin. During the defeat of Whaley Bridge in 1974, father and son took all ten wickets between them. Even more remarkably, nine of the wickets were recorded as, 'caught Cooper, bowled Cooper,' with father and son ably supporting each other's bowling by their performance in the field. Joe Lomas rather spoilt the score card by taking one of the catches!

The Chapel club was involved in another remarkable game in 1974, when they won the Bissenden Cup in a final against Dove Holes. The match, which was played at Hayfield, lasted for no fewer than nine days, apparently because rain stopped play on numerous occasions and various players had pressing business commitments!

The Bissenden Cup was to become a favourite tournament of the Chapel club. They have won the competition on eight occasions since its inception in 1969. Ian Hawtin was the all-round hero of the 1978 campaign, scoring 74 in the semi-final and taking five for 13 in the final. Stirring cup performances were matched by consistent results in the league. When the Chapel team, skippered by Ian Hawtin, won the Derbyshire and Cheshire League in 1975, they had lost only one match in their previous 47 games. Ian achieved a league record score of 185 not out against Hazel Grove and Joe Lomas was still topping the league averages with a remarkable 71.8.

Three members of the Cooper family were playing in the side during this period. Bryan and his son Martin were the only father and son to be selected in the same Derbyshire and Cheshire representative XI; Martin shared an opening stand of 74 with his uncle Norman in a match against Hawk Green in 1977 and he skippered the Chapel side which won the league and cup double in 1981. Martin also captained the U19 county side to victory in the National Trophy and played in several U25 matches for Derbyshire. Bryan Cooper was still representing the league at the age of 52 and, when he retired from playing in 1982 at the age of 58, he had become one of only a handful of players in the league to take over 1,000 wickets. He was made a life member and a trustee of the Chapel club. After spending 23 years as the chairman he became the president in 1991, with Martin Kelly taking over as chairman. Bryan and his brother Norman are still to be seen on the cricket field, because they have formed an umpiring partnership for the past 20 years, and Bryan's son, Martin Cooper, is the current chairman of the club.

When Chapel won the double in 1981 David Bailey made a major contribution by hitting a century against Hazel Grove and scoring 79 not out in the Bissenden Cup final. In Chapel's fifth successive appearance in the Bissenden Cup final in 1983, Ian Hawtin hit three successive sixes and Kevin Woodwiss scored 56 to clinch victory over Hazel Grove.

Star players in the 1990s included Gary Pheasey, his brother Neil, and Lee Bradley, all of whom played for the county's U19 team. In a match against Birch Vale in 1990 Gary Pheasey contributed 100 not out to Chapel's 224 for two and his brother had bowling figures of four for 18. Ian Durham was a successful opening batsman during the '90s, scoring 169 in Chapel's record-breaking 366 for three against Whaley Bridge – his knock was the second highest ever recorded in the Derbyshire and Cheshire League. Ian and Gary Pheasey were two of only three batsman in the history of the league to top 1,000 runs in a season. Ian Chipchase, who was one of the leading bowlers of the time, became the first Chapel bowler to take all ten wickets in a match – this was achieved in a game against Old Glossop in 1996.

Despite the presence of these outstanding individuals, fewer trophies came to the club in the 1990s, but fortunes were revived in 1997 when Chapel narrowly won the Bissenden Cup, with an Old Glossop batsman failing to score the winning runs off Martin Cooper's very last ball, having hit a six off the penultimate ball! Ian Chipchase, who bowled his allotted eight overs at the cost of only a single run, was awarded 'Man of the Match'.

The century ended with a thrilling millennium-year title chase between Chapel and Hawk Green. Chapel lost only one match in the entire season, whereas Hawk Green lost two, but poor weather ruled out play in Chapel's last match, while Hawk Green were able to play their fixture. In the final analysis Hawk Green won the title, with just one point separating the two teams after over 20 games played that season in an expanded league; almost a return to the glory days!

Chapel-en-le-Frith Town Football Club

Based on material supplied by Joanne Carrington (secretary), Doreen Vernon and Joe Lomas, and contributions from Kevin Kelly (chairman), Linda Vernon, Hector Carrington, Shaun King and Alastair Carrington.

Chapel-en-le-Frith is a town with a strong footballing tradition. In the early years of the twentieth century there were no fewer than four teams competing in local leagues: Chapel United and Chapel Favourites, who shared a ground near Bowden Lane; Chapel Celtic, who played at Rowton Grange; and Chapel Albion, who had a ground on Ashbourne Lane.

After the Second World War, Chapel Celtic enjoyed considerable success. The double-winning team, which won the Stockport and District League Championship and the Kennedy Cup, was captained by Les Heathcote and included: Peter Higgins, who briefly played for Stockport County and was the brother of John Higgins, the Bolton Wanderers centre-half; Roy Maycock, who had a trial with Sheffield Wednesday; and the tricky winger Joe Lomas, who was being watched by Aston Villa scouts and was also one of Chapel's leading cricketers.

The Chapel United team, which was packed with ex-servicemen, was also a good side. The matches against their Celtic rivals were always highly competitive and one particularly memorable local derby in the late 1950s ended with United achieving victory by five goals to three. In the mid-1950s United were approached by Celtic with a view to a possible merger. After initially rejecting the proposal, they finally agreed to an amalgamation in 1958.

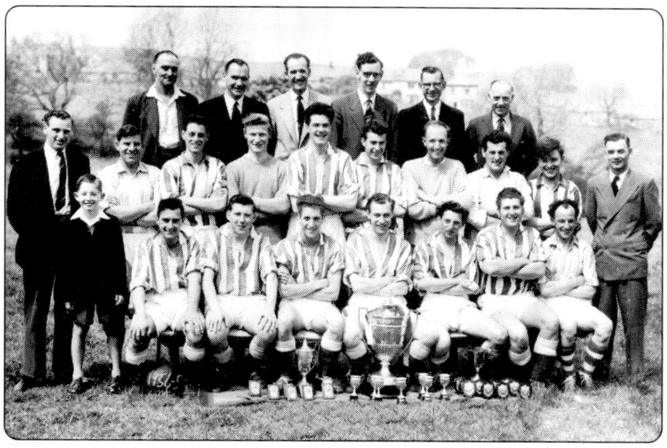

Chapel Celtic in 1956. Left to right, back row: *T. Trivett, K. Cawthorn, J. Vernon, R. Ogan, L. Middleton, R. Hoyle;* middle row: *R. Hallam, ? Bramwell, ? Gregory, R. Maycock, N. Woodcock, B. Worthington, N. Cooper, J. Lees, D. Nall, G. Sullivan;* front row: *? Sullivan, J. Lomas, W. Heathcote, R. Baldwin, C. Heathcote, B. Goodwin, J. Baldwin, B. Lloyd.*

The new club, which was christened Chapel Town Athletic Club, was managed by George Sullivan, who quickly signed up the best players from the two former clubs and added a few new faces. Messrs Maycock, Redfern, Higgins, Worthington, B. Goodwin, Bentley, Parr, and Les and Bill Heathcote all signed from the old Chapel Celtic. Messrs Cockhill, Jarvis, O'Hara, Bradley, Wright, Bowden, Woodcock, Lund and Mycock joined from the former United team. Joe Lomas, as befits the star player, was locked in contract negotiations, but new signings included Bill Turner from Chinley, Peter Whelan from Buxworth and Doug Brown, a former Sunderland player.

The club originally played their matches at the Memorial Park, a ground whose sloping surface required teams to play an uphill half and a downhill half, but the Chapel Athletic Club committee had their eye on a piece of land at Rowton Grange, adjacent to the cricket club, where they hoped to establish a proper Chapel sports centre, complete with football pitch and athletics track. Even though the area was earmarked for housing and local planners would only give a five-year guarantee that the ground would not be claimed by developers, the committee decided to launch a Ground Fund Appeal. The club was refused a government grant under the Physical Training and Education Act because the longevity of the ground could not be guaranteed, but the Appeals Committee, comprising K. Middleton, D. Eley, F. Frisby, R. Ogan, W. Ashworth and T. Heyes, lobbied local and national businesses, carried out house-to-house collections and contacted former residents of the town, with the aim of raising £1,835 for the purchase of four and a half acres of land from Yvonne Hartford, £2,000 for preparation of the football pitch and £1,500 for a pavilion and dressing rooms. Secretary K. Middleton's letter to potential donors included the following plea:

> *The surrounding land is scheduled for building development, but this ground, with the cricket field, will provide an oasis for sport, and future generations will be grateful to those who have helped obtain it.*

The ground was duly purchased, 300 yards of drains were installed, topsoil was placed on a layer of cinders and 1,500 tons of stone were moved by an army of volunteers to create a 160-yard access road, but the club had to 'make do' with an ex-RAF hut as a changing room. By 1960 Chapel Town was able to play all home games in the Manchester League at their new home, which they christened Rowton Park.

Five years later the club ran into debt. The crisis came to a head when only 31s. were taken in gate receipts at a match with Buxton Reserves which was watched by a mere 25 people. The club was already £1,000 in the red and, to make matters worse, the team lost 2-1 that day. Explaining that it would cost Chapel Town £200 to honour their remaining fixtures in the Manchester League that season, chairman Jack Vernon asked for more volunteers to act as agents for the club's football pool and the committee decided to send begging letters to former sportsmen. Fortunately, support was forthcoming and the club survived, but a decision was taken to play in the Fairfield League rather than the Manchester League.

By 1970 finances had recovered sufficiently to allow the club to begin fund-raising for a new pavilion. The committee hatched a scheme to raise £10 loans, many of which were actually given as donations. The new pavilion was duly built, allowing the club to add good changing and social facilities to their existing asset of an excellent enclosed pitch in an idyllic location.

In the 1970s the club left the Fairfield League to join the Hope Valley League. Success on the pitch was slow to arrive, but by the mid-1990s Chapel Town finally had a team which was ready to challenge for honours. The club won the Lawrence Cup and were league runners-up in 1994; they were runners-up again in 1995 and won both the Derbyshire Divisional Cup and the Dore Shield in 1996. Success came again in the millennium year, when they won the Derbyshire Divisional Cup and were runners-up in the league and the Lawrence Cup and semi-finalists in the Dore Shield. The following season saw Town win the Lawrence Cup, when they defeated Whaley Bridge in the final, thanks to an own goal.

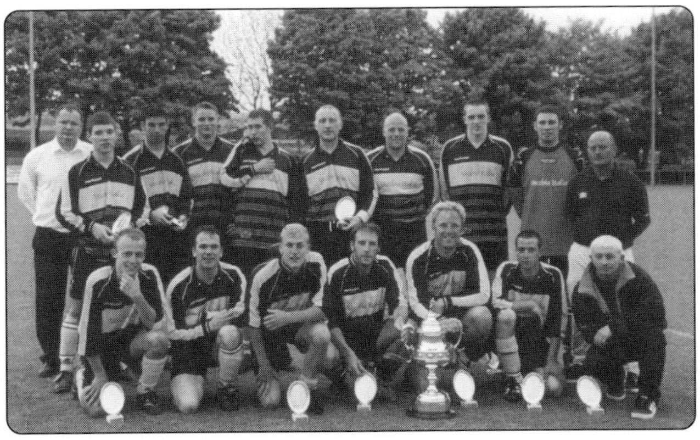

The team that won the Derbyshire and the Lawrence Cup. Left to right, back row: *Mark Fairey (manager), Nikki Hibbert, Terry Bradbury, Oliver France, David Lancaster, Julian Wildgoose, Kevin Yeomans, Ryan Stafford, Andrew Annison, Shaun King (manager);* front row: *Craig Hall, Paul Egerton, James Everall, Dean Williamson (captain), Glyn McNicholas, Simon Garner, Ian Pickford.*

At the time of writing the team manager, Stuart Timpson, and captain Leigh Williamson not only lead a successful team, they also have a fine home ground which is splendidly maintained by Shaun King. Former team manager Mark Fairey says, 'If you can't play on our pitch, you can't play on anything!'

Chapel Town Juniors

By Joanne Carrington.

Although various boys' teams had been operating at Rowton Park prior to 1990, Chapel Town Juniors was formally inaugurated on 9 September 1990. In the 1991–92 season, an Under-10 team was entered in the Rowsley and District Youth League. When this team became the Under-11 team for the 1992–93 season, a new Under-10 XI was formed; they quickly proved their worth by winning the Haddon Medal and becoming the first Chapel junior team to win honours. In 1993–94 the same team, playing as Under-11s, went on to win the Rowsley and District Division Two Championship and so gain promotion.

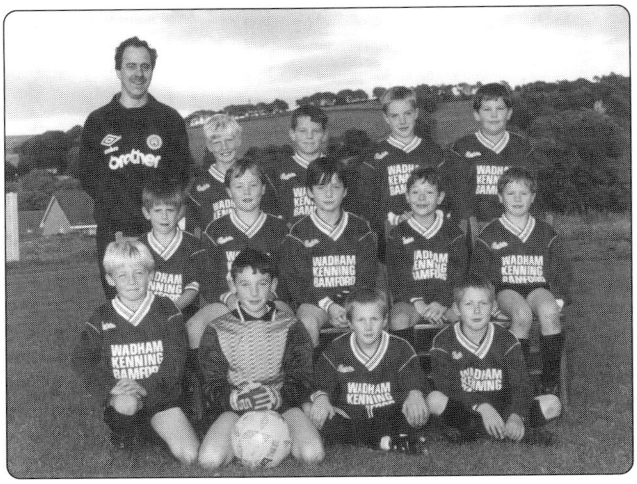

The Under-10 team that won the Haddon Medal in 1992. Left to right, back row: *Alastair Carrington, Phil Davies, Gary Hopkin, Ryan Stafford, Euan Moran;* middle row: *Paul Shear, Richard Beesley, Matthew Robinson, Nicki Hibbert, Chris Carrington;* front row: *Craig Hall, Rob McNaughton, Tom Hughes, David Lancaster.*

With the number of junior teams growing by the year, the logistics of meeting fixture requirements became difficult. It was decided to enter the Under-12 team in the Tameside League, whose matches take place on Saturdays, but keep the Under-10s and Under-11s in the Rowsley and District League, whose matches take place on Sundays.

By the 1996–97 season Chapel Town had no fewer than seven junior sides, ranging from Under-10s to Under-16s. Between 1995 and 2001 the club's junior teams won at least ten trophies, including the following:

1994–95:
Under-10s won the Woodford Cup.
Under-12s won the Sportsmanship award.
Under-13s won the League and the Dial-a-Phone Rosebowl.

1995–96:
Under-14s won the Knock-out Cup and the League Cup.

1996–97:
Under-12s won the League.
Under-14s won the Matlock Mercury Cup.

1998–99:
Under-14s won the League Cup.

2000–01:
Under-13s won the League.

The junior sides have also proved to be an excellent nursery for the senior team. The Chapel Town side which won the Lawrence Cup in 2001 featured no fewer than five players who had graduated from the junior teams: Craig Hall, Ryan Stafford, Dave Lancaster, Nikki Hibbert and Peter Compton. One former Chapel junior player, Ben Burgess, has even gone on to play in the Football League, initially for Blackburn Rovers and then for Stockport County.

In the 1999–2000 season small-sided soccer was introduced for juniors and the Chapel club entered two Under-10 six-a-side teams in the Tameside League. In the 2000–01 season two Chapel Under-10 six-a-side teams were entered in the Stockport Metro League. Let us hope these youngsters will be playing 11-a-side soccer as senior squad players in a few years time and helping to maintain Chapel Town's recent run of success.

Chapel Bowling Club

By Ron Cooke, secretary.

There are indications that a form of bowls was practised in Egypt as long ago as 5000BC. The earliest record of a game being played in this country is of a match which took place in Southampton in 1299. However, there is a bowling-green near the centre of Chesterfield which is scheduled as an ancient monument and is said to date from 1229. The green is used occasionally for special competitions.

Bowling was very popular in Britain during the Middle Ages, but fell into disrepute because it was said to be interfering with archery practice. The flat green game was revived in the nineteenth century and the laws of the game were written in Scotland in 1849.

There is a long tradition of bowls in Chapel-en-le-Frith. It is possible that there was a green of some description under what is now High Street as early as the eighteenth century and in the mid- to late-nineteenth century there was a green on land which is now part of the Memorial Park. The green was situated behind the old vicarage and was entered from High Street via the road which is still known as Bowling Green Lane.

The present green, at the north-eastern corner of the Memorial Park, was owned originally by the Royal Oak Inn, but was acquired by the Parish Council in the early 1920s when the Memorial Park was constructed. It has been maintained by the Parish Council ever since that time and the bowling club pays an annual rent for the use of the green and the shelter. Unfortunately, the excellent green originally used by the Ferodo Bowling Club is no longer used, although it is still in existence. Squirrel Green in Chinley was a popular hotel green and was the venue for the British Individual Championships in 1918.

A total of 180 bowling associations are registered with the Derbyshire Crown Green Bowling Association and 23 of these are in the High Peak area. Chapel-en-le-Frith has nine teams competing in local leagues, including two teams in the Men's Buxton League, two teams in the Men's North Derbyshire Bowling League, one team in the Men's Veteran Division, two teams in the North Derbyshire Ladies' Bowling League and two teams in the North Derbyshire Ladies' Veteran Bowling League.

At the time of writing four members of the Chapel club are involved in the local bowling administration: Fred Barnes, who is treasurer of the North Derbyshire Bowling Association; Bob Hall, who is chairman of the Buxton and District Bowling Association; Maureen Barnes, who is secretary, treasurer and registrar of North Derbyshire Ladies' County Association; and Ron Cooke, the secretary of the Chapel club, who is treasurer of the North Derbyshire League.

The club has between 80 and 90 members, who vary in age from 10 to over 70. The age profile of the Chapel club is a clear indicator that the game of bowls is not solely the province of pensioners, as many youngsters would like to believe. Young players are well represented at local, national and international level and there are league team players in Chapel who are as young as 15. Chapel Park is the venue for an annual Junior Open Competition, when under-18s and under-16s from a wide area compete.

During the season the club stages 11 competitions for members and holds an annual presentation evening. There are also four competitions open to any bowler registered with the British Crown Green Bowling Association. These are the Ladies' Rose Bowl for individual ladies, the Jean Joule Mixed Doubles Trophy, the Arthur Ford Singles Trophy for individual gents or ladies, and the Chapel Park Open Junior Competition for both boys and girls. The club attracts a large number of entries to these competitions because generous prize money is on offer as a result of sponsorship. Sponsors are the Derbyshire Building Society, Peak Press, Hall's Mica Hardware, the Vecchia Italia restaurant, High Peak Borough Council and Mrs Roma Coley, who has sponsored a club competition in memory of the late Arthur Coley.

The Chapel club won the High Peak Trophy in 1985, 2001 and 2002, and the Buxton League in

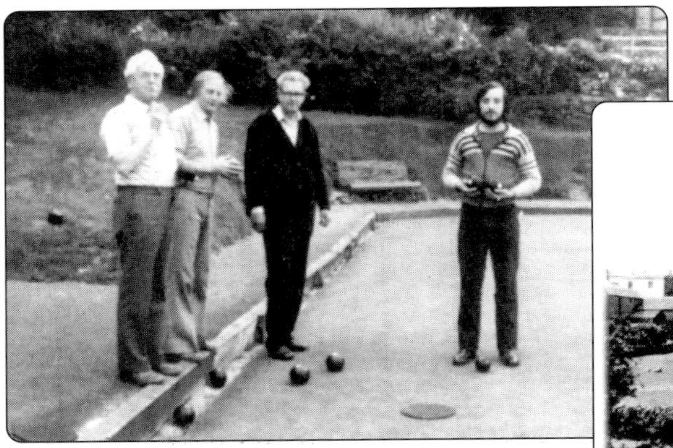

Arthur Cottrill, Bob Hall, Ron Bridge and Tim Norton at the bowling club.

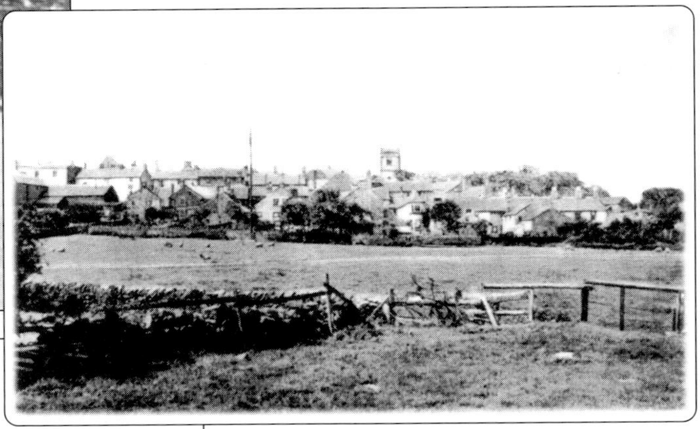

Above: *The scene in 1900. The bowling green is behind the wall and the trees in the centre of the picture.*

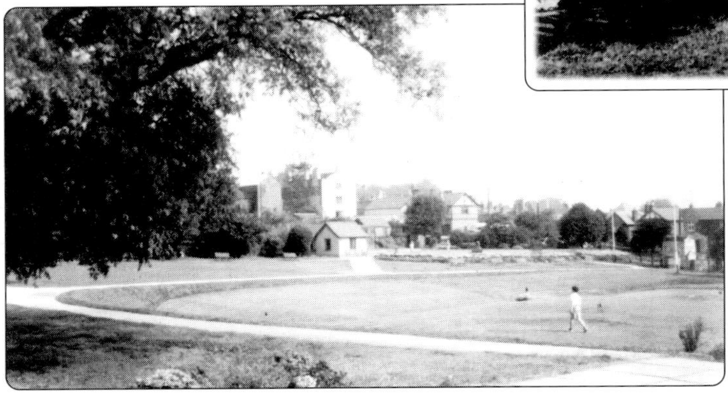

The bowling-green in the mid-1950s. Note the putting-green in the foreground.

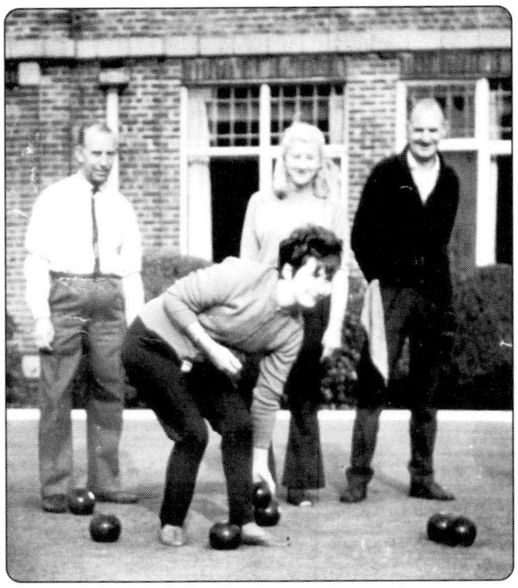

Bert Nichols, Jackie Buxton and Denis Barnes await their turn to bowl on the Ferodo green.

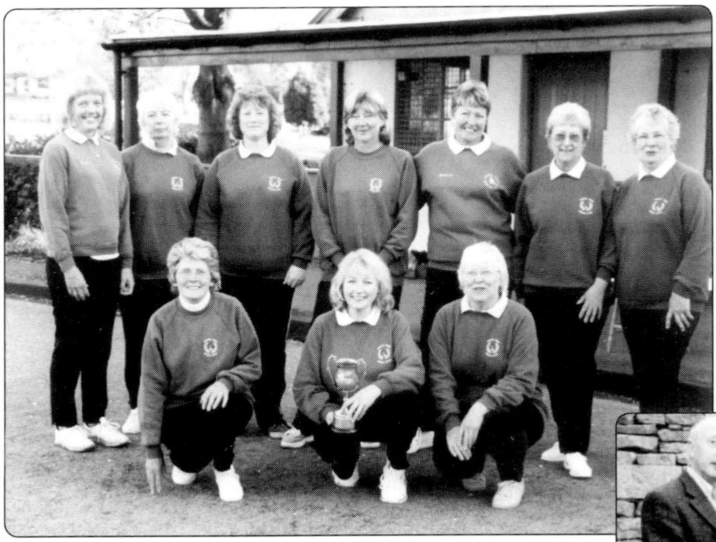

The Ladies A Team, winners of the Allan Smith Team Trophy, 2002. Back row, left to right: *Mary Timmins, Carole Sisson, Sheila Pountain, Jackie Buxton, Maureen Barnes, Carole Mone, Mary Merrick;* front row: *Elizabeth Ball, Caroline Hall, Linda Fletcher.*

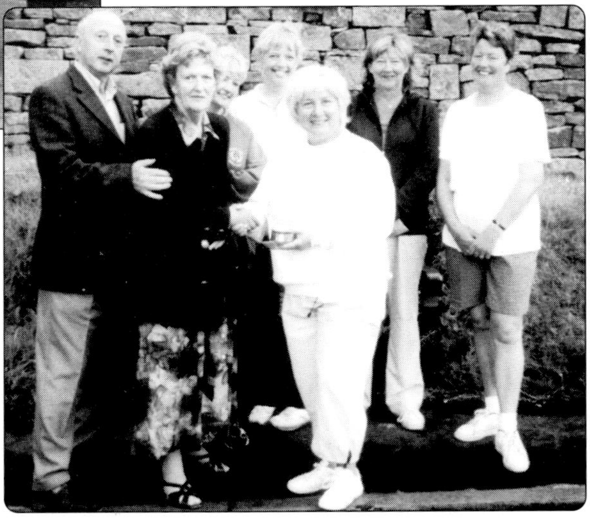

Right: *Bob and Jennifer Mulholland present Sue Wheatley with the Open Rose Bowl trophy in 2002. Caroline Hall, Mary Timmins, Jodie Buxton and Maureen Barnes are also in the picture.*

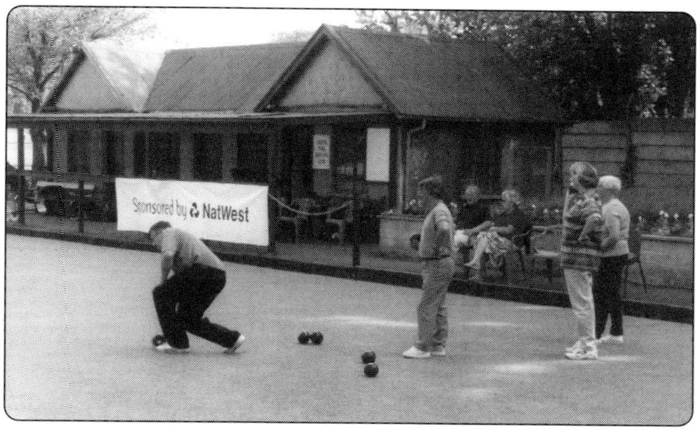

A NatWest-sponsored event at the bowling-green.

1977 and 1999; they were runners-up in Division One in 1984 and winners of Division Two in 2002, when Keith Middleton topped the league averages. Tim Norton, who topped the League Division One averages in 1987, was runner-up in the Derbyshire Yorkshire Bank Trophy in 1985 and 1986, and won the Derbyshire Senior Merit in 1994 and the North Derbyshire League Handicap in 1987. He has also won the White Cup on four occasions. The Chapel ladies' team won the Allan Smith Trophy in 2002. Four Chapel bowlers, Sam Hall, Keith Middleton, Tim Norton and Clive Lomas, have all represented Derbyshire.

Combs Sailing Club

Taken from an article which appeared in *Living Edge* magazine in March 2000.
(Thanks to Silk Press Ltd for permission to reproduce the piece.)

The alarm was raised at 7.15a.m. A massive overnight storm had lashed huge waves against the perimeter wall of Combs Reservoir; spray had blown over the top of the dam, the bank was becoming waterlogged and soil was spilling off the retaining wall onto the road below. By 9a.m. British Waterways inspectors had taken a decision to lower the water level in the lake, and it was not long before they were employing syphons and setting up pumps to accelerate the process, as well as instituting round-the-clock surveillance.

The local newspaper reported a 'tense situation'. A British Waterways employee told their correspondent that the water had 'found a weak spot'. Asked about the state of the dam wall, he replied that it was 'reasonably safe at the moment' – words that did little to reassure people living in the valley below the reservoir. J.W. Pritchett, chairman of the local Parish Council, articulated their fears in his statement to the press: 'When a banking starts to go, with 293 million gallons of water pushing behind it, it creates a serious situation.'

Eventually, the severe gales which had swept the country in January and February 1976 began to subside; British Waterways undertook their repairs and local MP Spencer le Marchant, who had asked to be kept informed about the situation, began to make reassuring noises, saying: 'The measures taken have removed any threat to life and property down the valley towards Whaley Bridge.'

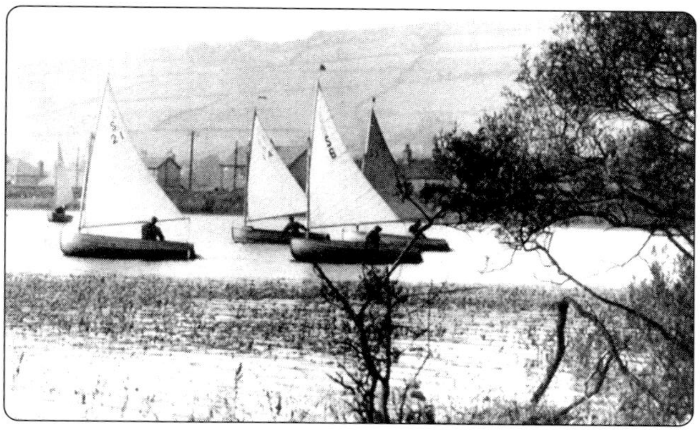

Sparklet-class boats on Combs Reservoir in the 1950s.

Meanwhile, committee members of the Combs Sailing Club, which had operated on the lake since 1950, had an important decision to make. Should they carry on sailing in a greatly reduced lake or take up an offer of alternative accommodation from the sailing club which uses nearby Errwood Reservoir? The committee showed its true bulldog spirit by resolving to carry on sailing at Combs – they would cope with the lower water level simply by extending their slipway.

Sandy Broadbent, a former commodore of the club, emphasises the importance of this decision in his book on the history of Combs Sailing Club,

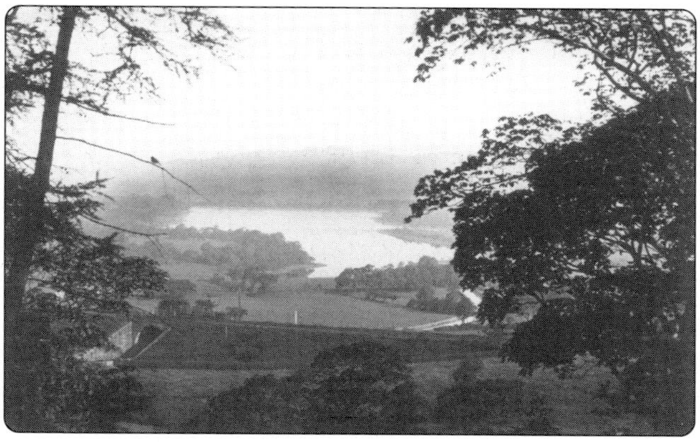

Combs Reservoir – with water.

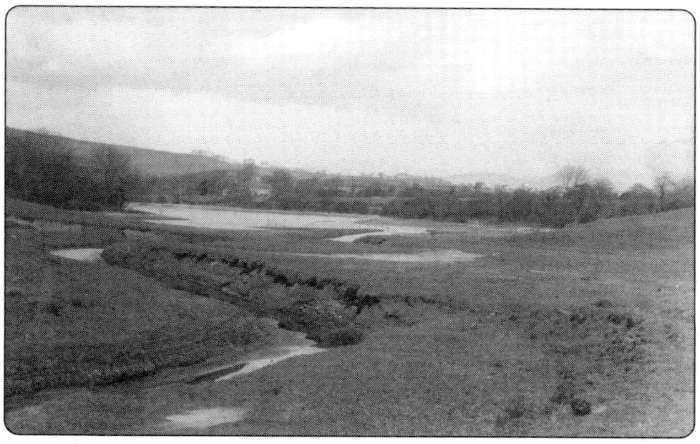

Combs Reservoir – without water!

which was published to coincide with the club's 50th anniversary. He believes the decision to carry on almost certainly saved the club from closure.

Repair work on the dam wall actually took eight years and water levels were reduced throughout this time. Had the committee known this was likely to happen, they would not have made the same decision. In addition the people of Whaley Bridge would not have been quite so reassured by the words of their MP had they known the results of a subsequent survey which found that the dam had been 'marginally stable for a long time'.

Combs Reservoir was built in 1794 to service the Peak Forest canal, which runs from Bugsworth Basin into the Manchester conurbation. The lake, covering some 80 acres, and its backdrop of High Peak hills make an attractive scene which is celebrated in the verse:

They rave about the glories of Buxton,
In lines that would fill many tomes,
Of the charms and beauties of Dovedale,
But give me the valley of Combs.

It is said that one nineteenth-century resident of Chapel-en-le-Frith, just two miles away, took his annual holidays at Combs!

Combs Sailing Club was founded in 1950 by Tommy Russell, a local builder. Tommy became the club's first commodore, an office he retained for 15 years. The rules of the new club were very strict: the use of any form of power, other than sailing, rowing or paddling, was 'strictly excluded' and membership was restricted to gentlemen (ladies were not admitted until 1965), at least two-thirds of whom had to live within a three-mile radius of the Hanging Gate pub, on the northern shore of the lake.

Philip Carpenter, one of the club's 34 founder members, wrote a wonderful letter of application, including a carefully crafted residency claim:

With regard to the rule which I understand limits membership of the club to one third resident more than three miles distant, you may be interested to know that I have taken the six inch map and measured the distance from the nearest point of the reservoir to the front door of my home and find it to be 17,590 feet. No doubt your limiting mileage represents nautical miles, fixed by the Admiralty at 6,080 feet, thus I live only 2.9 miles from the reservoir.

Philip became a stalwart member at Combs and later presented the club with a trophy he had made by sawing a ballcock in half. 'People will compete for anything,' he said.

The Sparklet, a round-bottomed clinker boat, was chosen as the standard craft for the new club, but a decision was taken in 1955 to change to the highly popular two-handed GP14 boat – more than 13,000 examples of this model have been made over the years. The Combs club also keeps some Optimist-class boats for use by junior members. Although no greater in length than a lounge sofa, they do a great deal to encourage young sailors. Sandy Broadbent says, 'One of the club's great strengths is that it is a family club.'

Dawn Fox-Davies, the club's secretary, who began sailing at Combs 13 years ago when she was pregnant with her youngest child, believes sailing is an educational experience for children because 'it gives them the chance to experience being in control of a situation.'

Combs Reservoir is situated over 600ft above sea level, so weather conditions are often quite extreme. Sandy Broadbent remembers a beautiful autumn day when, as duty officer, he had checked wind speeds at the boat-house, but failed to consider the conditions away from the sheltered shore. In the first event that day 29 boats capsized, five retired from the race and only one competitor remained dry! In conditions such as this, sailing is a test of speed and agility but, as Sandy explains, calm conditions are equally demanding because they examine the 'ability to balance, read conditions on the lake and take advantage of every breath of wind.'

The sailing club regularly welcomes new members and its future looks very bright, but the situation could have been so very different if the members had not chosen to carry on sailing after the great gale of 1976!

CHAPEL GOLF CLUB

By Mike Harrison, chairman of the Members' Committee in 2002 and a former chairman of the General Committee of Chapel-en-le-Frith Golf Club.

Knowing that Chapel Golf Club is set in the foothills of the Pennines, visitors are often concerned that they may be in for a mountainous round of golf, but they quickly discover that the course is surrounded by magnificent scenery and nestles in a valley of gently rolling parkland.

The club was founded in 1905 by Mr Ritchie of Bowden Hall, Mr Gaston le Peton of Combs and several other members of the local gentry. It is believed that the inaugural meeting took place at the Hanging Gate Inn, but there is no record of the exact date of this gathering or the names of those present. The club has been evolving ever since.

The original nine-hole course was situated on the north side of the old A6 and, as far as is known, extended from Cockyard to Roeside and almost up to Crossings Road – the site of some of the original tees and greens can still be seen today.

In 1912 the club rented land on the south side of the road, among picturesque scenery on the lea of Combs Moss, and a nine-hole course, slightly longer than the old course, was established there. Although the new course opened on New Year's Day in 1913, it was incomplete and the further work that needed to be done was postponed indefinitely when war broke out in 1914. Little golf was played during the First World War, but the club was sustained by about 60 members paying a nominal subscription of one guinea per year. Five acres of the course, including two greens, were ploughed up for food cultivation during the war and the course was also used as a training ground for the Volunteer Home Guard.

In 1919 the club began to get back on its feet and engaged as a new professional Len Saunders, who designed and laid out a new nine-hole course, much of which can be seen today, including greens laid down in 1919–21 to the famous McKenzie pattern. In addition to his duties as club professional, Mr Saunders acted as steward, secretary and greenkeeper, and was even in charge of the Cockyard Mission. He remained at the club until his retirement in 1956!

By the end of the 1920s Chapel Golf Club was well and truly on the map and was regarded as one of the best nine-hole courses in the county. In 1929 the course was recorded as covering 5,402 yards with 18 holes, a par of 68 and a Standard Scratch Score of 68. During the Second World War activities were again severely curtailed, but the club survived the difficulties.

In 1963 the club engaged Leo Feeney as its professional. He became much loved by members and very well known and respected throughout the county and beyond. Club members were devastated to hear of his death in a traffic accident in 1977. The Feeney family retain their connection with golf and the Chapel club to this day.

In 1969 land became available on the north side of the main road. Despite the club's poor financial position at the time, the plot was acquired and development began on nine new holes, which were completed in 1972. This expansion to an 18-hole course was a major step forward, because it allowed the club to increase its membership and so generate extra income. A new clubhouse was also built during this period, although this was only a prefabricated two-storey structure with limited planning permission. In 1972 the 18-hole course covered 6,089 yards, with a par of 70 and a Standard Scratch Score of 69.

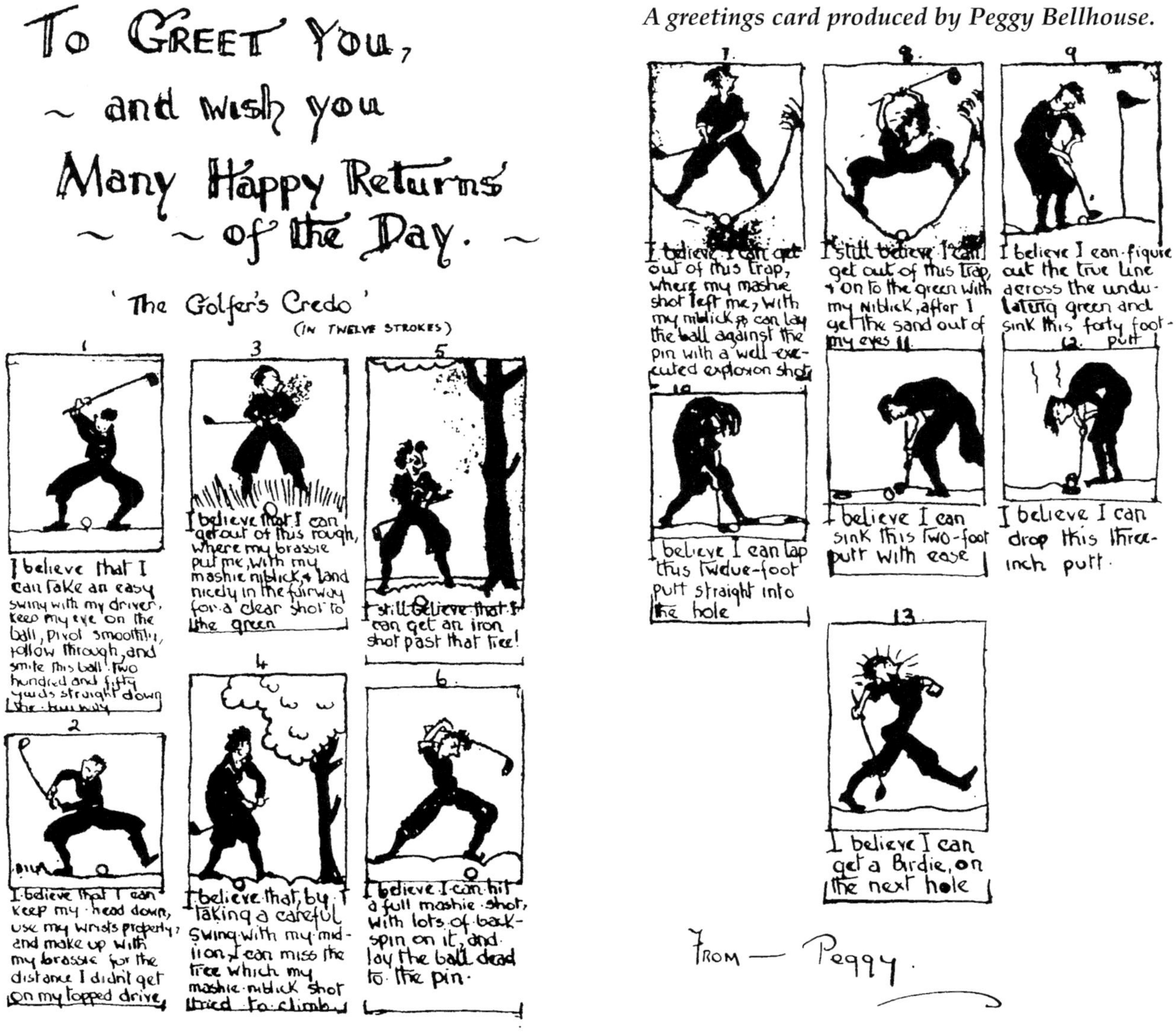

A greetings card produced by Peggy Bellhouse.

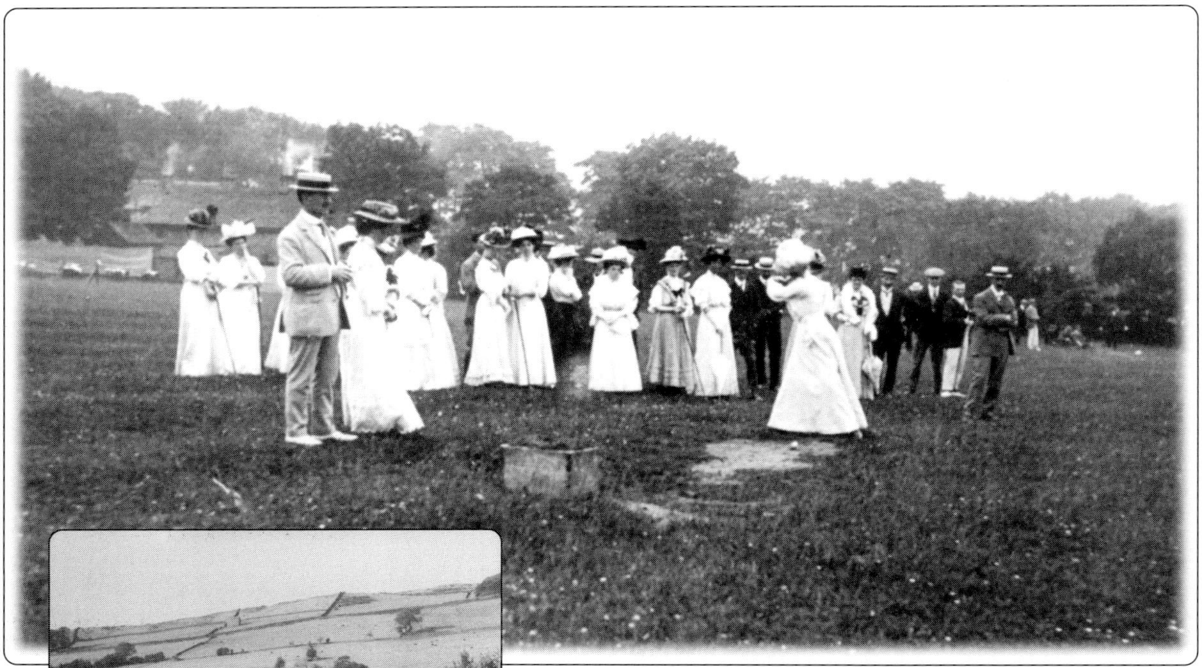

Chapel Golf Club ladies' driving competition, 1908.

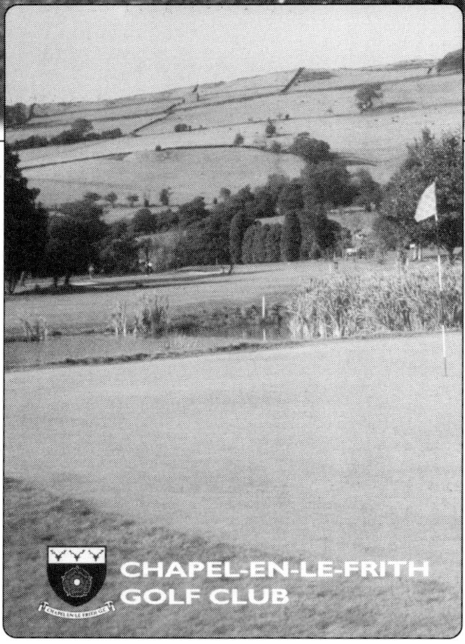

Club brochure with a cover picture of the golf club in an idyllic setting.

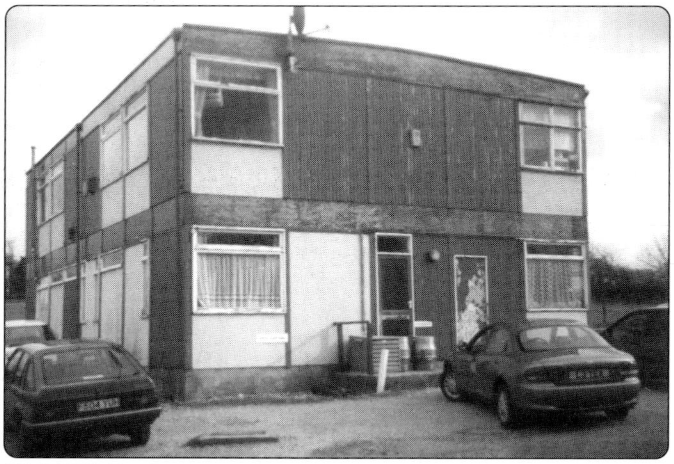

Right: *The old pavilion.*

Below: *The old pavilion being demolished.*

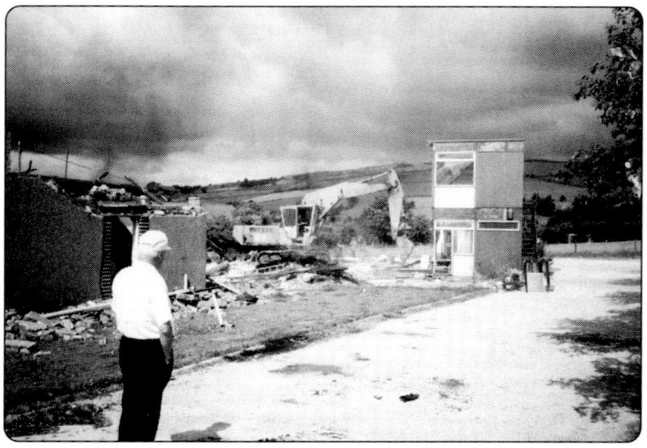

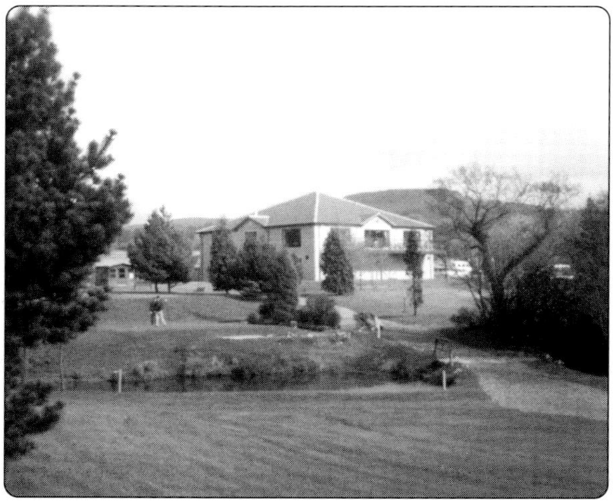

The new clubhouse, 1995.

Until the early 1980s the club was always seen as a nursery for golfers waiting to join more fashionable clubs in Cheshire and Manchester, where waiting lists were often lengthy, but as the years have gone by Chapel has become a club which attracts and retains members in its own right.

The front nine land had been leased from the time of the club's inception, so there were obvious concerns about security of tenure. By the 1990s the club found it was able to purchase the majority of land on the front nine, together with an additional area adjoining the back nine holes. Two new holes were developed on this land, allowing the club to embark on an ambitious plan to develop a new clubhouse on part of the existing golf course. Planning permission was granted and the new clubhouse was opened by the Duke of Devonshire in August 1995.

The club is justifiably proud of this facility, which provides unrivalled views from the balcony. Drinks from the bar and award-winning food are available throughout the day. A snooker room, men's and ladies' locker rooms and showers, and a well-stocked shop complete the facilities.

In 1999 further land was acquired alongside the picturesque Combs Reservoir. This purchase, which was supported by a grant of £55,000 and an interest-free loan of £20,000 from the Foundation for Sport and the Arts, allowed the development of three new holes and an extension to the front nine – the new holes were officially opened in May 2002. However, the back nine, normally regarded as among the best in North Derbyshire, have remained unchanged. This important development now makes Chapel an obvious choice to host representative matches at county level.

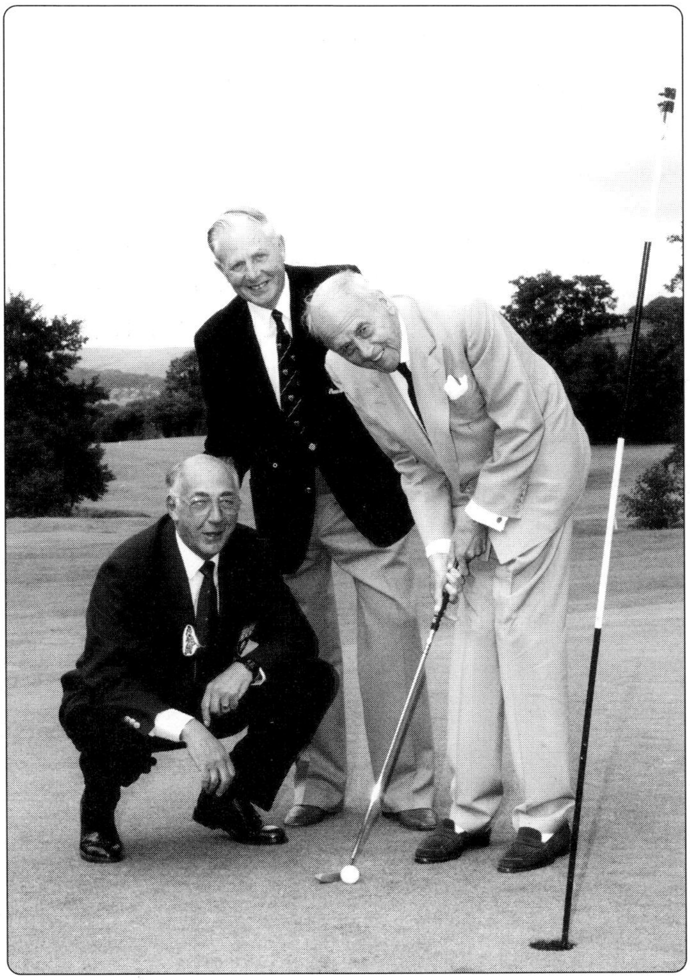

The Duke of Devonshire putting after opening the new clubhouse in 1995. Club Captain Derek Price and President Walter Chatterton are also in the picture.

In the May/June 2002 issue of *County Golfer – Derbyshire,* the Chapel course was described as, 'one of the most picturesque courses in the north Midlands.' The article added:

> *The overall effect of the new development has been to produce a golf facility which is the ideal blend of a challenging golf course with excellent clubhouse facilities situated in one of the most beautiful spots in the country.*

The Chapel Golf Club of today is a forward-looking and successful organisation, which has a very strong membership in both men's and women's sections. The club is also extremely proud of its junior section, which is very strong at the time of writing. Chapel has always been regarded as a 'friendly club', as well as a 'golfer's club'. It is noted for the hospitality shown towards members and guests alike.

Each year the club hosts approximately 60 golf-society gatherings and corporate golf days – many of the groups return year after year. In addition the club has an annual influx of over 2,000 casual visitors, who are drawn to Chapel by the prospect of playing golf in such beautiful surroundings.

The present course has a yardage of 6,434 yards, a par of 72 and a Standard Scratch Score of 71. The current professional is David Cullen, who has been at Chapel since 1986; he is rated among the top coaches in the county and is always on hand for helpful advice, personal lessons and golf clinics.

The club will be celebrating its centenary in 2005 and is looking forward to meeting the challenges that the next 100 years will bring.

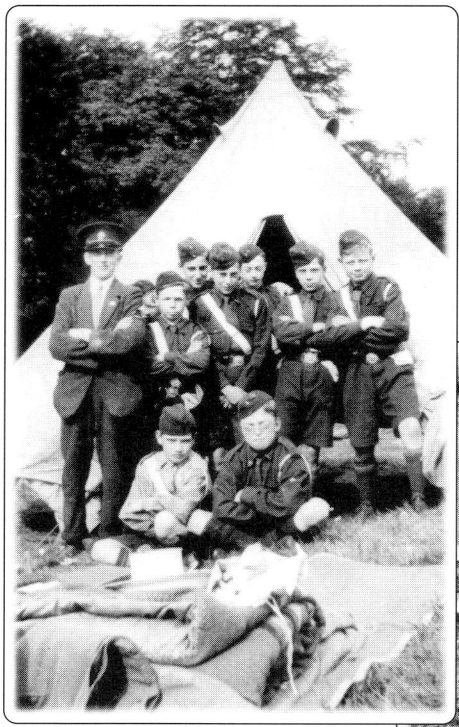

Left: *First camp at Hassop in 1927.* Left to right, back: *Edward Carrington, Bill Belfield, Norman Jowitt, Fred Callender, Wesley Cluett, Reg Wheritt, Harry Robinson, Harold Middleton;* front: *Harold Mellor, Sam Salt.*

Below: *Queuing for grub at Bridlington in 1936. Harry Minshull is serving up to Alan Firth, Les Lister, ?, Harry Hibbs, Herbert Lomas, Harold Middleton, Bill Frith, Robert Cooper, Sam Lomas, Joe Ford, Ken Prime, Jack Williamson, Arthur Element, Harold Cox, Reg Eyre, Fred Element and Donald Muir.*

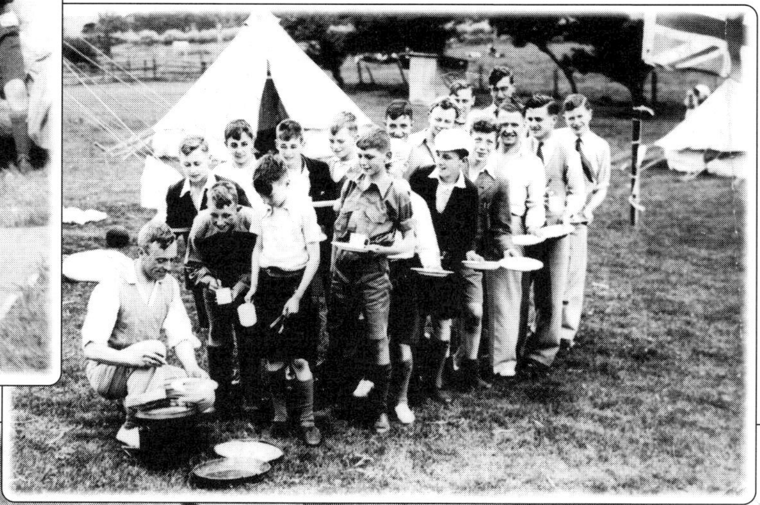

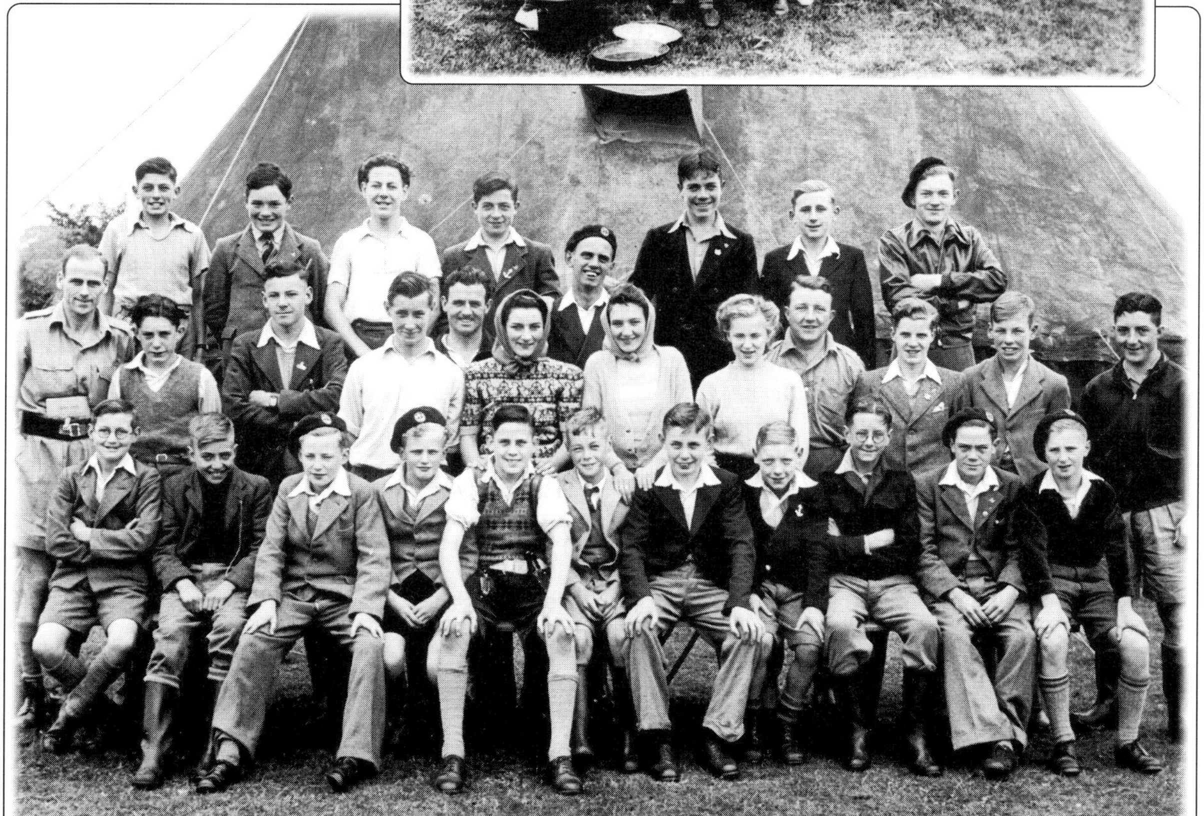

The first Boys' Camp at Bridlington after the war, in 1948. Left to right, back row: *Brian Mycock, Ralph Harper, Philip Young, Tony Alexander, Derek Evans, Brian Bailey, Les Footitt, Graham Harper;* middle: *Roy Lomas, Alec Mycock, Norman Margerisson, Gordon Minshull, Fred Element, Muriel Lomas, May Lomas, Nora Element, Sam Lomas, Harold Manning, Barry Bentley, Herbert Lomas;* front: *Billy Hulley, Clive Bowler, Barry Thompson, John Thompson, John Element, Alan Minshull, Derek Ogan, Arthur Williams, Frank Hulley, Thomas Merrick, Colin Bennett.*

Chapter 9

THE YOUNG ONES

Young people in towns and villages throughout the country habitually complain, 'There is nothing for us to do.' It is of course true that many facilities which were commonplace in the past, such as rural cinemas and park tennis courts, have disappeared. The young people of Chapel-en-le-Frith have certainly suffered in this respect, but they cannot complain about a lack of youth organisations in the town. Thanks to the sustained hard work of many dedicated townspeople, Chapel parish has thriving groups of Boys' and Girls' Brigades, Scouts, Cubs and Brownies. The Youth Club has recently transferred to its new home in the old Infant School and is now offering an impressive range of facilities.

At the time of writing a new skateboard park in the Memorial Park is being planned by the Parish Council, via the Chapel-en-le-Frith Regeneration Committee, and a Community Leisure Centre opened in May 2003 on the new High School site. Hopefully, the present generation of young people in Chapel-en-le-Frith will feel that the town does offer them something to do. Let us hope they will also follow the fine example set by the town's young people in the past, many of whom graduated to become leaders of the youth organisations which they attended.

CHAPEL-EN-LE-FRITH BOYS' BRIGADE COMPANY (WHICH IS UNITED WITH THE BOYS' LIFE BRIGADE)

By Peter Goddard, captain of the 1st Chapel Company and author of a booklet, published in 2001 to celebrate 75 years of the Boys' Brigade in Chapel-en-le-Frith.

Origins of the Boys' Brigade

William Alexander Smith, a Glasgow Sunday school teacher and a member of the local Volunteer Regiment, came up with the idea of a Boys' Brigade after realising that it was far easier to keep a Company of Rifle Volunteers keen and interested on the parade ground than it was to sustain the attention of a group of boys on Sunday morning.

The first unit, known as the 1st Glasgow Company of the Boys' Brigade, was formed on 4 October 1883 at Woodside Mission Hall. A total of 59 boys joined in the first few weeks, and 35 of them stayed on and agreed to the firm regulations. Smith adopted the motto, 'Sure and Steadfast', and set out the following clear objectives for his new organisation:

The advancement of Christ's kingdom among boys, and the promotion of habits of reverence, discipline and self respect and all that tends towards a true Christian manliness ['obedience' was added at a later date].

By 1917 the new organisation had became so popular throughout the country that it became necessary to establish a junior section (for 9–12-year-olds), known as the Boy Reserves.

The success of Smith's organisation gave rise to the setting up of many similar groups, including the Church Lads' Brigade, the Jewish Lads' Brigade, the Catholic Boys' Brigade, the Girls' Brigade and the Boys' Life Brigade.

The Boys' Life Brigade was founded by Dr John Brown Paton, a retired principal of Nottingham Congregational Institute. Like many Nonconformists, he disliked the militarism of the Boys' Brigade, particularly the use of a model rifle in drill. Brown placed the emphasis of his organisation on life saving and adopted a red cross as his emblem.

The union of the Boys' Brigade and the Boys' Life Brigade was first discussed in 1913, but this did not become a realistic possibility until 1924, when the Boys' Brigade withdrew from the Cadet Force and discontinued rifle drill. The amalgamation took place on 1 October 1926 and a new emblem was introduced which incorporated the anchor of the Boys' Brigade and the red cross of the Boys' Life Brigade.

Chapel-en-le-Frith Company of the Boys' Brigade, 1926–42

The 1st Chapel Company was inaugurated on 19 September 1926 in the schoolrooms of Town End Methodist Church, just 12 days before the Boys' Brigade and Boys' Life Brigade merged. Thirteen boys were enrolled by Captain Harry Minshull and Warrant Officer Edward Carrington. F.O. Stables became the president, but was succeeded a few months later by W.H. Marshall, and a ladies' committee was also formed to support the activities. The new company adopted the Boys' Life Brigade uniform, later known as the Boys' Brigade B uniform.

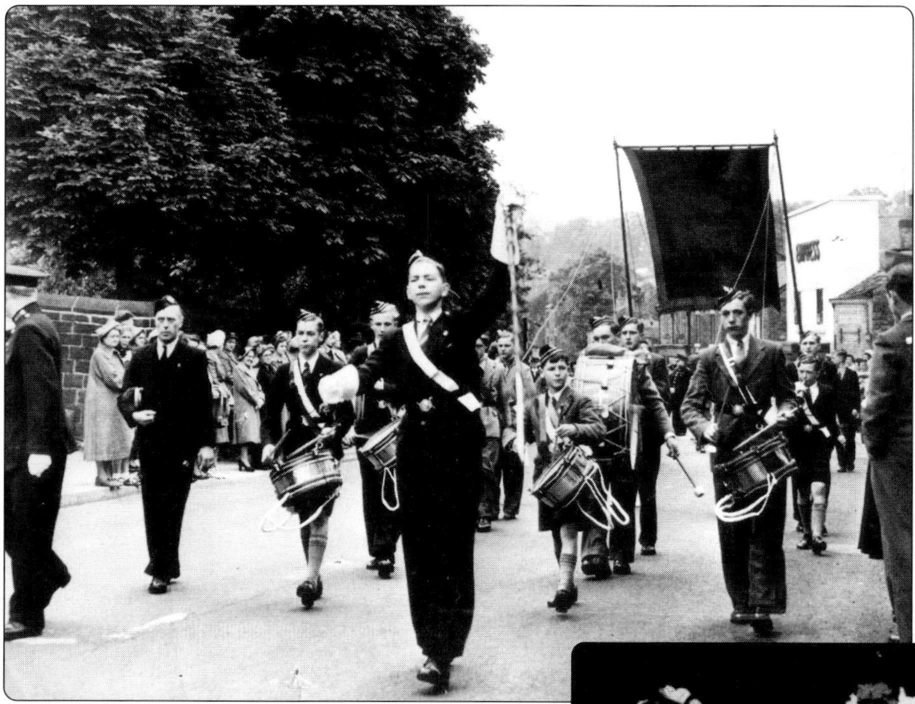

The band of the Boys' Brigade leading the Sunday school anniversary procession in 1952. The picture includes: Harry Minshull, Alan Minshull, Barry Thompson, Richard Osbourne, Arthur Williams, Keith Williams, George O'Brien, Ralph Harper, Stephen Derbyshire, Clive Bowler, Nicholas Campbell, Colin Bennett.

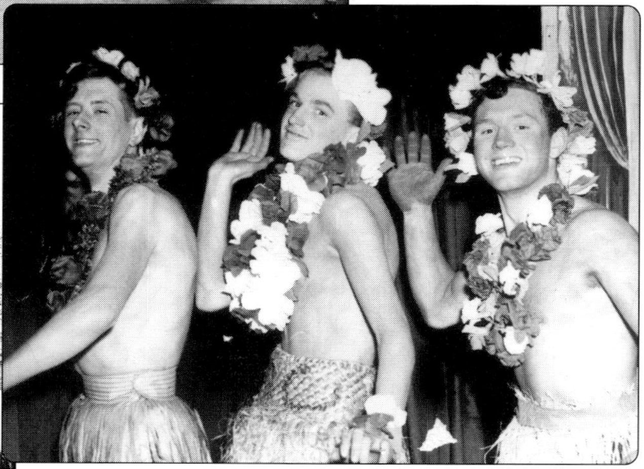

Frank Hulley, John Thompson and Ralph Harper attempting a Hawaiian dance in 1954.

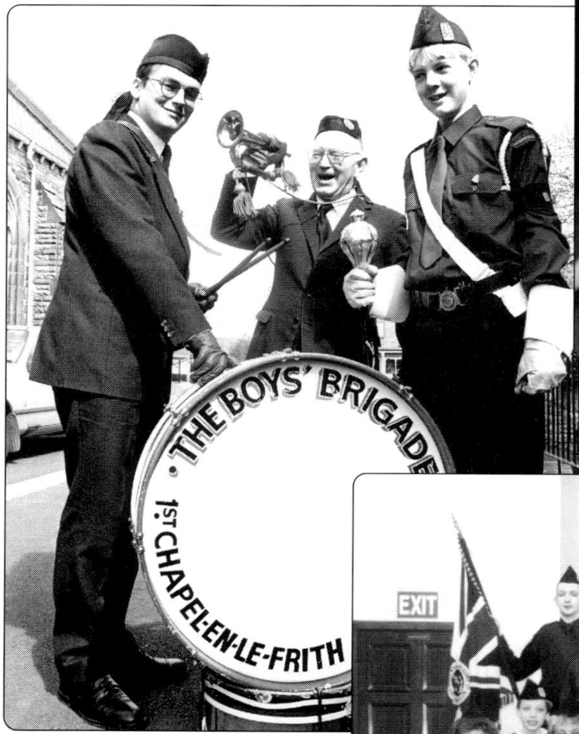

Celebrating the 70th anniversary in 1996. Left to right: *Peter Goddard, Captain of the 1st Chapel Company, with Graham Harper and Dale McNicholas.*

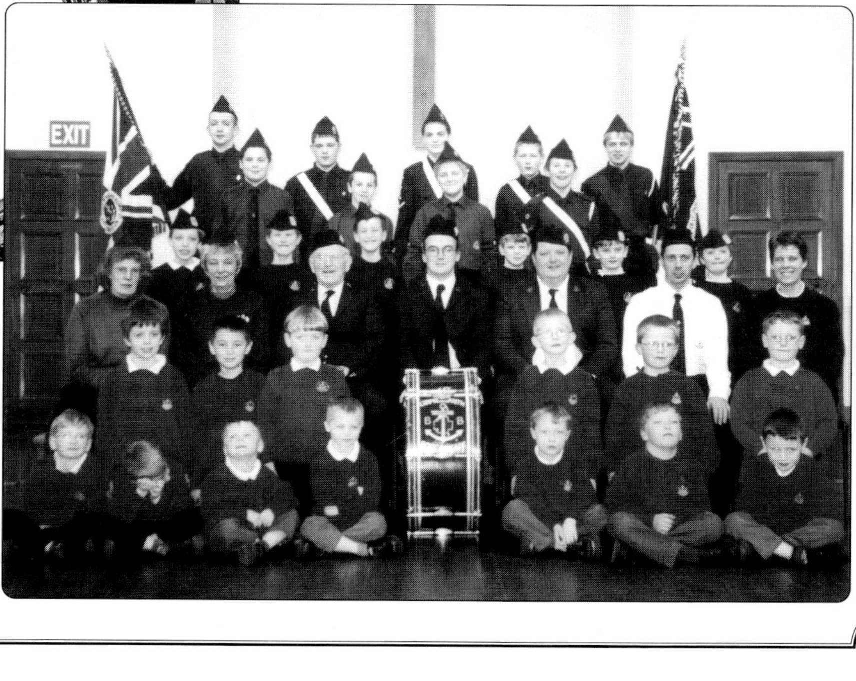

A photograph of the Company taken in 2001.

Harry Minshull, who formed the first company in Chapel, was a member of a staunch Methodist family. At 11 years of age he joined the 62nd Manchester Company of the Boys' Life Brigade and later the Alfreton BLB, with whom he became captain. On moving to Chapel-en-le-Frith he found work at Hunter's shop (now the Vecchia Italia) and attended Town End Methodist Church, where he became a trustee, a member of the choir and a Sunday school teacher. He lodged for a time with Mr and Mrs Brocklehurst, whose son Leslie became an early member of the Boys' Brigade.

The Chapel company attracted boys from Cockyard, Whaley Bridge, Chinley and New Mills, as well as Chapel, and one boy even cycled each week from Disley, passing two other BB companies in New Mills along the way.

Badge work was very popular; many boys gained the 'ambulance badge' under the guidance of Dr Kennedy; and the 'physical training badge' programme included work with Indian clubs, parallel bars and the vaulting horse, as well as outdoor sports, such as cricket, football, paper-chases and bridge building. Alec Muir recalls that early physical training classes were held in the garage behind Hunter's shop. A drum and bugle band was formed a year after the group started, but the practices proved to be so unpopular with local residents that the captain decided to hold them in a quarry near Ford Hall. Eventually, the band became proficient enough to lead church parades, but they always had to be careful not to frighten any of the horses which led the six horse-drawn milk floats in the town.

Camps became an annual event after the success of the first one, which was held in 1927 at Hassop, near Bakewell, and is remembered by Reg Eyre as 'a wonderful experience'. On two occasions, violent storms washed out the camps and the boys had to dry out around the camp-fire all night.

Alice Cluett (the future Mrs Minshull) set up the 1st Chapel Girls' Life Brigade shortly after the girls held their first camp, and she also started the Life Boys (now the junior section).

Display concerts, designed to demonstrate company activities to parents, friends and supporters, became an annual fixture and featured a band, comprising accordion, thimbles, washboards, mouth organs, bazookas and drums.

The Chapel company prospered throughout the 1930s and, in 1933, three representatives from Chapel attended the Boys' Brigade golden jubilee celebrations in Glasgow. In 1939 war was declared while the boys were on camp in Bridlington; Harry Minshull was called up to the Royal Army Service Corps and he arranged for Reg Eyre to become acting captain, but the company was suspended in 1942 due to wartime difficulties. A total of 23 members of the company served in the Forces. Three of these, James Adams, Leslie Adams and Eric Maddison, never returned.

Chapel-en-le-Frith Company of the Boys' Brigade, 1946–60

The company was restarted after the war on 19 February 1946, with 20 boys being enrolled at the Methodist schoolroom by Captain Minshull and Lt Fred Element. Among them was 14-year-old Graham Harper, who had seen an advert at the Empress cinema. In 2003 Graham is still an officer with the company. By June 1946 there were 35 members, the band was re-formed and the first camp was held the following summer at Bridlington – a coachload of parents visited the boys at Forty Foot Road.

In 1951, 21 years of activity were celebrated with a visit by the 14th Manchester Pipe Band from Levenshulme, but the company had to go through a gradual postwar rebuilding programme and it was not until 1953 that the Life Boys was resurrected by Alice Minshull and Keith and Mary Millward. In 1953 a coronation concert was held with the newly formed Girls' Life Brigade Company. Arthur Williams represented Chapel at the coronation celebrations and Sgt Richard Osbourne was the representative at the Sir William Smith centenary celebrations at Eton.

During their first 30 years the company had met in the schoolrooms of the Methodist Church, but this involved the weekly chore of moving all the desks to the side of the hall and then moving them back at the end of the meeting. In 1954 a former prisoner-of-war hut from Dove Holes was purchased and plans were made for the company to have its own club room by placing the hut on a site at Reddish Green, obtained from Sam Longson.

The Chapel company helped in the formation of the 1st Chinley company and the 1st Buxton company, and went on to hold a joint camp with the Chinley company at Torquay. The camp was made memorable by one of the lads swallowing a miniature souvenir horseshoe from Cockington Forge. Thankfully, it was passed on the return journey!

In 1956 the company president of 30 years, W.H. Marshall, died and his post was taken by his son, a local GP and old boy, Dr W.E.S. Marshall.

An international camp was held in Jamaica to celebrate the 75th anniversary of the Boys' Brigade in 1958 and Cpl Terry Gill was chosen to attend as the representative for the whole of Derbyshire. The High Peak group of the BB was formed, comprising the Chapel, Chinley and Buxton companies, and various events were held between the three groups. The following year saw a joint church parade held at Fairfield Methodist Church. And so, as the 1950s drew to a close, the BB was stronger than it had ever been in the High Peak area.

Chapel-en-le-Frith Company of the Boys' Brigade, 1961–80

The 'swinging sixties' began with the Chapel

Company in a very good position, with 36 officers and boys in what is now the company section and 30 in the junior section, but the Buxton and Chinley companies both closed down in the early part of the decade.

In 1963 a swimming gala was held at the Palace Hotel in Buxton to celebrate the 80th anniversary of the Boys' Brigade. In that same year Ron and Joan Lomas arrived from Winsford, in Cheshire, and became actively involved in the company. In the following year a new coffee bar was constructed in the club room. Gang shows, which included sketches and songs, became popular in the '60s and the later ones were staged jointly with the Girls' Brigade. In 1966 the company visited the Lancashire and Cheshire District BB Show at Blackpool Tower Circus for the first time.

Captain Minshull now had difficulty attending parades due to ill health and so Ron Lomas became the acting captain. In 1966 a presentation, attended by over 200 old boys, parents and friends, was held to celebrate Harry Minshull's retirement after 40 years as the captain. Ralph Harper took over as company captain.

In 1967 a new company colour was dedicated at the March Parade service, with old boys contributing to part of the cost and attending the service. The construction of the new Junior School at Warmbrook meant that the schoolrooms were now released for use by the brigade. The club room was sold to Sam Longson and was finally demolished during the early 1980s.

In 1968 Chapel Memorial Institute presented an inscribed bugle in memory of Frank Kirkham, a long-time supporter of the company. Captain Harry Minshull died on 13 February 1969 at the age of 63. He was much loved by his family and well respected and remembered by the many hundreds of boys whose lives had been touched by him.

Proceeds from a garden party at Cromwell House enabled the purchase of three new side drums, but a new fund-raising idea hit the streets in 1970, when the BB laid out a line of pennies by the kerbside, using coins collected from passers-by. The 'Mile of Pennies' became a regular event that would last for 30 years.

In 1971 the company transferred from the North Midland District of the BB to the Lancashire and Cheshire District, and became part of the Stockport and District Battalion. The uniform was changed in the following year from cap, belt and haversack with blazer to a shirt uniform with a new-style hat. The BB set up a pilot scheme for a pre-junior section, with various names being proposed, such as Robins and Cabin Boys. Chapel decided on the term Anchor Boys and this was the one which was eventually adopted by the BB. Their uniform was a navy-blue jumper, with a red anchor on the left breast, and a new-style hat with no badge. In the following year Mrs Minshull presented the band with a new mace.

The Lancashire and Cheshire District became the North West District in 1974, the year in which Town End Methodist Church celebrated its centenary. In the following year the Parish Church celebrated its 750th anniversary with a 'Youth Frolics Concert' – the BB band performed and the juniors put on a semaphore demonstration.

Chapel BB's golden jubilee year was celebrated by a host of events, including a parade service led by the district pipe band and attended by the 131 boys and officers that made up the company at that time, as well as dozens of old boys. A committee of old boys raised money to purchase a bell lyre for the band, as well as a plaque celebrating the golden jubilee and the role played by Captain Minshull. The company also helped the formation of the East Cheshire Battalion and three boys, Chris Nicholls, Phillip Newton and David Youd, formed part of the guard of honour for the Duke and Duchess of Gloucester at Salmesbury Airport, Preston.

The Queen's silver jubilee was celebrated by the building of a bonfire on the summit of Eccles Pike and 60 boys took part in a Diddymen's party item at Blackpool. The Anchor section was made official and the red jumper was introduced. Alan Tideswell moved up to the company section and became the first boy to have progressed through all three sections. The 1980 camp, held at Llandudno, was made memorable by two of the frame tents blowing away in the middle of the night. Luckily, they were 'mess' tents and therefore unoccupied!

Chapel-en-le-Frith Company of the Boys' Brigade, 1981–2000

The new decade began with the company looking forward to the BB centenary year in 1983. Old boy Robert Hulley donated two pairs of cymbals in 1981 and ten-year-old David Kennedy became the youngest ever bass drummer in the band. Sgt John Goddard and Cpl David Tideswell attended a centenary year international camp at Scone Palace in Scotland, the company participated in the centenary parade in Chester and several local events were held, including a garden fête, a dinner at the King's Arms and a torch procession and bonfire on Eccles Pike. The year was also rather special in that a record five boys from the Chapel company were awarded the Queen's Badge. A centenary fund was set up to raise money for a marquee for use at camp and over £1,000 was raised, including £600 by the chaplain, Revd Kevin Savage, who undertook a 100-mile sponsored walk.

Ralph Harper stepped down as captain in 1985 after 38 years with the company, including 19 as captain. His successor was Michael Berry, who was immediately faced with the task of transferring the company from the East Cheshire Battalion to the

Manchester and District Battalion. The following year some of the BB officers started a church youth club 'Pop In', which is still going strong today. In 1987 the company acquired its first minibus and the band performed at the opening of the Chapel bypass. In 1988 the company went to camp in Wales (at Betwys-y-Coed on this occasion) and again lost two tents in a gale – the kitchen and the captain's tent. It would be ten years before they ventured into Wales again!

In 1990 Ron and Joan Lomas moved back to Winsford, having given many years' service to Chapel BB. At this time the interior of the church was being remodelled on more flexible lines and a new coffee bar and lounge were being added; the school-rooms were used as a temporary church before being sold for housing. Warrant Officers David Kennedy and Ian Vernon, Cpl Roy Whittle and Anchor Boy leaders Emma Berry and Lesley Vernon all undertook a parachute jump in aid of church funds and raised over £1,000.

Captain Berry retired from the company in 1994 and was replaced by Peter Goddard. In April 1994 Cpl John MacMillan and Cpl William Carver were chosen to parade in a royal review at Windsor Castle and the new captain accompanied them. The day was made special, not only by the glorious weather, but by the Queen taking time to talk to both boys. The company also performed 'Neolithic Nonsense' in a display at the International Brigade Council meeting, held that year in Manchester, and Simon Hopkins, John MacMillan and Ben Jackson all played in a special battalion band organised for the weekend.

The company built a huge bonfire on Eccles Pike to celebrate the 50th anniversary of VE Day in 1995, using a number of wooden pallets donated by Ferodo – the boys had to camp out at the Pike throughout the weekend to look after the wood!

The 70th birthday of Chapel BB in 1996 was celebrated with a display of photographs and memorabilia, and a grand parade with old boy Ron Lomas as guest preacher. Chapel Parish Council presented the company with a new side drum, Lt Graham Harper was presented with a plaque to mark his 50th year with the BB, and Dr Marshall was presented with a plaque to mark his 40th year as the company president. Sadly, Dr Marshall died later that year. His post as president was filled by ex-captain Ralph Harper and ex-captain Michael Berry and Graham Harper were appointed as vice-presidents.

In 1997 the company was presented with a new Queen's colour in memory of Norman Vernon, who had put in many hours behind the scenes, helping at camp and driving and maintaining the minibus. His wife Linda and children Lesley and Ian have all been officers. In the following year the company was presented with a new colour in memory of Alec MacMillan, whose son John is an officer and one of the company's Queensmen.

In 1988 a new king-size marquee, incorporating a kitchen, was bought, in order to put an end to soakings between food preparation and consumption. In the millennium year, when every boy was given a candle, buttonhole badge and certificate, four boys received the President's Badge (the second highest award in BB) and five boys gained the Duke of Edinburgh Bronze Award. A new uniform for all sections was introduced in April 2000.

The year 2001 marked 75 years of BB in Chapel. Alan Minshull, an old boy, Queensman, ex-officer and son of the company's founder, was the special guest at the annual inspection and display. King's and Queen's Badge holders were also invited to help congratulate Jonathan Hall, the latest Queensman – the Queen's Badge is the highest award in the Brigade.

Some 300 old boys were invited to a celebration weekend in May 2001, which included an exhibition of photographs and memorabilia and a social. Messages of goodwill were received from the USA, Canada, Australia and New Zealand, and 'volunteers' from the audience tried to remember how to play bugles and drums and put on a display. The special parade service was taken by Revd John Goddard, a Queensman of the company and a Baptist minister, and Revd Kevin Savage, a former chaplain of the company and now a chaplain in the Army.

In July 2001 Lois Thornley persuaded Sgt Jonathan Hall, Lt Lesley Vernon and Capt Peter Goddard to join her in a charity abseil from the roof of Manchester Town Hall, with the aim of raising money for the British Lung Foundation. In 2002 Sgt Jonathan Hall was chosen from thousands of members to represent the Brigade at a Royal Garden Party to celebrate the Queen's golden jubilee, and was even spoken to by the Duke of Edinburgh, who had spotted his Duke of Edinburgh Award badge.

The 1980s and '90s saw a change in attitude towards uniformed organisations (especially single-sex ones) and many companies closed as a result, but this trend now seems to have been reversed – uniforms are even returning to schools! Staffing has become a problem because many more people work irregular shifts and many more boys who go through the sections have to leave Chapel to attend university or find work. Nevertheless, membership has increased steadily over the last couple of years and, as in the early years of the company, new recruits have been attracted from surrounding towns and villages. It is a testimony to the support of the local people that the 1st Chapel-en-le-Frith Company has met the challenge of the last 76 years and is in a good position to serve the town for many years to come.

Chapel-en-le-Frith Girls' Brigade

By Jeanette Saxby and Julie Murdy,
former and present captains of the company.

The Girls' Brigade is an international and interdenominational organisation for girls of all ages.

Since its foundation in 1893 the Girls' Brigade has become known worldwide as an enjoyable, interesting, challenging and relevant provider of activities, skills, care and Christian love for hundreds of thousands of young people. The organisation was formed in July 1965 by the union of the Girls' Brigade of Ireland (founded in 1893), the Girls' Guildry (founded in 1900) and the Girls' Life Brigade (founded in 1902).

The Girls' Life Brigade, which was founded by the National Sunday School Union (now known as the National Christian Education Council) was a church-based international movement, with a varied programme for four age groups. Its aim was 'to help and encourage girls to become responsible, self-reliant, useful Christian women.' International membership at the time of union was 120,000.

All these movements were designed to supply weekday activities for members of Sunday schools and churches and to provide opportunities to develop mind, body and spirit in preparation for a life of useful Christian service and witness. Methods have been adapted over the years, and the union of the three organisations in the Girls' Brigade can be seen as a strengthening of purpose in the face of the challenge of the present day.

The aim of the Girls' Brigade is to encourage girls to become followers of Jesus Christ through self control, reverence and a sense of responsibility, in order to find true enrichment of life. Its motto is 'Seek, Serve and Follow Christ.'

In 1928 a Girls' Life Brigade company was formed in Chapel by Mrs Alec Minshull, the wife of the captain of the Boys' Brigade. The company was based at Town End Methodist Church and continued until 1941 under various captains, including Mrs Dorothy Stewart.

In 1952 the 1st Chapel-en-le-Frith Girls' Life Brigade was formed, again based at Town End Methodist Church. A total of 21 girls joined the company, which was led by Captain Ivy Potts. Gela Evans was lieutenant and the company's president was Mrs Sam Longson. One of the first events was a mammoth jumble sale to raise funds for work within the company. Jumble sales, coffee mornings and sales of work, including the presence of the 'handkerchief girl', became the main fund-raisers. Soon after its formation the Chapel company found itself in the midst of the coronation celebrations of 1953. Displays were organised at the time by Mrs William-Boote, who also co-ordinated the participation of the girls in a joint coronation concert with the Boys' Brigade.

In 1954 the company was expanded to include a cadet section (now Explorers) led by Mrs Minshull and assisted by Mrs Rogan. The first cadet on the register was Barbara Singleton (née Ford), who has been the company president since 1982. Band instruments were also acquired and, with Frank Moss agreeing to train the girls, a company band was soon performing at monthly church parades. This arrangement initially caused a dispute because the captains of the Girls' and Boys' Brigades could not agree on a format to allow both their bands to play during the parade. As a result the Boys' Brigade started from Ashbourne Lane and the Girls' Life Brigade started from the Town Hall, with the two bands arriving simultaneously at the church!

In 1955 the band competed in the National Band Competition in London and members of the company attended the annual display at the Royal Albert Hall in the evening. In 1958 four Chapel girls took part in a PT display of the Manchester Division at the Royal Albert Hall. Mrs Ivy Potts remained as captain until 1959, when Mrs Kathleen Thompson (née Longson) took over until 1960. At this point the company had reached a low ebb and struggled on without a captain for four years, with Mrs Alec Minshull assisting until Mrs Linda Harper took over in 1964.

The year 1965 was important for the Brigade nationally, with the Girls' Life Brigade of England and Wales, the Girls' Guildry of Scotland and the Girls' Brigade in Ireland amalgamating to form the Girls' Brigade. A new uniform was introduced to include a warm blazer, which proved to be ideal for parades in Chapel-en-le-Frith!

The old Girls' Life Brigade colours were laid up in 1966 and the new Girls' Brigade colour was dedicated at a parade service led by Revd Donald Hirst, who was also company chaplain. The year 1966 also saw Ralph Harper take over as band instructor, a position he held until 1985.

In the following years the company grew in strength and extended its range of activities. In 1971 the Girls' Brigade took part in the Chapel Youth Carnival, the first of the carnivals we still see today. In 1975 the youth organisations of Chapel joined together to produce a gang show, called 'Festival of Frolics', held at Chapel-en-le-Frith's secondary school. The girls performed some maypole dancing and put on a joint gymnastics display with the boys. The jubilee celebrations of 1977 culminated in a reunion of ex-members, which featured an impromptu 'Old Girls' Band', which has become a regular feature at each subsequent reunion.

The company became a regular visitor to the Girls' Brigade Rally of the North, an event which is held every two years at Blackpool Tower Circus. Many girls remember the coach journeys on Bowers' buses, the couple of hours freedom which you enjoyed if you were in the senior section, the bracing weather and the stick of rock to remind you of the trip – not to mention the show itself! In 1979 the band had the honour of being chosen to play at the rally and gave two performances, each before an audience of over 2,000. The 21 members of the band rehearsed for several weeks before going to Blackpool and had a chance to try out their routine when they were a guest band at Taxal Scouts' Bands Open Night.

Below: *Officers at the Royal Albert Hall in 1957.*
Left to right: *Betty Cooper, Wendy Frith, Kathleen Watson, Mrs Potts, Margaret Potts, Sheila Marshall, Kathleen Longson.*

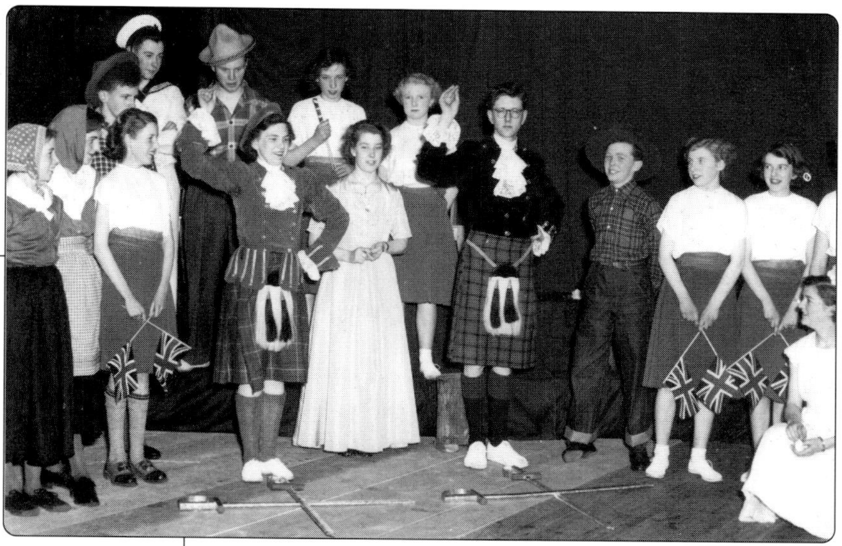

Above: *Coronation concert, 1953. The group includes: Joyce Frith, Doreen Ogan, John Thompson, Betty Taylor, Alan Minshull, Kathleen Longson, Wendy Frith, Frank Hulley, Jean Allsop, Nick Campbell, Mildred Jackson, Ann Merrick.*

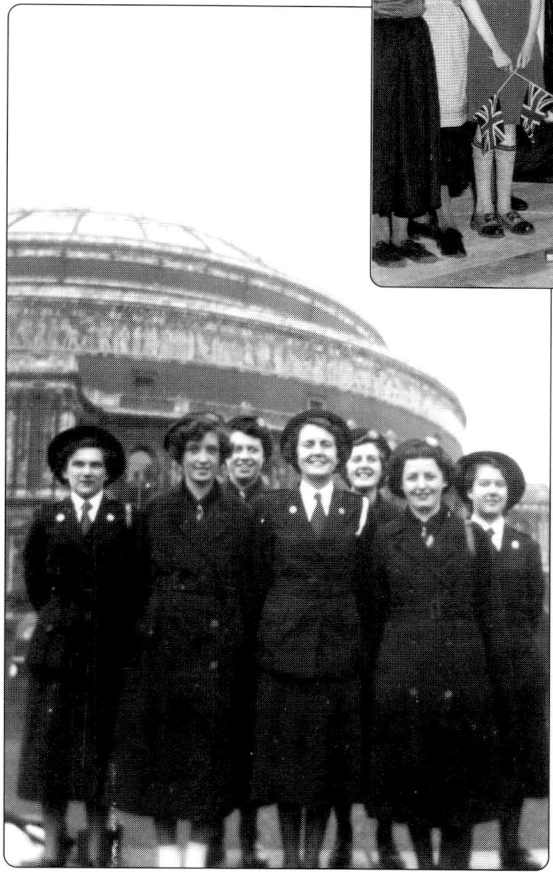

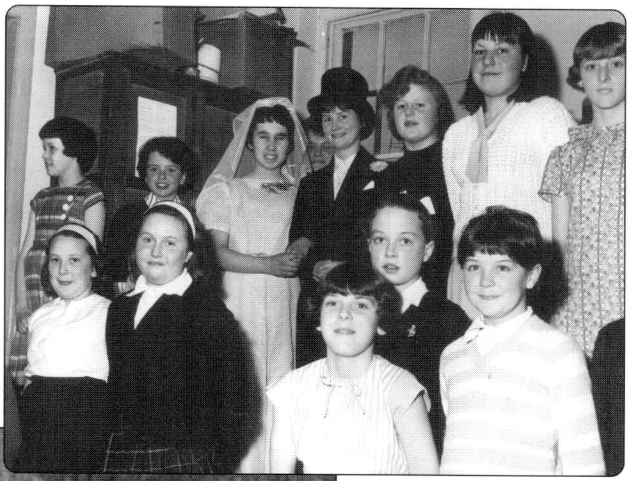

Above: *Girls' Brigade Gang Show, 1966. Group includes: Gillian Helps, Susan Bunting, Carol Burt, Adele Lane, Kath Hardy, Stephanie Lane, Jane Saunders.*

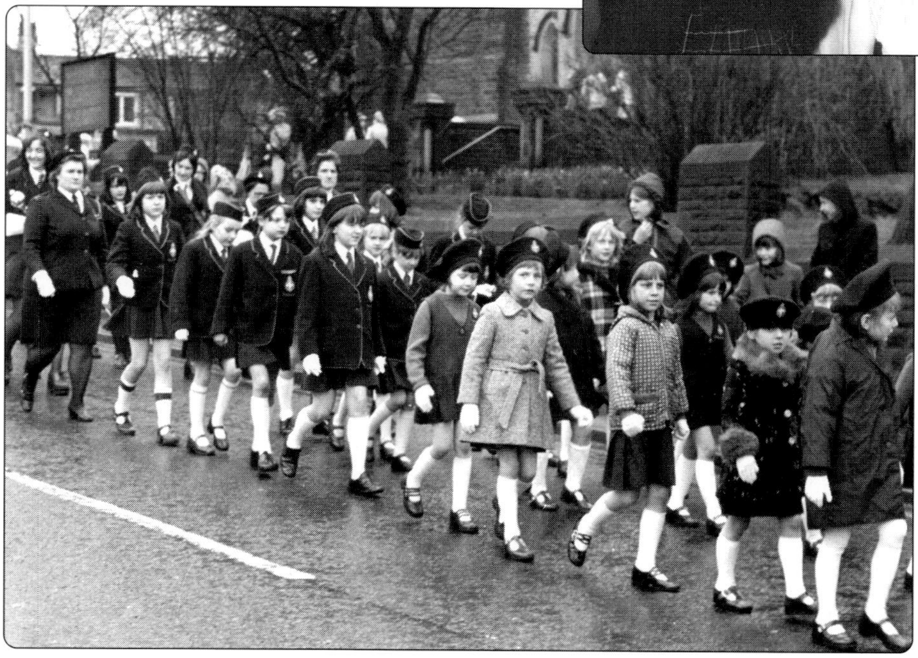

Left: *Girls' Brigade at the Boys' Brigade Jubilee Parade in 1976.*

Below: *Girls' Brigade at the Queen of the Peak Competition in the Ferodo canteen in 1979.* Left to right: *Karen Piper, Sharon Wilson, Claire Preston, Amanda Ridgeway, Amanda Muller, Jennie Taylor, Julie Whitehead. Judy Shipstone is at the organ. Jeanette Cohen was Queen of the Peak.*

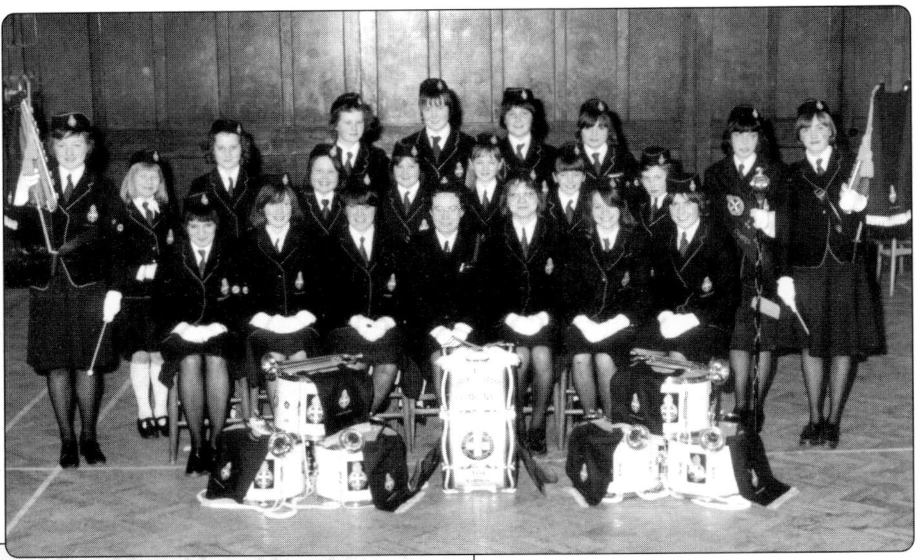

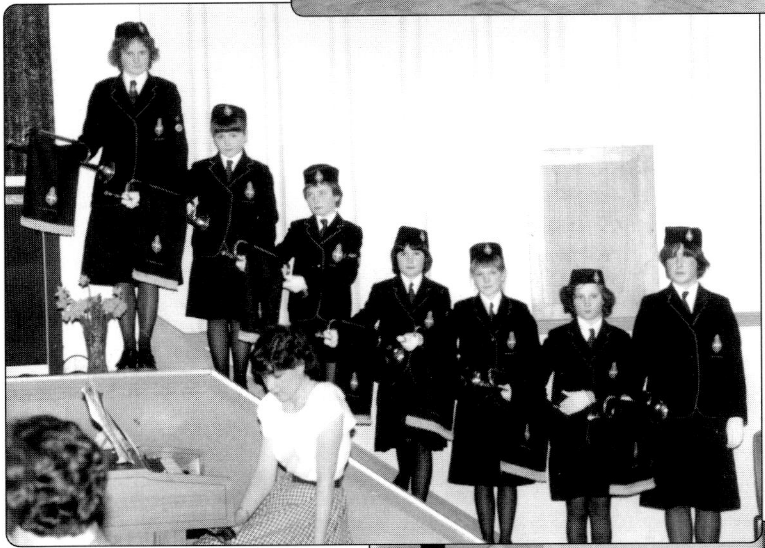

Above: *Blackpool Rally Band Display in 1979.* Left to right, back row: *Karen Piper, Alison Burgess, Maureen Wild, Joanne Wood;* middle row: *Debbie Element, Sarah Myers, Jennie Taylor, Michelle Wallis, Amanda Ridgeway, Amanda Muller, Sharon Wilson, Claire Preston, Judith Wild, Louise Muller;* seated: *Debbie Atwell, Jeanette Cohen, Michelle Banks, Linda Harper, Kathleen Barnes, Ann Alger, Julie Burgess.*

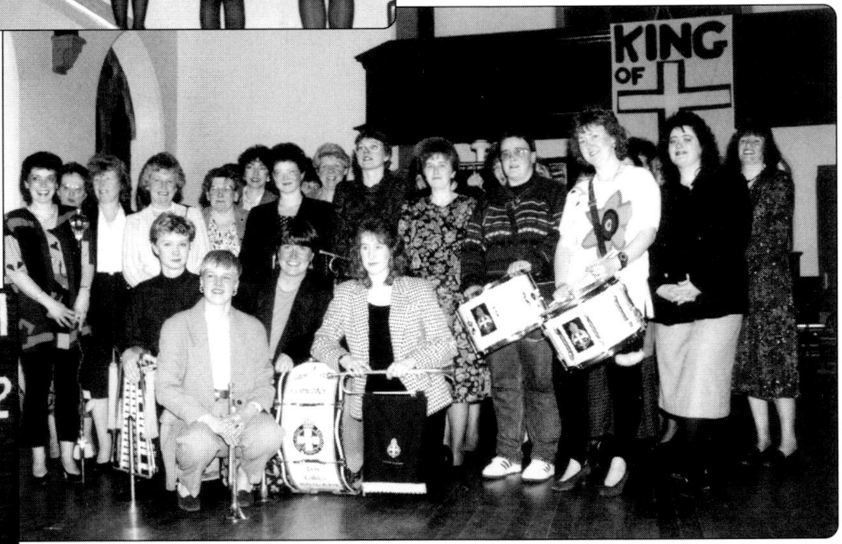

Below: *The 40th anniversary celebration tapestry presented to the Company.*

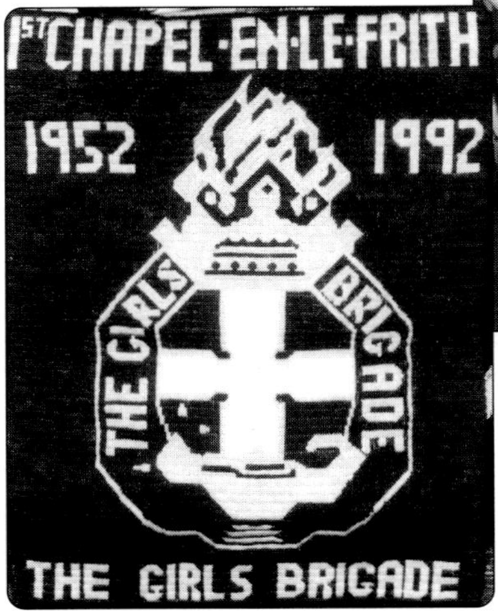

Above: *The 40th anniversary celebrations in 1992. The group includes* (standing): *Judith Wild, Linda Harper, Sheila Marshall, Betty Taylor, Ann Hibbs, Helen Brook, Kathleen Barnes, Valerie Nadin, Maureen Wild, Alison Burgess, Karen Bradbury, Gillian Helps;* kneeling: *Helen Harper, Carolyn Youd, Julie Burgess, Kay Dunk.*

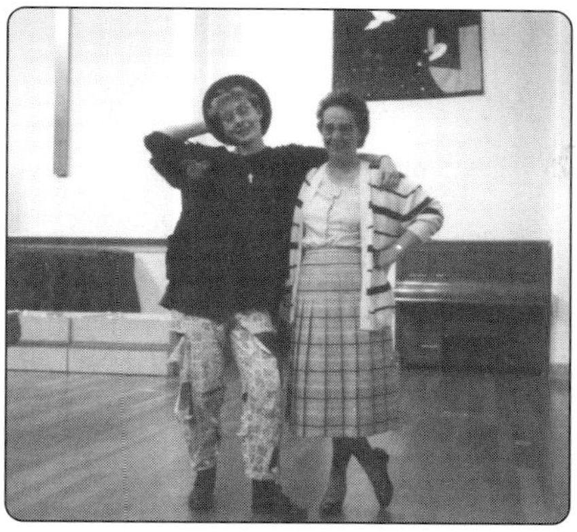

Helen and Linda Harper provided 70 years of service in total!

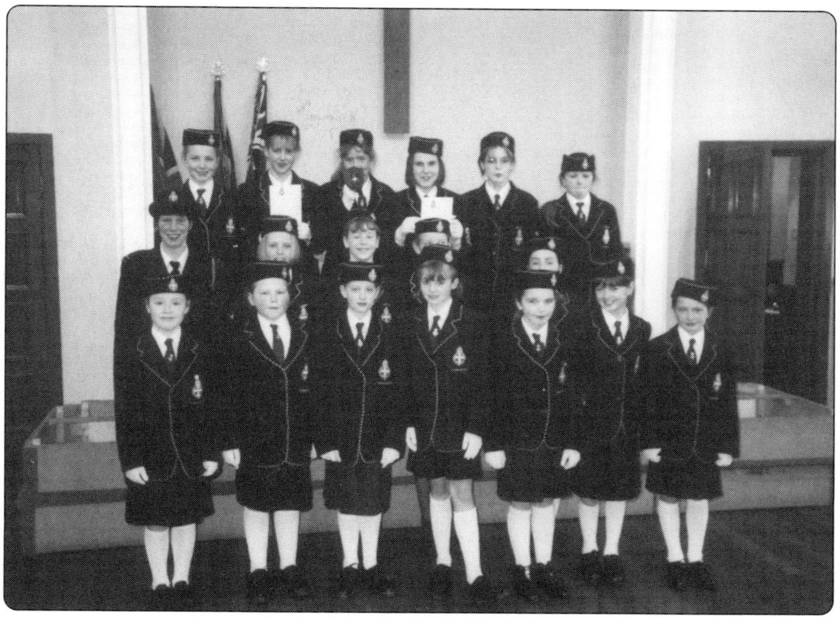

The 1995 Divisional Drill Competition.

By the beginning of the 1980s membership was up to 70 girls and waiting lists were introduced for all sections of the company. A group of members travelled to the National Rally at the Royal Albert Hall in 1985 to see Clare Grundy from Chapel receive the Distinguished Service Award from Lord Coggan for helping to save a man's life on Bowden Lane.

At the close of the summer session in 1985 Mrs Linda Harper retired as company captain and was replaced by Mrs Jeanette Saxby (née Cohen). Linda had been a member of the company from its formation in 1952, becoming an officer in 1962 and captain in 1964. Although retired from the company, Mrs Harper became deputy commissioner for the Manchester Division for a further 11 years. She remained as a reserve officer until 2002, completing a total of 50 years' service in the Girls' Brigade. Her daughter, Helen Harper, has completed 20 years' service with the Chapel company, so one family can boast an unprecedented total of 70 years' service!

During the late 1980s the company began the first of many youth-hostel camps, Eyam, Ravenstor and Castleton being among the first. By using local camps transport costs could be kept low. In fact, the girls, including one girl who was only eight years old, walked everywhere, carrying all their equipment and clothing. Once they arrived at the youth hostel the girls were kept busy with organised activities, lots of food, dormitory inspections, including checks for toothpaste in the sinks, and, of course, midnight feasts!

Manchester Divisional drill, badge work and competitions were entered eagerly and with some success: in 1986, the junior section (eight to ten years) won the cookery competition and was congratulated for being the only team seen to have washed their hands properly before they started. The senior section (11 to 13 years) won a prize for their skills at DIY, by tiling a section of board and rewiring a plug, among other tasks. The Explorers competed with a piece of artwork and a senior girl, Elizabeth Helps, took on the Brigadier (14+ years) task of decorating an Easter cake. This splendid display of teamwork resulted in the Chapel company taking the overall trophy.

In 1987 the Chapel company took part in the Girls' Brigade Regional Parade held in York. This proved to be an amazing sight, with a parade of 800 girls, followed by a service in a packed York Minster.

In 1990 Mrs Jeanette Saxby (née Cohen) married at Town End Methodist Church with the whole company in attendance. She moved to live in Wales, where she served with the 1st Old Colwyn Company. Mrs Elizabeth Cox took over as captain of the Chapel company.

During Mrs Cox's captaincy membership figures remained high, with numbers in the Explorer section alone reaching 30. In 1992 the company celebrated its 40th anniversary with a reunion of old members at Town End Methodist Church and in 1993 the National Girls' Brigade celebrated its centenary. The Manchester Division of the Girls' Brigade held a teddy bears' picnic and issued all members with centenary mugs.

In 1994 Mrs Cox stepped down as captain, but remained as an officer, and Mrs Saxby returned to take over the captaincy. The company continued to participate in divisional events, winning first place in the Divisional Sports Day in 1994 and first place in the Divisional Drill Competition (2nd tier) in 1995.

The year 1995 also saw the introduction of a new uniform for both girls and officers. A sweatshirt bearing the Girls' Brigade badge replaced the blazer and the wearing of hats became optional. A less fitted suit in a lighter shade of navy-blue also replaced the officers' uniforms. An activity uniform for all sections, including officers, was also introduced; it comprised navy-blue trousers, polo shirt and Girls'

Brigade sweatshirt – a much more practical outfit for outdoor activities and games.

Mrs Julie Murdy took over as captain in 1998, a year in which the girls took part in an activity camp at Shell Island in Wales. Abseiling, rock climbing, land yachting and obstacle courses were all included. The company continued to take part in district, regional and national events. In 1999 Nonie Lambert won the competition to design the cover for the Blackpool Rally programme. Nonie was presented with the prize at the rally, where she and her mum had the privilege of sitting in the prime seats while the rest of the company had to sit in the 'gods'. In 2000 Nonie won first prize in the District Millennium Competition with her ideas of how the Girls' Brigades in Manchester could best celebrate the millennium. In 2001 the Brigadier section took part in the national competitions.

The company continues to take part in Greater Manchester District activities and many local events. Over the years they have been asked to attend and lead activities such as the Chapel well dressing ceremony, Peak Forest well dressing, and act as escorts for Chapel's carnival royalty on their visit to Whitestones and Eccles Fold. All of these events are now included in the regular activities of the company.

The year 2002 marked a special milestone because it was the 50th anniversary of the Chapel company, and the occasion was made even more memorable because it coincided with the Queen's golden jubilee. An exhibition of company photographs and memorabilia, a reunion, a party and a celebratory parade service marked the event.

Chapel-en-le-Frith Scout Group

By Tony Read (group Scout leader in 2003), with contributions from Ron Davidson (former group Scout leader) and Gerald Williams (whose father was group Scout leader).

The Scout Movement

The Scout movement was born in 1907, when Robert Baden-Powell took a group of boys from widely differing backgrounds on a week's camp on Brownsea Island. The camp was a huge success, so much so that Baden-Powell's friend, Sir William Smith (the founder of the Boys' Brigade) persuaded him to write a series of booklets entitled *Scouting for Boys*. A new booklet was produced each fortnight, and the series proved to be an instant hit, despite costing four pence per copy, a not insignificant amount in Edwardian times. Boys from all over the country embraced the Baden-Powell ideas, and patrols of Scouts began appearing everywhere. By 1908 there were already over 10,000 lads involved nationwide.

It was intended that the starting age for Scouts would be 11 years of age but, with so many younger boys desperate to join the movement, it was decided to form Wolf Cubs, with programmes and characters woven around Rudyard Kipling's *Jungle Book.*

Chapel Scouts

The precise date on which Scouting commenced in Chapel-en-le-Frith is not entirely clear, although 25 November 1925 is believed to be the date when our first Scout troop was registered and it is clear that there was a Scout troop in Chapel by 1926, because a faded photograph exists showing boys from Chapel camping at Monsal Dale. By this time Scouting had become international, with over one million members worldwide.

Over the years Chapel Scouts have depended on a great many gifted and dedicated people. Among the early Scout and Cub leaders were Edgar Vernon (Scoutmaster), Billy Wilkins (group Scoutmaster), and Miss Prain and Sheila Eyre, who ran the Cub pack. George Ainscow became group Scoutmaster in 1938 and led the group through the difficult war years. He later became High Peak Scouts' district secretary and was eventually awarded an MBE for services to Scouting. The Scouts and Cubs continued to meet every week throughout the war years, when punctual attendance was required, uniform had to be worn whenever possible and a weekly subscription of a penny was collected.

In 1940 'Skip' Williams moved to Chapel-en-le-Frith and his enthusiasm for the Scout movement soon became apparent to people in the town. He had joined the Scouts in 1908 and had become a Rover Scout leader while living at Chorlton, Manchester. He filled the same role in Chapel and ensured that there was an active and demanding programme for the boys throughout the period up to 1945, when Scout leaders Reg Fox and Bernard Fox (no relation) were demobilised and able to resume their running of the Scout troop. Skip became group Scoutmaster and led the group for the next 30 years. He was a great believer in outdoor activities and hiking,

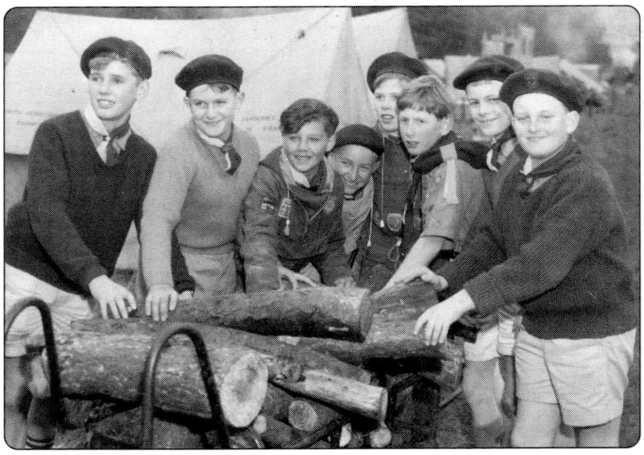

A jamboree at Chatsworth in 1965. Left to right: *Ian Watt, Philip Davidson, Stuart Wilson, Ian Harrison, Ian Charles, Colin Prime, Geoff Brearley, Richard Green.*

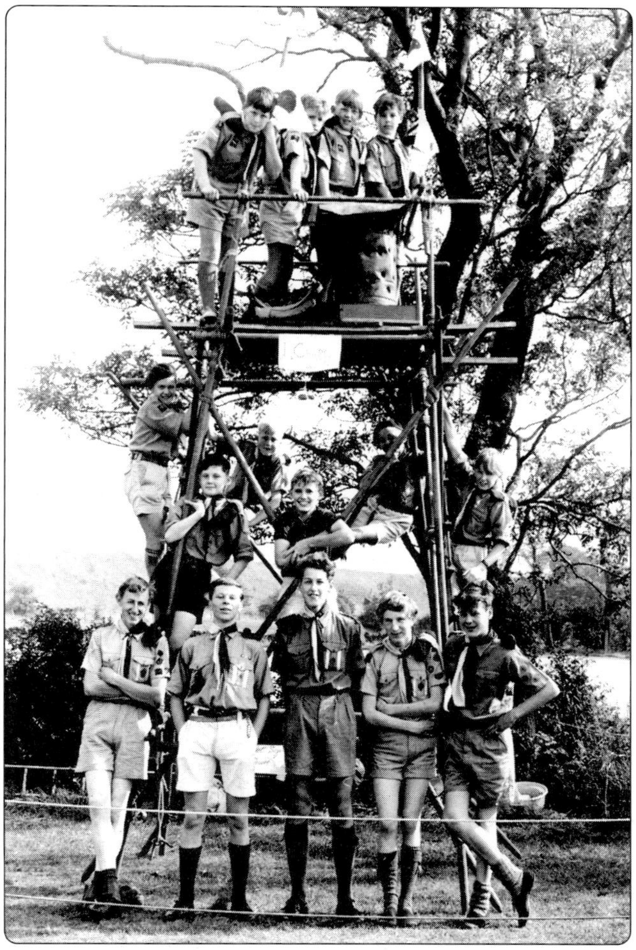

Pioneering polers at Long Lane School in the late 1960s.

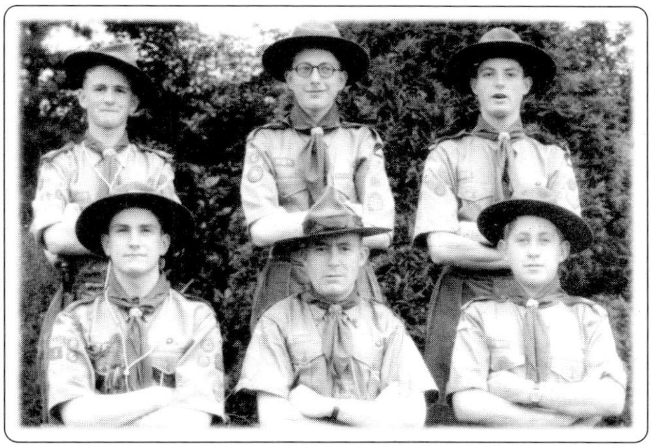

Chapel Scouts in 1947.

sailing, rafting on Johnny Middleton's pond, camping, 'wide-games' on Eccles Pike, and even skiing, including an amazing cross-country ski excursion from Chapel to Edale, became the order of the day. Under Skip's leadership the troop performed very well in swimming galas, sports days and other such competitions, but skills and badges were not neglected. Many Chapel Scouts gained the King's Scout and later the Queen's Scout awards. In the late 1930s Cornwall badges for bravery were presented to George Foden and Wallace Askey – very high honours indeed!

International jamboree camps had started to be held before the war, but it was not until 1947 that Chapel Scouts got the opportunity to attend. In that year a group of lads, led by Skip, attended a jamboree at Moisson, in France. The group consisted of Colin Longson, Roy King, Trevor Hill, Arthur Booth and Andrew Fisher. Colin Longson later became the district commissioner for High Peak Scouts, Trevor Hill became a minister of religion and Arthur Booth became a doctor. Since that time Chapel Scouts have attended most world jamborees, even though their locations have become more and more far flung. In recent years Chapel boys have attended jamborees in Chile and Korea.

During the 1970s it became possible for older Scouts (17 to 20 years old) to go on expeditions for Explorer Belts. Working in pairs, the Scouts are taken abroad, where they embark on a trek and carry out specified tasks. One such trek started at Corinth and involved a week-long hike through southern Greece. The Scouts were provided with letters of introduction to local people and were required, during a seven-day period, to make contact with a local Scout, learn a Greek dance, attend a church service, try the local food and make new friendships. Another adventure involving Chapel lads took place in Morocco, and several Chapel boys repeated the Moroccan trip in the 1990s as part of the High Peak Mountaineering Group, spending ten nights camping at 13,000ft in the Atlas mountains and climbing Mount Toubkahl, the highest peak in the range.

Ron 'Kim' Davidson joined the group in 1963 and gradually took over the running of the group, carefully maintaining the traditions which had been established. He took over from Skip as group Scout leader in 1975, but Skip didn't retire and was a regular visitor to the hut and always on hand to give help and sound advice.

For more than half a century the Chapel Scout headquarters was a wooden hut on Eccles Road. The building was already second-hand when it was acquired, but it was always well-maintained and, after the Scouts moved to their new brick-built headquarters in 1982, it was occupied for a while by the Chapel Town Band, until it was unfortunately destroyed by fire. Its last service to the Scouts was to provide some of the wood for the group's bonfire night celebrations!

The new Scout headquarters was a tremendous boost to the group. The funds to pay for its construction were raised in only six years and the building is a testament to the tireless efforts of many dedicated individuals. Over the years fund-raising has become an increasingly important part of the Scouts' programme. In the 1930s, and in many subsequent years, the annual jumble sale was the major source of revenue for the troop. Some idea of the changing value of money can be judged by the fact that a sale which raised £2.15s.6½d. in 1936 was regarded as a success!

By the 1990s other methods of fund-raising, such as HQ-letting, packing customers' bags in Safeway, sponsored walks and novelty events such as 'frog racing', proved to be more profitable than jumble sales. The group held its last jumble sale in 2000, but there are people who have fond memories of pushing a heavy trek cart around Chapel for several days prior to the sale, in order to collect jumble, from house to house, often in some extreme weather conditions.

Many other things have altered in Chapel's 80-year Scouting history. Uniforms have undergone marked changes: broad-brimmed hats are no longer worn and shorts are not part of the modern uniform – youngsters who parade on Remembrance Sunday today may think themselves lucky not to have to march through the streets with their exposed knees turning blue due to lack of protection from rain, sleet or gales!

The group grew quickly in the 1980s and by 1985 there were two Scout troops, known as Williams (named after Skip) and Pathfinders, and two Cub packs, known as Kinder and Bowden. Leaders in those days included Eric Jackson, David Bird, Jim Perkins, Peter Ripley and David Parker in Scouts, and Gill Carrington, Jean Clough, Doreen Bird and Marion Parker for Cubs. A Beaver Colony, for boys aged between six and eight years, was established in 1985 by Marian Jackson and Ann Stewart, and quickly became a great success. With the new influx of boys the total membership of all sections exceeded 100.

Ron Davidson retired in 1993 as group Scout leader. Roddie Maclean became the new Pathfinder leader, the group appointed Tony Anderson as group Scout leader and his wife Christina took over the running of Kinder Cubs. Ann Piper from Chapel Milton took charge of the Beaver Colony, greatly supported by her husband Donny, and she later took charge of Bowden Cubs, when Jean Clough became assistant district commissioner for Cubs.

Unfortunately, the Williams troop folded in the '80s and the Beaver Colony also ceased to function through lack of leaders. However, with a great deal of help from the High Peak district, especially Jean Barton, Jean Clough and Elaine White, Tony Read, who is the group Scout leader at the time of writing, succeeded in re-establishing the Beaver Colony. In 2003 it is thriving group and is enthusiastically led by Jane Green and Ruth Carter.

The Chapel Scout group of 2003 consists of two Cub packs, a Scout troop and a Beaver Colony. The current leaders, Roddie Maclean, Peter Bywater, Ann Piper, Tom Birch, Paul Read, Steve Ryan, Jane Coleman, Ros Price, Tony Brewin, Jane Green, Ruth Carter and, when available, John Read, do a first-rate job keeping Scouting alive and well in Chapel-en-le-Frith. They are supported by an industrious group Scout committee, which has always been a strength of the Chapel group. Over the years the group has been fortunate in having the involvement of a number of very dedicated people, including Reg Fox, a long-serving chairman, Alan Taylor, who was group secretary for nearly a quarter of a century, and Bob Brearley, who was treasurer for a similar period. The future seems equally assured; with Chapel Scouts looking forward to another 80 years of success and fully intending to remain an integral part of the fabric of the town.

Chapel Youth Club

By Bernice Wood, youth centre clerical worker.

The minutes of a Youth Club management committee meeting, held on 16 February 1969, included a statement by a Mr Wald that there had been a youth club in the town in 1945/46, but there were no other known records of a youth club existing in Chapel at this time. However, a newspaper cutting dated 1948 reported that halloween was celebrated at Chapel Youth Club, where Mr A. Wathall and Mr W.A. Hudson were leaders. It is also known that the North West Area Youth Drama Festival was held in Chapel-en-le-Frith on 4 December of that same year.

A lads' club was formed in 1953 and accommodated in two huts, which had been purchased by Derbyshire Education Authority from T. Shepley & Co. Ltd and were located between Dane House and the Parish Church. By 1953 girls were also attending the club.

The first recorded management committee meeting dates from 1952, when committee members included Dr Marshall, Mrs Barber, Mr Millward, Mr Ward, Mr Wathall, Revd Canon Green, Father Whitehouse and Miss Riley. The minutes record that the Youth Club leader was E. White and that two members, Trevor Beswick and Vernon Wakefield, had attended a weekend course in Buxton, entitled 'Youth at the Helm'. There was a balance of only 16s.6½d. in the Youth Club account, but an appeal for funds was about to be launched in the local press. Activities for the autumn term included: a public-speaking contest at Whaley Bridge, a talk about racing pigeons, a so-called 'rubber' of games, and a potato-pie supper to commemorate the anniversary of the opening of the club.

The leader's report of 22 January 1953 stated that Chinley Youth Club members had visited Chapel Youth Club for a quiz and a whist drive. It was reported in April of that year that Chapel members had done well in a cross-country running race in Buxton and had been runners-up in an area quiz competition in Glossop. However, three members had been suspended for gambling and some members had come into the club 'worse for drink' on one or two evenings.

Mr Woodward of Hayfield gave the Youth Club some packing cases free of charge. These were delivered by Sam Longson and the material from them was used to re-line the games room. The re-lining and redecorating proved to be a considerable task, requiring members to work every night from 14 May until the end of June.

In June 1954 the club membership dropped to 30 because some members had been called up to serve in the Forces.

In December 1965 there was a break-in at the youth centre. The police caught the intruders and discovered that the miscreants were all club members. The offenders were brought before the committee, before whom they made their apologies and pleaded to remain as members. Revd Austin and his committee decided to let them off with a caution.

The club closed down between February 1965 and December 1966 to allow a small Army hut to be prepared on the Eccles Road site. Ron Hill, who had the grand title of warden of the Peak Park County Youth Clubs, was responsible for the running of the Chapel club, as well as that at Tideswell. The club had a balance of £45 at the time and it was decided to use some of this money to purchase a badminton set and a gramophone, on the understanding that members would bring their own records.

By September 1967 the club had 44 members, ran cricket and netball teams, and organised football training at Long Lane School (now Chapel High School). That year the members enjoyed trips to Lea Green and Blackpool, and two girls from the club collected £6.3s. for the National Society for the Prevention of Cruelty to Children. Club dances were held at the Constitutional Hall, with a group called the Bin Band and disc jockeys called Kevin and Brent.

A separate youth coffee bar, called Our Place, operated from April 1969 until July 1970 at the old Civil Defence building (now Chapel Pets) on Market Street. When the building was sold and the facility closed, most of the members joined Chapel Youth Club.

The second stage of the Eccles Road youth centre, comprising hall, lounge, office and toilets, was completed in 1970. The following year David Wood was employed by Derbyshire Education Authority as a full-time youth worker at the centre. When the Youth Club became operational on Eccles Road a number of residents in the vicinity expressed concern about 'the probability of excessive sound levels of offensive pop music at Sunday-night activities of the Youth Club.' When the sound levels were checked it was apparently found that loud music played at the club could not be heard in the surrounding roads!

In the early 1970s the Eccles Road centre was open for seniors on four nights per week, when it was staffed by paid workers. On one other evening voluntary members ran a junior club. The site was also used by Long Lane and Bank Hall Schools, adult yoga classes, a playgroup, the Guides, the Crusaders and the Mothers' Union. A letter written by the Mothers' Union in 1970 indicates that the group had been desperate for new premises to replace their base in the upper floor of the Infant School, which was reached by an iron ladder. Their letter read, 'As our members have become infirm, they have been unable to attend meetings.'

In 1973 the Youth Club had a full programme of activities. A 48-hour dance marathon raised £180, just under half of which went to the mobile physiotherapy unit; a float in the shape of a paddle-steamer was entered in the Chapel carnival; a summer play week was held for junior members and 11 senior members went to a camp in Devon. The members' committee of the time included A. Baxter, I. Fell, D. Waterhouse, C. Middleton, J. Allen, C. Bunting, D. Neill, J. Bramwell, J. Kerr and P. Buckle.

A light-hearted monthly newsletter was produced and posted on the wall for members to read. One extract reads:

Due to the number of broken windows in the school building, balls can only be taken in the yard if a member of staff is present. This should safeguard both the windows and yourself.

It also contained the following observation:

Is it true that Alan Baxter and Wayne Thomas are trying to start a skinhead revival in Chapel? Seems to me that they are twelve months out of date. Never mind lads, they say baldness is sexy!

One sports report read:

Our table tennis team was hammered when they went over to Chinley. However, let's remember our lads have only been playing for four weeks, whereas the others have been playing for years.

In 1973 Elaine Simmons was employed as an ancillary worker at the club and later became a part-time leader. Elaine also ran the junior club, which opened in 1971 and finally closed in 1998. She is still with the Youth Club to this day as a member of the management committee and an occasional voluntary helper. John Barnes (who worked as a leader-in-charge on occasions when full-time workers were not available) and Geoff Hibbert did a great deal to keep the club running through the 1960s and '70s.

Simon Fuchs took over as full-time leader in 1975 and remained with the club for four years, during which time he facilitated a wide range of activities for both seniors and juniors. Trips were taken to the cinema, there was ice-skating and sailing on Combs Reservoir; a discussion on drugs, led by Mrs Gordon; and a showing of the film 'Live and Let Die'. Under the guidance of Mrs Simmons a group of girls started to make a blanket for a pensioner who lived in a caravan near the site, and a folk group was formed and guitar classes held. A floodlit hard play area was completed in 1977, allowing the members to play outdoor games.

Jo Polak was employed as a youth worker for a short time in the mid-1980s, but Pat Bowers, who had started working as a volunteer in 1971, took over as leader-in-charge in 1986. Elaine Simmons and Eileen Heyes worked alongside Pat for a period of ten years, giving stability to the club and helping to keep membership high. During this time the club was redecorated by members, with the help of Neil Bennett's artistic input. The redecoration included a mural on the coffee-bar walls depicting scenes in the town. With the help of High Peak Community Arts, the members also worked on a drugs project, which involved discussions, video, drama, photographs and the production of a magazine that was circulated to other clubs. Mary Cohen, who ran a women's group, worked alongside the Youth Club at the first health drop-in.

Youth workers need many skills, not least competence in first aid. After a particularly harrowing evening in 1996, Geraldine Dean, a worker-in-charge, wrote a poem entitled 'A Youthworker's Nightmare or Thumbthings Amiss', recalling an evening when one Youth Club member got himself shackled in a pair of handcuffs and had to be taken to Buxton hospital to be set free.

After working at the Fairfield Centre for four years, Mark Robinson became a team member in 1997 and worked at the Chapel and Chinley clubs for a further four years. Mark enjoyed sport and music and encouraged the members to go on activity weekends.

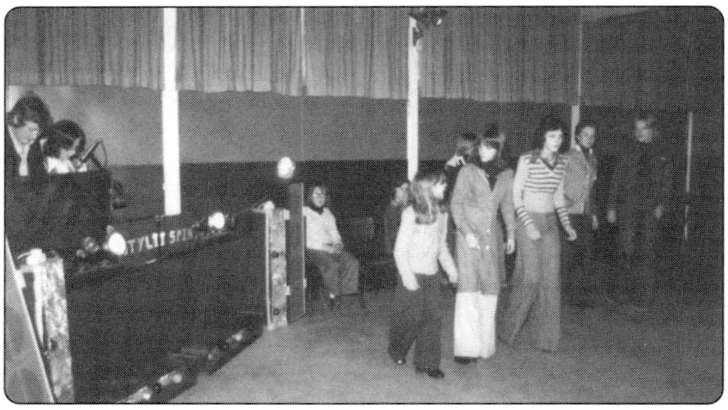

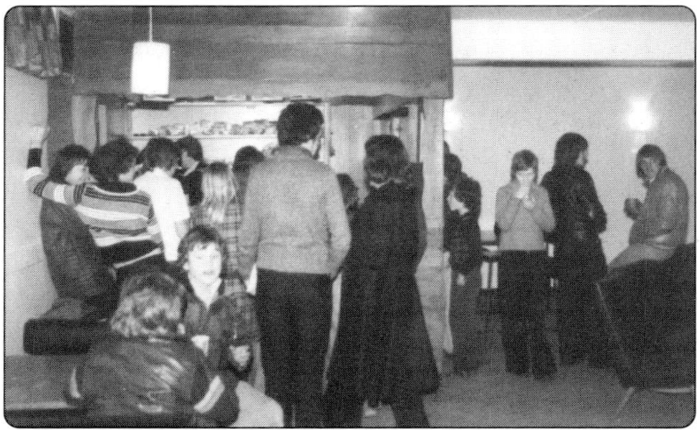

Both pictures above: *Chapel Youth Club in their old centre.*

The discos which were held at this time attracted young people from as far away as Disley, Glossop, New Mills and Buxton. Club members fought to retain the discos by writing to the local press and petitioning the local council, but the dances became a victim of their own success, because the staff were unable to control the 250 teenagers who descended on the town on Friday evenings. Complaints from local residents finally forced the discos to close.

The Youth Club moved into its new home in the old infant-school site on 11 August 2001. New technology arrived in the form of an up-to-date personal computer, whose delivery had been arranged by Councillor Charles. The new machine gave members access to the internet and replaced a ten-year-old Apple Mackintosh, which was still in working order and was donated to the Glossop Centre.

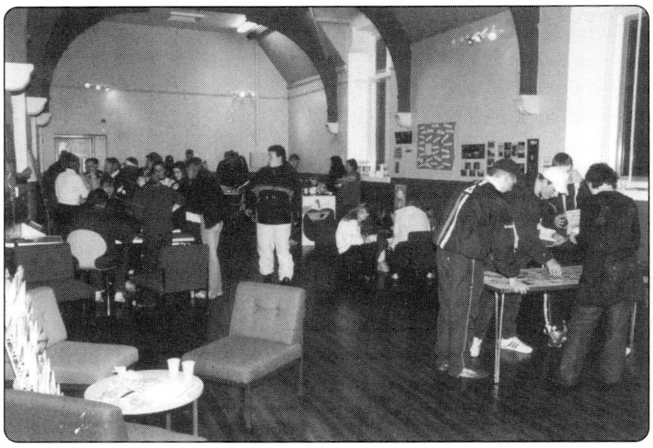

The Youth Club's new centre in the old infant-school building.

Unfortunately, team member Mags Davies left shortly after the new facility was opened, but she was replaced by Kevin Skermer. By the time of the official opening of the new centre on 30 November 2002, membership had risen to 150. Kevin's development plan envisages Chapel Youth Centre as a specialist Youth Arts and Technology Centre – a computer room has already been set up by Dan Taylor, from Derbyshire County Council, and Paul Draycott, Chapel Senior Club worker-in-charge.

The opening ceremony was attended by over 200 people who were entertained by Lost Cause, Three Must Get Beers and Rastiraka (three bands which had been formed by Youth-Club members) and a girl dance group called Twisted Angels.

Mike Davies, who stood in for Councillor Bob Janes, unveiled a metal plaque which had been produced by members working with Peter Sharp, an activity leader. Frances Hibbert presented the club with a gold disc obtained by Lloyd Cole and the Commotions for 'Drastic Plastic', and donated by Lloyd's parents. Lloyd was a former pupil of the Infant School whose building is now occupied by the Youth Club.

Staff working at the new club alongside Kevin

Skermer at the time of writing are : Paul Draycott, Judith Ashurst, Margaret Hallam and Angela Henderson, and dance tutor Heather Jones.

Combs Brownie Pack

By Janet McNicol, Brownie Guider.

The 1st Combs Brownie Pack was registered in 1958, with six children meeting in a house in Combs. Numbers grew rapidly and the meeting-place for the pack was moved to the gymnasium above the old Chapel-en-le-Frith Infant School, and later to the main hall of the school, but summer meetings continued to be held in Combs village, where there are fine opportunities for exploring the countryside.

When the Infant School moved to a new site in 1999 the Brownies were left with nowhere to meet in Chapel-en-le-Frith, but were able to return to Combs and, thanks to the Combs Village Hall Committee, they now meet in the Village Hall.

Combs Brownies form a busy, active pack of girls, aged from seven to ten years, and there is a waiting list of eager children wishing to join. The Promise is at the centre of all activities: loving God, serving Queen and country, and helping other people. The weekly meetings are arranged around ideas which have been put forward by the Brownies themselves, within a programme designed to encourage the girls to become involved in all kinds of fun and rewarding activities.

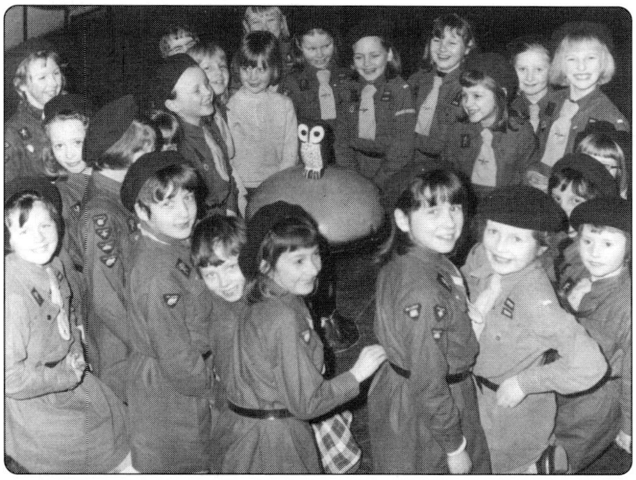

Combs Brownies in 1967.

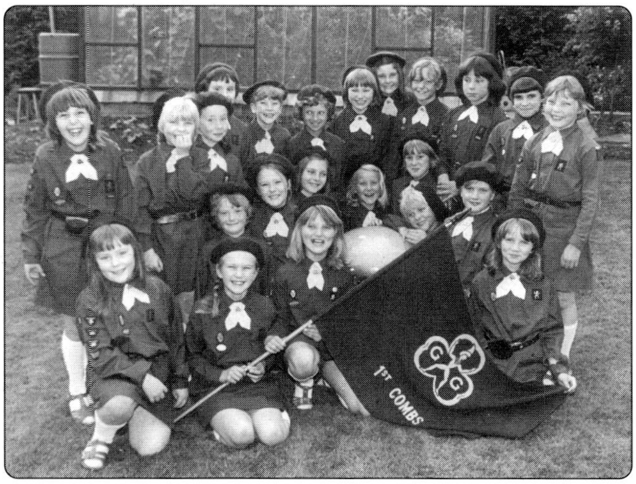

Combs Brownies at the dedication of the new flag in 1980.

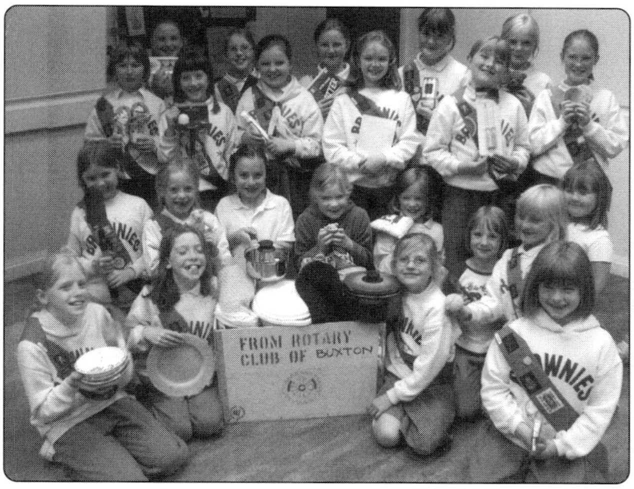

Packing a Rotary International emergency box in 2002.

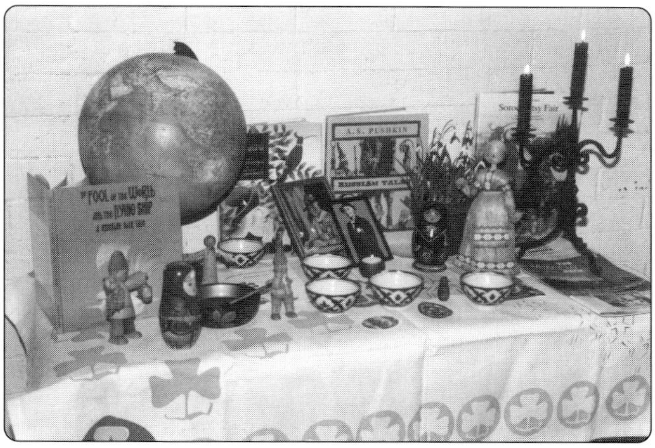

Thinking display in 1999, with Russia as the theme.

'Pack Holiday', with treasure hunts, cooking, crafts, exploring, and lots and lots of laughter, is one of the highlights of the year.

The visits that are arranged to various places often help the Brownies to complete badges or challenges, and the pack raises money for many charities and appeals. They have sponsored children in the Holy Land, 'adopted' a dolphin in Scotland, sponsored nest boxes in the Goyt Valley and an inshore lifeboat near Skegness, and planted trees and plants for various events.

Many projects, such as the Environment Challenge, Book Aid or the Rotary International emergency box scheme, have been undertaken with enthusiasm. The list of activities is very long and includes producing pantomimes, quad-biking, pottery, constructing bird boxes, keep-fit and dance routines, archery, toe-wrestling and fire prevention. In fact, no two meetings are the same and it would take several books to record all the things undertaken by the pack.

In 1961 the first 'Easter Sale' was held. This is now an annual event, held on the day before Palm Sunday, and is the only occasion in the year when the pack raises money for itself. The Brownies often organise other events, such as the Charities Fair, which are designed to make money for other organisations.

The leaders are all trained volunteers and the pack is always happy to welcome visitors and show them their crafts and skills. Since 1958, when the pack was set up, there have been many changes. The uniform and the programme of activities are now much altered, but the values of the Promise and the enthusiasm of the children remain constant.

The Guide Movement in Chapel-en-le-Frith

By Elizabeth Stafford (High Peak divisional commissioner and assistant Guider with Chapel 1st Guides), with help from Muriel Carrington (former Guide leader) and Elaine Radford (former assistant Guide leader).

Chapel-en-le-Frith Girl Guides (as they were then known) started in 1923, after an advertisement placed in the local press had attracted a tremendous response. Several girls were selected to become patrol leaders and the first captain gave them some initial training in her own home. Once these girls were ready, the company was opened to others and meetings began to take place in the local Drill Hall. The Guides wore a navy dress, wide-brimmed felt hat and a pale-blue triangular scarf – the whole uniform would have cost 2s.6d. and subscriptions were 2d. per week.

The company was officially registered on 24 November 1924 and their Guide colours, which now hang in St Thomas Becket Church, were dedicated on 2 May 1926.

In 1928 a spacious wooden hut was erected by a local carpenter, at a cost of £129, on a piece of land on the Warmbrook estate, which had been either donated or sold cheaply to the Guides by a local man. The building was officially opened on 8 September 1928.

The earliest record of Brownies in Chapel-en-le-Frith was a meeting in the new hut on 1 September 1928, although it is believed that the pack may have been formed at an earlier date. The Guides and Brownies met in the Warmbrook hut for many years until both units were closed for a time. However, it is known that both the Guides and the Brownies were meeting during the war years and taking part in the war effort. One Brown Owl of the day remembers that the Brownie pack was inundated with evacuees.

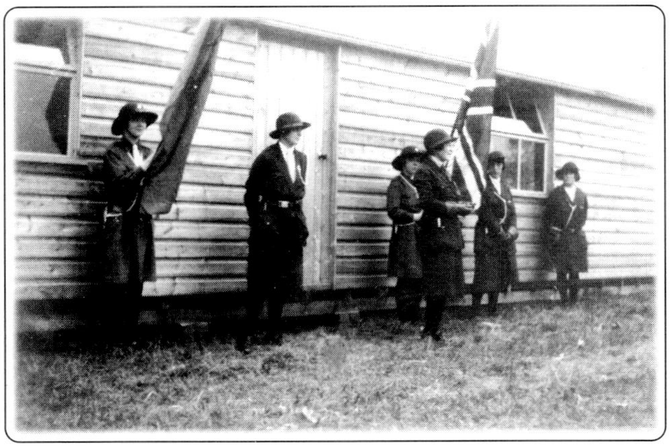

The opening of the Guide hut on 8 September 1928.

The Brownie pack was re-registered on 25 January 1950 as 1st Chapel-en-le-Frith St Thomas Becket Brownies, and the Guide company was re-registered on 25 June 1958 as 1st Chapel-en-le-Frith St Thomas Becket Guides. They both continued to meet in the old Guide hut, which was also in use as an ancillary classroom for Town End's school. In 1966 the Guides and Brownies had to move to a new home as the hut was no longer fit for use. The building was sold to a farmer for use as a chicken house and the rest of the land at Warmbrook remained empty for some time. In the early 1970s the Guiders and the Guides started to raise money for a new hut and the then Local Association (interested friends of the movement) joined in the project. In 1976, after a great deal of hard work, the Guides and Brownies were able to move into their new headquarters, which had been erected on the same plot of land as the original hut. The official opening took place on 9 September 1976, almost 48 years to the day after the official opening of the first hut.

Over the years several girls gained the Queen's Guide Badge, once the highest award in Guiding. Although names and uniform changes have taken place, Guiding continues to be what Baden-Powell had envisaged: a game with purpose, which tries to provide opportunities for the girls to develop personal faith and values, to think for themselves and make their own decisions, learn to work and share with others, to develop a sense of tolerence, self awareness, self respect and confidence, to appreciate the environment, and to learn about the world and its peoples and cultures. The movement, now known as Girl Guiding, with its modern uniform to fit with today's lifestyle, welcomes all girls irrespective of creed, race or colour, provided they are willing to make the Guide Promise, which asks that a Guide does her best to love her God, serve her Queen and country and keep the Guide Laws. Both the Guide and the Brownie units continue to meet weekly in their headquarters on Barlow Road, in order to follow the Guiding game.

The Guider at the time of writing is Katy Tanfield, with Elizabeth Stafford as assistant Guider. The two exchanged roles when Elizabeth became division commissioner after being Guider for over 30 years. Rachel Shaw is an assistant Guider. The Brownies are led by Sarah Bailey, who is assisted by her mother Christine. Vera Scowcroft was Brownie Guider for the previous decade and worked for many years with Deborah Bailey.

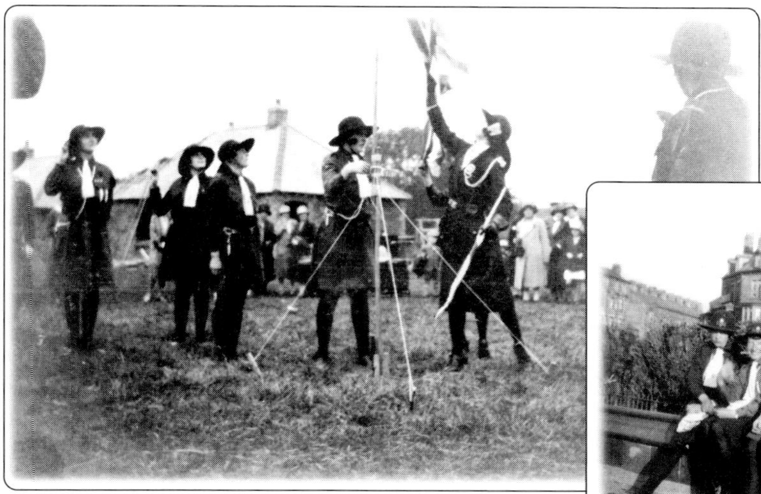

The opening of the Guide hut on 8 September 1928.

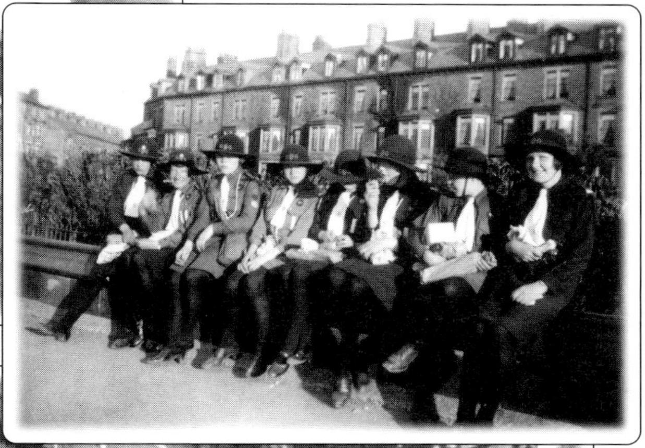

1st Chapel Guides on holiday in Heysham, 1928.

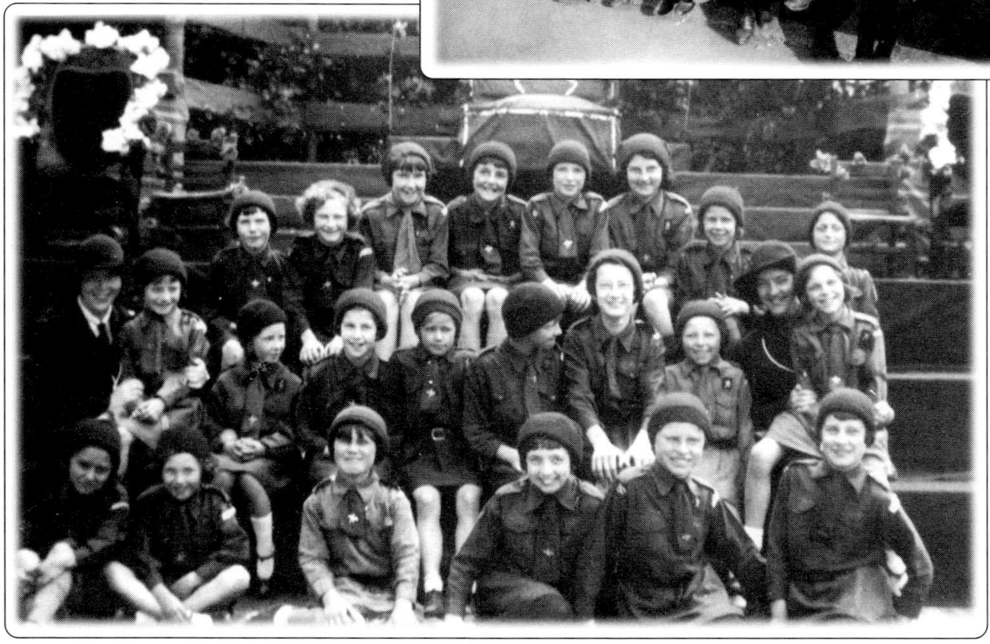

1st Chapel Brownies at the Peak Forest Rose Queen Festival, 1932.

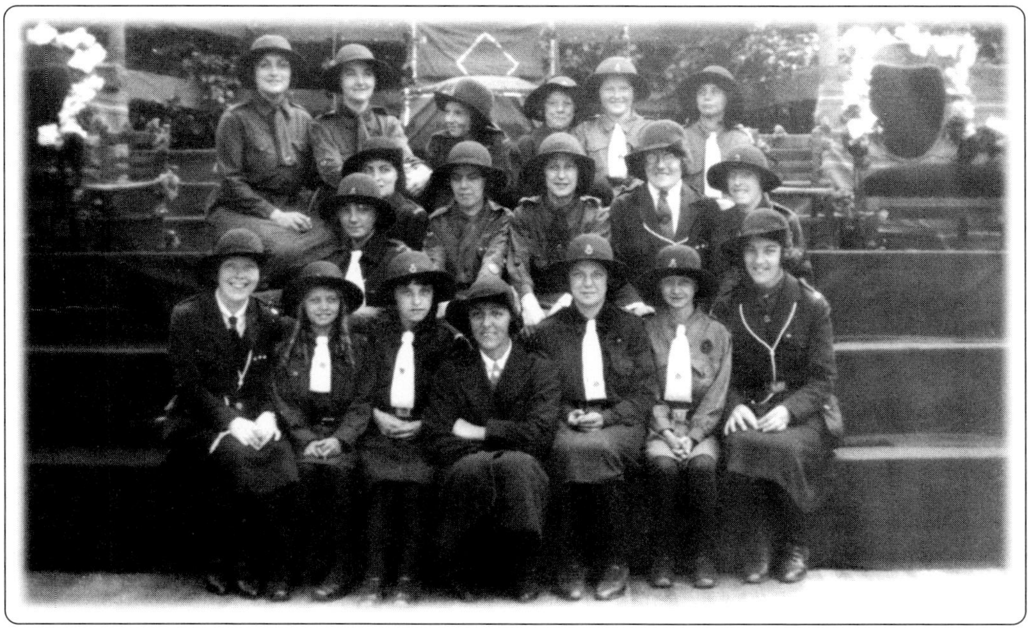

1st Chapel Guides at the Peak Forest Rose Queen Festival, 1932.

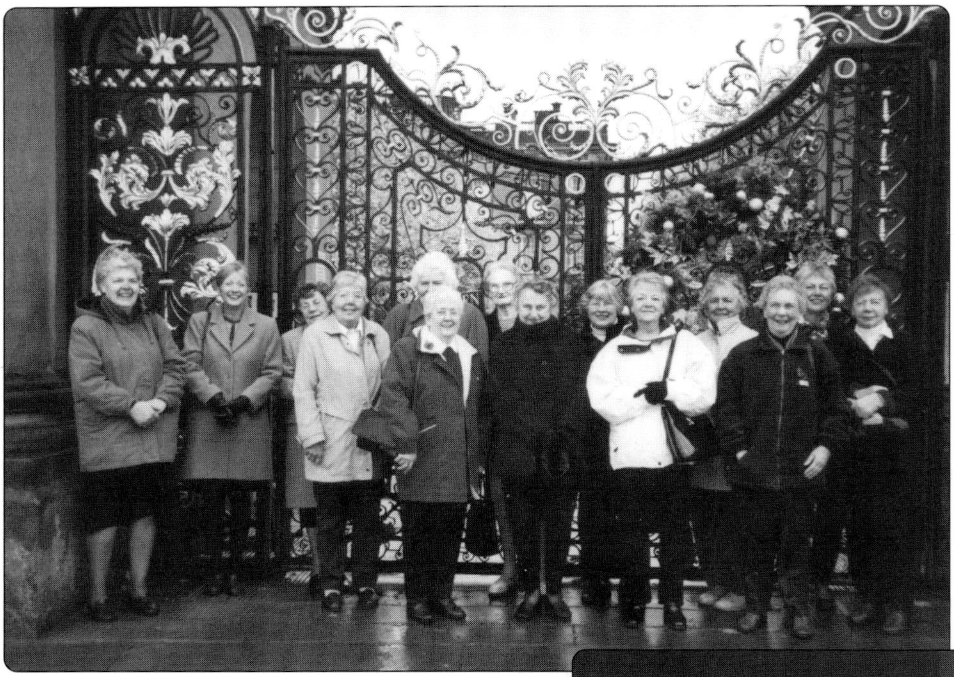

Left: *Members of Chapel WI on a visit to Chatsworth House in 2001.* Left to right: *Christine Asbury, Gwen Armishaw, Dorothy Hall, Dorothy Shuker (guest), Jean Shirt, Margaret Bywater, Ethel Smith, Gwen Goddard, Beryl Silvester, Norma Muller, Doreen Vernon, Ada Hudson, Joyce Taylor, Marie MacKenzie.*

Below: *Daffodils planted by the WI bringing colour to the junction of Spencer Road and Crossings Road in the spring of 2000.*

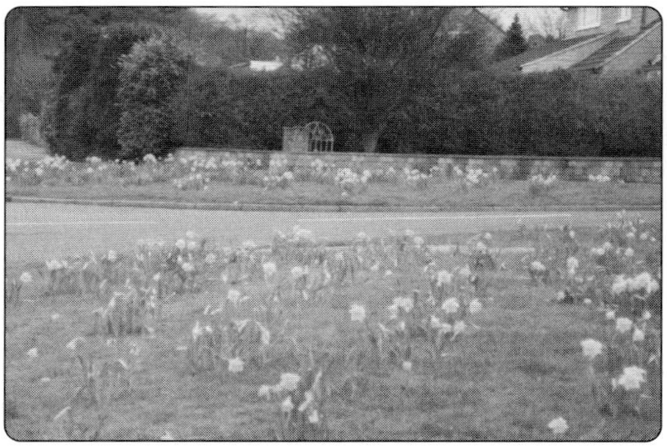

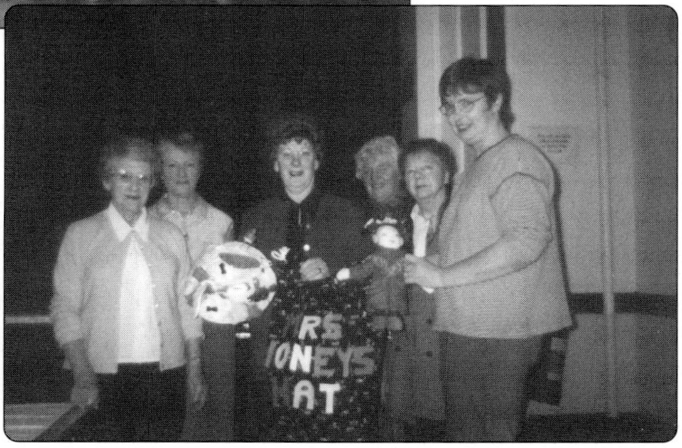

Above: *Presenting a story sack (Mrs Honey's Hat) to Jeanette Saxby* (on right) *of Peak School, Alderbrook. WI members present are: Doreen Reidpath, Joyce Taylor, Jean McDowell, Jean Shirt, Marie Mackenzie.*

Below: *Toys knitted for children in Bosnia.*

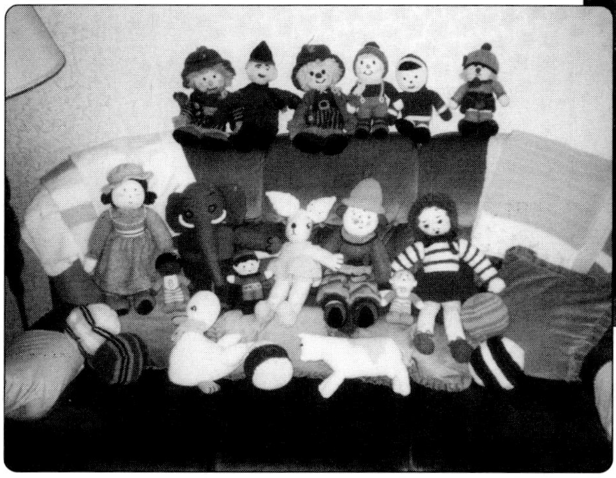

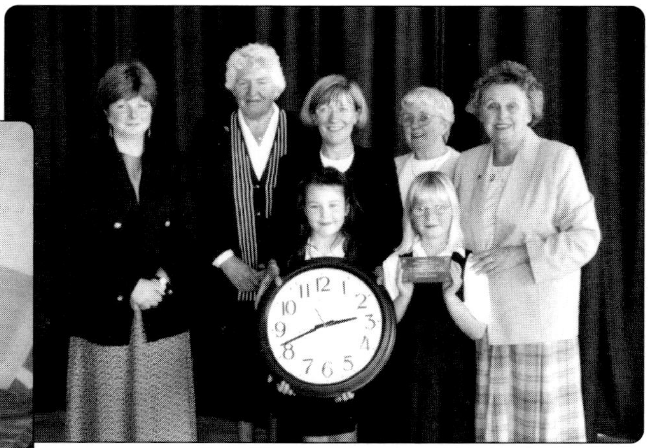

Above: *Presenting a clock to the new Chapel Infant School.* Adults (from left to right) *are: Anne Western (chair of governors), Jean Shirt, Sue Taylor (head teacher), Margaret Bywater, Gwen Goddard.*

Chapter 10

STRICTLY FOR THE LADIES

In the days when wives rarely went out to work, Women's Institutes and Townswomen's Guilds not only gave women a chance to escape the drudgery and isolation of housework, but also gave them a wide range of educational opportunities and a chance to socialise.

Chapel-en-le-Frith had one of the earliest Townswomen's Guilds in the country and supported no fewer than three Women's Institutes. Although labour-saving devices have made housework less time consuming, many women now have paid employment outside the home. Consequently, very few ladies have the time to attend daytime meetings or the inclination to sacrifice a precious few hours with their family to attend evening meetings.

These social changes have brought about the demise of the local branch of the Townswomen's Guild as well as one of the Women's Institutes. The remaining two WIs continue to thrive and the role played by all of these organisations over many years should not be underestimated.

THE WOMEN'S INSTITUTE

Compiled from contributions by Christine Ashbury (press secretary of Chapel WI), Jean McDowell (president of Chapel WI in 2002) and Joyce Taylor (president of Chapel WI in 2003).

The Women's Institute movement originated in Stoney Creek, Ontario, USA; it was started as a domestic-science class by Adelaide Hoodless, who believed that her own child had died as a result of ignorance about hygiene. The movement spread to Britain in 1915, initially as an aid in the drive for greater food production during the First World War. The first UK institute was founded at LlanFairpwllgwyngyllgogerychwyrndrobwyllllantysiliogogogoch in Anglesey, under the aegis of the Agricultural Organisation Society. Four years later, the Women's Institutes became independent, by which time there were already 1,405 WIs in England and Wales.

The rules of the WI require that no sectarian or party-political matters should be discussed at any meeting. Members pay a yearly subscription, which entitles them to a voice on their County Federation and the National Federation of Women's Institutes (NFWI).

The NFWI has over 250,000 members in the UK and therefore carries considerable clout. Each year, resolutions are put forward at an annual meeting of members. Important recent resolutions include a demand for more women in local government, a request for positive help for the unemployed and Government legislation against food irradiation. Other issues of current concern include the adequate training of staff working with older people, a sustainable future for agriculture and the provision of a school nursing service.

All the WIs in the High Peak are affiliated to the Derbyshire Federation of Women's Institutes, which is a very active organisation with a varied programme of activities, including walks, orienteering, white-water rafting, 'reading aloud' evenings and health-awareness days. Members of all the institutes of the Derbyshire Federation have also contributed to a new edition of a book about Derbyshire villages, which is splendidly produced and has full-colour illustrations.

The Kinder Group of WIs comprises: Chinley and Buxworth, Chapel-en-le-Frith, Sparrowpit, Horwich End and Hayfield. The Combs WI closed in December 2002.

CHAPEL-EN-LE-FRITH WOMEN'S INSTITUTE

Chapel-en-le-Frith Women's Institute was formed in September 1984. By the following year, there were 70 registered members. This figure fell to 33 in 2002.

Over the years, the members have enjoyed many outings. Visits to country houses have always been popular and have included trips to Harewood House, Erddig Hall, Sandringham and Lyme Hall. A visit to Chatsworth House even included a tour of the 'backstage' areas and a chance to view the stunning Derbyshire Dales from the roof of the great house. The members have also visited Buckingham Palace, and enjoyed seaside frolics at Llandudno and Bridlington, and taken a ride on a canal boat from Skipton.

Chapel WI members have a penchant for dressing up and putting on a show, especially on a carnival float. Three of their themed floats have obtained first prize in Chapel carnival: 'Last Night of the Proms' in 1986, 'Women Through the Ages' in 1987; and 'Keep Chapel Tidy' in 1990.

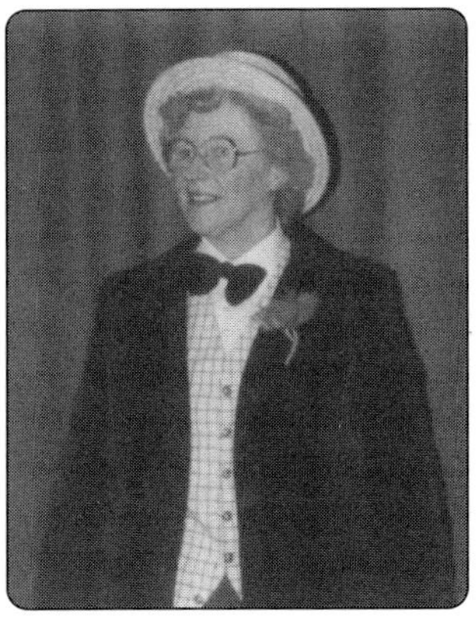

Left: *Mary Williamson performing in the* Good Old Days, *1982.*

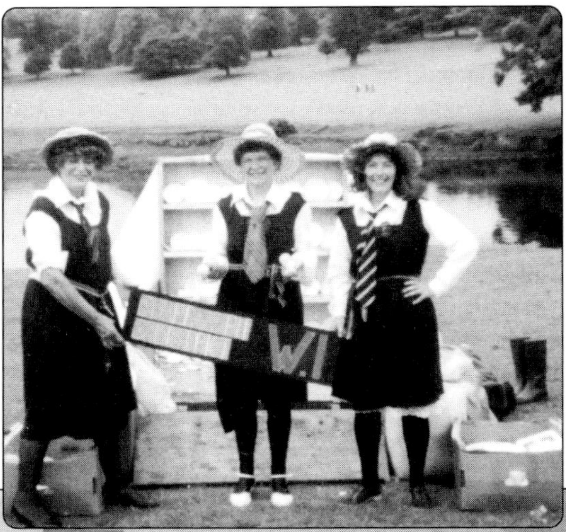

Right: *St Trinian's pupils from Sparrowpit WI organising plate smashing at Chatsworth Fair in 1984.* Left to right: *Joan Guilding, Joan Jackson, Liz Hollis.*

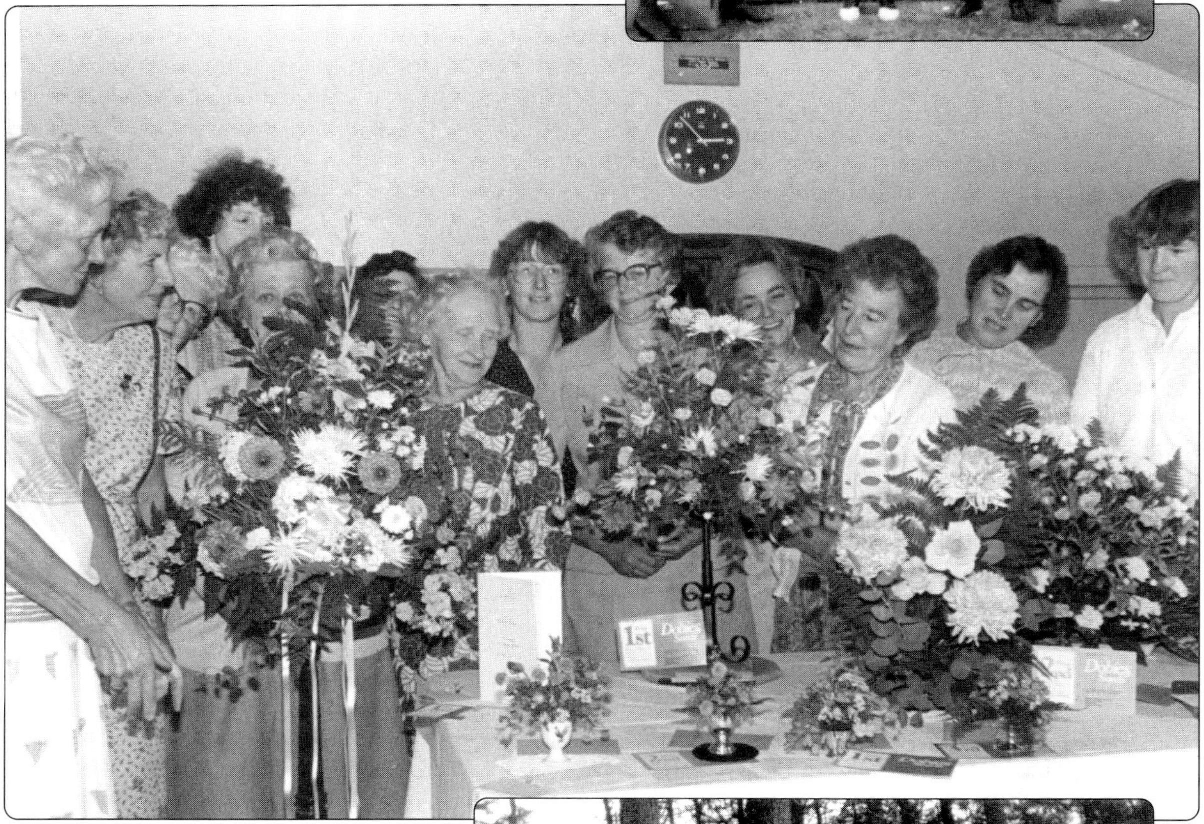

Sparrowpit WI at the Produce Show, 1984. Left to right: *Mrs Taylor (county chair), Mrs Guilding, Mrs Hallam, Mrs Morten, Mrs Hearnshaw, Mrs Cartledge, Mrs Fletcher, Mrs Hayward, Mrs Stafford-Salt, Mrs Phillips, Mrs Moorcroft, Mrs Buckley.*

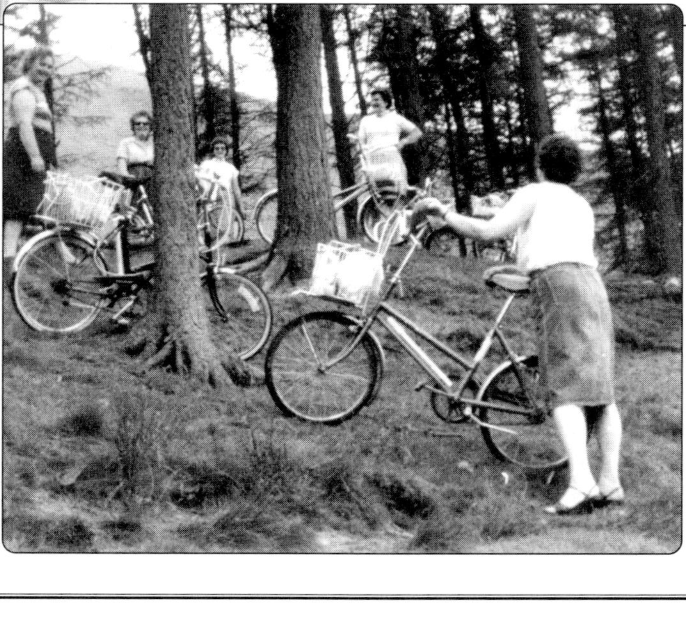

Cycle trail in the Goyt Valley. Left to right: *Dorothy Moorcroft, Enid Phillips, Susan Moorcroft, Phyllis Cartledge, Judith Morten.*

WI activities obviously give a great deal of pleasure to members, but many of them are also designed to serve the community. The Chapel group has been especially generous to local medical groups, with donations being given to the mobile physiotherapy unit, the High Peak Hospice, the Heart Start Appeal, the Ambulance Service and the Buxton Scanner Appeal. They have also made contributions to the purchase of nebulisers for local surgeries.

The ladies of Chapel have put their knitting skills to good use. Knitted and crocheted blankets have been produced for elderly people in the area and knitted toys have been made for children in Bosnia. Local children have also benefited from WI altruism. Members put together a 'story sack' for Peak School, Alderbrook, and presented a clock for the school hall at the new Chapel-en-le-Frith Infant and Nursery School on 16 September 1999 – the pupils can now time the length of school assemblies!

Over the years, WI members have planted daffodils on the roadside at the Jolly Carter, Manchester Road, the Hanging Gate pub on Bowden Lane, and at the junction between Crossings Road and Spencer Road. The resultant spring display does a great deal to bring a splash of early brightness to the town.

Like other WIs in Derbyshire, the Chapel branch has been involved in contributing to the new edition of the book on Derbyshire villages. Gwen Goddard wrote the piece on Chapel-en-le-Frith for the publication.

When they are on holiday, Chapel members often visit Women's Institutes in other villages. Chapel members have been guests at WI meetings in Cornwall, the Isles of Scilly and even New Zealand, so proving the value of belonging to an international organisation!

Sparrowpit Women's Institute

Compiled from archive material kindly loaned by Enid Phillips (press officer for Sparrowpit WI).

Sparrowpit WI was formed in October 1977 by Mary Williamson, Joan Guilding and Joan Jackson; it therefore celebrated its silver jubilee in the Queen's golden jubilee year. Mary was the first president and was followed by Joan Jackson, who gave up her post in 1981, but ensured members would be kept in good order by presenting the WI with a gavel made by her husband, John. Joan Guilding took over the presidency, but moved in 1986 to the Lake District, where she was subsequently visited by members from Sparrowpit, who were keen to pinch a few Lakeland recipes.

One of the earliest activities was a Produce Show, with displays of a wide range of foodstuffs produced by members. This became an annual event, which has not missed a year since its inception and was even held twice yearly for a short time. Holding a show in a marquee at Sparrowpit, which is over 1,000ft above sea level, can often be a hazardous affair – the marquee blew away in 1980, but the show carried on regardless.

The WI meets in the Village Hall on the third Tuesday of every month, with the single exception of February, when the weather is often at its worst in Sparrowpit. However, members are in the habit of going for a meal in February to High Peak College, which is situated at Harpur Hill, whose altitude is very nearly as great as that of Sparrowpit!

The WI members have also formed the habit of entering their food produce, as well as their craft work, in the annual Bakewell Show, where competition is very fierce and judging is extremely rigorous. For example, one judge's report on a patchwork entry read, 'Somerset patchwork would be easier in a circle. All points must be even and should be flat. Glue should be used very sparingly when attaching numbers.' Undeterred by the threat of criticism, members have regularly entered work and picked up a number of prizes.

Craft work and food production are, of course, traditional WI activities. In 1983 the National Federation began a concerted effort to change the image of the organisation, hoping to appeal to women from a wider age range. Enid Phillips caught the mood of the campaign in a poster she produced for the Chatsworth Show, which read, 'We are not all jam and Jerusalem. Our interests and activities are varied. Join us at the Chatsworth County Fair and see what we have to offer.' Just to prove their claims were not merely propaganda, the group initiated regular cycle-trail tours in the Peak District. There had been criticism in the press that 'WIs are full of ladies in sensible shoes'. However, the new vice president, Kath Dance, responded to this criticism in literal fashion when she wore a pair of bright red brogues at the AGM – they had actually been loaned to her because she had forgotten to bring along replacements for her driving shoes.

The ladies of Sparrowpit WI have proved to be great thespians over the years. Their shows have included: *The Good Old Days*, which they have performed at a number of venues; *The Sparrowpit Flappers*, which involved members dancing energetically in their 1920s' outfits; and *Oh What a Lovely War*, which featured a clothes-line hung with scanties.

In their earliest days, the group began the tradition of an annual carol concert, which is now held jointly with other WIs in the area. The Sparrowpit choir performs regularly. A press release for one of their sing-songs read, 'The ladies of Sparrowpit love to sing – they think it has something to do with the 'air' in their area, which they tell us is over 1,000ft above sea level.'

The members have also been richly entertained by visiting performers. These include: Fraser Martin, the hypnotist; entertainer Ray Rush, whose act

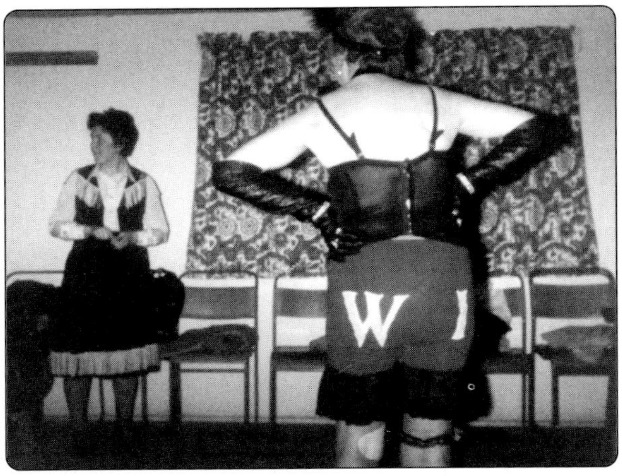

Sparrowpit WI's new-year concert, 1985. Pictured are Liz Hollis and Joan Guilding.

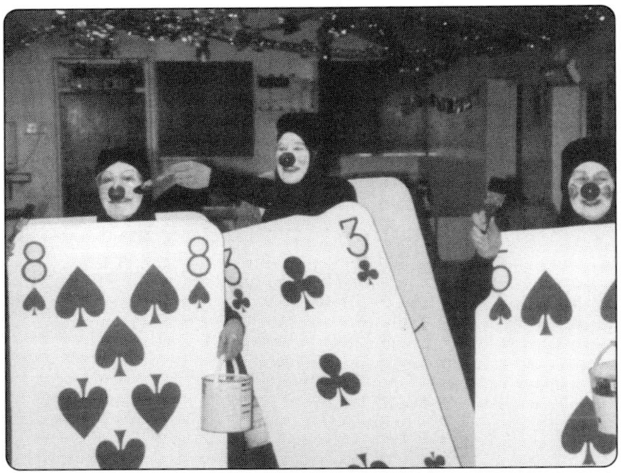

'Three right cards' at the Christmas party in 1992: Enid Phillips, Jenny Sherrett, Aileen Guzman.

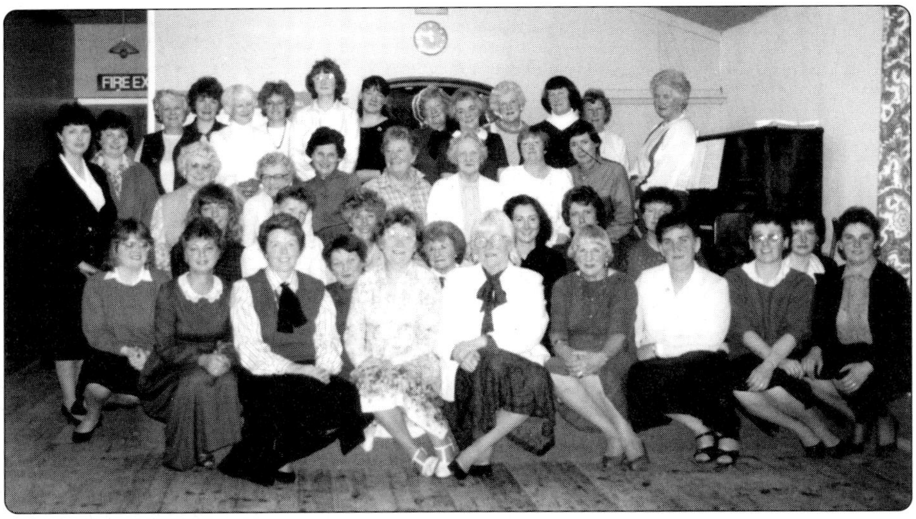

Sparrowpit WI's tenth anniversary, 1987. Left to right, back: *Louise Hadfield, Sheila Barrett, Dorothy Morten, Dorothy Steeples, Kath Dance, Jean Harrison, Myra Hearnshaw, Sandra Morten, Muriel Hallam, Christine Salt, Margaret McCary, Phyllis Cartledge, Clara Vernon, Ann Goddard;* third row: *Ivy Froggatt, Bessie Beswick, Phyllis Cartledge, Enid Phillips, Daisy Fletcher, Lorna Bennett, Pearl Kay;* second row: *Beryl Edge, Hilary Batterbee, Louise Buckley, Hazel Bowyer, Rosie Harding, Jessie Gregory, Alison Jackson-Bass, Eileen Cohen, Linda Peach, Susan Evans;* front: *Sheila Kelly, Liz Hollis, Joan Jackson, Mary Williamson, Joan Guilding, Dororthy Moorcroft, Mary Hayward, Judith Morten.*

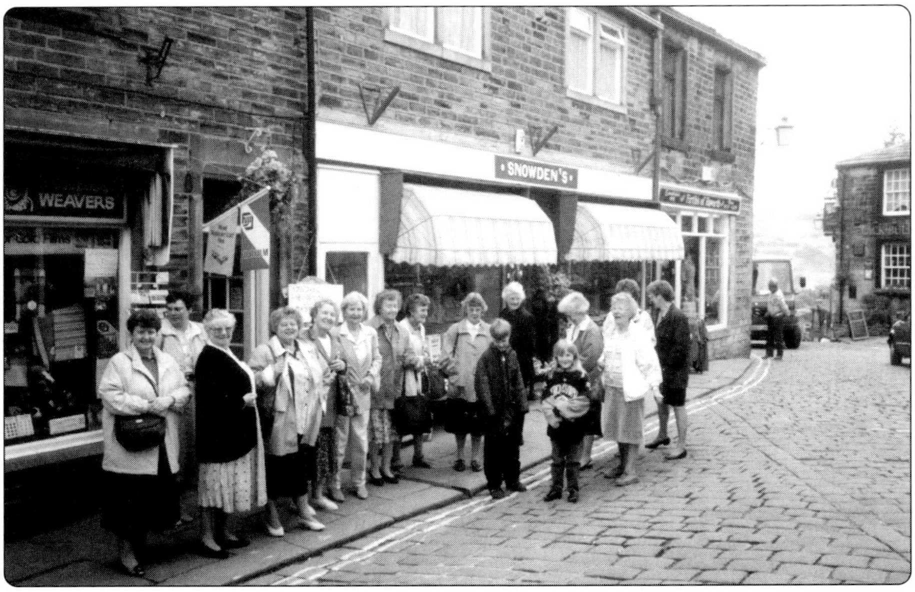

Sparrowpit WI trip to Haworth in 1995. Left to right: *Linda Peach, Judith Morten, Chris Barker, Shirley Barber, Elsie Lomas, Eileen Cooper, Mary Johnson, Phyllis Cartledge, Aileen Guzman, Dorothy Reynolds, Christine Salt, Enid Phillips, Sheila Kelly, Mary Hayward. The two children are Nicola and Stuart Williamson.*

involved putting the president in a sack, and a talk by Clarence Daniel on ghosts and headless men. The group has even been entertained by a pet owl.

Shopping trips, particularly at Christmas, are very popular with the members, who obviously have shopaholic tendencies. They visited the Meadowhall Centre in Sheffield when it first opened, and they now have a particular liking for the Ridings Centre at Wakefield. The Sparrowpit members are a well-travelled lot, whether their journeys be for shopping or cultural purposes. They have visited ancient towns such as York, Lincoln, Hereford and Lichfield, they have taken to the water at Scarborough, Llandudno and Windermere, and even ventured as far afield as Paris and Antwerp. Some members have attended the AGMs of the National Federation and short courses at Denham College, which Enid Phillips likens to 'stepping into a novel by Jane Austen'. Members have also watched a Torvill-and-Dean ice show, taken a cruise on the *Judith Mary* at Whaley Bridge, visited Cadbury World and taken tea at Betty's Café in Harrogate. Television studios seem to hold a particular fascination for the members – they have watched the making of 'Cluedo' and 'Coronation Street', and visited the studios of Pebble Mill and BBC North.

Treasure hunts, fashion shows, limerick competitions and 'prettiest scarf' competitions are among other events, and members have contributed to the new WI publication about Derbyshire villages. The WI has produced 'story sacks' for Warmbrook School, planted daffodils to beautify Sparrowpit and made high teas for groups who visit the hamlet on trips into the Peak District.

Many people have contributed to the life of Sparrowpit WI but one of a number of contributing WI husbands deserves a special mention. In 1997, Mary Williamson's husband Fred was run over by a tractor, resulting in a crushed forehead and fractures to his cheek, ribs and nose. He nevertheless staggered three quarters of a mile home and recovered to resume his customary role as auctioneer at the Produce Show and general WI handyman.

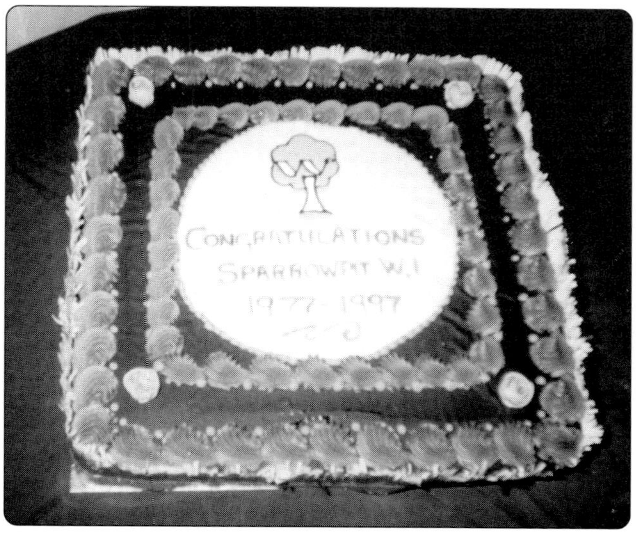

20th anniversary cake, made by Frank Redfern.

Anniversaries are always seen as significant occasions. All the past presidents were present at the tenth anniversary, Frank Redfern made a cake for the twentieth anniversary, and the WI and the Institute Committee combined to buy a seat for the village to mark their silver jubilee and the Queen's golden jubilee.

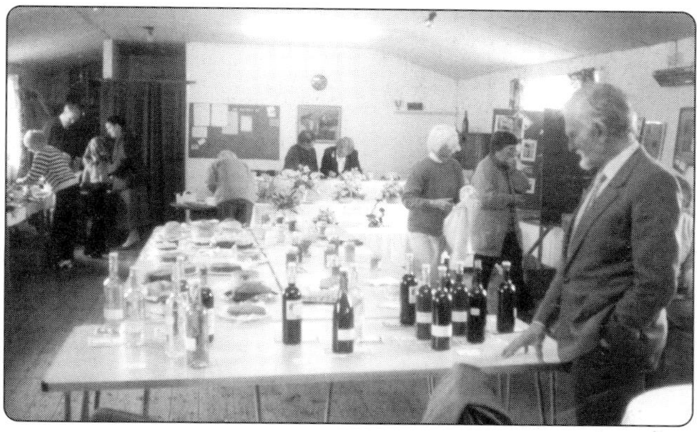

Produce Show, 1998, in the presence of the wine taster.

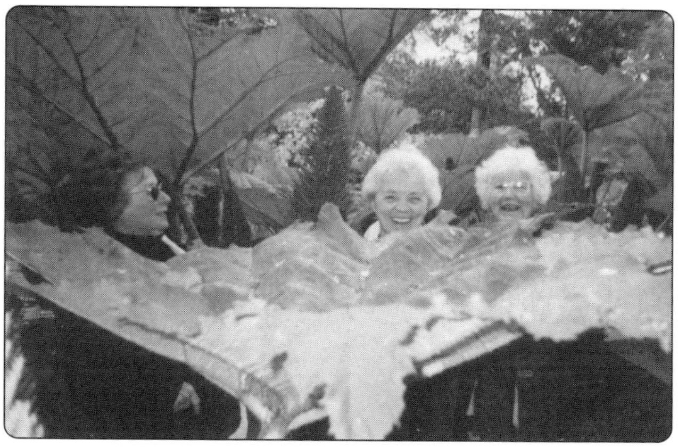

Lost on safari: Mary Hipwell, Christine Salt and Enid Phillips in 1995.

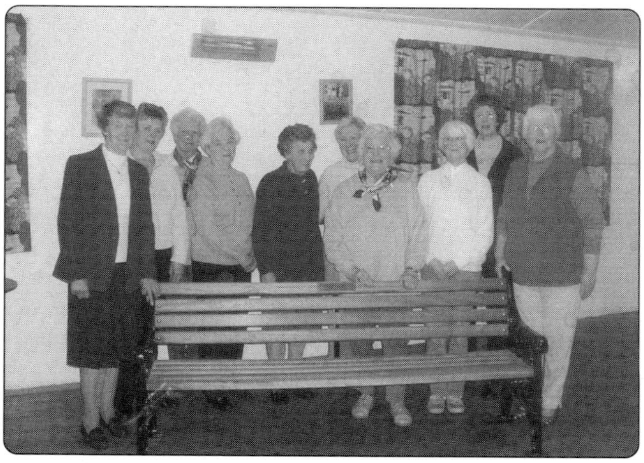

Presentation of the jubilee seat to the Sparrowpit community. Left to right: *Phyllis Cartledge, Sheila Barrett, Dorothy Batena, Christine Salt, Phyllis Cartledge, Rosie Harding, Enid Phillips, Kath Dance, Myra Hearnshaw, Mary Williamson.*

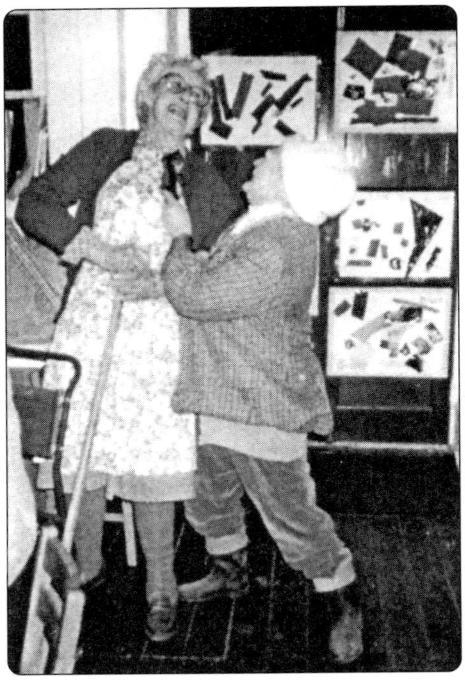

Combs WI's 21st anniversary sketch with Marion Crowther as Nora Batty and Elaine Sant as Compo.

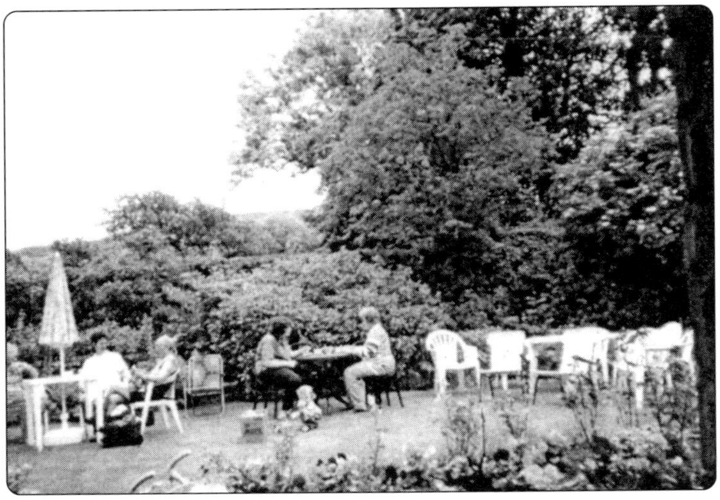

Above: *Afternoon tea at Grace Holmes' house.*

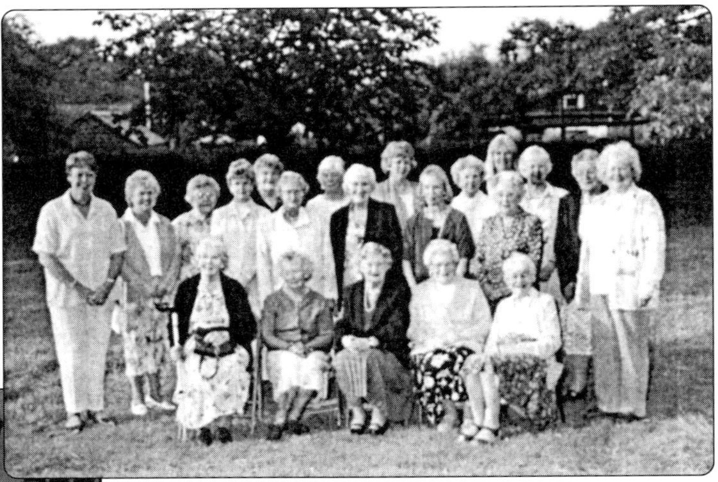

Above: *Combs WI on the occasion of long-term member Bertha Challis leaving to live with her family in Kent.* Left to right, standing: *Liz Goodwin, Pat Goodwin, Margery Hollinrake, Barbara Gregory, Betty Goodchild, Lottie Howgate, Una Laing, Bertha Challis (with dark coat), Rowena Wallen, Judy Whitehead, Joan Nicholson, Patricia Hampson, Lucy Parkin, Joyce Bratt, Grace Holmes, Jean Evanson;* seated: *Jay Lorimer, Pam Liebert, Jessie Gledhill, Mary Jackson, Nan Phillips.*

Below: *Tenth anniversary celebrations in 1983.*

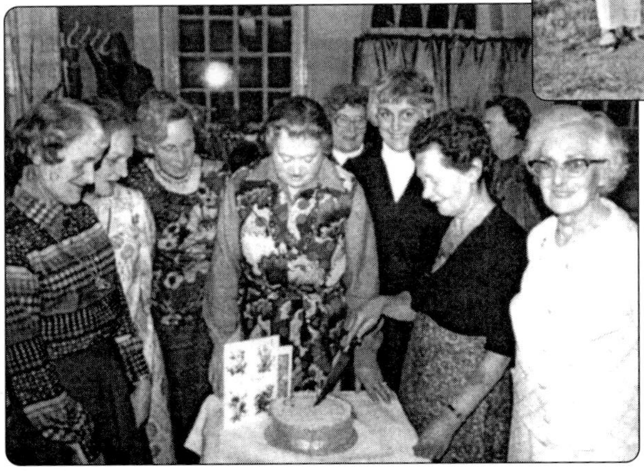

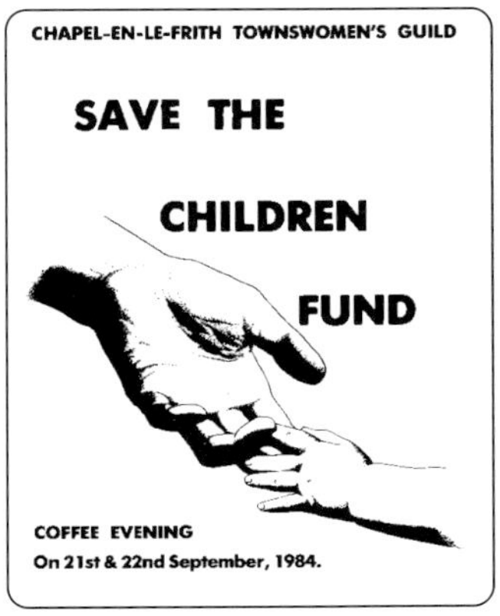

Cover of the programme for the Save the Children Coffee Evening in 1984.

Right: *21st birthday cake for Combs WI.* Left to right: *Ann Jones, Nan Phillips, Jessie Gledhill, Kath Dance, Mary Jackson, Pam Liebert.*

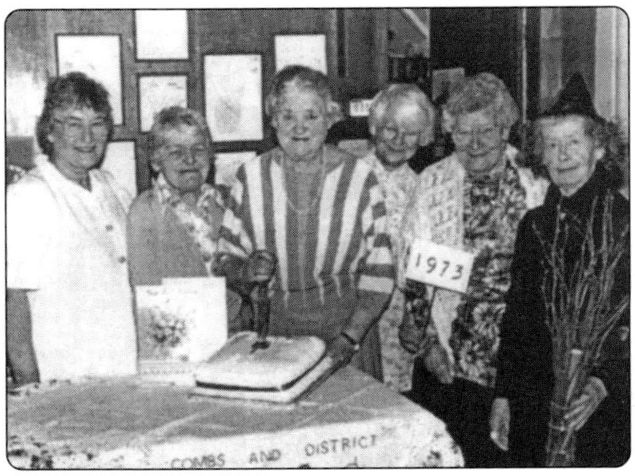

Combs & District Women's Institute

By Jean Evanson (the last president of Combs and District WI).

The Combs and District WI was formed in May 1973, largely thanks to the drive of Jessie Gledhill, who had been an active member of Chinley WI and had moved to Combs from Chinley with her husband Percy. She worked with her fellow founder members, who included Nan Phillips, Lucie Parkin and Mary Jackson, to raise interest and support.

The meetings were held in Combs Methodist Chapel/School on the evening of the third Tuesday in each month. Activities included a drama group, with Elaine Sant as the key organiser. The members also attended monthly cookery lessons, which were held at Hope Valley College, with Ms Warrington as the first tutor of the class. They also had members from other WI groups in surroundings areas and Ms Warrington came to Combs to give demonstrations.

The group supported a series of arts and crafts classes, which were held in Bertha Challis' house. The work which resulted was put on display in an annual exhibition for the entire village to view.

When Derbyshire WIs were asked to submit a play based on their locality, Peggy Bellhouse wrote one entitled *Scene 80* (the manuscript is still retained by the committee) and the play was performed at Derby Assembly Rooms in a competition which lasted all day. The ladies were assisted by John Sant, who worked with the backstage team and helped with the stage lighting. They received a certificate for their play and their performance; the day at Derby was a talking point for years!

A key activity for Combs WI had always been fund-raising, which often took the form of garden parties at Grace Holmes' property. Members from Kettleshulme even walked over the hills to Combs to take part in this event. More recently, Joyce Holmes has hosted strawberry teas. In addition to the regular meetings, there have been visits to herb gardens, stately homes and sightseeing trips.

Sadly, Combs WI closed in December 2002, because of a drop in membership. Residents are preparing plans to open a mixed-interest community group, which will include partners and friends and will meet in the Village Hall. Perhaps this could act as a model for other WIs to follow in the future!

Chapel-en-le-Frith Townswomen's Guild, 1930–2000

Mike Smith delves into the archives of Chapel Townswomen's Guild, which have been donated to the Chapel-en-le-Frith Amenity Society.

The Chapel-en-le-Frith Townswomen's Guild was the first to be formed in the Stockport Federation and one of the earliest to be formed in the country. It had a varied programme of activities from the very outset. Members danced, sang, rambled, flower arranged, played whist, gave monologues and performed in one-act plays, picking up a second prize at the Buxton Drama Festival of 1940. They organised bring-and-buy sales, White Elephant stalls, produce stalls and, in the years before the war, '1s. stalls'. Christmas parties, annual dinners and outings were always well attended. Trips were organised to many locations, including country houses, factories, parks and historic towns, and some members attended AGMs of the National Federation, which met in locations such as Cardiff, the Isle of Man, Blackpool and the Royal Albert Hall.

Members of Chapel TWG had no excuse for not being well informed. The subjects of talks given at their regular meetings ranged from the experiences of Churchill's wartime secretary and the life of Kathleen Ferrier to the creation of the Pennine Way and canoeing and potholing in the Peak District. Chrichton Porteus came to talk about his life as an author and Harry Buxton related his experiences as a press photographer. Members always had early news of technological developments: they had talks on man-made fibres at the time of their first appearance; they had a demonstration on how to use a washing machine and, in 1974, they had a presentation about computers, but this may not have been very enlightening because the speaker entitled his presentation, 'Computers, by someone who knows nothing about them.'

As people began to travel more widely, TWG members and others were called upon to relive their experiences. Through listening to illustrated talks, the ladies could travel to Italy, Norway, Iceland, Russia, Africa, Jordan, Israel, British Guiana, Australia, the Falklands and the Himalayas, to name but a few places. They even heard about a trip on the Orient Express. Health, well-being and what would now be called lifestyle issues were always well to the fore. There were talks on 'Housework with Ease', 'Childbirth without Tears' and 'Preventing Overtiredness and Stiffening-up'. Miss Rawlinson spoke on 'Happiness' and Joan Wilcock expounded on 'The Fun of Growing Older'.

Competitions have always been a feature of the TWG. In 1935 alone, there were competitions for the best pot of bulbs, the best jar of marmalade, the best cake from a given recipe, the best 6d. tray cloth and the best use of 2oz of wool.

Bring-and-buy and table-top sales were often held at meetings and the money raised was used for good causes. Over £2,000 was raised for the children of Bangladesh; £450 was donated to the Buxton Scanner Appeal; £500 was given to Christie's Hospital and £455 was raised for the St John Ambulance Brigade.

The TWG also made donations to the town, including a copper-beech tree for the Memorial Park in 1974 and a battery wall clock for the Parish Council, given on the occasion of Chapel TWG's 40th birthday – the clock still hangs in the room where council meetings are held.

Unfortunately, changing patterns of work helped to force the closure of the TWG, which ceased to function in the millennium year. As Mrs Fullaway, one of the founder members explained, 'When the guild was formed in 1930, most married women did not go out to work and so could attend afternoon meetings. This is no longer the case.' However, many Chapel ladies have benefited from TWG activities during its 70-year existence and they have always tried to follow a creed laid down in their song, which was composed by Mrs Potter, their president from 1964 to 1969:

Sing with the Guild of women,
With ideas old and new,
In art, and crafts, and drama,
Social studies too.
Heedless of creed or party,
They maintain their high ideals,
To become much better citizens,
Responsive to appeals.
Sing to the Guild of women,
And keep their standards high,
In work, and play, and studies,
Let no chance go by.

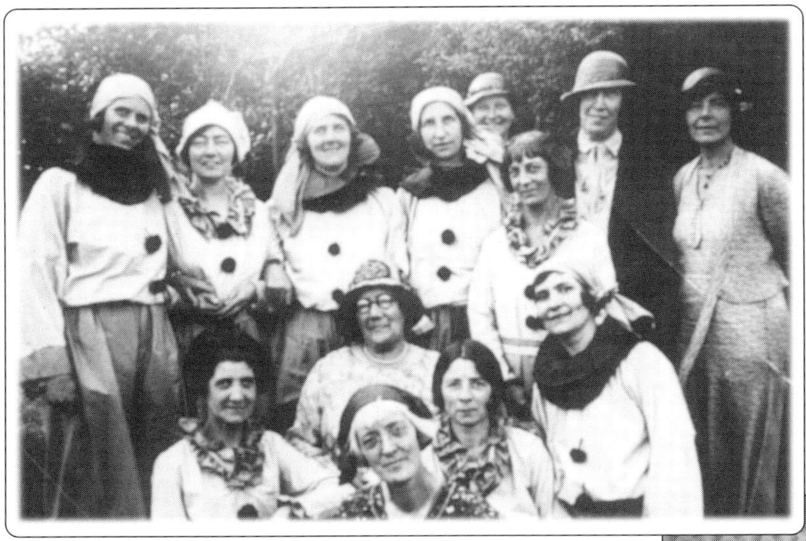

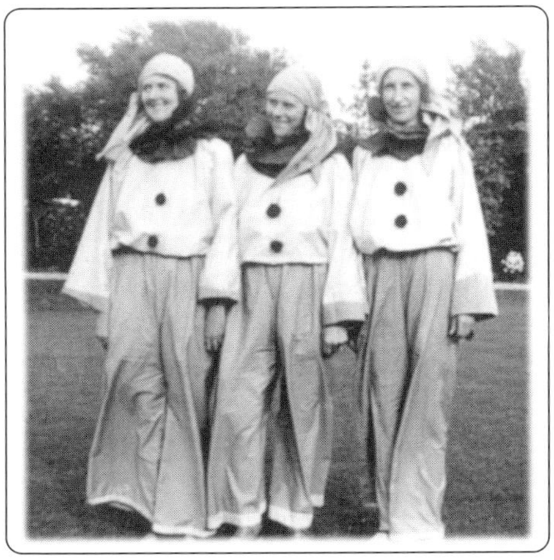

Above: *TWG members in 1934. The group includes: Mrs Hadfield, Mrs Bennett, Mrs Wilson, Mrs Heather, Mrs Slack, Mrs Spencer, Mrs Ford.*

Above right: *Mrs Heather, Mrs Slack and Mrs Wilson in 1934.*

Right: *Seven TWG members – not identified by name!*

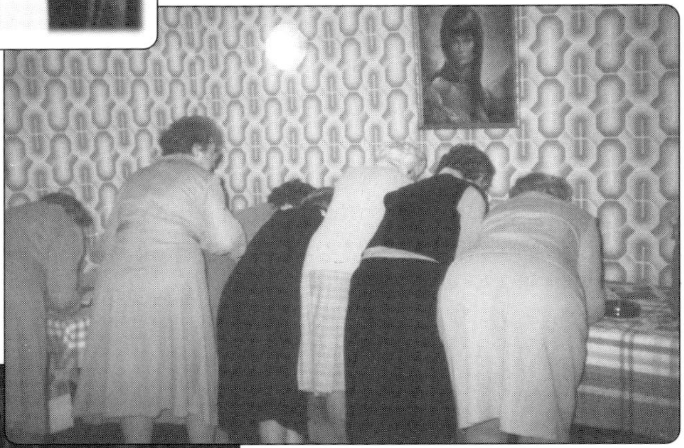

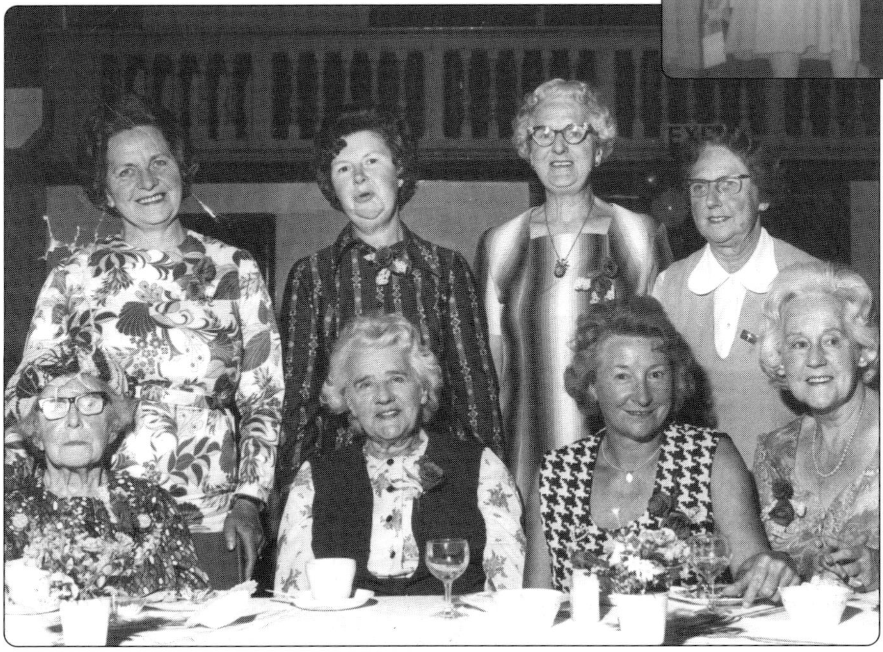

Chairmen and vice-chairmen at the 40th anniversary celebration in 1970. The group is thought to comprise, standing, left to right: *Mrs Bradbury (1968–70), Mrs Thornley (vice-chair 1970), Mrs Kendrick (1959–61, '67), Mrs Carrington (1957–58);* seated: *Mrs Ibbotson (1952), Mrs Gregory (1953–54), Mrs Ellison (1955–56), Mrs Shirley (vice-chair 1964–66).*

Chapter 11

All the World's a Stage

The Chapel Amateur Players have been entertaining the people of Chapel-en-le-Frith ever since 1921. Their highly polished productions of farces, comedies, murder mysteries, 'old tyme music hall' and pantomimes remain very popular with local people.

The town acquired its first purpose-built cinema in 1924. Residents could enjoy going to the movies at their much-loved picture palace until 1961, when the rising popularity of television killed off so many local cinemas. The movies have enjoyed a revival in recent years, but cinema has not yet returned to Chapel-en-le-Frith.

Chapel Players

Compiled from archive material kindly loaned by Baz Brown.

In March 1921 members of the newly formed Chapel-en-le-Frith ex-servicemen's Operatic and Dramatic Society put on their first show, comprising a number of orchestral pieces, a selection of songs performed by a male voice choir and a one-act play called *Fifteen and Sixteen*. This ambitious opening effort reflected the tripartite nature of the new organisation, which was made up of dramatic, choral and orchestral sections. However, it was the staging of the full-length play *What Happened to Jones?* in the following year that was to define the shape of things to come. In 1927 the male voice choir left the group to become an independent society, the orchestra remained as a supplier of incidental music and the members of the drama section, having realised that opera would be unlikely to figure in any of their upcoming programmes, changed the name of the society to Chapel-en-le-Frith Amateur Players.

William Braylesford Bunting, who would later write the definitive history of Chapel-en-le-Frith, was the first president of the society, and Arthur Marchington, who produced no fewer than 21 plays for the group, along with John Marchington, took on the role of joint chairman for the first 18 years. Subscribing vice-presidents were recruited to provide a steady source of income, but funds were barely adequate in those early days. The programme for the farce *Lord Richard in the Pantry* contained the following plea:

The committee is earnestly desirous of enrolling as many vice-presidents as possible. This means of attaining a more regular income will do much to relieve the committee of financial anxiety and at the same time will enable them to go forward with greater confidence.

By the early 1930s the number of vice-presidents had grown considerably, financial anxieties had eased and appreciative audiences were being fed occasional murder mysteries and a regular diet of farce and comedy, performed by stalwarts such as Jack Jagger, Ida Simpson, David Lyall, Edith Bentley, Beatrice Marchington and the splendidly named Vincent Duckmanton. Ambrose Cooke and his orchestra provided musical accompaniment for many of the productions, George Muir and Edward Lingard were regular producers and almost all the plays were performed at the Constitutional Hall. A brief move to the Town Hall in 1931 and 1932 was abandoned after it was realised that the venue did not lend itself to the creation of the off-stage effects required for productions like *The Ghost Train.*

The war years brought obvious problems, but chairman William King and actors such as Bea Price, Vincent Duckmanton, Emrys Jones, Frances Eaton, Muriel Carrington, Joe Wildgoose and Fred Warhurst kept the society going. With the single exception of 1940 plays were performed throughout the years of conflict and the society played its part in the war effort by raising the spirits of local people with a succession of comedies.

The proceeds from productions staged both during and immediately after the war were donated to organisations such as the Chapel-en-le-Frith War Service Department and the Soldiers', Sailors' and Airmen's Families' Association, but the state of the group's finances dictated that this generosity would have to come to an end at some stage. In the programme for the 1949 production of *The Girl Who Couldn't Quite,* the society announced, rather sheepishly and alongside a reminder that the players had raised over £800 for charity in the previous ten years, that proceeds from this particular play would have to be used for the renewal of scenery and equipment.

In the postwar period the number of productions increased markedly, with as many as five plays being staged in some years, and high standards were set. The critic for the *High Peak Reporter* was particularly

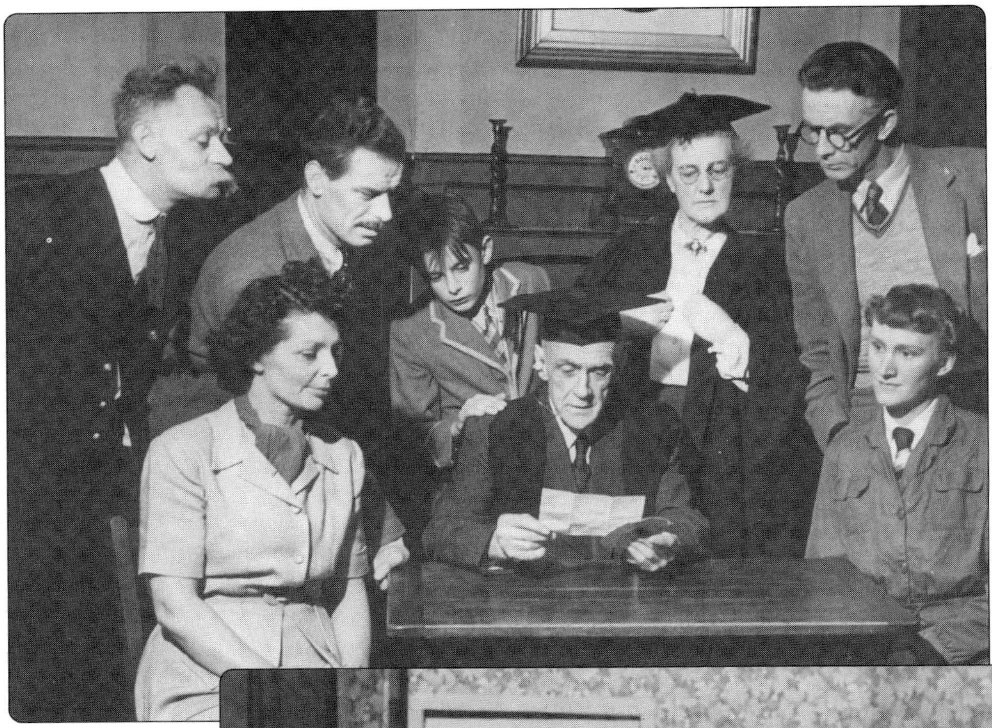

Production of The Happiest Days *in 1954 with* (left to right) *Bill Perks, Bea Price, Gerald Williams, Harry Brindley, Joe Wildgoose, Catherine Goddard, Jack Jagger, Una Price.*

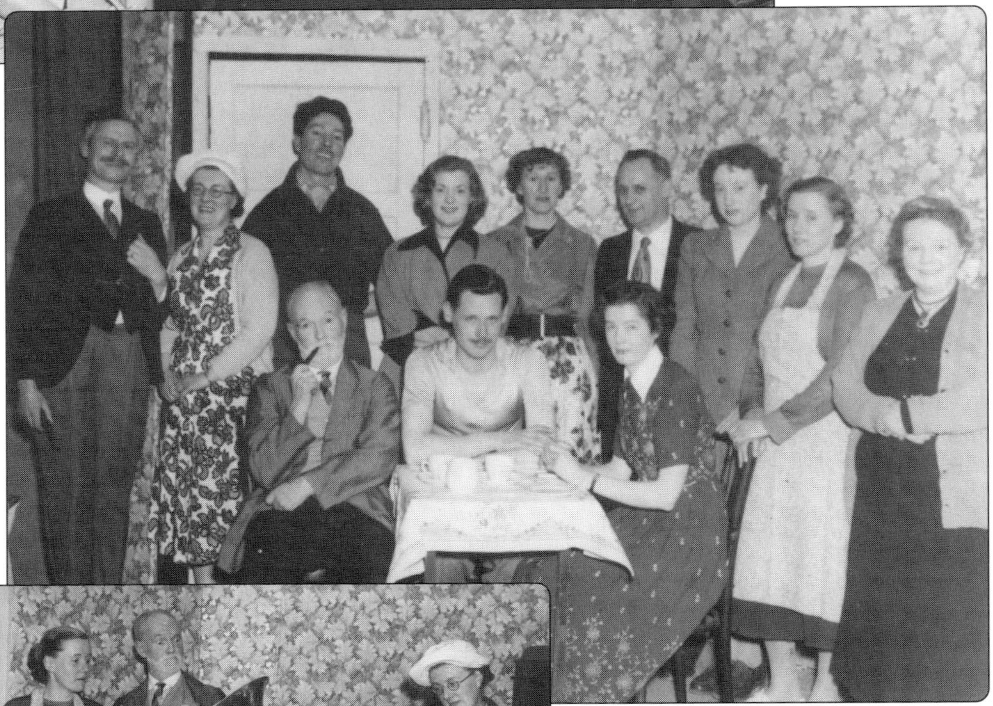

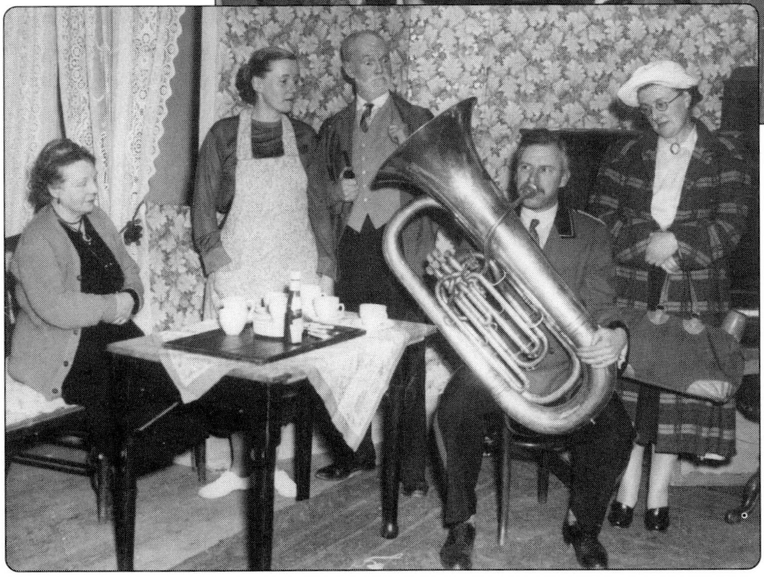

Above: Bed, Board and Romance *in 1954.* Standing, left to right: *Harry Brindley, Bea Price, Albert Phillips, Audrey Simpson, Catherine McIntosh, Joe Wildgoose, Margaret Davies, May Fletcher, Frances Eaton;* seated: *Emrys Jones, Eric Clarke, Edith Wharmby.*

Left: Bed, Board and Romance *with* (left to right): *Frances Eaton, May Fletcher, Emrys Jones, Harry Brindley, Bea Price.*

impressed with the Chapel Players' 1948 production of *See How They Run,* which he described as:

> *... the most outstanding thing they have ever done in this realm of entertainment. They made more of some of the scenes than many professional companies would have done.*

In the first 30 years of its existence the society had staged 89 plays and involved over 200 local people in productions, but the players lacked a permanent home of their own until 1952, when they were given a chance to purchase the Constitutional Hall. A total of 60,000 1s. shares were raised, half being purchased by the members of the society and half being bought by local business people and benefactors. This arrangement gave rise to some problems, because people outside the society retained a considerable voice in the operation of the hall. However, privately owned shares made their way over the years into the hands of society members, either by purchase or donation. By 1966 the players had become the majority shareholders and by the time of the millennium they had acquired some 80 per cent of the shares.

As soon as the decision was made to purchase the hall, fund-raising became a priority. The society put on a number of 'sales of work' and they held regular garden parties at Greyfriars, courtesy of Mrs Wilson, who became the president of the group. In all their money-raising literature, Chapel Players were anxious to stress that their purchase of the hall was designed:

> *... to preserve the Constitutional Hall as a centre for cultural and recreational facilities, not only for ourselves, but for all the other organisations in and around Chapel-en-le-Frith who have used the hall in the past and, we hope, will continue to do so in the future.*

Bryan Marchington produced many of the plays in the 1950s, although two of the leading actors, Bea Price and Fred Barnes, also took their turn at production, and a team of committed actors, including Muriel Carrington, Joe Wildgoose, David Smith, May Fletcher, Pamela Wolstenholme, Frances Eaton, George Muir, Alfred King and Mabel Wood, ensured standards were maintained. The players won the Derbyshire Trophy on five occasions during the '50s and picked up a number of other awards. The critics were equally complimentary: a review of the 1956 production of *The Secret Tent* included praise for convincing portrayals of 'emotional strain' by Eileen Turner, 'dignity' by Muriel Carrington, 'insincerity' by Bea Price and 'a combination of authority and tact' by Albert Phillips.

In the 1960s, '70s and '80s enthusiastic members, such as Ann Cook, Ian Stubbs, Dennis Crumpton, Richard Gibbon, Judy Benning, Mike Gallagher, Baz Brown, Peter Liebert, Paul Holman, David Mowl and John Gilberthorpe, became regular performers alongside the society's long-standing actors, and the players decided to cash in on the popularity of the BBC's programmes from Leeds' City Varieties by staging 'Old Tyme Music Hall', in addition to regular plays. Either Christopher Ellis or John Gilberthorpe would take on Leonard Sachs' role of chairman and singers such as Judi Bostin would tease the audience with renditions of music-hall classics, including 'I was a Good Little Girl Till I Met You' and 'Oh Mr Porter'.

More 'bums on seats' were encouraged by the purchase of new cushions in 1971, when the hall was also redecorated, and a pantomime was staged for the first time in 1978. Pantomimes proved to be very popular with the public and Mike Cullen, John Gilberthorpe and Melvyn Wright all put on memorable performances as dames. The early pantomimes were produced by Betty O'Brien and Glen Eva, but Warner and Sheila Christie took over their production in 1990. In 1995 the society celebrated the 40th anniversary of VE Day by staging a selection of sketches and songs made popular in the two world wars.

The society remained very active and successful throughout the 1980s and '90s, thanks to the enthusiasm of both the actors and those working backstage. Two stalwarts among many perhaps deserve a special mention: Eric Young, who was responsible for the 'electrics' for many years until Baz Brown took over, and Glynne Jones, who was the president of the Chapel Players for a long period and later secretary of the holding company – his knowledge of the workings of local authorities proved a valuable asset and he was made an honorary life member in recognition of his services.

By the time of the society's 75th anniversary in 1996 the players had put on 220 plays, 19 pantomimes, eight music halls and three Christmas shows. It was decided to celebrate the occasion with an anniversary review and a performance of *The Ghost Train,* which had previously been staged in 1932 and 1971. The Chapel Male Voice Choir was invited back to perform and conductor Harry Redfern was made an honorary life member because of his dedication to the players as their musical director. Unfortunately, this special year also saw the death of Bea Price, who began her long and distinguished career with Chapel Players by taking a two-line part as a schoolgirl in 1927. The society's librarian and press officer, Jill Dick, wrote in the commemorative programme that Bea's first entrance in a play would often be greeted by spontaneous applause and she recalled that a press report in 1974 had described her as 'probably Chapel's most well-known and best-loved character actress.'

The 75th anniversary programme also contained a piece by Muriel Carrington, who had taken on a

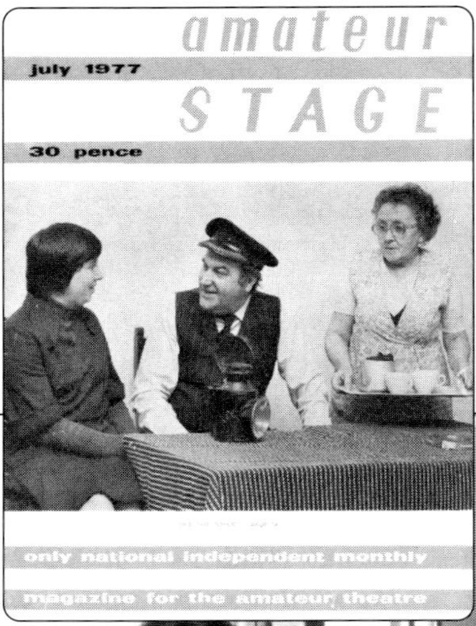

Cover of the Amateur Stage *in 1977, featuring Chapel's production of* Off the Rails *with Ann Hallworth, Colin Wilson and Ann Cook.*

Production of The Chocolate Factory *in 1982.* Left to right, back row: *Andrew Sherwood, Pamela Higginbotham, Julia Charles, Joe Wildgoose, Paul Holman, Ian Stubbs, Warner Christie, Hellen Cullen, Kash Bennett;* front row: *Bea Price, Emma Gibbon, Jason Christie, Rachel Bullock, Andrea Fowler.*

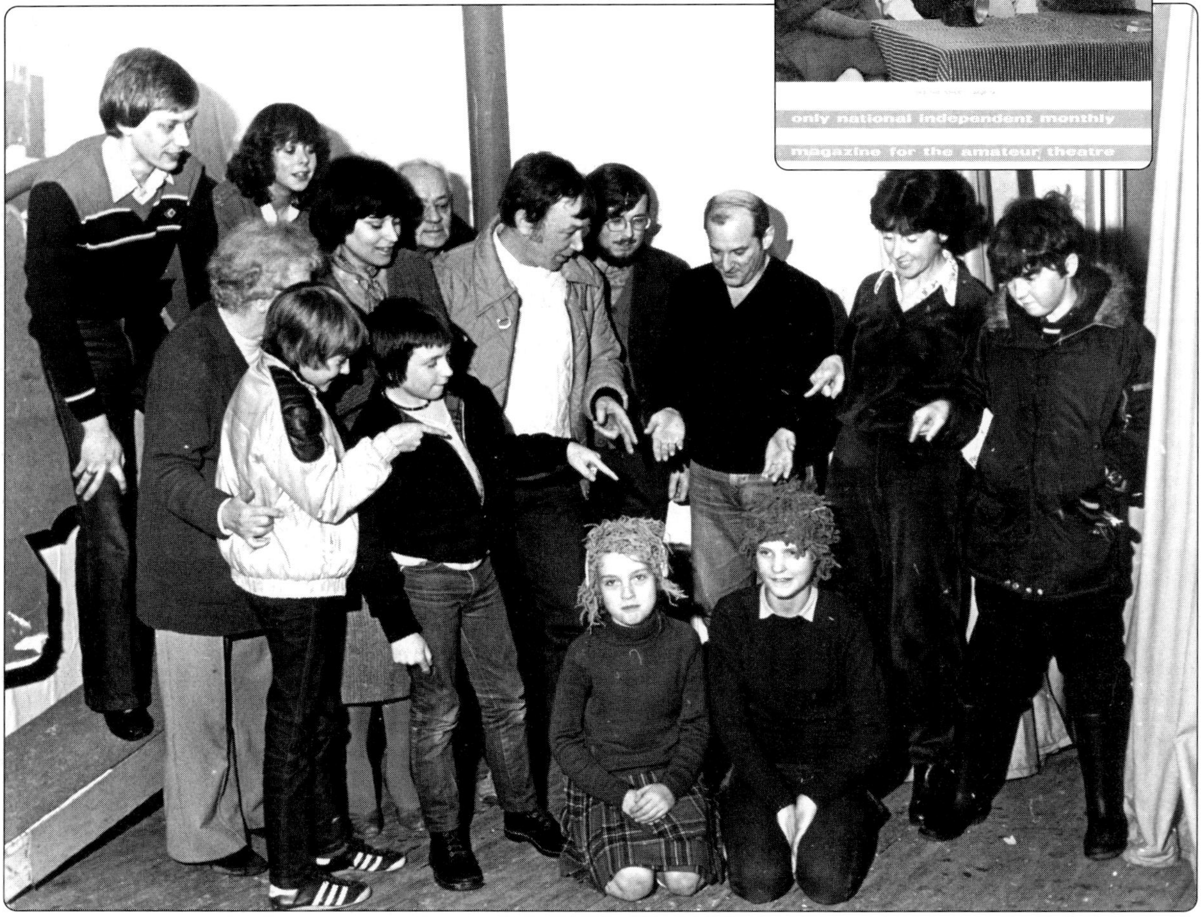

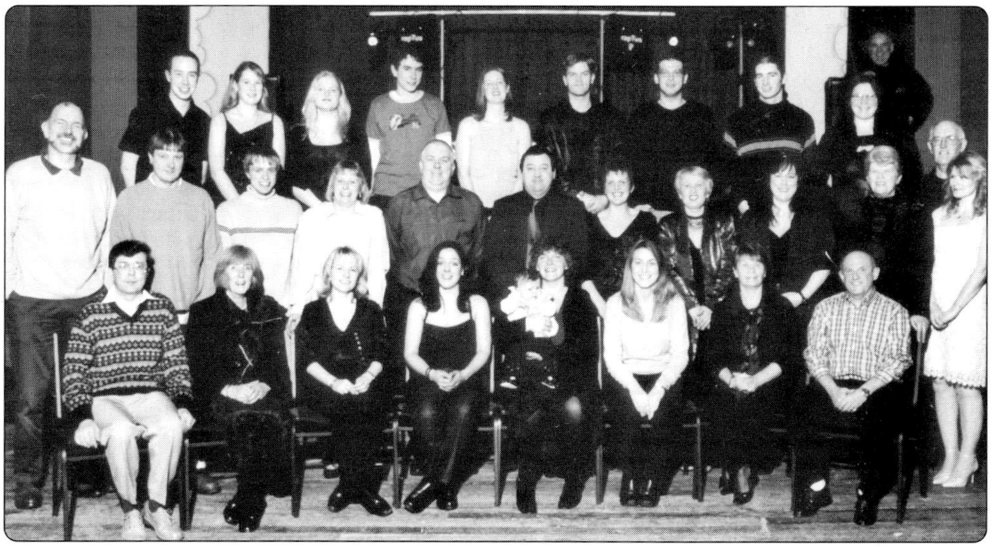

Group photograph of the Chapel Players, 2001.

plethora of roles with the society, including actress, producer, prompt, property manager, wardrobe mistress and overseer of make-up. Muriel recalled the low-tech days when coconut shells were used to imitate horses' hooves and dried peas were rolled around in a tin box to simulate rain. Sheila and Warner Christie, who had produced two dozen pantomimes by this stage, spoke of the satisfaction of including all the members of the society in these productions, but also of the heartache involved in turning down scores of children who would turn up annually to audition for parts in the pantomime chorus. Peter and Pam Liebert, who had been in charge of properties for many years, remembered an occasion when a pornographic magazine used in one production so enthralled the actor when he picked it up that he forgot his lines. Producer David Mowl recalled the manufacture of a rotating, double-decker set, representing two floor levels of a house, for a production of *Noises Off*. As the stage of the Constitutional Hall is only 11ft high in total, the actors had to 'duck or grouse' as they went through doors only 5ft high.

To celebrate the 75th anniversary chairman Baz Brown invited as many past and present members as possible to a grand reunion. Large numbers turned up, including Arthur Hirst, who played Richard Winthrop in the 1970s production of *The Ghost Train*. Many of those who were unable to attend sent their good wishes. Glen Eva, who had been responsible for pantomimes in 1986 and 1988, sent greetings from her home 'under the stunning blue skies unique to Provence' and recalled being presented with an 'Oscar' for being 'the producer who threw the best tantrum' and Sheila Finn, writing from Hornsea, said she 'really missed bullying everyone into knowing their lines.'

The millennium was also celebrated in style with a special show of songs, sketches and poems spanning the century. Sheila and Warner Christie produced a section which included Angela Buttrill singing 'When I take my Morning Promenade', Karen Webster performing 'Don't Dilly Dally' and the chorus belting out old favourites such as 'The Old Bull and Bush', and 'Pack Up Your Troubles'. Chris Mason produced a section devoted to the 1960s which included a performance by Gemma Hazlewood and Tom Jackson of Sonny and Cher's 'I Got You, Babe' and a rendition by Chris Mason and Wendy Rains of 'Cryin' in the Rain'.

Writing in the millennium programme, Baz Brown said, 'On joining Chapel Players, I little thought that 25 years later I would still be here celebrating the end of one century and the beginning of another.' Reflecting on the technological changes which have been introduced, he reminded readers, 'Thirty years ago our stage was still lit by gas.' Writing in the 75th anniversary programme, Warner and Sheila Christie had expressed the hope that 'perhaps one of our members will find his or her vocation in life and go on to greater things – Who knows?' In fact, several recent members have done so. Kash Bennett and Andrea Hartle now pursue careers connected with the theatre and Jonathan Hall, who wrote the script for the 2001 pantomime, Gareth Edwards and Gemma Hazlewood are all taking higher education courses in the field of music and drama. Most importantly, the players continue to entertain the people of Chapel-en-le-Frith in fine style, as they have been doing for the last 81 years.

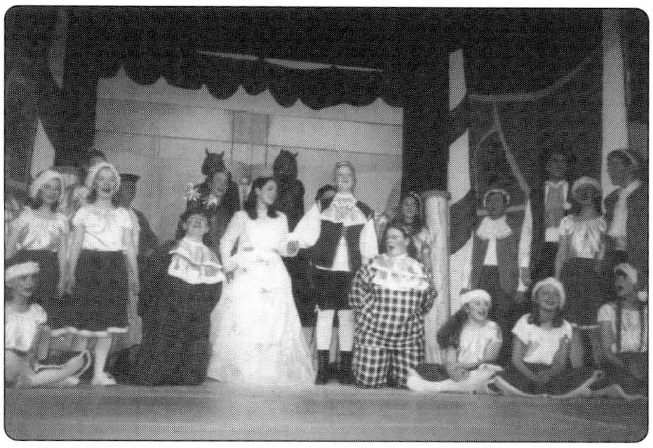

Pantomime production of Sleeping Beauty, *2001.*

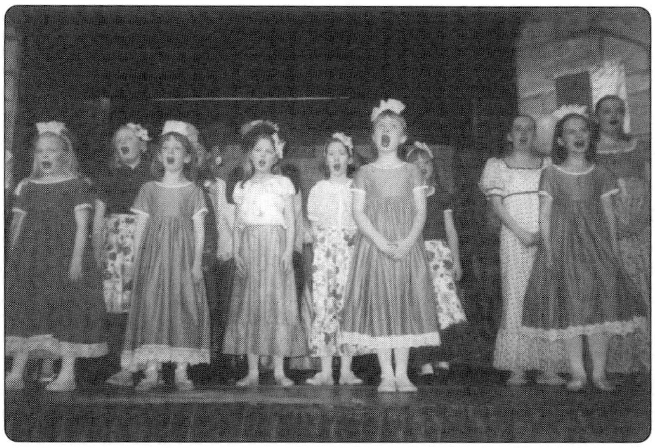

Pantomime chorus in Cinderella, *2002.*

Picture Palace

An adaptation of an article from *Living Edge* magazine (August 2001), with extracts from *The Story of the Empress Cinema and Moving Picture Shows in Chapel-en-le-Frith* by Sam Winfield. Extracts are reproduced by permission of Silk Press Ltd and quotations from Sam's book are reproduced with his permission.

Sam Winfield's research suggests that:

> *... moving pictures probably arrived in Chapel-en-le-Frith at the turn of the century, being brought by showmen from Sheffield or possibly Manchester. The shows would be 20 to 30 minutes long at the most and were presented in empty shop premises or in hastily erected booths at fairs and in the Wakes Week.*

Sam has also discovered, from an old copy of the *Kinematograph Year Book*, that Stratton Wells was running a picture palace of some 450 seats in the town in the second decade of the twentieth century, but a purpose-built picture house was not erected in Chapel-en-le-Frith until 1924, when the Empress cinema in Market Street was opened by Eldred and Alice Fletcher. The cinema was managed by their son Eldred junr and his wife Eva, who lived with their daughter Beryl in accommodation which was located directly above the auditorium – they even had their own garden at the rear of the building.

In its heyday the cinema showed three different programmes each week; admission prices were 1s.6d. and 2s.6d., and it was possible to make a regular booking in the 'posher' seats – one particular row was almost entirely occupied by the local vicar, his wife and their six children. Donna Kadzewska, who still lives a stone's throw from the site of the old cinema, told me about the weekly trips she made with her family to their regular seats, which placed them behind a man who bore a remarkable resemblance to the actor Raymond Massey. On one occasion, the man's seat was left empty and several people turned around in surprise when they heard Donna's mother exclaim, 'Raymond Massey isn't here tonight'. Donna also recalls one summer evening when she went along to the 'first house' to see *Red Dust*, staring Clark Gable and Jean Harlow. All the doors and windows of the auditorium had been opened that night to allow some air into the hot auditorium. When she arrived home, Donna went up to her bedroom and was able to hear the entire film again through her open window!

Donna also recalls the highly entertaining, flamboyant piano playing of Sarah Wildgoose, who was employed to add atmosphere to the early films. However, not everyone was impressed: Donna remembers overhearing one member of the audience complaining, 'I don't think much to it here. When you pay this price in London, you get an organ coming up through the floor.'

There was great excitement in March 1930 when the first talkies were shown at the Empress, actually ahead of their showing in the larger Buxton cinemas. The Empress was modernised in the 1930s, probably in response to competition from the local Constitutional Hall, which also had film shows and advertised itself, rather grandly, as The Regent. An all-white, slab frontage was added to the Empress, giving it a rather incongruous appearance in a street of gritstone cottages. Sam Winfield reports that the auditorium was enlarged at this stage, creating seating for over 300 people, and that auditorium lighting was provided by planet-like globes encircled by discs. One of the cinema's great selling points was the American soda fountain in the foyer, and Eva Fletcher was known as a very generous host, for she would often give free admission to poor families and to youngsters from the local children's home. Top brass bands gave Sunday concerts at the Empress in the early 1940s to raise money for the war effort and the programme was interrupted in May 1941 for an announcement that HMS *Hood* had been sunk.

Sometimes the soundtrack would not synchronise with the film and complete breakdowns would occur fairly regularly, but this was all part of the entertainment, for the audience would shout in unison on these occasions, 'Fetch Eldred'. Almost invariably, Eldred had to be brought in from the back garden where he had escaped from the heat of the projection box. Many people in the town remember Italian prisoners being allowed to march from the prisoner-of-war camp at Dove Holes to watch films at the Empress. Beryl Hall, who once worked as an usherette for the Fletchers, recalls great excitement among the local girls when weekend hikers from Manchester attended the cinema; Norma Muller told me that she and her husband had done their courting on the back row at the Empress, and Sam Winfield records that patrons flocked to see the newsreel at the cinema in 1947 when their own town was featured in coverage of the extensive snowfalls of that winter.

The Empress finally closed as a cinema in 1961, but carried on as a bingo hall for a decade before it was demolished. John Barnfield even recalls occasional striptease shows being held in the former cinema during this period and can remember that he and his friends would climb up a tree in the grounds of the manse across the road for a free view of the performers as they left the stage. The site where the cinema once stood is now occupied by the new Shoulder of Mutton, built in 1971 to replace the old public house of the same name which occupied an adjacent site, where there is now a pub car park. Sam Winfield suggests that some former patrons of the Empress took bricks or other mementoes from the site as souvenirs when the cinema was being demolished.

When Sam Winfield was researching the history of the Empress, he made an appeal for information through the local newspaper. One of his respondents

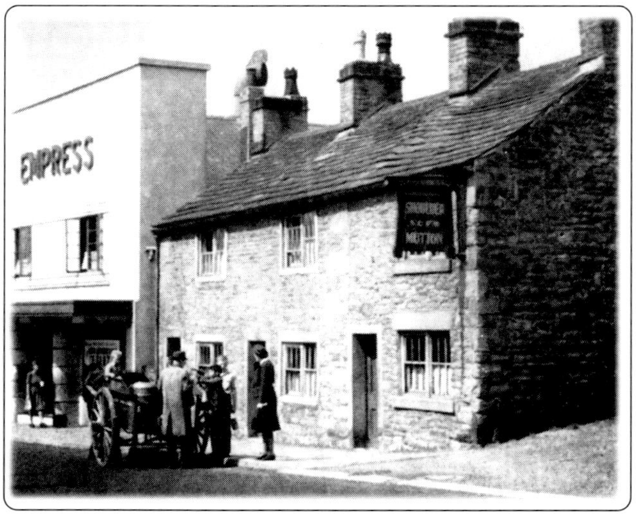

The Empress Cinema, now demolished.

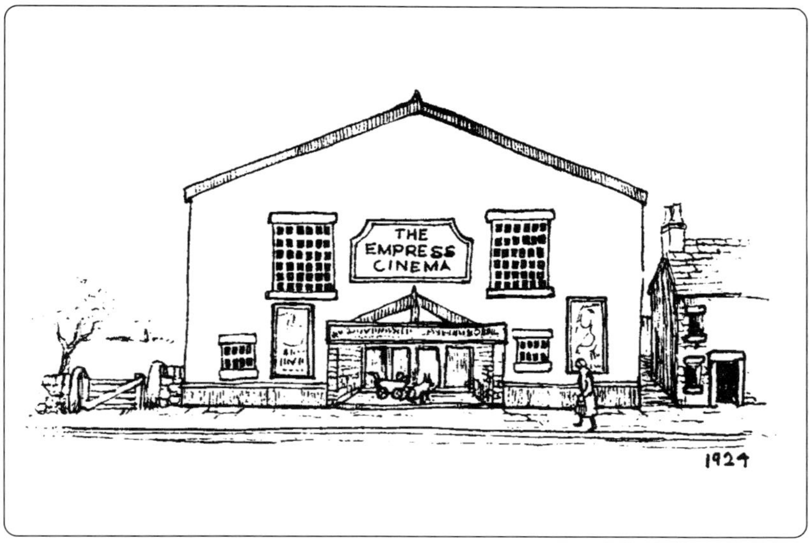

The old cinema frontage in 1924, drawn by Beryl Pilkington (née Fletcher).

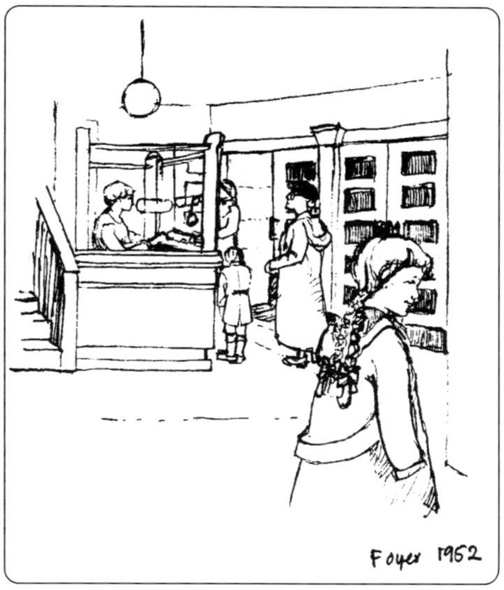

The foyer in 1952, drawn by Beryl Pilkington (née Fletcher).

was Beryl Pilkington, the Fletchers' daughter, who lived above the cinema auditorium for the first 24 years of her life. Beryl was able to supply Sam with useful information, but she was unable to let him have photographs, programmes or posters from the Empress' great days, because her mother had burned them all when the cinema closed down. However, she does still possess a silver ring which was made for her by one of the Italian prisoners of war; she also has the artistic skills to transpose her memories of the building to paper, and has made some drawings for Sam's monograph.

Beryl recalls films being delivered in a car by Mrs Heathcote, who was usually accompanied by her pet monkey, and she has many vivid memories of her childhood at the Empress, such as playing hide-and-seek behind the large cinema screen and having birthday parties with private screenings for her guests. She also remembers being the envy of her school friends, because she had a rather special home address: The Empress Cinema, Chapel-en-le-Frith.

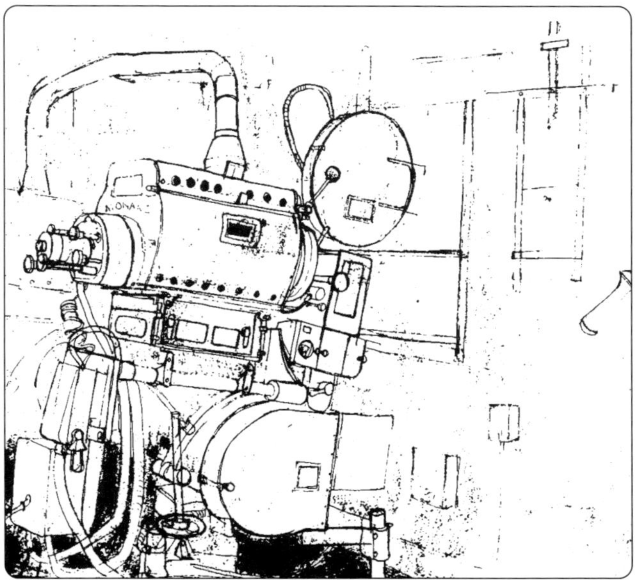

The projection room at the Empress, drawn by Beryl Pilkington (née Fletcher)

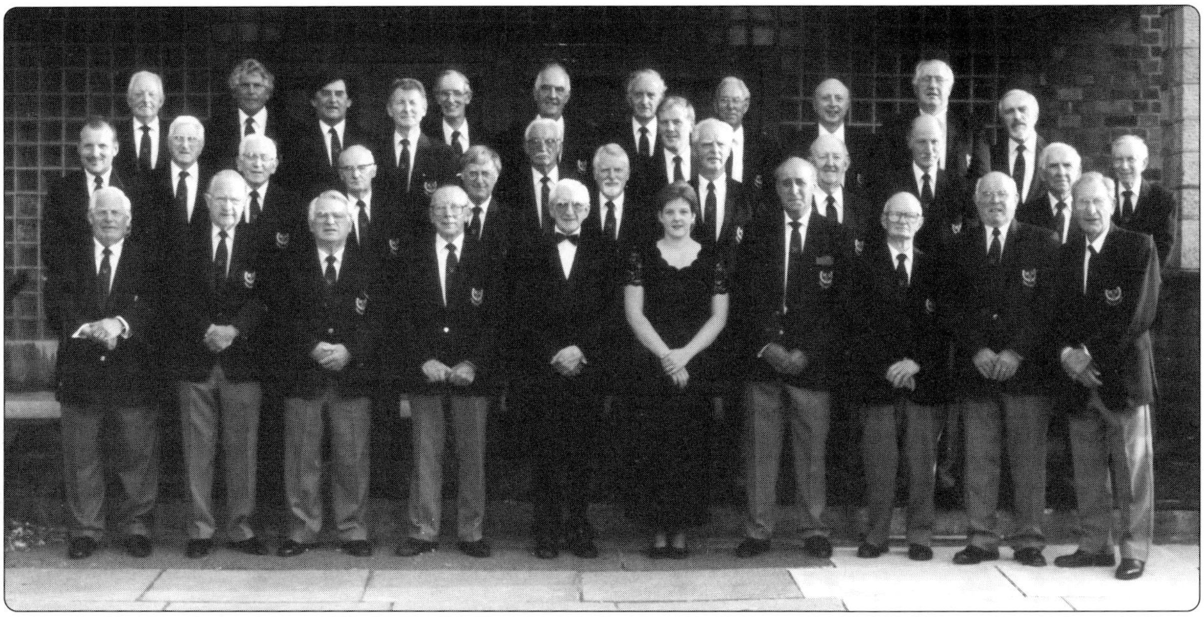

Chapel-en-le-Frith Male Voice Choir, 2001. Left to right, back row: *Peter Burgess, Roy Buxton, Derek Blair, Roy Danson, Bill Goddard, Arthur Hunstone, Edward Green, Brian Clamp, Bob Mulholland, John Chirgwin, David Youngs;* middle row: *Geoff Read, Ben Hill, Russell Wallace, Norman Shirt, Walter Higginbotham, Alan Howe, Peter Bowes, Robert Ford, Geoff Bradbury, Bob Colligan, Dennis Richards, Duncan McNanney, Vic Calver;* front row: *Ron Hartle, Russell Crompton, David Hughes, Alan Moore, Harry Redfern, Karen Drummond, George Gooch, Hubert Mellor, Derek Boardman, Dan Bletchler.*

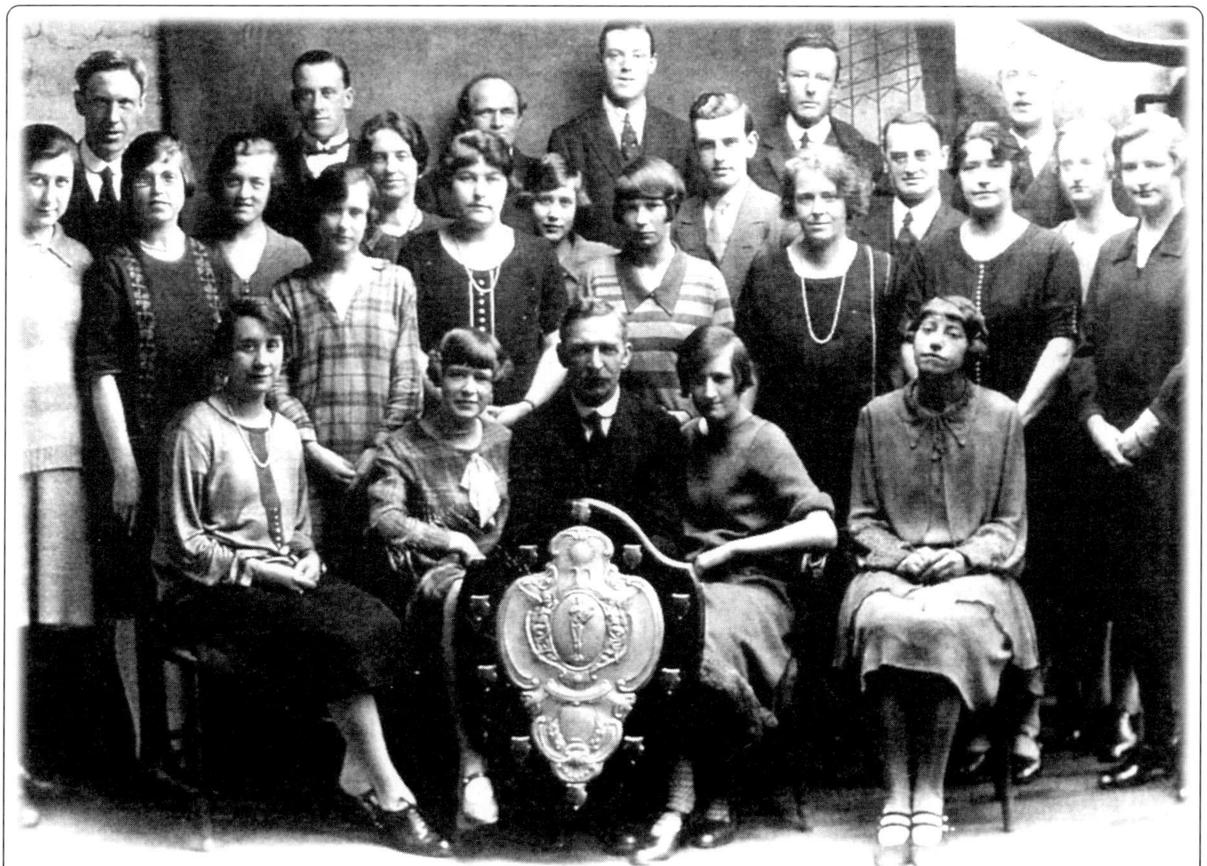

The mixed church choir, which won a first prize at the Derbyshire Music Festival in 1930. Edward Carrington was the conductor.

Chapter 12

MAKING MUSIC

As in the rest of the North of England there is a strong musical tradition in the High Peak, and especially in Chapel-en-le-Frith. The town's male voice and ladies' choirs, which both have high standards, attract members from all parts of the Peak District, and a number of children in the town are members of the Kinder Children's Choir, which has gained a very high reputation in just a decade of existence.

The High Peak is also an area with a strong brass band tradition and, over the years, Chapel-en-le-Frith has supported three brass bands – the Volunteer Band, the Ferodo Works Band and the Town Band.

CHAPEL-EN-LE-FRITH MALE VOICE CHOIR

Compiled with the assistance of Roy Danson, press officer of the Male Voice Choir.

The Chapel-en-le-Frith Male Voice Choir was formed after the First World War as one of three sections (orchestra, choir and drama group) in the Chapel-en-le-Frith ex-Servicemen's Operatic and Dramatic Society. Originally, performances of the society involved a series of one-act plays, a selection of songs by the choir and a number of orchestral pieces. In 1927 the Male Voice Choir left the group to form an independent society. Town End Methodist Church was their first home and Tom Longson was their conductor for many years.

The choir competed successfully in local festivals, but also sang purely for entertainment. Numbers were depleted during the Second World War, but the choir continued to function and there were celebrity concerts with artists such as Isobel Bailey and Heddle Nash. Then, as now, much of the choir's activity was for charity, but a prime aim has always been to provide an evening of good singing and entertainment, with something for all tastes, from composers such as Verdi, Rodgers and Hammerstein, to Lloyd Webber.

Anniversary concerts have always been rather special. The Fairey Band, conducted by Harry Mortimer OBE, were guests at the golden jubilee concert in 1969, and the CWS (Manchester) Band were guests at the 1979 diamond-jubilee concert, when the programme carried a piece by Bert Longson about the choir's origins:

One night after I had been to a choir practice at Town End Wesleyans, I was talking to George Muir, Joe Lomas and Joe Pearson, at the bottom of the school yard. Then we started singing and a schoolmaster who was staying with Alice Middleton came across the road and said, 'With voices like that you ought to be able to form a male voice choir.' So we went round all the ex-servicemen. Amongst them was Sam Ibbotson and Tom Sidebotham, and we went carol singing. We gave the money collected to the Amateur Dramatic Society, which was effective in starting the Amateur Players. After a while, we couldn't carry on as we were losing members, and so we threw it open and three people, dear friends of mine, Alf King, Joel Potter and Wilton Ward, joined us. By the way, Mrs Tom Shepley was our first accompanist, and my uncle, Tom Longson, was our first conductor.

At the 80th anniversary concert the choir performed at Town End Methodist Church with their guests, Nigel Ogden, the organist and Radio Two broadcaster, and Adrian Blakeley, a member of the BBC Daily Service Singers.

At the time of writing the choir in 2003 has about 40 members and they come from all corners of the Peak District and beyond. They always welcome new members, insisting that no previous experience is necessary.

Harry Redfern is the present conductor and musical director in 2003, and he was formerly an accomp-anist. Harry also plays a prominent part in other musical activities across the High Peak and is to be found in the orchestra pit for musical productions by the Chapel Players. Thanks to Harry, the choir performs programmes with a blend of old and new, classical and popular, sacred and secular. Karen Drummond, Head of Music at St Augustine's School, Oldham, is the accompanist. Previous accompanists have included Dorothy Wild and Carol Reid.

The group rehearsed for many years in the canteen at the Ferodo works, but the building was demolished in 2000. It now rehearses in the Becket Room of the Parish Church. After more than 80 years of existence, the Chapel-en-le-Frith Male Voice Choir is one of the most enduring cultural institutions in the town and is testament to the strong musical traditions in the area.

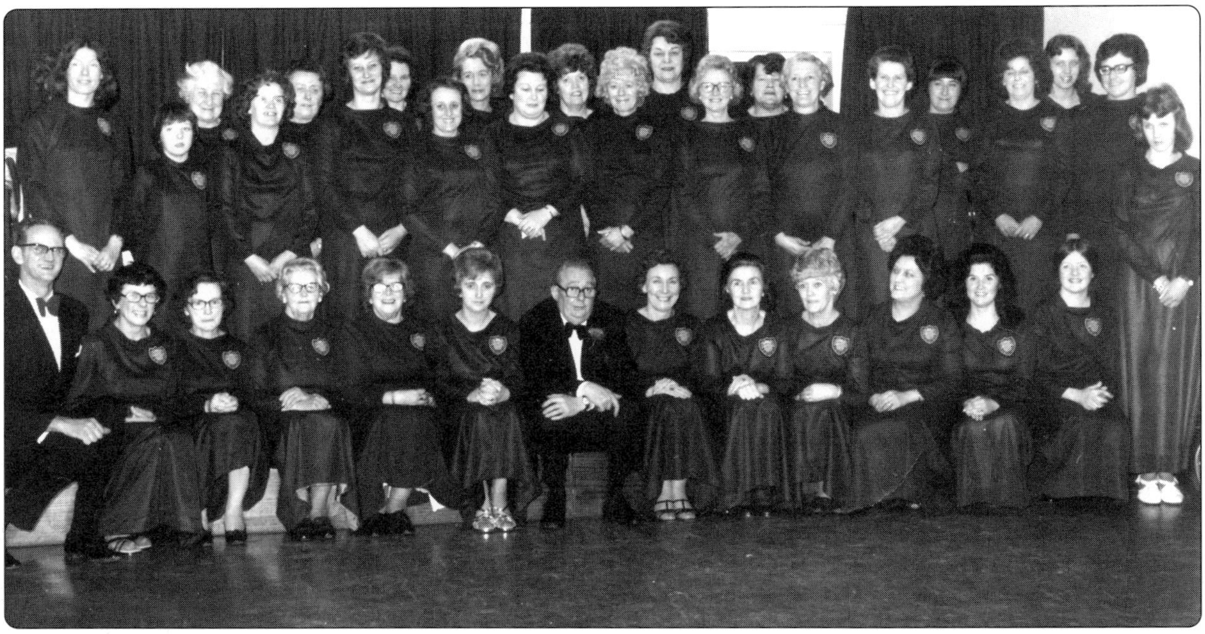

Chapel Ladies' Choir, 1975. Left to right, back row: *J. Pocock, I. Bagshawe, E. Ainscow, M. Evans, K. Mitchell, M. Trimmer, D. Yates, L. Gibson, C. Mone, D. Mitchell;* middle row: *G. Brodkin, S. Tideswell, G. Hinde, P. Brodkin, O. Nadin, B. Hinks, Mrs Quibell, P. Rawles, K. Mellor, A. Hancock, K. Whyte;* front row: *D. Evans, E. Salt, Mrs Brierley, N. Reeves, C. Baxter, R. Holden, A. Hudson, D. Woodiwiss, G. Esterhuizen, J. Morris, B. Craven, A. Trimmer.*

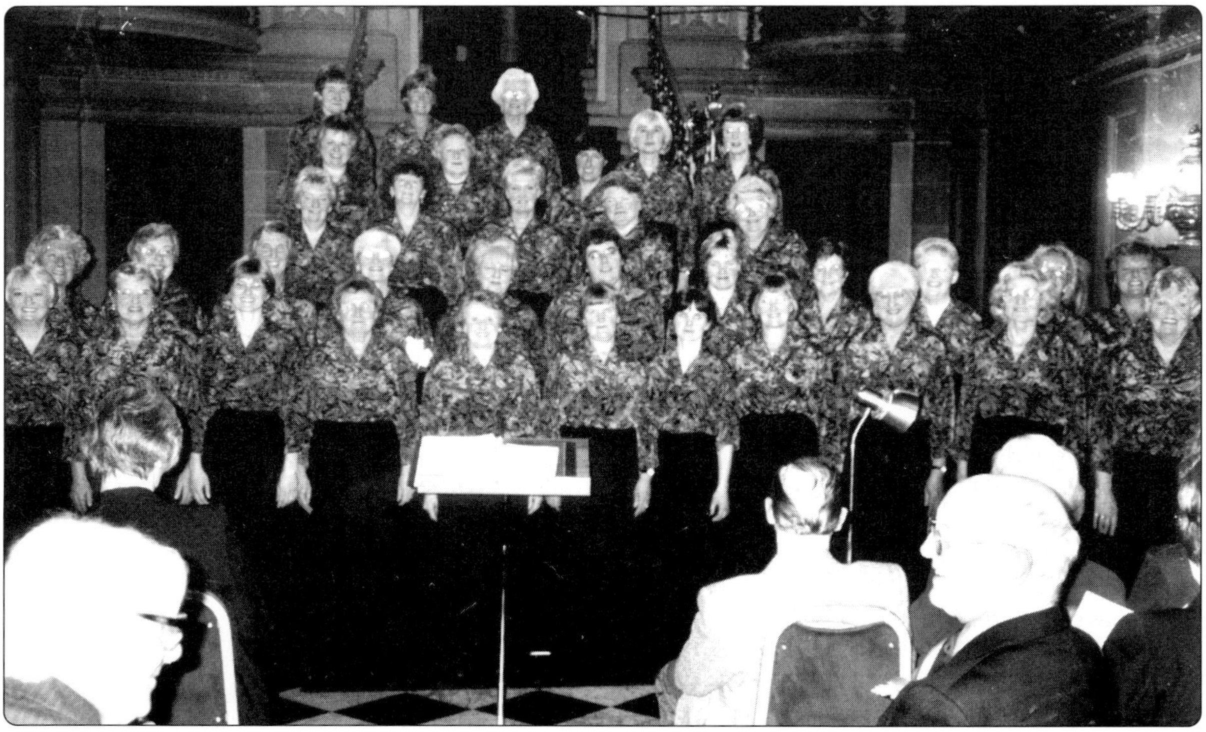

Chapel Ladies' Choir in the Painted Hall at Chatsworth, November 2000. Left to right, back row: *J. Dowell, M. Towey, M. Williamson;* fourth row: *S. Barratt, B. Engleby, A. Phillips, M. Cooper, M. Hearnshaw;* third row: *B. Haggata, A. Weston, M. Davies, P. Sutherland, U. Burton;* second row: *M. Hyde, M. Marchington, M. Bradbury, D. Martin, S. Cousins, P. Plant, M. Hibbert, N. Stephens, K. Naden, B. Robson, B. Johnson;* front row: *M. Brignell, E. Brightmore, J. Fitzgerald, M. Hipwell, P. Turner, J. Knibb, C. Garland, J. Cooke, M. Oakley, B. Taylor, M. Trimmer.*

Chapel-en-le-Frith Ladies' Choir

By Mary Davies (secretary of the Ladies' Choir), with contributions from other choir members.

In 1974 Ray Holden, then licensee of the Roebuck, and Eva Salt, a well-known Chapel resident, discussed the possibility of forming a ladies' choir. Advertisements were placed in the local newspaper asking for ladies who were interested. Many came forward and the choir was formed under the baton of Mr Holden.

Unfortunately, Ray died within a year and the baton was taken over by Victor Handforth, at that time conductor of the Chapel Male Voice Choir, and Ray Orritt of Chapel Town Band, until a permanent conductor came along, namely George Jacobs.

When George was unable to continue because of ill health, the choir's pianist, Kath Nadin, approached Norma Gough, who began a month's trial run, but has been the choir's musical director ever since. She will be celebrating 25 years in the post in April 2003.

Norma was born in Bradford and cannot remember a time when she didn't sing. She continued with her singing through school and college, gradually taking on more and more work, singing with choirs and performing as a soloist in many operettas, oratorios and musicals. Under Norma's leadership the choir has grown in size and musical stature.

In 2003 the choir is about 40 singers strong and its members are not only drawn from Chapel-en-le-Frith, but from all corners of the Peak District. Most of the performances take place locally, but the choir has also sung in the Anglican Cathedral in Liverpool, the Painted Hall at Chatsworth, and much further afield, in France, Belgium and Holland. In 1982 the choir twinned with the Gesangwerein Schwalheim, a musical choir from Bad Nauheim in Germany, and regular exchanges have taken place since that time, with many friendships being formed. The choir also has regular exchanges with two Welsh choirs, Carmel Ladies' Choir from Llanwrst and Betws-yn-Ros Male Voice Choir.

The choir provides a varied programme at its concerts, with the intention of appealing to all tastes. We are fortunate to have as our accompanist Alison Wheeldon, who began playing for the choir in 1980, having been spotted at a school concert by Norma. After over two decades she is still playing, often performing duets with Llinos Hodgson, who has been a great friend to the choir and substitutes for Alison when she is unavailable. Mrs Bradbury MBE was the choir's first president, serving it well with support and encouragement. She was succeeded in October 2000 by Councillor Mrs Ann Young, who continues the tradition set by Mrs Bradbury.

The choir still has four founder members: May Hipwell, Kath Nadin, Maureen Trimmer and Pauline Turner, who can each boast 29 years of choral singing – quite a record!

So what of the future? The choir grows yearly and, in general, no lady who has the commitment and the desire to sing is turned away. Programmes are devised to be of interest to a wide audience and the choir is determined that the proud tradition of choral singing, which is deeply rooted in the North of England, should continue in this corner of the Peak District. Any lady who feels inclined to join the choir should come along to Chapel Town Hall on any Monday evening at 8p.m. A warm welcome awaits!

Chapel-en-le-Frith Town Band

By Robert Mulholland, president of the Town Band.

The brass band has been part of the cultural life of Chapel-en-le-Frith since the middle of the nineteenth century, when standardisation of instrumentation was adopted by groups of brass musicians in the towns and villages of the North of England. In later years the brass-band movement swept across the British Isles and eventually to many countries around the world, where it thrives to this day.

In earlier centuries groups of musicians, playing brass, reed and string instruments, had provided music for services in churches and at community social functions in Chapel-en-le-Frith. However, it is believed that a particular group of brass players, who had provided music at Chapel-en-le-Frith Parish Church, formed themselves into the Town Band in 1882, at a time when their services were no longer required at the church due to the installation of the new organ.

Brass bands were hugely popular sources of entertainment in the nineteenth century and it said there were 40,000 in existence in Britain around 1900. In the early part of the twentieth century a number of bands were active in and around Chapel-en-le-Frith, including the Town Band and the Volunteer Band, and there were also bands in Chinley and Bugsworth, as well as in Whaley Bridge, Dove Holes, Peak Dale and Fairfield. There was great rivalry between the bands and there are stories of competitions between them, which involved their playing while marching up the steep, cobbled incline of Church Brow.

By the end of the Second World War the only surviving band was the Town Band, which then entered the most successful period in its history. In the late 1940s the band gained championship status at various competitions in the North of England and competed, under the direction of Frank Moss, a local musician, against the cream of the country's brass bands in the prestigious Belle Vue Championships. For major competitions the band was often coached by the country's leading band conductors, including three members of the legendary Mortimer family: Fred Mortimer, conductor of the Foden's Motor Works Band, and two of his sons, Harry and Alex.

In the early 1950s Frank Moss and a number of players left the Town Band to form the Ferodo Works

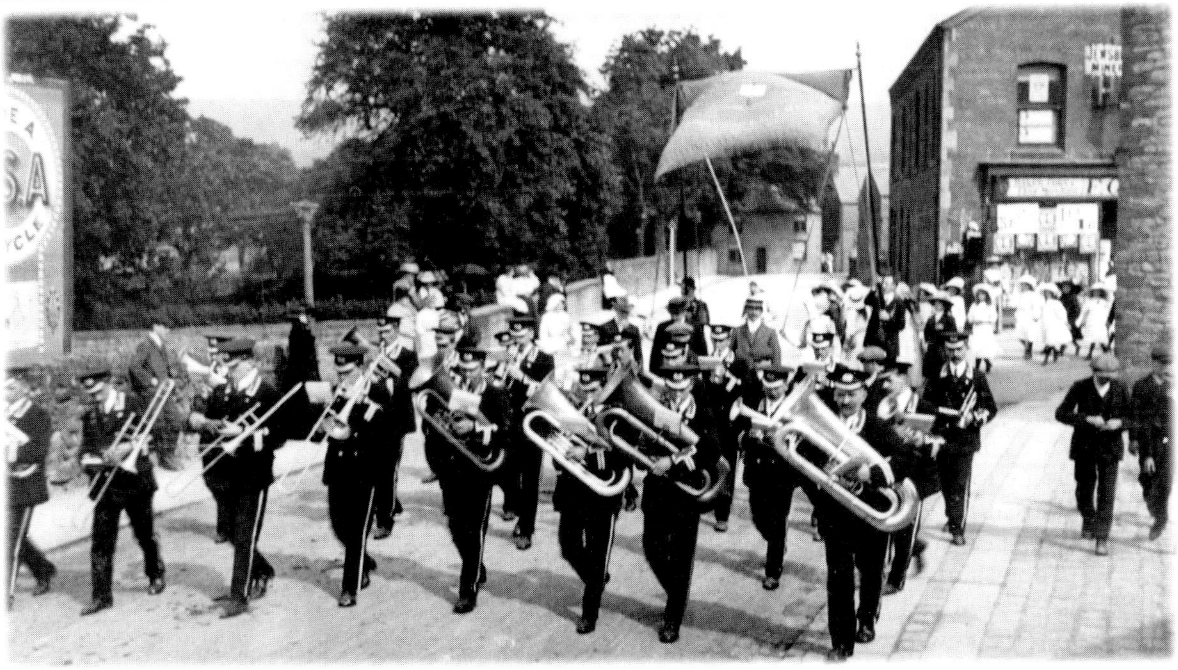

The Town Band in 1912.

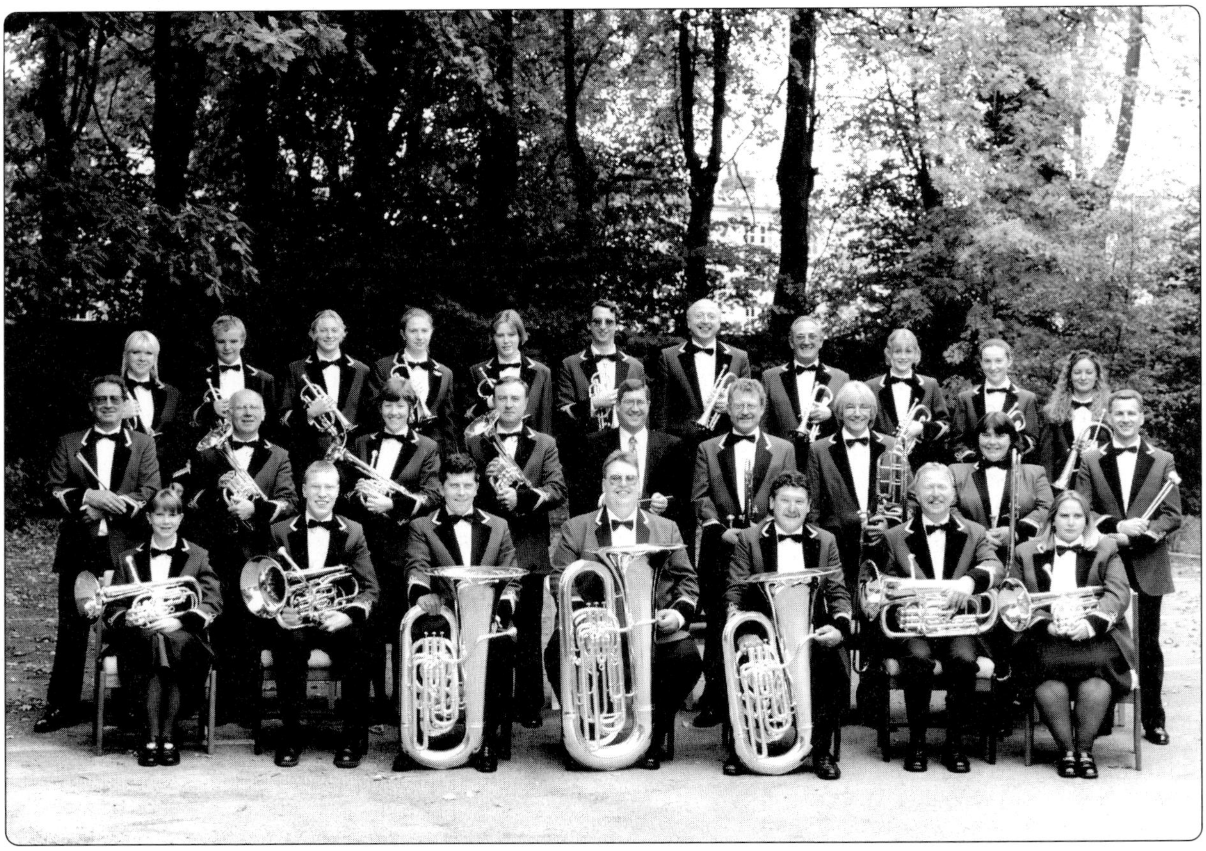

A picture of the Town Band in 1997. Left to right, back row: *Nicola Longden, David Gartside, Tanya Shepherd, Louise Bailey, Philip Marsland, Robert Mulholland, Gordon Booth, Leanne Shepherd, Amy Thomas, Christine Brydon;* middle: *Tony O'Reilly, Jeffrey Owen, Linda Bailey, David Ford, Peter Christian (Musical Director), Barry Thompson, Bill Grindey, Sarah Jackson, Geoffrey Bradley;* front: *Karen Mellor, Andrew Dodd, David Shear, Mark Nicholls, Tony Carter, John Groake, Emma Hartle.*

Band, where they were generously supported by the company. The Ferodo Works Band became one of the country's leading brass bands, winning the Belle Vue Championships in 1955 under the direction of George Hespe. Although the Town Band was left to recover from the loss of some of its players, it too attained a high standard, winning the National Championship of Great Britain (Second Section) in the same year, under the direction of Joe Cooke, another local musician. After a period of several years the Ferodo company withdrew its sponsorship and their works band folded.

For the past half century the Town Band has fulfilled engagements throughout the district and competed in competitions in many parts of the country, providing entertainment for audiences, introducing many young people to the joys of music making and helping to raise thousands of pounds for various charitable causes within the locality.

The band flourished in the 1980s with an influx of many young people under the direction of Gordon Booth, a former Royal Marines bandsman. In 1994 he and his wife Jean were awarded a Dedicated Service Award in recognition of their services over 11 years. Following Gordon's retirement the band continued to progress under the direction of Geoffrey Bradley of Tintwistle, and later Peter Christian of New Mills, a former member of the Black Dyke Mills, Foden's and Fairey Aviation Works Bands. Competing in the National Championships the band played at a number of leading venues, including Wembley Arena, Symphony Hall in Birmingham, and the Royal Concert Hall in Nottingham, progressing from the Fourth to the Second Section of the competition. In October 2000 the band, under the direction of Peter Christian, competed for the first time in its history at the Royal Albert Hall, London, in the finals of the National Brass Band Championships of Great Britain (Second Section), representing the Midland Region. In the summer of 2002 the Town Band, in collaboration with Whaley Bridge and Fairfield Bands, presented a highly successful 'Proms in the Park' event in the Memorial Park, which raised a substantial sum for the High Peak Hospice.

KINDER CHILDREN'S CHOIRS OF THE HIGH PEAK

By Robert Mulholland, trustee of the Kinder Children's Choirs of the High Peak.

The Kinder Children's Choirs of the High Peak have been one of the major success stories in the cultural life of the High Peak during the last decade. Founded ten years ago by their musical director, Joyce Ellis, an internationally known opera singer who now resides in the High Peak, the choirs quickly gained a national and international profile, with successes in major competitions, appearances in prestigious concert venues, on CDs and in a series of BBC and Granada television programmes.

The choirs involve 100 children and young choral students between the ages of eight and 18, from all parts of the High Peak and beyond, and are administered by a registered charitable trust. There are five choirs in the system, ranging from training groups to a Youth Choir and the highly successful Concert Choir. They perform a wide repertoire, ranging from the religious works of the English choral tradition to contemporary choral music and arrangements from the musical stage and pop music.

Miss Ellis was inspired to form the choirs in order that she could pass on her early experience in the choral system to new generations of children. The specific aim of the Kinder Children's Choir Trust is to provide an educational training programme in vocal and choral skills and to offer an introduction to music education, along with the excitement of a performing platform with professional attitudes and approach. Children are not precluded for reasons of cost and there is no audition or voice test for anyone wishing to join the choirs, but candidates go through a training programme before they can become fully-fledged members.

The trust promotes an appreciation of choral singing among both participants and their audiences through the choir's educational activities, through their performances, locally, nationally and internationally, on the concert platform, and through recordings, radio and television performances. The artistic life of the choir reflects their uncompromising commitment to quality, innovation, challenge, variety, new music and equality of opportunities.

The choirs have gained an international profile in competitions, prestigious concerts and in a series of appearances on Granada and BBC television. They won the children's section at the International Eisteddfod in Llangollen, competing against 29 choirs from around the world. They have been the Choir of the Day and semi-finalists in the Sainsbury Choir of the Year on BBC television and were invited to perform at the Music for Youth Gala Concert at the Royal Festival Hall; they have shared the concert platform with the London Symphony Orchestra, the Royal Liverpool Philharmonic, and the Chorus of Opera North, and have made four concert tours to Germany. They performed at St Paul's Cathedral in the service of thanksgiving for the Children's Society to mark the 100th birthday of the Queen Mother, and the choir recently produced their third CD, entitled 'Can You Hear Me?'

The trust has contacts with Derbyshire Education Authority and has won the financial support of High Peak Borough Council, the Granada Foundation and the Arts Council of England. In 1999 it was awarded a Lottery grant of £60,000 towards the cost of new equipment, including staging and instruments for rehearsal and performance. It also has strong support from Government bodies, and District and County Councils. The choirs have their rehearsal and study headquarters at the Chinley Independent Chapel Sunday School on the edge of the parish of Chapel-en-le-Frith, which is a central location for the High Peak.

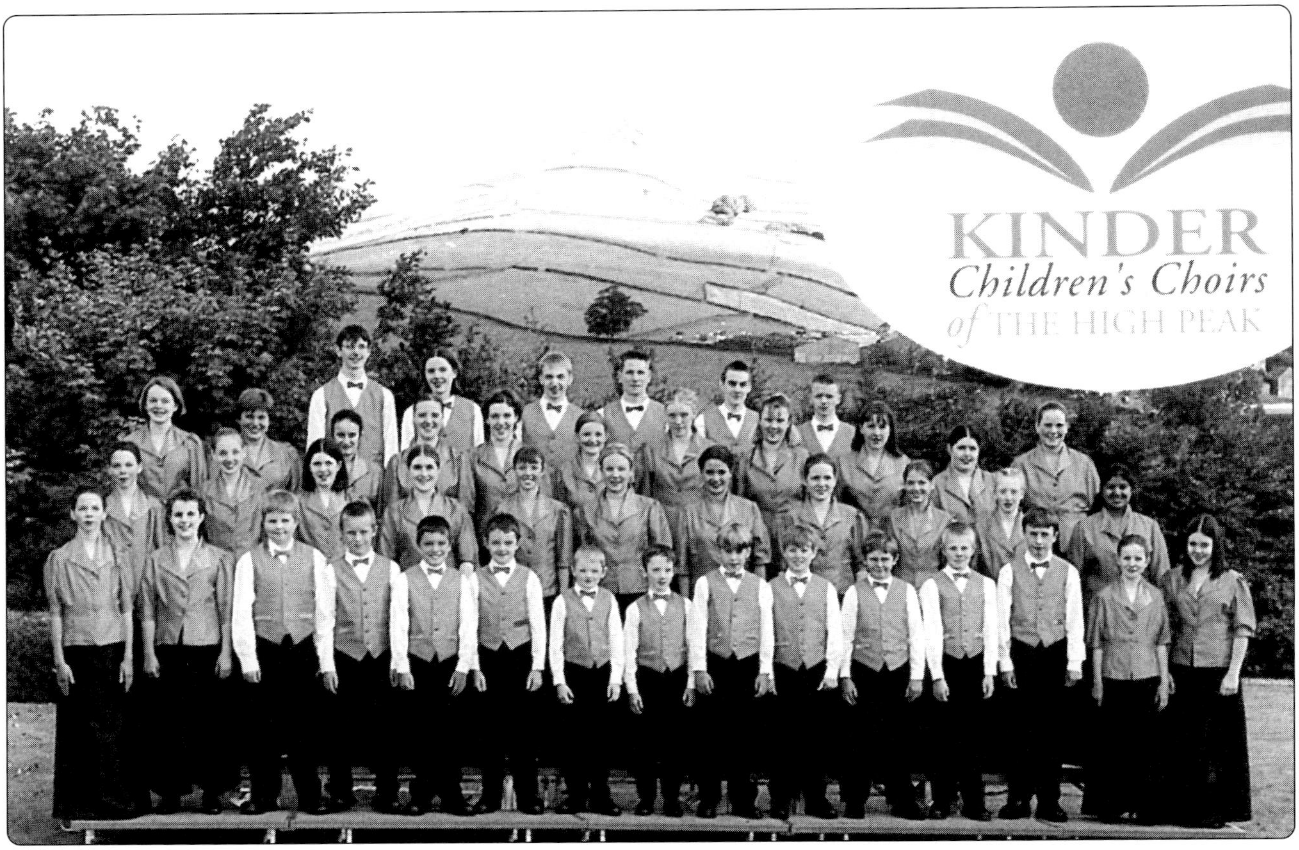

The Kinder Children's Choirs of the High Peak.

Subscribers

Ken Ichiro Aida, Hiroshima, Japan
Maurice and Gwen Armishaw, Chapel-en-le-Frith
Doris Ash, Matlock, Derbyshire
Kevin David Ashton, Chapel-en-le-Frith
M. Bailey, Dove Holes, Derbyshire
Sandra M. Ball, Chapel-en-le-Frith, Derbyshire
Mr Stuart Barber, Chapel-en-le-Frith, Derbyshire
Harry Barker (deceased) 4 November, born Chapel-en-le-Frith 1912
William H. Bates, Higher Crossings, Chapel-en-le-Frith
Victor W. Baxter, Chapel-en-le-Frith, Derbyshire
Fred Beresford, Chapel-en-le-Frith
The Beresford Family, Chapel-en-le-Frith, Derbyshire
Reg Birchenough, Chapel-en-le-Frith, Derbyshire
Peter Booth, Chapel-en-le-Frith
Edmund and Nigel Bradbury, Chapel-en-le-Frith, Derbyshire
Sean Brady, Chapel-en-le-Frith, Derbyshire
Mr and Mrs Brown, Chapel-en-le-Frith, High Peak
Jane Brownlow, Cullompton, Devon
Mrs Edna Burt
Doreen Buttrill, Chapel-en-le-Frith, Derbyshire
Brian G. and Margaret (née Ainscow) Bywater, Chapel-en-le-Frith
Terence R. Cartledge, Chapel-en-le-Frith, High Peak
Roger Cartledge
1st Chapel-en-le-Frith Company, The Boys' Brigade
A.M., G.E. and R.J. Clarey, Chapel-en-le-Frith
Aileen Clayton, Chapel-en-le-Frith, Derbyshire
Mr N. and Mr S. Coley, Chapel-en-le-Frith
Combs Infant School
G. Bryan Cooper, Whitehough, High Peak
Mrs H.J. Craven, Combs, High Peak
M. Davies, Chapel-en-le-Frith
Ernie Drabble M.B.E., Glossop, Derbyshire
Judy Dyson, Ash Vale, Surrey
Robert H. Else, Chapel-en-le-Frith, Derbyshire
Jean and Mike Evanson, Combs, High Peak, Derbyshire
Eyre, Chapel-en-le-Frith, Derbyshire
Betty Fitzgerald, Buxton, Derbyshire
Mr J.R. Fletcher
G.B. and L.M. Fletcher, Chapel-en-le-Frith
Charles D. Flintham, ex Chapel-en-le-Frith
Olive Fraser, Bagshaw, Chapel-en-le-Frith
Andy and Honor Fraser, Buxton, Derbyshire
Lynne Frith Gleave, Chapel-en-le-Frith
Ivy Froggatt, Sparrowpit, Derbyshire
Mr T.S. Gill, Southwell, Nottinghamshire
Peter J. Goddard, Brighouse
Revd John M. Goddard, Barrow-In-Furness, Cumbria
Jackie Goddard, Chapel-en-le-Frith, Derbyshire
Florence Marjorie Goddard, Chapel-en-le-Frith, Derbyshire
Aileen M. Guzman, Chapel-en-le-Frith
Derek Hall, born Chapel Milton, lives Chapel-en-le-Frith
Harry Hall, Chapel-en-le-Frith, Derbyshire
Eric Hallam, Chapel-en-le-Frith
Ralph and Linda Harper, Penrhyn Bay, Llandudno
Helen Harper, Chapel-en-le-Frith, High Peak
Maureen Heaps, Bushey, Hertfordshire
Judith Hearnshaw, Chapel-en-le-Frith
Myra and John Hearnshaw, Blackbrook, Chapel-en-le-Frith
Mrs D. Helps, Chapel-en-le-Frith
Mr P. Helps, Chapel-en-le-Frith
Elizabeth A. Hibbert, Walthamstow
J. Peter Hibbert, Chapel-en-le-Frith, Derbyshire
Frances M. Hibbert, Chapel-en-le-Frith, Derbyshire
William A. Hibbert, Surrey
James E. Hirst, Chapel-en-le-Frith, Derbyshire
John Hodgkinson, Chapel-en-le-Frith, Derbyshire
Wilfred Hollinrake, Chapel-en-le-Frith
Megan Hollinrake, Chapel-en-le-Frith, Derbyshire
Russell Jackson Hoyle, Chapel-en-le-Frith
Rosina S. Jamieson, Chapel-en-le-Frith, High Peak
Mrs J. Jeffcock, Chapel-en-le-Frith, Derbyshire

Stephen P. Kenyon, Chapel-en-le-Frith
Rob Kenyon, Chapel-en-le-Frith, Derbyshire
Hilary Kenyon, Chapel-en-le-Frith
S.H. and L.M. King, Chapel-en-le-Frith, Derbyshire
Mike and Sue Kirby, Chapel-en-le-Frith
J.D. and M. Leach, Chapel-en-le-Frith
John Joseph Lomas, Great Longstone, Derbyshire
David C. Lomas, Chapel-en-le-Frith, Derbyshire
John V. Lomas, ex Chapel-en-le-Frith
Sue Lucas, Combs, Derbyshire
H. Eric Lumb, Chapel-en-le-Frith
Nigel Macbean, Haughton, Darlington, Durham
David Macbean, Chapel-en-le-Frith, Derbyshire
Mr W.H. Marshall, Chapel-en-le-Frith, Derbyshire
Dr W.E.S. Marshall, Chapel-en-le-Frith, Derbyshire
Mr R.C.F. Marshall, Chapel-en-le-Frith, Derbyshire
Roger T. Marshall, Dove Holes, Derbyshire
Guy and Beryl Martin, Chapel-en-le-Frith
Guy David Martin, Chapel-en-le-Frith
Bryan McGee, Blackbrook, Chapel-en-le-Frith
Albert McInnes, Chapel-en-le-Frith, Derbyshire
Patrick McNicholas, Chinley, Derbyshire
J. McNicol, Chapel-en-le-Frith
Marlene A. Meakin, Chapel-en-le-Frith, Derbyshire
William Mellor, Chapel-en-le-Frith, Derbyshire
David Brian Merrick, Meir Park, Staffs.
Irene M. Middleton (née Crane), Tideswell, Derbyshire
Friar, John Derek De Montalt (Moult), Late of Molte Hall
Malcolm W. Moore, Chapel-en-le-Frith, High Peak
Jean Morris, Chapel-en-le-Frith, Derbyshire
Basil G. Naden, Dove Holes, Derbyshire
V. Needham, Chapel-en-le-Frith
G.A. Needham, Chinley
David Needham and Anne Buckley, Chapel-en-le-Frith, Derbyshire
Su Nolan, Highbury, London
Mr George and Mrs E. O'Brien, Hale, Nr Altrincham
Christine M. O'Gara, Chapel-en-le-Frith, Derbyshire
Dr Richard V. Osborne
Mr and Mrs I.G.M. Parker, Combs, Chapel-en-le-Frith
V.I. Parker, for Sir G. Goodman family
Arnold Peach, Chapel-en-le-Frith, Derbyshire
John and Paula Pheasey, Chapel-en-le-Frith
Enid Phillips, Chapel-en-le-Frith, Derbyshire
Beryl Pilkington, Chapel-en-le-Frith, Derbyshire
David and Joan Prime, Chapel-en-le-Frith, Derbyshire
Lilian Pritchard, Chapel-en-le-Frith, Derbyshire
Gwen Proudlock (née Bywater)
Mrs Sandra Quinn (née Joule), Queensland, Australia
Mrs J.A. Reid, Hook Green, Kent
D. and D. Ripley, Chapel
L.M. and P.D. Robinson, Chapel-en-le-Frith, Derbyshire
A. Rowbotham, Chapel-en-le-Frith, Derbyshire
Rachel Shaw, Woolley Bridge
Margery Sherwood and Trevor George Gilman,
Dorothy and Patricia Simpson, Chapel-en-le-Frith, Derbyshire
John and Dianne Smith, Chapel-en-le-Frith
Miss N.M.M. Smith, Bagthorpe
Marie Smith, Chapel-en-le-Frith, Derbyshire
Mr A.R.M. Smith, Mains of Mayen
Mr M.P.M. Smith, Lima
Mr P.W.M. Smith, Wirksworth
Mr Allan F. Steeples, Sparrowpit
Mrs D.F. Stewart, Chapel-en-le-Frith, Derbyshire
Miss Charlotte H. Tait-Mellor, Chapel-en-le-Frith
Stuart and Anne Taylor, Wadebridge, Cornwall. formerly of Chapel-en-le-Frith
Alan and Joyce Taylor, Chapel-en-le-Frith
Margaret A. Taylor, Old Hall Farm, Wormhill
Eric and Sybil Taylor, Chapel-en-le-Frith
Derek and Sheila Tideswell, Chapel-en-le-Frith, Derbyshire
David I. Timmins, Chapel-en-le-Frith, Derbyshire
T. and M. Trimmer, Chapel-en-le-Frith, Derbyshire
Rebecca Gray and Simon Tyler, Chapel-en-le-Frith
Anthony and Angie Vernon, Chapel-en-le-Frith, Derbyshire
Diana Walkden, Tideswell, Derbyshire
John F.W. Walling, Newton Abbot, Devon
D.J. Wallis, Chapel-en-le-Frith, Derbyshire
Patricia White (née Ford), Manurewa, Auckland, New Zealand
Peter L. Williams, Chapel-en-le-Frith, Derbyshire
William and Lynne Wilson, Tunstead Milton
Georgina Wilson, Chapel-en-le-Frith, Derbyshire
Bernice Wood, Chapel-en-le-Frith, Derbyshire
Robert Wright M.C.I.P.S., Lower Eaves, Chapel-en-le-Frith
Dr and Mrs D.W. Yalden, Chapel-en-le-Frith
Peter D. Yeomans, Burrfields, Chapel-en-le-Frith
Kelvin H. Yeomans, Crossings Avenue, Chapel-en-le-Frith
David P. Youd
Cllr Mrs Ann S. Young, Chapel-en-le-Frith
Mary Young

Community Histories

The Book of Addiscombe • Canning & Clyde Road Residents Association & Friends
The Book of Addiscombe, Vol. II • Canning & Clyde Road Residents Association & Friends
The Book of Axminster with Kilmington • Les Berry and Gerald Gosling
The Book of Bampton • Caroline Seward
The Book of Barnstaple • Avril Stone
The Book of Barnstaple, Vol. II • Avril Stone
The Book of The Bedwyns • The Bedwyn History Society
The Book of Bickington • Stuart Hands
Blandford Forum: A Millennium Portrait • Blandford Town Council
The Book of Bramford • Bramford Local History Group
The Book of Breage & Germoe • Stephen Polglase
The Book of Bridestowe • R. Cann
The Book of Bridport • Rodney Legg
The Book of Brixham • Frank Pearce
The Book of Buckfastleigh • Sandra Coleman
The Book of Buckland Monachorum & Yelverton • Hemery
The Book of Carharrack • Carharrack Old Cornwall Society
The Book of Carshalton • Stella Wilks and Gordon Rookledge
The Parish Book of Cerne Abbas • Vale and Vale
The Book of Chagford • Ian Rice
The Book of Chapel-en-le-Frith • Mike Smith
The Book of Chittlehamholt with Warkleigh & Satterleigh • Richard Lethbridge
The Book of Chittlehampton • Various
The Book of Colney Heath • Bryan Lilley
The Book of Constantine • Moore and Trethowan
The Book of Cornwood & Lutton • Compiled by the People of the Parish
The Book of Creech St Michael • June Small
The Book of Cullompton • Compiled by the People of the Parish
The Book of Dawlish • Frank Pearce
The Book of Dulverton, Brushford, Bury & Exebridge • Dulverton & District Civic Society
The Book of Dunster • Hilary Binding
The Book of Edale • Gordon Miller
The Ellacombe Book • Sydney R. Langmead
The Book of Exmouth • W.H. Pascoe
The Book of Grampound with Creed • Bane and Oliver
The Book of Hayling Island & Langstone • Rogers
The Book of Helston • Jenkin with Carter
The Book of Hemyock • Clist and Dracott
The Book of Herne Hill • Patricia Jenkyns
The Book of Hethersett • Hethersett Society Research Group
The Book of High Bickington • Avril Stone
The Book of Ilsington • Dick Wills
The Book of Kingskerswell • Carsewella Local History Group
The Book of Lamerton • Ann Cole & Friends
Lanner, A Cornish Mining Parish • Sharron Schwartz and Roger Parker
The Book of Leigh & Bransford • Malcolm Scott
The Book of Litcham with Lexham & Mileham • Litcham Historical & Amenity Society
The Book of Loddiswell • Reg and Betty Sampson
The New Book of Lostwithiel • Barbara Fraser
The Book of Lulworth • Rodney Legg
The Book of Lustleigh • Joe Crowdy
The Book of Lyme Regis • Rodney Legg
The Book of Manaton • Compiled by the People of the Parish
The Book of Markyate • Markyate Local History Society
The Book of Mawnan • Mawnan Local History Group
The Book of Meavy • Pauline Hemery
The Book of Minehead with Alcombe • Binding and Stevens
The Book of Morchard Bishop • Jeff Kingaby

The Book of Newdigate • John Callcut
The Book of Nidderdale • Nidderdale Musuem Society
The Book of Northlew with Ashbury • Northlew History Group
The Book of North Newton • Robins and Robins
The Book of North Tawton • Baker, Hoare and Shields
The Book of Nynehead • Nynehead & District History Society
The Book of Okehampton • Radford and Radford
The Book of Paignton • Frank Pearce
The Book of Penge, Anerley & Crystal Palace • Peter Abbott
The Book of Peter Tavy with Cudlipptown • Peter Tavy Heritage Group
The Book of Pimperne • Jean Coull
The Book of Plymtree • Tony Eames
The Book of Porlock • Denis Corner
Postbridge – The Heart of Dartmoor • Reg Bellamy
The Book of Priddy • Albert Thompson
The Book of Princetown • Dr Gardner-Thorpe
The Book of Rattery • By the People of the Parish
The Book of St Day • Joseph Mills and Paul Annear
The Book of Sampford Courtenay
with Honeychurch • Stephanie Pouya
The Book of Sculthorpe • Gary Windeler
The Book of Seaton • Ted Gosling
The Book of Sidmouth • Ted Gosling and Sheila Luxton
The Book of Silverton • Silverton Local History Society
The Book of South Molton • Jonathan Edmunds
The Book of South Stoke with Midford • Edited by Robert Parfitt
South Tawton & South Zeal with Sticklepath • Radfords
The Book of Sparkwell with Hemerdon & Lee Mill • Pam James
The Book of Staverton • Pete Lavis
The Book of Stithians • Stithians Parish History Group
The Book of Stogumber, Monksilver, Nettlecombe
& Elworthy • Maurice and Joyce Chidgey
The Book of Studland • Rodney Legg
The Book of Swanage • Rodney Legg
The Book of Tavistock • Gerry Woodcock
The Book of Thorley • Sylvia McDonald and Bill Hardy
The Book of Torbay • Frank Pearce
Uncle Tom Cobley & All:
Widecombe-in-the-Moor • Stephen Woods
The Book of Watchet • Compiled by David Banks
The Book of West Huntspill • By the People of the Parish
Widecombe-in-the-Moor • Stephen Woods
The Book of Williton • Michael Williams
The Book of Witheridge • Peter and Freda Tout and John Usmar
The Book of Withycombe • Chris Boyles
Woodbury: The Twentieth Century Revisited • Roger Stokes
The Book of Woolmer Green • Compiled by the People of the Parish